THE CULT OF SAINT KATHERINE OF ALEXANDRIA IN LATE-MEDIEVAL NUREMBERG

T0330872

For Jean
For all my friends and family

In memoriam

Alexander and Valerie Simon
Nicholas Ainsworth
Robert Hood
Malcom and Margaret Emery
Frank Shaw

The Cult of Saint Katherine of Alexandria in Late-Medieval Nuremberg

Saint and the City

ANNE SIMON

Institute of Germanic and Romance Studies, University of London

Routledge
Taylor & Francis Group

LONDON AND NEW YORK

First published 2012 by Ashgate Publishing

2 Park Square, Milton Park, Abingdon, Oxfordshire OX14 4RN
711 Third Avenue, New York, NY 10017

Routledge is an imprint of the Taylor & Francis Group, an informa business

First issued in paperback 2018

British Library Cataloguing in Publication Data
Simon, Anne.
The cult of Saint Katherine of Alexandria in late-medieval
Nuremberg : saint and the city.
1. Catherine, of Alexandria, Saint–Cult–Germany–
Nuremberg–History–To 1500. 2. Nuremberg (Germany)–
Religious life and customs. 3. Religion and sociology–
Germany–Nuremberg–History–To 1500.
I. Title
282.4'3324'0902-dc23

Library of Congress Cataloging-in-Publication Data
Simon, Anne.
The cult of Saint Katherine of Alexandria in late-medieval Nuremberg : saint and the city / by Anne Simon.
pages cm
Includes bibliographical references and index.
ISBN 978-1-4094-2071-2 (hardcover) 1. Catherine, of Alexandria, Saint–Cult–Germany–
Nuremberg–History–To 1500. 2. Catherine, of Alexandria, Saint–Cult–Germany–Nuremberg–
History–16th century. 3. Nuremberg (Germany)–Religious life and customs. I. Title.
BX4700.C45S56 2012
235'2–dc23

ISBN 978-1-4094-2071-2 (hbk)
ISBN 978-1-138-37972-5 (pbk)

Contents

List of Plates

Preface

Any study of a city with as rich and complex a history as that of Nuremberg – and with such a wealth of archives and primary source material – will inevitably fail to do complete justice to every aspect of the topic under investigation. Any study of a saint whose cult was as widespread and popular as that of Saint Katherine of Alexandria in the Late Middle Ages will face similar problems of selection and omission. With world enough and time I would ideally have looked at Patrician wills, letters, late-medieval drama, variants on the legend and miracles of Saint Katherine in manuscript and print, altars, murals and windows etc. in churches around Nuremberg – the list of possible sources is endless. Similarly, a comparison of the cult of Saint Katherine to those of Sebaldus and Lawrence, patron saints of the city's two principal churches, or to that of Saint Dominic, founder of the order to which the Katharinenkloster belonged, would doubtless have shed revealing light on the importance of Saint Katherine to the city, as well as of saints' cults generally. However, this would also have resulted in a very different – or unmanageably lengthy – work, one in which Saint Katherine herself may have been submerged. Moreover, in trying to convey the interrelatedness of diverse aspects of Nuremberg life, played out as it was within mighty city walls and controlled as it was by a powerful Council, I may have written against the grain in places; or, indeed, presented arguments that overlap from one chapter to the next. So tightly knit were the ruling Patrician families, their identities and interests that overlap is almost inevitable. However, precisely therein lies the fascination of Nuremberg and of the saint who functioned virtually as the city logo, so I hope the reader will bear with any shortcomings this study will have. The same forbearing reader may consider the density of the footnoting one such shortcoming. However, information about the saint, the city and the Patricians who governed it has been culled, often piecemeal, from a wide variety of primary and secondary sources, not all of them particularly accessible; and it seemed crucial both to provide the evidence on which my arguments were based and to document its sources.

In the course of researching and writing one incurs many debts, which it is a pleasure to acknowledge. My sincere thanks go to the Deutscher Akademischer Austauschdienst and the Arts Faculty Research Fund, University of Bristol, for their funding of the archival research necessary for this book; as well as to the British Academy for the conference grant that enabled me to present part of Chapter 4, 'Showcasing a Saint', at the annual conference of the Medieval Academy of America, Vancouver 2008. Further thanks are due to the staff of the Germanisches Nationalmuseum Nuremberg and the Stadtbibliothek Nuremberg for their resourcefulness, patience and helpfulness; these are wonderful, civilized places to work. To Frau Margot Lölhöffel and Frau Christina Plewinski of the Stadt Nürnberg goes my gratitude for their kindness and generosity towards my students and for sharing with me their knowledge of and enthusiasm for their wonderful city. My debt to friends runs deep: without them this work may never have seen the light of day. Particular gratitude is due to Professor Marketa Goetz-Stankiewicz for the unwavering friendship, encouragement, support and belief in me that have sustained me for 30 years; to Dr Heike Bartel for her loyal friendship, for her helpful and sensitive reading of my work and for having greater faith in my scholarship than I have myself; and to Dr Rolf Keitel for his steadfast, generous, wise and supportive friendship. To Nicholas Ainsworth, Dr Jeffrey Ashcroft, Dr Ferdi Besselmann, Sharon Baker, Dr Birgit Beumers, Margaret Boakes, Henrietta Cassar, Elsie and David Cassidy, Juliet Cox, Professor David Darby, Peggy Davis, Majella Drew, Ron and Sue Diederichs, Deborah Draffin, Gunlög Eliasson, Malcom, Margaret and Ainslie Emery, Iris and Peter Fenger, Professor John Flood, Bertha Garrett, Michaela Gigerl, Alice Hawkins, the Hood family, Alison Maclaine, Father Tony MacDonald, Caroline McIntyre, Ilse Mozga, Professor Eva Neumann and Dr Wolf Zeitz, Professor Gaby Neumann, Professor Ivan Parvev, Professor Silvia Ranawake, Christa Santi, Professors Frank and Gisela Shaw, Steve Webb, Lynn Wharton and my other friends from Frimley and Camberley Grammar School my heartfelt thanks for their generous, supportive and unconditional friendship, which over the years has given me greater comfort, strength and delight than they may realize; and to Dr Ulrich Freudenstein for thoughtful care and laughter in painful times. To the students who took my Nuremberg option at the University of Bristol I owe thanks for their enthusiasm, commitment and contribution to my own knowledge of the city, as well as for the sheer fun of the classes. To Sam Atkins, Harriet Swindall, Ian Tompkins, Deborah Whitehead and Rike Borchers in particular I owe a huge and lasting debt for their loyalty, support and friendship during an exceedingly difficult year. Professor Henrike Lähnemann, Dr Liz Andersen and Dr Cyril Edwards also went far above and beyond the call of friendship and collegiality and to them, too, I am enormously and enduringly grateful. Tom Gray, my editor at Ashgate, has been a model of patience and understanding; to him, also, my sincere thanks; as to Dr Volker Schier for his generosity in and care over providing the images for this book. Finally, my deepest debt is to my parents, Alexander and Valerie Simon, whose belief in the value of education and personal sacrifice for the sake of mine made everything possible; and, above all, to my sister Jean Webb for her loyalty, her concern for my wellbeing, her unwavering support and her unfailing ability to make me laugh and forget the brutal, disillusioning vicissitudes of academic life.

Anne Simon,
Torquay, 2012

Acknowledgements

Aspects of the discussion on Jezebel first appeared in *Violence, Culture and Identity. Essays on German and Austrian Literature, Politics and Society*, ed. Helen Chambers (Oxford: Peter Lang, 2006), pp. 47–64.

The images of the Volckamer, Konhofer and Kaiser windows, of the Memminger Altar (all Lorenzkirche) and the Löffelholz Altar (Sebalduskirche) were kindly provided by Dr Volker Schier.

The images of the Fütterer Altar (formerly Katharinenkloster; now Lorenzkirche) were kindly provided by Herr Eike Oellermann.

Chapter 1
Saint and the City: Nuremberg and the Cult of Saint Katherine of Alexandria

On 2 January 1945 the Katharinenkloster in Nuremberg was destroyed by an Allied air raid, one of over 40 that ultimately left some 95 per cent of the historic city centre in ruins. Now only the shell of the church and a few convent buildings act as markers of a community which at its height in the second half of the fifteenth century was a centre of intellectual activity and reform. The Katharinenkloster, a Dominican convent, may have originated from a hospice for the care of the sick and impoverished;[1] it was endowed on 27 May 1293 by the Nuremberg Patrician Konrad von Neumarkt and his wife Adelheid, neé Pfinzing;[2] and confirmed on 2

---

[1] It stood outside the city walls until 1379. Müllner mentions an institution by the Pegnitz in which nuns cared for the sick from Nuremberg and elsewhere. Konrad von Neumarkt and his wife gave them 'die Hofrait oder Grund, darauf sie gewohnet, mit ihren Zugehörungen' [the farms with outbuildings or land on which they lived with everything that went with it] as well as land in and tithes from various other properties in the villages around Nuremberg. Two-thirds of the income was for the use of the nuns; one-third for the care of the sick (Johannes Müllner, *Die Annalen der Reichsstadt Nürnberg von 1623*, vol. 1 *Von den Anfängen bis 1350*, ed. and intro. Gerhard Hirschmann (Nuremberg: im Selbstverlag des Stadtrats zu Nürnberg, 1972), pp. 270–1). In the Middle Ages Saint Katherine was a popular patron saint of 'Spitäler und Siechenhäuser' [hospices and alms houses for lepers] (Peter Assion, *Die Mirakel der Hl. Katharina von Alexandrien. Untersuchungen und Texte zur Entstehung und Nachwirkung mittelalterlicher Wunderliteratur* (Diss. Heidelberg 1969), p. 97).

[2] The Neumarkt are first mentioned as an important Nuremberg Patrician family in 1259. Descended from imperial *ministeriales*, they were members of the *Stadtrat* (City Council); Konrad von Neumarkt himself was *Reichsschultheiß* (Imperial Sheriff). The Pfinzing were a leading and long-established Nuremberg Patrician family, first mentioned in 1233 in a document from the monastery in Heilsbronn. In the fourteenth century they already played an important role in Nuremberg trade, having connexions to Italy and South-East Europe. In 1264 Mercklin Pfintzing was sent by Nuremberg Council to Mainz to negotiate mutual freedom from customs' duties (Müllner, *Annalen*, vol. 1, p. 213). Marquardt Pfintzing was *Pfleger* [trustee] of the Egidienkirche in 1269; Bertholdt in 1383 (Müllner, *Annalen*, vol. 1, p. 116); Hanß Pfintzing, his wife Anna and their son Wentzel endowed the celebration of mass there on the anniversary of their death, as did Veit Pfintzing (Müllner, *Annalen*, vol. 1, p. 117). Bertholdt Pfintzing was Sheriff of Nuremberg in 1227 (Müllner, *Annalen*, vol. 1, p. 175). A Berthold Pfintzing was also Sheriff in 1280 and administrator of the *Reichsvogtei* (Imperial Stewardship)

May 1295 by Arnold von Solms,[3] Bishop of Bamberg, who also granted the convent letters of indulgence for anyone who gave it alms, helped with the care of the sick and the poor and visited it on the anniversary of its consecration and feast day of its patrons. The convent church, endowed by Kraft Lang, was consecrated on 28 October 1297.[4] As the foundation attracted nuns from Patrician families[5] it had

at the same time (Müllner, *Annalen*, vol. 1, p. 219). Another Bertholdt Pfintzing was *Pfleger* of the *Siechkobel* (leper hospital) Sankt Johannes in 1356 (Müllner, *Annalen*, vol. 1, p. 211); Endres Pfintzing was *Kirchenpfleger* of the Lorenzkirche in 1390 (Müllner, *Annalen*, vol. 1, p. 58); Sebaldt Pfintzing was *Pfleger* of the Klarissenkloster in 1418 (Müllner, *Annalen*, vol. 1, p. 73). A family connexion with the Katharinenkloster continued: an Elß Pfintzingin was a nun there in 1452 (Müllner, *Annalen*, vol. 1, p. 274). The family died out in 1764. Information on the Katharinenkloster and Katharinenkirche is taken from Walter Fries, 'Kirche und Kloster zu St. Katharina in Nürnberg', *Mitteilungen des Vereins für Geschichte der Stadt Nürnberg*, 25 (1924): 1–143 and illustrations; and the *Stadtlexikon Nürnberg*, ed. Michael Diefenbacher and Rudolf Endres (Nuremberg: Tümmels, 1999; 2nd edn 2000), p. 524; on the Neumarkt family p. 739; on the Pfinzing pp. 821–2. For the Pfintzing see also Müllner, *Annalen*, vol. 1, pp. 219–20; for the Neumarkt Müllner, *Annalen*, vol. 1, pp. 225–6. Unless otherwise stated translations are the author's own.

 [3]   Müllner has 6 May (Müllner, *Annalen*, vol. 1, p. 271).

 [4]   Kraft Lang and Konrad von Neumarkt both lie buried in the convent church (Müllner, *Annalen*, vol. 1, p. 271). In the course of the fourteenth and fifteenth centuries convent and church attracted further letters of indulgence and grants of land and goods (e.g. four cart-loads of firewood a week from the imperial forest (1366)) as well as the protection of King Wenzel III of Bohemia (1271–1305), Emperor Ludwig (1337) and Emperor Karl IV (1358). Emperors Sigmund (1431) and Friedrich (1444) confirmed the convent in all its freedom and privileges, as did Emperor Charles V (Müllner, *Annalen*, vol. 1, pp. 272–3).

 [5]   For example, Cunegunda (d. 1478) and Catharina Holzschuherin (d. 1453) (Johann Gottfried Biedermann, *Geschlechtsregister des Hochadelichen Patriciats zu Nürnberg* (Bayreuth: Friederich Elias Dietzel, 1748; reprint. Neustadt an der Aisch: Christoph Schmidt, 1982). The Patrician Hans VI Tucher's daughter Barbara, from his first marriage to Barbara Ebner, and Sebald Rieter's elder sister were also nuns in the Katharinenkloster. See Randall Herz, 'Hans Tuchers des Ä. "Reise ins Gelobte Land"', in Klaus Arnold (ed.), *Wallfahrten in Nürnberg um 1500. Akten des interdisziplinären Symposions vom 29. und 30. September 2000 im Caritas Pirckheimer-Haus in Nürnberg, Pirckheimer Jahrbuch*, 17 (2002): 79–104 (p. 94); and Ludwig Grote, *Die Tucher. Bildnis einer Patrizierfamilie*, Bibliothek des Germanischen National-Museums Nürnberg zur deutschen Kunst- und Kulturgeschichte 15/16 (Munich: Prestel, 1961), p. 64. The votive picture endowed by the Jerusalem pilgrim Hans VI for the family tomb in the Sebalduskirche in 1485 includes the Katherine wheel representative of the monastery at Sinai (Grote, *Die Tucher*, p. 63). Müllner mentions a number of abbesses or prioresses from Patrician families: Mechthildt Mufflin (1329); Margretha Volckamerin (1391); Katharina Mentlerin (1394); Elizabeth Schurstabin. A Felicitas Tucherin was prioress there in 1536 (Müllner, *Annalen*, vol. 1, pp. 273–4). Moreover, members of leading Patrician families were assigned to the convent as *Pfleger*: Cunradt Groß (1329); Jobst Tetzel der Ältere (1394); Peter Mendel (1420); Sigmundt Stromer (1430) (Müllner, *Annalen*, vol. 1, p. 275).

close ties to those governing Nuremberg, since these families provided 34 members of the 42 strong, all-powerful *Kleiner Rat* (the other eight were master craftsmen).[6] Eventually, the Katharinenkloster became one of the largest women's foundations in South Germany, boasting 70 sisters in 1470.[7] After a first, largely unsuccessful, attempt in 1396, the convent adopted reform in 1428, although not without opposition on its part and the intervention of the City Council.[8] It subsequently became renowned both for the learning of its nuns, many of whom were active as scribes and illuminators, and for the size of its library.[9] Indeed, whilst the nuns did

---

[6]   The number of Patrician families was finally set by the *Tanzstatut* (Dance Statute) of 1521, which restricted to 42 those families eligible to dance at balls at the *Rathaus* (Town Hall). This closed group, which alone was eligible to serve on the *Kleiner Rat*, Nuremberg's governing body, was further subdivided into 20 old and seven new families and 15 only eligible for Council service since 1440 (*Stadtlexikon Nürnberg*, p. 1063).

[7]   It resisted the Reformation, with the result that after March 1525 the City Council allocated it Protestant preachers and confessors and in June 1525 refused it the right to accept novices, at the same time allowing Nuremberg citizens to remove their relatives from the convent, even against the latter's will. The last prioress died in 1596.

[8]   According to Karin Schneider and Werner Williams-Krapp, the main incentive for reform was the Council's desire not to lose the considerable fortune of Kunigunde Schreiberin, widow of Nikolaus Schreiber and member of the Patrician Groß family (Konrad Groß had founded the Heilig-Geist-Spital and been financier to Ludwig der Bayer). On her husband's death she wished to enter a strictly observant foundation and, like other wealthy Nuremberg women before her, was contemplating Schönensteinbach in Alsace. Her husband had been buried in the church of the Dominican monastery in Nuremberg in 1428 (Karin Schneider, 'Die Bibliothek des Katharinenklosters in Nürnberg und die städtische Gesellschaft', in Bernd Moeller, Hans Patze and Karl Stackmann (eds), *Studien zum städtischen Bildungswesen des späten Mittelalters und der frühen Neuzeit*, Abhandlungen der Akademie der Wissenschaften in Göttingen Philologisch-historische Klasse Dritte Folge 137 (Göttingen: Vandenhoeck & Ruprecht, 1983), pp. 70–82 (p. 77); Werner Williams-Krapp, 'Die Bedeutung der reformierten Klöster des Predigerordens für das literarische Leben in Nürnberg im 15. Jahrhundert', in Falk Eisermann, Eva Schlotheuber and Volker Honemann (eds), *Studien und Texte zur literarischen und materiellen Kultur der Frauenklöster im späten Mittelalter*, Studies in Medieval and Reformation Thought 99 (Leiden and Boston: Brill, 2004), pp. 311–29 (pp. 318–19)).

[9]   For an account of the library and the nuns active as scribes, see Fries, 'Kirche und Kloster', pp. 47–57; and Marie-Luise Ehrenschwendtner, 'A Library Collected by and for the Use of Nuns: St Catherine's Convent, Nuremberg', in Jane H.M. Taylor and Lesley Smith (eds), *Women and the Book. Assessing the Visual Evidence* (London and Toronto: British Library and University of Toronto Press, 1996), pp. 123–32. Karin Schneider says of the convent: '[E]s dürfte zu Ende des 15. Jh.s die größte Sammlung deutschsprachiger Handschriften besessen haben, die aus dem Spätmittelalter bekannt ist' [At the end of the fifteenth century it may well have possessed the largest collection of German-language manuscripts known from the Late Middles Ages] (Schneider, 'Bibliothek', p. 70).

execute outside commissions,[10] many of the manuscripts they copied were intended for their own use and housed in the library, which had been in existence since the mid-fourteenth century.[11] The sisters were permitted to take their personal libraries with them upon entering the convent;[12] women donated books to the foundation;[13] the nuns were given books by their wealthy relatives;[14] and books were left to the

---

[10] For example, when she entered the Katharinenkloster, Klara Keiperin took with her a German translation of the *Compendium theologicae veritatis* (now attributed to the Dominican theologian Hugh Ripelin of Strasburg (c. 1205–c. 1270); formerly attributed to Albertus Magnus) that had been copied for a member of Nuremberg's upper classes (either Klara Keiperin's father Konrad Paumgartner or her husband Fritz Keiper) by the founder of the convent scriptorium, Kunigund Niklasin, in the 1430s and then illuminated in the Dominican monastery (Williams-Krapp, 'Die Bedeutung der reformierten Klöster', p. 320).

[11] At that time it may well have housed only 45 volumes. See Elizabeth Schraut, *Stifterinnen und Künstlerinnen im mittelalterlichen Nürnberg*, Ausstellungskataloge des Stadtarchivs Nürnberg 1 (Nuremberg: Selbstverlag der Stadt Nürnberg, 1987), p. 45. For the type and use of manuscripts see Petra Seegets, 'Leben und Streben in spätmittelalterlichen Frauenklöstern', in Berndt Hamm and Thomas Lentes (eds), *Spätmittelalterliche Frömmigkeit zwischen Ideal und Praxis*, Spätmittelalter und Reformation. Neue Reihe 15 (Tübingen: Mohr Siebeck, 2001), pp. 24–44.

[12] Katharina Tucher took 24 manuscript books with her as a dowry on entering the convent c. 1433 after her husband's death (Schneider, 'Bibliothek', p. 73; Schraut, *Stifterinnen*, p. 29 (who puts the number at 23)). She was active as a scribe and recorded her own mystical visions. Her books included the *Schwabenspiegel* (an important medieval law codex); a German version of the *Lucidarius* (a medieval encyclopaedia); popular 'religiöse Erbauungsliteratur' [religious devotional literature] such as Heinrich Seuse's *Buch der ewigen Weisheit* or the *Buch von den sechs Namen des Fronleichnams* by the monk of Heilsbronn, a nearby Cistercian monastery; a Psalter; saints' lives (e.g. Sebaldus); a *Historienbibel* and five prayer books (some sisters owned as many as 10) (Schneider, 'Bibliothek', pp. 74–5). Another rich widow, Kunigunde Schreiberin, also took 19 manuscripts into the convent with her. She made a considerable contribution (also financial) to the reform of the convent in 1428. Her library included a medical treatise; a Psalter; mystical writings; saints' lives; a treatise on how to live a married life pleasing to God; and the *Vierundzwanzig goldene Harfen*, a collection of sermons by the Dominican Johannes Nider, who carried out the reform of the convent (Schneider, 'Bibliothek', pp. 76–7). Indeed, quoting a letter from the prioress of a reformed convent to a prospective nun, Williams-Krapp points out that by the time of the Katharinenkloster reform women who wanted to enter an observant Dominican convent were more or less expected to bring with them a basic library that included, amongst other things, a Psalter, a diurnal (for the daytime canonical Hours) and a processional (Williams-Krapp, 'Die Bedeutung der reformierten Klöster', p. 324).

[13] For example, Anna Schürstabin, whose daughters Margaretha and Dorothea and granddaughter Apollonia were in the convent (Antje Willing, *Literatur und Ordensreform im 15. Jahrhundert. Deutsche Abendmahlsschriften im Nürnberger Katharinenkloster*, Studien und Texte zum Mittelalter und zur frühen Neuzeit 4 (Münster: Waxmann, 2004), p. 48).

[14] Schraut, *Stifterinnen*, p. 27; Schneider, 'Bibliothek', p. 78.

convent as a whole.[15] Between 1451 and 1457 Sister Kunigund Niklasin drew up a list of all books in the nuns' private possession, most of which were prayer books. Between 1455 and 1457 she catalogued the convent library, which, on its dissolution in the course of the Reformation, held about 500 volumes.[16]

One manuscript from the collection achieved an impact beyond the convent walls, namely Germanisches Nationalmuseum Hs. 877 (1421), a compendium copied by Fridricus Lenckner for Cecilia Rötin (d. 1469), who took it into the convent with her and was herself active as a scribe.[17] On 28 July 1474 Hans Sensenschmid, the first Nuremberg printer, published *Der Heiligen Leben*, the augmented German translation of Jacobus de Voragine's *Legenda aurea* and an ambitious, richly illustrated work.[18] The *Heiligen Leben* appeared in

---

[15] Schneider, 'Bibliothek', p. 79. Williams-Krapp records that in his will of 1449 the Patrician Franz Pirckheimer, after (presumably mainly Latin) book bequests to the family, left half his remaining German books to the Katharinenkloster and half to the Augustinian convent in Pillenreuth near Nuremberg (Williams-Krapp, 'Die Bedeutung der reformierten Klöster', p. 325).

[16] Schraut, *Stifterinnen*, p. 45. Another estimate puts the number of vernacular manuscripts at well over 600 (Falk Eisermann, review of Antje Willing, *Literatur und Ordensreform im 15. Jahrhundert. Deutsche Abendmahlsschriften im Nürnberger Katharinenkloster*. Studien und Texte zum Mittelalter und zur frühen Neuzeit 4 (Münster: Waxmann, 2004), in *IASL Online* at http://iasl.uni-muenchen.de/rezensio/liste/Eisermann3830913311-1032.html. Fries points out that Niklasin's catalogue was a list of material suitable for reading during meals; it did not cover the entire library holdings (Fries, 'Kirche und Kloster', p. 48). Furthermore, Karin Schneider suggests that the Latin codices, especially liturgical ones, were not catalogued (Schneider, 'Bibliothek', p. 71); while Antje Willing postulates a (no longer extant) catalogue for Latin works alone, since they were usually catalogued separately from vernacular ones (Willing, *Literatur und Ordensreform*, p. 31). She characterizes the contents of the convent library as follows (the letters are part of the shelf-mark): A bibles; B catechetical treatises; C German Psalters; D liturgical works; E collections of sermons; F Leopold Stainreuther's German translation of the *Rationale divinorum officiorum* of Wilhelm Durandus; G five works on the rituals for Dominican nuns; H writings (in Latin and German) concerning the rules and constitution of the Dominican Order, including its constitution, instruction for novices and so forth; J (the largest group) hagiography and the *Lucidarius*; K medical and legal texts; L prayer books and *Ars moriendi* literature (pp. 35–6).

[17] See Assion, Mirakel, pp. 66–8.

[18] Sensenschmid moved to Nuremberg from Bamberg and began printing there in 1469; his first datable work is the *Comestorium viciorum* by Franz von Retz (1470), of which he and Dr Heinrich Rummel, Patrician and lawyer, donated a copy to the Carthusian monastery in Nuremberg (Franz Machilek, 'Klosterhumanismus in Nürnberg um 1500', *Mitteilungen des Vereins für Geschichte der Stadt Nürnberg*, 64 (1977): 10–45 (pp. 16–17)). Sensenschmid's edition of *Der Heiligen Leben* is the first richly illustrated Nuremberg print, boasting over 250 woodcuts. Saint Katherine's legend (fol. cclijr–cclxj^r) is introduced by a small image showing Saint Katherine kneeling in front of a wheel, flame-like rays of Grace falling from the sky, a

24 editions between 1471 and 1500, the *Winterteil* of Sensenschmid's edition containing a life of Saint Katherine of Alexandria taken almost verbatim from this Katharinenkloster manuscript.[19] That this printed version of Saint Katherine's legend and miracles is some 14,400 words long, seven times longer than the average saint's life in the *Heiligen Leben*,[20] and that it takes as its source a manuscript produced in the nearby convent, furnishes just one indicator of the extent to which Saint Katherine was rooted in the spiritual, cultural and community consciousness of Nuremberg from at least the late-thirteenth century onwards. Indeed, such was her presence that the entire city could be read as a map of devotion to her. Hence, the purpose of this chapter is to explore the following: first, the shaping of urban space through the cult of Saint Katherine; second, her role in moulding, marking and reflecting Patrician identity through cultural patronage; third, her iconography as transformer and redeemer of meaning; fourth, her iconography as reminder of and vehicle for saint and city further afield. Finally, the role of visualization and memorization strategies in this process of recursive reflexion will be tested.[21] Four texts illustrate

---

bearded Maxentius behind her and two men prostrate in front of her (fol. cclij[r]). *Der Heiligen Leben* was first published by Günther Zainer in Augsburg in 1471. The oldest *Der Heiligen Leben* manuscript is listed in Niklasin's catalogue (Assion, *Mirakel*, p. 55).

[19]   See Assion, *Mirakel*, pp. 66–8. The oldest manuscript version of *Der Heiligen Leben* dates to around the end of the fourteenth century and was also produced in the Katharinenkloster Nuremberg. It is now in the Stadtbibliothek Nürnberg, Cod. Cent. IV, 43. Williams-Krapp calls *Der Heiligen Leben* 'das erfolgreichste volkssprachliche Legendar des europäischen Mittelalters' [the most successful vernacular legendary of the European Middle Ages]. According to him, 198 manuscripts are extant, most of them from the fifteenth century; of these, 60 are monastic in provenance (24 of these from Dominican convents). Approximately 36 manuscripts known to have been owned by lay people and 41 printed editions testify to the work's popularity amongst the lay (Werner Williams-Krapp, 'Ordensreform und Literatur im 15. Jahrhundert', *Jahrbuch der Oswald von Wolkenstein Gesellschaft*, 4 (1986/7): 41–51 (p. 45)).

[20]   Bruce A. Beatie, 'Saint Katharine of Alexandria: Traditional Themes and the Development of a Medieval German Narrative', *Speculum*, 52 (1977): 785–800 (p. 785 and p. 793). Beatie draws largely on Fries. See also Bruce A. Beatie, 'St. Katharine of Alexandria in Medieval German Illustrative Cycles: A Problem beyond Genre', in Hubert Heinen and Ingeborg Henderson (eds), *Genres in Medieval German Literature*, Göppinger Arbeiten zur Germanistik 439 (Göppingen: Kümmerle, 1986), pp. 140–56; and D.L. d'Avray, 'Katharine of Alexandria and Mass Communication in Germany: Woman as Intellectual', in Nicole Bériou and David L. d'Avray (eds), *Modern Questions about Medieval Sermons. Essays on Marriage, Death, History and Sanctity*, Biblioteca di Medioevo Latino 11 (Spoleto: Centro Italiano di Studi sull'Alto Medioevo, 1994), pp. 401–8.

[21]   For the term 'recursive reflexion' I am indebted to Dr Rolf Keitel, TRIUMF, University of British Columbia.

particularly clearly both the integration of Saint Katherine into urban spiritual life and the latter's echoes beyond Nuremberg city walls; these will form the basis for discussion: Sensenschmid's *Der Heiligen Leben*, Hans Tucher's *Reise zum Heiligen Grab* (Augsburg: Johann Schönsperger, 1482; reprint Nuremberg: Konrad Zeninger, 1482), Stephan Fridolin's *Schatzbehalter* (Nuremberg: Anton Koberger, 1491) and Marquard vom Stein's *Der Ritter vom Turn* (Basel: Michael Furter for Johann Bergmann von Olpe, 1493).

Saint Katherine of Alexandria was the fourth-century virgin saint and mystic bride of Christ martyred by the Roman Emperor Maxentius, who wanted her as a bride for his son and tried to undermine her belief in Christ, whom she had wed in a vision. He summoned 50 philosophers to attempt this task; Saint Katherine's faith, erudition and eloquence enabled her to convert them to Christianity instead, a triumph resulting in their immediate martyrdom by fire. Maxentius ordered that Saint Katherine be torn to shreds on a spiked wheel especially devised for this purpose; however, in response to her prayer an angel shattered it, 4,000 pagans perishing as collateral damage. Maxentius' wife, Faustina, and his captain of the guard, Porphyrius, also suffered death on their conversion to Christianity by Saint Katherine. Eventually Saint Katherine was beheaded, whereupon milk instead of blood flowed from her neck. Her reconstituted body was translated by angels to Mount Sinai, where it now rests in the Greek Orthodox monastery; at one time healing oil flowed from the saint's bones.[22] Known for her beauty and intellect, Saint Katherine was the patron saint of young girls, nursemaids, scholars, teachers, universities, schools and libraries.

If this was Saint Katherine's legend, what image of her prevailed in the convent and the wider city? In Sensenschmid's *Der Heiligen Leben* she is characterized as follows:[23]

> ES was eyn edler reycher Kung yn Cipperen land in der inselen in einer stat dy hyeß Solomina / der hyeß Costis der hett eyn tochter dye hyeß Katherina / vnd die was zu mal weiß vnd schon vnd kensch [*sic*] vnd tugentlich Vnd da sie bey sechs iaren waz da ließ man sie zu schul gen / da lernet sie gar wol / vnd da sie klug ward yn der ku*n*st des ward sy gar volkummen darin d*a*z man iren gleychen niedert fand / vnnd man hieß sie ein bewerte Meisterinn in den siben hochsten kunste*n*.[24]

---

[22]   The legend of Saint Katherine is included in the *Legenda aurea*. See Jacobus de Voragine, *The Golden Legend. Readings on the Saints*, trans. William Granger Ryan, vol. 2 (Princeton: Princeton University Press, 1993), pp. 334–41.

[23]   The printed edition rather than the Germanisches Nationalmuseum manuscript is taken as the basis for discussion due to its greater accessibility.

[24]   *Der Heiligen Leben*, fol. cclij[r]. All subsequent references to this work will be given in the text. According to Saint Katherine's legend she was born in Famagusta. However,

[There was once a noble, rich king on the island of Cyprus in a town called Solomina. His name was Costis and he had a daughter called Katherine who was wise, beautiful, chaste and virtuous. When she was six years old she was sent to school, where she excelled at her studies and because she cleverly mastered the curriculum she became so perfect in her studies of the *trivium* and *quadrivium* that her equal could not be found and she was known as a tried and tested Master of the Seven Liberal Arts].

First, Katherine is located in terms of both geography and lineage. Cyprus was known to Nuremberg merchants through trade and as a stopping point on the way to the Holy Land.[25] Solomina or Salamis is near Famagusta, which itself had a reputation for the wealth of its merchants, as recorded, for example, by Ludolf von Sudheim on his pilgrimage to the Holy Land: 'In a warehouse in this city there is more aloeswood than five carts can carry; I say nothing about spices, for they are as common there as bread is here, and are just as commonly mixed and sold'.[26] He notes further:

> There are also in Cyprus exceeding rich citizens and merchants, and no wonder, seeing that Cyprus is the furthest (east) of all Christian lands, wherefore all ships both great and small, and all merchandise of whatsoever kind and from whatsoever country, must needs come first of all to Cyprus, and can in no wise pass by it. (pp. 43–4)

---

near Famagusta is the ancient port and capital of Cyprus, Salamis (or Constantia), of which Solomina may be a corruption. The city was destroyed by earthquakes in 332 and 342 AD.

[25]   The ship carrying Hans Tucher and his party on their pilgrimage struck anchor in Limassol for three days, so they took the opportunity to go ashore and hear mass (Hans Tucher, *Die 'Reise ins Gelobte Land' Hans Tuchers des Älteren (1479–1480)*, ed. Randall Herz, Wissensliteratur im Mittelalter 38 (Wiesbaden: Reichert, 2002), pp. 366–7). Tucher does not mention any Cyprus connexion to Saint Katherine, although he does record the presence of her right arm and her hand in the chapel of the Hospitaller Grand Master on Rhodes (p. 365) and note that pilgrims to Cyprus usually visit the port of Salines, 10 miles from Famagusta (p. 367).

[26]   Ludolf von Sudheim, *Ludolph von Suchem's Description of the Holy Land and of the Way Thither. Written in the Year 1350*, trans. Aubrey Stewart, Palestine Pilgrims' Text Society 27 (London: Palestine Pilgrims' Text Society, 1895), pp. 42–3. Ludolf's report was first published in Latin by Heinrich Eggesteyn in Straßburg between 1475 and 1480. A German version published by Johannes Zainer appeared in Ulm in 1473. The work must have been known in Nuremberg as Tucher draws on it for his account. Ludolf does mention Saint Katherine: 'Near Famagusta there is another city on the sea-shore named Constantia or Salamina, which once was an exceeding noble, famous and beauteous city, as its ruins bear witness ... In the same city was born S. Katharine the Virgin, and a chapel stands on the place of her nativity to this day' (p. 42).

Famagusta, then, places the saint within a familiar urban trading environment. Her royal lineage means that her martyr's crown is foreshowed by a princess's; that she is of suitable rank to be the bride of the King of Heaven; and that she belongs to a family-based ruling elite, a status with which the governing Patrician readers of *Der Heiligen Leben* would have identified and which corresponded to that of the Patrician nuns.

Second, Katherine is described as 'weiß vnd schon vnd kensch vnd tugentlich',[27] so it was her wisdom that, for the nuns of the Katharinenkloster, was her most significant quality and set the mould for her image in the city as a whole. The highlighting of wisdom reinforces the convent's identity as a place of learning, locates it within the history of women's contribution to the history of salvation and provides the nuns with a purpose: the acquisition and transmission of spiritual wisdom.[28] Saint Katherine's wisdom and virtue are further expressed by her beauty as the outward manifestation of inner worth; her chastity confirms the nuns in their renunciation of marriage and embrace of their new identity as brides of Christ. Indeed, a prayer at the end of the *Der Heiligen Leben* account of Saint Katherine's life and miracles cites her status as Christ's spouse as a channel for her intercession on the petitioner's behalf:

> Nun helff vns dye heylig iunckfraw Sant Katherin vmb got vnsern herren Jhesum Cristum iren lyeben gemaheln erwerben durch all ir wirdikeyt dye sye ewigklich mit ym hat / daz wir hye menschenn werden nach gottes lob / vnnd vnsers lebens eyn gucz end vnd dar nach das ewig leben / das helf vns got der vater vnd gott der sun vnd got der heylig geist Amen. (fol. cclxj^r)

> [Now may the holy virgin Saint Katherine, for the sake of our Lord God Jesus Christ, her beloved spouse, help us to manage, through her eternal worthiness in His eyes, to become people worthy of God's praise on this earth, to die a good death and then attain eternal life. May God the Father, God the Son and God the Holy Ghost aid us. Amen].

Not only does Saint Katherine provide a model for nuns, who as brides of Christ may use their prayer to help their Patrician families and community; she also provides one for young female readers of *Der Heiligen Leben*, who through their

---

[27]   'wise, beautiful, chaste and virtuous'.

[28]   Indeed, Felix Fabri refers to Saint Katherine's skull as 'that treasure-house of heavenly wisdom, the virgin's sacred head' (Felix Fabri, *The Wanderings of Felix Fabri*, trans. Aubrey Stewart, 2 vols, The Library of the Palestine Pilgrims' Text Society 10 (London: Committee of the Palestine Exploration Fund, 1897), p. 600).

own virtue and chaste fidelity to their spouse may recreate the holy union in their own lives, thus serving their community and providing a model in their turn.

Third, the importance of the saint's learning, though part of her legend, is significant, both for the convent and the city as a whole. It is said of her that she 'lernet ... gar wol', eventually becoming known as 'ein bewerte Meisterinn in den siben hochsten kunste*n*'.[29] In other words, Katherine had enjoyed an education in the Seven Liberal Arts that formed the medieval university curriculum; this alone singles her out as exceptional at a time when German women at least were denied access to the few universities in Europe. In collecting and copying manuscripts, the nuns were following Katherine's model by acquiring learning on a smaller scale.[30] They were also contributing to a broader civic tradition of learning which had, in the fourteenth century, seen the founding of Latin schools connected to the Lorenzkirche (mentioned 1325), the Sebalduskirche (mentioned 1337),[31] the Heilig-Geist-Spital (mentioned 1339) and the Egidienkloster (mentioned 1396).[32] From 1400 onwards private schools provided a practical education designed to meet the needs of merchants and artisans.[33] Somewhat later, in 1503, another Nuremberg convent,

---

[29]   'she excelled at her studies'; 'a tried and tested master of the Seven Liberal Arts'.

[30]   *Der Heiligen Leben* also contains Saint Katherine's miracles (fol. ccliiij^r–cclxj^r), slightly trickier for the nuns to emulate. No mention has been found of a school in the Katharinenkloster (apart from the *Schreibschule*). The degree to which the nuns knew Latin is impossible to determine with absolute certainty: although the convent library included works in Latin, Willing, for example, assumes most of the sisters knew none (Willing, *Literatur und Ordensreform*, p. 28). Peter Ochsenbein speculates that in the course of the fourteenth and fifteenth centuries Dominican nuns' knowledge of Latin became increasingly limited to that necessary for the liturgy and prayer. However, he also suggests that if male Dominican mystics (such as Meister Eckhart) preached in German, it was also due to their limited competence in Latin and lack of ability to formulate complex ideas in that language (Peter Ochsenbein, 'Latein und Deutsch im Alltag oberrheinischer Dominikanerinnenklöster des Spätmittelalters', in Nikolaus Henkel and Nigel F. Palmer (eds), *Latein und Volkssprache im deutschen Mittelalter. Regensburger Colloquium 1988* (Tübingen: Niemeyer, 1992) pp. 42–51 (p. 42)). Fries, on the other hand, assumes a considerable command of Latin by the Katharinenkloster nuns post-reform (Fries, 'Kirche und Kloster', pp. 47–8; see Chapter 2).

[31]   A further school was built next to the Sebalduskirche in 1465 (Johann Jacob Carbach, *Nürnbergisches Zion / Das ist: Wahrhaffte Beschreibung Aller Kirchen und Schulen in= und ausserhalb Der Reichs=Stadt Nürnberg* (s.l., 1733), p. 4.

[32]   Poor pupils paid no fees. The curriculum was based on the *trivium* and consisted of Latin (in which pupils learnt to read and write), grammar, logic and music (i.e. singing).

[33]   *Stadtlexikon Nürnberg*, pp. 614–15 and pp. 958–9. Moreover, from the second half of the fifteenth century onwards the Patriciate started to send its sons to university: for example, Berthold IV Tucher attended the University of Vienna and in turn sent his five sons to Heidelberg, where they were joined by their cousin Sixtus (Grote, *Die Tucher*, p. 65).

the Klarissenkloster, also became an intellectual force as Caritas Pirckheimer (1467–1532), the exceptionally well-educated sister of the Humanist Willibald Pirckheimer, was elected Abbess.[34] Caritas Pirckheimer enjoyed a reputation for learning and was in correspondence with the likes of Konrad Celtis (first German Poet Laureate and editor of Hrotsvit von Gandersheim), Sixt Tucher[35] and her own brother.[36] Moreover, just as Saint Katherine herself had converted the heathen philosophers, so nuns from the Katharinenkloster in Nuremberg were subsequently dispatched to reform other convents. These included Tulln an der Donau in Lower Austria (1436); Pforzheim, Baden-Württemberg (1443); the Kloster zum heiligen Grab, Bamberg (1451); Hohenaltau, Bavaria (1465); Medingen by Dillingen (1472); Gotteszell by Gmund (1478); the Kloster zum heiligen Kreuz, Regensburg (1483); and Engelthal (c. 19 miles east of Nuremberg) (1513). The exchange of books and correspondence between the two prioresses, Angela Varnbüler (St. Gallen) and Kunigunda von Haller (Nuremberg), from 1476 on also led to the Nuremberg convent's exercising of considerable influence on the reform of the Katharinenkloster in St. Gallen.[37]

In the late-fifteenth century, then, the Katharinenkloster was a politically well-connected, culturally active and intellectually open presence within a city where printers enjoyed close links to the monasteries and Patrician merchants socialized and debated with leading Humanist scholars such as Willibald Pirckheimer. In addition to Katharinenkloster manuscripts containing Saint Katherine's legend, miracles and prayers to her for the nuns' own use, daily devotion to the saint was shaped and guided by the statues and paintings of her found within the confines of the convent.[38] Moreover, representations of the saint abound in Nuremberg churches,[39] including that of Saint Sebaldus, the

---

[34]   The also well-educated Apollonia, daughter of Herdegen I Tucher, was Prioress in the Klarissenkloster; she read Latin and the works of Saint Jerome, loved the mystics and corresponded with Nuremberg Humanists and Konrad Celtis (Grote, *Die Tucher*, pp. 64–5).

[35]   Provost of the Nuremberg Lorenzkirche from 1496.

[36]   Indeed, in 1511 Albrecht Dürer dedicated the printed edition of his *Marienleben* to her. See *Stadtlexikon Nürnberg*, p. 827; and Charlotte Woodford, *Nuns as Historians in Early Modern Germany* (Oxford: Clarendon, 2002).

[37]   See Thomas Käppeli, *Dominikanerinnenkloster St. Katharina. Ein Abriß seiner Geschichte* (Wil: St. Katharina, 1957), pp. 10–12.

[38]   Some of these are now in the Germanisches Nationalmuseum, Nuremberg, and include two depictions of Saint Katherine's mystic marriage to Christ, one a painting by Hans Pleydenwurff's workshop (donated 1468 and 1475); the other a carved altar shrine (Nuremberg 1480).

[39]   Due to the destruction of Nuremberg during the Second World War and the allocation of works from the Katharinenkloster to other churches in the city it is not possible to say with absolute certainty where images of the saint originally stood. However,

city's patron saint.[40] The Sebalduskirche stands at the bottom of the present-day Bergstraße, in the late-fifteenth century home to a number of wealthy Patrician families, to Albrecht Dürer's own goldsmith father and to such artists as Michael Wolgemut, to whom Dürer was apprenticed for three years. Patricians and, in all likelihood, Dürer himself, worshipped in the Sebalduskirche, which houses numerous examples of Patrician patronage. One such is a carved wooden altar in the West choir, the Löffelholz Altar (c. 1462–4), dedicated to Saint Katherine and depicting on the left the miracle of the wheel and on the right her execution, in other words the two stages of her martyrdom.[41] On the painted wings are found the disputation with the philosophers and the burning of the philosophers.

---

in present-day Nuremberg statues, carvings, stained-glass windows and pictures of the saint on altarpieces are present in the following churches: the Marthakirche, Klarissenkirche, Jakobskirche, Egidienkirche Sebalduskirche, Lorenzkirche and Frauenkirche.

[40]   Saint Sebaldus was a Benedictine hermit who worked with Saint Willibald in his missionary activity in the Reichswald (Imperial Forest). He died circa 770 and became patron saint of Nuremberg in the eleventh century. Associated with such miracles as helping a farmer to find his lost oxen or turning icicles into firewood, he was prayed to for protection against cold weather. His feast day is 19 August. His relics were housed in a silver shrine (1391) within an ornate brass housing cast in 1507–19 by Nuremberg's leading metal-caster, Peter Vischer (1460–1529), with the help of his two sons. The shrine is decorated with the coats-of-arms of the free imperial city and the Holy Roman Emperor, functioning as a statement of both Patrician wealth and pride and of Nuremberg's eminence within the Holy Roman Empire. It was customary to open the casket containing Sebaldus's relics from time to time, such as 22 July 1503 (Müllner, *Annalen*, vol. 1, p. 15).

[41]   For information on Saint Katherine and her iconography see: Diane Apostolos-Cappadona, *Dictionary of Women in Religious Art* (New York and Oxford: Oxford University Press, 1998; 1st edn New York: Continuum, 1996), pp. 66–8; Sally Fisher, *The Square Halo & Other Mysteries of Western Art. Images and the Stories that Inspired Them* (New York: Harry N. Abrams, 1995), pp. 140–2; James Hall, *Hall's Dictionary of Subjects & Symbols in Art*, intro. Kenneth Clark (1st edn 1974; London: John Murray, 2000), pp. 58–9; and Peter and Linda Murray, *The Oxford Companion to Christian Art and Architecture* (Oxford and New York: Oxford University Press, 1996), p. 95. An altar dedicated to Saint Katherine also stood in the crypt at the West end of the Sebalduskirche, probably erected immediately upon completion of building work on that part of the church. The earlier altar is first mentioned in connexion with the confirmation of earlier indulgences for the Sebalduskirche by the Bishop of Bamberg, Leupold von Gründlach, on 3 July 1298. See Franz Machilek, 'Dedicationes Ecclesiae Sancti Sebaldi. Die mittelalterlichen Kirch- und Altarweihen bei St. Sebald in Nürnberg', in Helmut Baier im Auftrag des Evang.–Luth. Pfarramtes St. Sebald (ed.), *600 Jahre Ostchor St. Sebald – 1379–1979* (Neustadt a. d. Aisch: Ph. C. W. Schmidt, 1979), pp. 143–59 (p. 148). This altar was moved from the crypt to the West choir and re-consecrated by 1357 at the latest. According to Müllner's *Annalen*, an altar dedicated to Saint Katherine stood 'ob der Crypta. Hat Cunradt Schatz, ein Vicarier gestiftet' [above the crypt. Cunradt Schatz endowed a curateship] (Müllner, *Annalen*, vol. 1, p. 17).

The altar was donated in 1462/4 by Wilhelm Löffelholz (1424–75) in memory of his wife Kunigunde Paumgartner (d. 1462),[42] one of the four daughters of the immensely wealthy Konrad VI Paumgartner, one of the richest and most respected men in Nuremberg.[43] Kunigunde was the widow of Hieronymus Ebner; Wilhelm married her on 28 February 1446.[44] A merchant family, the

---

[42]   She died on 7 March 1462, having borne 10 children. The inscription on the altar reads: 'Anno domini m cccc liii an s Thomas tag de Aqiin verschied frav Kunigund Wilhelm Loffelholtzin, der got gnadt' [On Saint Thomas Aquinus' Day in the year 1453 Frau Kunigunde Löffelholz departed this life. May God have mercy on her soul]. For this and what follows see Friedrich Wilhelm, Die Sebalduskirche in Nürnberg. Ihre Baugeschichte und ihre Kunstdenkmale, rev. and augmented by Th. Hampe, E. Mummenhof and Jos. Schmitz (Vienna: Gerlach & Wiedling, 1912), p. 137. On Kunigunde's death Wilhelm Löffelholz wrote: 'gar eines selig=lieblichen Endes dergleichen nit viel gehört noch gesehen wäre worden verschieden'. He continues: 'Sie war eine gar verständige, schön fromb Hausfrau und einer mittelmäßigen Läng, die auch wol sticken und würken kunnt, wie manz das sieht an den Altar=Tuchern in den Tumkirchen zu Bamberg und Würzburg und in Nürnberg auf St. Katharinen=Chörlein (der Löffelholz=Kapelle) zu St. Sebald' [She died a blessed, beautiful death such as is rarely seen or heard ... She was a prudent, admirably pious housewife of medium height, who was a talented embroiderer and needlewoman, as can be seen on the altar cloths in the cathedral churches in Bamberg and Würzburg and in Saint Katherine's Choir (the Löffelholz Chapel) in the Sebalduskirche]. See die historische Commission bei der königl. Akademie der Wissenschaften (ed.), Allgemeine Deutsche Biographie, vol. 19 (Leipzig: Duncker & Humblot, 1884), p. 93. Kunigunde Löffelholz had, then, embroidered altar cloths for Saint Katherine's altar in the West choir, a connexion to the altar established by the family during her lifetime. For the nature and purpose of endowments see Ralf Lusiardi, Stiftung und städtische Gemeinschaft. Religiöse und soziale Aspekte des Stiftungsverhaltens im spätmittelalterlichen Stralsund, Stiftungsgeschichten 2 (Berlin: Akademie Verlag, 2000).

[43]   Wilhelm Löffelholz also commissioned a Latin Book of Hours, the *Löffelholz-Gebetbuch* (third quarter of the fourteenth century; possibly bound 1468; now Germanisches Nationalmuseum Hs 1736). My thanks to Dr Volker Schier for drawing my attention to this volume.

[44]   The occasion was marked by a *Gesellenstechen* (tournament): 'Dies Gestech hat der alte Berthold Volckamer in seiner Behausung an S. Egidiengaß in eine große Stuben auf ein ausgespannetes Tuch, jeglichen Stecher mit allen Farben und Kleinoden, mit Fleiß malen lassen, welche Behausung nachmals Herr Christoff Teczel der Älter und Losunger erkauft, und das vielgedachte Gestech verneuen lassen, wie es dann in derselben Behausung noch zu sehen, und sein davon in Stech- und Schönbart-Bücher viel Kopien gemacht worden, wie es dann auch Cunrad Haller in sein Buch von den nürnbergischen Geschlechten also malen lassen' [Berthold Volckamer the Elder had this tournament painted with great attention to detail on a stretched canvas in a large room in his house on the Egidiengasse. Every jouster is depicted in all his colours and jewels. This house was later bought by Herr Christoff Tetzel the Elder, city *Losunger* (Sheriff), who had the much-lauded tournament picture restored. It can still be seen in the same house and numerous copies have been made of it in jousting and Schönbart books, like the one Conrad Haller had painted in his *Buch von den Nürnbergischen Geschlechten*] (Müllner,

Löffelholz had established themselves in Nuremberg in 1420;[45] from 1440 onwards they had been members of the *Kleiner Rat*. They were also culturally active: Johann Löffelholz (1448–1509), for example, was a Humanist poet (under the pseudonym 'Cocles') and friend of Konrad Celtis.[46] The choice of iconographic programme for the altar, possibly by Wilhelm Löffelholz himself,

---

Annalen, vol. 1, pp. 377–9). Fleischmann describes the occasion as 'eine wahre Prunkhochzeit ... bei der 39 junge Männer des vordersten Standes ein Gesellenstechen abhielten'. He continues: 'Dieser Versuch des Stadtadels der Nachahmung ritterlicher Umgangsformen gilt als sehr beachtlich, weil die Verehelichung von Angehörigen zweier junger, sehr wohlhabender Geschlechter den Anlass dazu gegeben hat. Dank der zeitgenössischen bildlichen Aufzeichnung eines Teilnehmers hat dieses Ereignis lange nachgewirkt, denn der Rat ließ es noch 1621 im Gang des zweiten Stockwerks des Wolffschen Rathausbaus als Stuckrelief an der Decke in einer Länge von etwa 65 Metern verewigen' [a truly magnificent wedding ... at which 39 young men of the leading class held a tournament ... This attempt by the urban nobility to imitate chivalric manners is considered very significant because the marriage of members of two young, very prosperous houses furnished the occasion for it. Thanks to a contemporary visual record by a participant this event resonated for a long time, since in 1621 the Council had it immortalized in a 65-metre-long stucco relief on the ceiling of the corridor on the second floor of the town hall designed by Wolff] (Peter Fleischmann, *Rat und Patriziat in Nürnberg. Die Herrschaft der Ratsgeschlechter vom 13. bis zum 18. Jahrhundert*, 3 vols, Nürnberger Forschungen 31 (Neustadt an der Aisch: Schmidt, 2008), vol. 2, *Ratsherren und Ratsgeschlechter*, pp. 672–3).

⁴⁵ The Löffelholz were originally *ministeriales* of the Bishops of Bamberg. In 1420 Burkhard Löffelholz was the first member of the family to come to Nuremberg and gain the *Bürgerrecht* [right to citizenship]. The family were admitted to the *Großer Rat* as early as in 1421. Hans der Alte was the first member of the family to be admitted to the *Kleiner Rat* in 1440; he served as *Jüngerer Bürgermeister* [Junior Mayor] in 1440 and 1444. Wilhelm I Löffelholz was the only surviving son of Hans der Alte and Barbara Haidin, whose wealthy father belonged to the retinue of the Burgraves of Nuremberg. He married Kunigunde Paumgartner on 7 February 1446 (Fleischmann, vol. 2, *Ratsherren*, pp. 671–2). Wilhelm I Löffelholz was *Ratsherr* [councillor] in 1454, 1469–71, 1473, 1474; *Alter Bürgermeister* [Senior Mayor] in 1464, *Septemvir* in 1473. He represented Nuremberg on various diplomatic missions, including at the *Reichstag* [imperial diet] in Regensburg in 1471 at which a campaign against the Turks was discussed. In 1475 Wilhelm Löffelholz was sent by the *Rat* to the Bishop of Bamberg and to Markgrave Albrecht to ask them to promote, with Emperor Friedrich, Nuremberg's wish to rid the city of Jews. Fleischmann says two of Wilhelm's daughters entered the Katharinenkloster, but not by which wife (p. 673). The Löffelholz seem also to have had a particular link to the Augustinerkloster, as Wilhelm Löffelholz was *Pfleger* there in 1467 and Müllner mentions the following as having 'ihre Jahrtäg und Begängnus in diesem Kloster gestiftet' [endowed masses for the anniversary of their death and burial in this monastery]; some also lay buried there: Christoff Löffelholtz; Wilhelm Löffelholtz (1475); Johann Löffelholtz (1492); Wolffgang Löffelholtz (1521) (Müllner, *Annalen*, vol. 1, p. 159). In 1452 Johann Löffelholtz can be found amongst the brothers in the Carthusian monastery; he had a new chapel built and gave the monastery over 600 florins (Müllner, *Annalen*, vol, 2, p. 81 and p. 344).

⁴⁶ *Stadtlexikon Nürnberg*, p. 639.

foregrounds Saint Katherine's use of her learning and eloquence in the service of God, her martyrdom and the glorious fate of those who heed her word and the Word. Obviously these elements are familiar from the legend, but they do echo and reinforce the textual image of the saint presented in *Der Heiligen Leben* and the original Katharinenkloster manuscript. On the outside of the *predella* are painted the members of the donor's family: on the left Wilhelm Löffelholz with four sons and the Löffelholz, Löffelholz-Dietner and Löffelholz-Stromer-Sachs coats-of-arms; on the right Kunigunde with four daughters, Löffelholz's new wife, Barbara Hirschvogelin, and the Löffelholz-Züngel, Löffelholz-Kreß and Löffelholz-Stromer coats-of-arms.[47] Although primarily a memorial to Wilhelm Löffelholz's first wife, the altar performs another function, namely as a statement of family identity, family piety and family connexions, of the family's location within the social and governing elite of the city. It identifies the saint as part of the Löffelholz family and their lineage. In typical donors' pose on the *predella* they serve as witnesses to Saint Katherine's martyrdom and literally support her in it, through their devotion establishing a model for other worshippers in the church. Past, present and future generations of the family kneel "under" the saint, symbolically under her protection, a privileged relationship to which the Sebalduskirche and wider urban community bear witness in their turn.

The altar, then, sets the family within the history of salvation; it signals their closeness to a major saint and to the wisdom and virtue she embodies; and it carries out a visual dialogue with similar assertions of piety and status by other Patrician families such as the Volckamer, the Behaim[48] and the Haller.[49] Altars,

---

47   Barbara Hirschvogelin was the daughter of Wilhelm Hirschvogel and Christina Haller and widow of Sebald III Tucher. She was born on 19 July 1442; married Wilhelm Löffelholz in 1464; and died on 25 September 1494, having borne Wilhelm seven children (Biedermann, *Geschlechtsregister*, fol. Qqr (Tabula CCCV)). Fleischmann says five children (vol. 2, p. 673).

48   The Behaim von Schwarzach supposedly came from the area round Pilsen in Bohemia; they are documented in Nuremberg from 1285 onwards. From 1319/23 they served on the *Kleiner Rat*. In the fourteenth and fifteenth centuries they were amongst the most important Patrician trading companies in Nuremberg, engaged in long-distance trade and mining. Their best-known representative, Martin II Behaim, maker of the first globe (1492), belongs to a junior line. The family were raised to the *Reichsfreiherrenstand* [status of barons of the Holy Roman Empire] in 1681 and incorporated into the Bavarian nobility in 1809. The family died out in 1942 (*Stadtlexikon*, p. 131).

49   The Haller von Hallerstein may have come originally from the Tyrol; they are documented in Nuremberg from 1293 onwards and are the only family to have served without interruption on the *Kleiner Rat* in 1318 and from 1332 to 1806 (dissolution of the Holy Roman Empire). They acquired considerable wealth through trade and financial dealings. Berthold Haller (d. 1379) founded the Heilig-Kreuz-Pilgerspital (1352/3),

sculptures, epitaphs, stained-glass windows donated by leading Nuremberg Patricians – all form a complex web of visual associations which locate the donor families within, as well as shape the spiritual identity of, a key symbol of Nuremberg's civic identity. Monuments including depictions of Saint Katherine are, amongst others, the Haller windows in the East choir (1381–6); the Haller Altar (1440); the Imhoff Epitaph (1413);[50] various altar cloths;[51] and the *Tucher-Gedächtnisbild* (Tucher Epitaph) (1513), a memorial to Lorenz Tucher (1447–1503), who had been provost of the Nuremberg Lorenzkirche between 1478 and 1496 and who, on his death in 1503, had left half his fortune for the care of the poor. The memorial was painted by Hans Süß von Kulmbach after a sketch by Albrecht Dürer and depicts the Virgin enthroned with the Christ Child on her lap, Saint Katherine on her right and Saint Barbara on her left.[52] Lorenz Tucher himself is shown kneeling on Katherine's right, Saints Lawrence and Peter behind him, their hands on his shoulders. The choice of artists for this and other works in the Sebalduskirche makes a very clear statement about the Patricians' financial clout.[53] Thus the Löffelholz, Tucher and other Patrician families used Saint Katherine as a billboard for advertising their place within the spiritual economy, financial hierarchy and familial network of the city. Conversely, the choice of saint demonstrates her importance within this spiritual economy and within the devotional and self-promotional landscape of the ruling Patricians. Moreover, this statement of her pre-eminence is made within the sacred space that houses the relics of the city's patron saint. The tomb of Saint Sebaldus,

---

a shelter for pilgrims, poor priests and students, and was financier to Emperor Karl IV. In the mid-fifteenth century the family's land-holdings in the city and the surrounding countryside far surpassed those of other Nuremberg families. The Haller were laid to rest in the Sebalduskirche (*Stadtlexikon*, p. 396). Ulrich Haller endowed the Erhard Altar in the Sebalduskirche, one of the 12 main altars in the church (Müllner, *Annalen*, vol. 1, p. 16).

    50   The von Imhoff were a merchant family who first came to Nuremberg in 1340; Hans III. Imhoff (d. 1398) founded the family trading company. They owned land and property in the Nuremberg area and served on the *Kleiner Rat* from 1402 (*Stadtlexikon*, p. 469). The epitaph is for Anna Rotflasch (d. 1413), the second wife of Konrad Imhoff (d. 1449), and shows Saint Anne with the Virgin and Christ Child flanked by Saints Katherine and Nicholas. See also Müllner, *Annalen*, vol. 2, p. 187.

    51   These include one donated c. 1425–30 by Konrad Kreß (d. 1430) and his wife Walpurga, née Waldstromer (d. 1433), which depicts Katherine, flanked by various female saints, kneeling before the wheel as it is destroyed by fire from Heaven. It belonged to the Katherine Altar (Leonie von Wilckens, 'Die Teppiche der Sebalduskirche', in *600 Jahre Ostchor St. Sebald*, pp. 133–42 (p. 135)).

    52   Dürer's sketches for the picture are reproduced in Grote, *Die Tucher*, plates 51, 52/3.

    53   As well as Dürer and Hans Süß von Kulmbach, we find works by Peter Vischer and Veit Stoß.

decorated with the free imperial city's coat-of-arms,[54] stands in the East choir of the church, so Saint Katherine's presence in the Sebalduskirche allies her directly with the Holy Roman Empire. As the Löffelholz Altar stands in the West choir the two saints, Katherine and Sebaldus, together frame and protect the community worshipping in the church. According to Ernst Eichhorn, Saint Katherine was co-patron of the West choir (with Saint Peter, to whom the Sebalduskirche had originally been dedicated) and by 1500 had almost attained the status of a patron saint to Nuremberg as there was barely a church in the city without an altar dedicated to her.[55] Furthermore, the Sebalduskirche stands directly opposite the city hall, where the Patrician families represented in the church met to govern the city, so Saints Sebaldus and Katherine stood guard over the very governance of Nuremberg.

That Saint Katherine was much venerated in Nuremberg may be due to that city's trade links to Venice, whose patron saint she was (along with Mark, Nicholas, George and Justina of Padua), and Alexandria; and to its Patricians' active tradition of pilgrimage to the Holy Land and Mount Sinai.[56] The choice of Saint Katherine for the *Tucher-Gedächtnisbild* serves as a reminder of the Tucher family connexion to the saint[57] and to Alexandria itself, where they enjoyed close trade and personal

---

[54]   Nuremberg was elevated to a free imperial city by Emperor Friedrich II's *Freiheitsbrief* in 1219.

[55]   Ernst Eichhorn, 'Der Sebalder Engelschor. Ein Beitrag zur mittelalterlichen Sakralarchitektur Nürnbergs', in *600 Jahre Ostchor St. Sebald*, pp. 94–116 (p. 113, fn. 126).

[56]   See, for example, the accounts of their pilgrimage to the Holy Land and Mount Sinai (1479–80) by the two Nuremberg Patricians Hans VI Tucher and Sebald Rieter: Hans Tucher, *Reise zum Heiligen Grab* (Augsburg: Johann Schönsperger, 1482); and Reinhold Röhricht and Heinrich Meisner (eds), *Das Reisebuch der Familie Rieter* (Tübingen: Bibliothek des litterarischen Vereins in Stuttgart, 1884). Other Nuremberg families with a tradition of pilgrimage include the Pfinzing, Haller, Muffel and Ketzel. See Klaus Arnold, 'Wallfahrten als Nürnberger Familientradition um 1500', in *Wallfahrten in Nürnberg um 1500*, pp. 133–41 (p. 134). Arnold points out the strength of the pilgrimage tradition in some families: 'In Nürnberg haben sich im Gefolge solcher Wallfahrten neben Bauwerken und Texten jedoch noch weitere Realien erhalten, die von der Pilgertradition ganzer Familien Zeugnis ablegen. So finden sich die Pilger- und Stammtafeln der Familie Ketzel' [In the wake of such pilgrimages objects other than buildings and texts have been preserved in Nuremberg that bear witness to the pilgrimage tradition of whole families. Thus we have the pilgrimage and genealogical tables of the Ketzel family] (p. 135). These include a plaque portraying all the members of the family that undertook a pilgrimage, now in the Germanisches Nationalmuseum.

[57]   Another example is the Tucher chapel in Sixtus Tucher's garden house in the Grasersgasse, near the Carthusian monastery (Grote, *Die Tucher*, plate 49), which was decorated with scenes from Saint Katherine's life by Hans Süß von Kulmbach in 1517; they were commissioned by Anton II Tucher. Moreover, the Haus zur Krone (Bindergasse 26, on the corner of the Bindergasse and Neumarkt), the ancestral home of the principal Tucher

relations with the resident Venetian merchants involved in the spice trade there.[58] In May 1479 Hans Tucher[59] undertook a pilgrimage to the Holy Land, Sinai and Egypt in the company of other Patricians: Sebald and Eustachius Rieter,[60] Sebald

---

line, boasted a chapel for which Anton II Tucher obtained papal permission for the annual celebration of mass in 1511. Its walls were decorated with murals by Hans Süß von Kulmbach depicting scenes from the life of Empress Faustina, converted by Saint Katherine to Christianity (Grote, *Die Tucher*, p. 22). Grote also makes explicit the Tuchers' immensely strong sense of family identity (pp. 18–19). Moreover, Sebald Tucher gave a manuscript (c. 1430) of the first half of the 'Winterteil' of *Der Heiligen Leben* to the Katharinenkloster (Assion, *Mirakel*, p. 61).

[58]   Hans Tucher and his companions stayed with the Venetians in Alexandria and knew some of them personally, not least since within the family trading company Tucher and his sons were responsible for trade with the Venetians (Grote, *Die Tucher*, p. 33). From 1440 to 1575 the Tuchers rented chambers and storage ('Kammer und Gewölbe') in the Fondaco dei Tedeschi on a permanent basis and young male members of the Tucher family were sent to Venice to learn the family business (Grote, *Die Tucher*, pp. 32–3). Through Venice the Tuchers imported spices, drugs and fruit such as pepper, saffron, ginger, raisins, almonds, pomegranates, cinnamon, dates, canella, cloves, galingale and sugar (Grote, *Die Tucher*, p. 35). Trade relations between Nuremberg and Venice probably began in the second half of the thirteenth century and flourished, as in 1347 the *Signoria* remarked that trade with Venice had enabled Nuremberg to go from rags to riches (Ludwig Veit, *Handel und Wandel mit aller Welt*, Bibliothek des Germanischen National-Museums Nürnberg zur deutschen Kunst- und Kulturgeschichte 14 (Munich: Sporer, 1960), p. 11). This trade was so prosperous that Nuremberg disobeyed Emperor Sigismund's trade prohibition when he was at war with Venice (1418) and a number of Patrician merchants were fined (Müllner, *Annalen*, vol. 2, p. 229; pp. 233–4); the lion of Saint Mark was mounted on the houses of Nuremberg merchants who traded mainly with that city and Nuremberg's constitution was modelled on that of Venice (Veit, *Handel*, p. 11). Fabri allows us a glimpse of the further reaches of the spice trade: 'On the shore of the Red Sea which was on our side we saw a very notable seaport, which in old times was called Berenice or Ardech, but now is called Tor. Ships which come bearing aromatic spices from India anchor at this port, and from thence the spices are carried into Egypt, and from Egypt across the Mediterranean Sea even to our own country' (Fabri, *Wanderings*, p. 574).

[59]   Hans VI Tucher (1428–91) was the younger brother of the city *Baumeister* (Head of Buildings and Works), Endres II; he sat on a commission to oversee the building of the Sebalduskirche towers; became a member of the *Kleiner Rat* in 1476 in place of Endres, who entered a Carthusian monastery; and *Jüngerer Bürgermeister* in 1481. From 1486 he was responsible for expanding and cataloguing the *Ratsbibliothek*, the library of the City Council (Saint Katherine is the patron saint of libraries). His mother, Margaretha, was a member of the Patrician Paumgartner family (and hence must have been related to the Kunigunde Paumgartner in memory of whom the Löffelholz Altar was commissioned). Hans Tucher lies buried in the Sebalduskirche.

[60]   The Rieter made their fortune in long-distance trade, are known to have been resident in Nuremberg since 1361 and members of the *Kleiner Rat* since 1437 (*Stadtlexikon*, p. 902).

Pfintzing and Martin Löffelholz.[61] On his return in March 1480 he wrote and published an account of his journey, the *Reise zum Heiligen Grab*. Included in Tucher's work is a description of his sojourn at Saint Katherine's monastery on Sinai, to which his party is guided by a star:

> Jtem auff dem weg durch die wusten sahen wir alczeyt vmb mittenacht, oder vngeuerlich ein stund darnach, einen gar hellen lichten ster*e*n auffgeen. Der ster*e*n ging auff sud sud ost, das ist czwischen dem auff gang vnd mitag medan gegen dem auffgang, der ster*e*n die gegent des gepirgs Sinaÿ anczeÿget, darnach sich alle geferten vnd pilgram auff dem weg Sant Katherina pey nacht richten mussen. Der wirt auch Sant Katharina ster*e*n gena*n*t. Denselbe*n* ster*e*n sahen wir deß morgens gerad vber dem closter Sant Katharina begrebtnuß scheÿnen.[62]

> [On the way through the desert we always saw, around midnight or about an hour later, a radiantly bright star come up in the sky. The star rose to the South South East, that is, between the dawn and mid-day meridians but more towards dawn; it identifies the area round Mount Sinai and all travellers and pilgrims on the way to Saint Katherine's have to orientate themselves by it at night. It is also known as Saint Katherine's Star. We saw the same star shining in the morning directly over the monastery where Saint Katherine lies buried].

The obvious analogy to the Magi following the star to Bethlehem serves three purposes: first, it marks Tucher and his companions as select and privileged witnesses to, even "re-enactors" of, one of Christianity's defining events;[63] second, it marks the monastery and the saint's relics as particularly holy and privileged, since not only does the star guide the pilgrims to them, it shines directly above them in the morning just as the Star of Bethlehem shone above Christ's manger (Matthew 2:9–10); third, the nature of the analogy signals the significance of the saint for the pilgrims. Tucher's comparison of Saint Katherine's monastery to the Heilsbronner Hof in Nuremberg serves not just as a point of comparison for readers at home but as an imaginative mental and emotional situating of Katherine's tomb and relics within the imperial city: 'Jtem das closter ligt jn einem grund zwischen hohen gepirgen vnd mit einer maẅr vmbfangen jn der

---

[61] Thomas and Christoff Löffelholz also undertook a pilgrimage to the Holy Land in 1498.

[62] Tucher, '*Reise*', p. 523. Saint Katherine is referred to as 'du edels gestern d[*er*] tugent' [you noble star of virtue] in a Katharinenkloster prayer (Stadtbibliothek Nürnberg, Cod. Cent. VII, 65, fol. 5ʳ).

[63] Naturally Tucher's party were not the only ones to see Saint Katherine's star (Fabri does, for example), but few reports mention it or do so in such detail.

weÿten vnd grösse als hailßprun*n*er hoff zu Nuremberg gelege*n*'.[64] The possibility of the Heilsbronner Hof serving as a site of imaginative devotion to the saint is strengthened by the lengthy description – of the Sinai monastery, Saint Katherine's sarcophagus and the oil that used to flow from her bones – that can be mapped onto the Nuremberg site.[65] The monks open Saint Katherine's sarcophagus for the pilgrims' worship:

> Jtem am vij. tag octobris, frue vor tags, sperret man vns Sant Katherina sarch auff vnd lyes vns alles jr heiliges gepein, als vor*e*n steht verzeichent, gar eygentlichen sehen, kussen, vnd ettlich vnser geret daran berur*e*n, das alles gar andechtiglichen vnd begirlichen zusehen ist. Man gab vns auch der paumwollen, darjnnen jrss heiligen gepeins jm sarch gelegen ist. Man lyeß vns auch sunder wollen jn das wirdig oll, das an der stat der prynnenden pusch pry*n*net, gedunckt an jr heiliges pein, bestreichen, das die bruder gar fur ein wirdig peyzeichen den pilgra*m*men zugeben schaczen.[66]

> [On the 7th October before dawn Saint Katherine's sarcophagus was opened for us and we were allowed to see and kiss her very bones ourselves (as recorded above) and to touch them with the vessels we had brought with us, all of which is devout and desirable to behold. We were also given pieces of the cotton wool in which her holy bones had rested in the coffin. Further, we were allowed to dip different cotton wool into the worthy oil that burns on the site of the Burning Bush and to stroke her holy bones with it. The monks consider this a worthy distinction for pilgrims].

The pilgrims are granted not just sight of and, in the kiss, intimate physical contact to the relics, but the opportunity to take back with them to Nuremberg "part" of Saint Katherine in the form of oil-soaked cotton wool that has touched her bones,[67] thereby translating their own "relic" of her to their home city and intensifying both

---

[64]   'The monastery lies on the floor of a valley between high mountains and is surrounded by a wall as broad and as high as that of the Heilsbronner Hof in Nuremberg' (Tucher, '*Reise*', p. 524). The Heilsbronner Hof lay to the immediate north of Nuremberg's other main church, the Lorenzkirche, and had been purchased in either 1254 or 1296 by the Cistercian monastery in Heilsbronn as a base from which to administer its property near Nuremberg, as a central collection point for tithes and as a trans-shipment centre for the monastery's wares. A small chapel dedicated to Saint Nicholas was erected for the private use of the monks and abbots staying at the Heilsbronner Hof (*Stadtlexikon*, p. 433).

[65]   Tucher, '*Reise*', pp. 525–9. The description of the Sinai runs from pp. 522–50, though the pilgrims do visit sites not directly connected to Saint Katherine, e.g. the spot where God handed down the Ten Commandments to Moses (p. 536).

[66]   Tucher, '*Reise*', pp. 548–9.

[67]   By the time of Tucher's visit oil no longer flowed from the saint's bones, hence the cotton wool is dunked in oil that burns where the Burning Bush used to stand.

its and their families' bond to the saint.[68] Saint Katherine becomes a holy presence experienced tangibly by a number of Nuremberg Patricians and integrated into their family lives and worship. Their initial mental image of the saint may have been shaped by *Der Heiligen Leben* (and similar texts) and by devotional images of her throughout the city but, conversely, their experience on Sinai may have shaped their emotional and spiritual experience of the saint – and the Heilsbronner Hof – when back home. In these visitors, at least, an emotional, spiritual and locational dialogue between Nuremberg and Sinai may have been established; each place, in the pilgrims' minds, superimposed on the other.

From Sinai Tucher and his party go on to Alexandria itself, where they stay with the Venetians and visit the shrines connected to Saint Katherine's martyrdom:

> Jtem erstlich der kercker, darjnnen Sant Katherina xij tag one leipliche speyß gefangen gewesen ist. Das ist ein kleinß gewelblein, darzu ein heyden zu negst dopey wonende den schlussel hat. Der schleust auff den pilgramen oder anderen cristen, wenn sie deß begeren vmb ein madin. Der gelten xxv ein ducaten.

---

[68]   It was also customary to touch the relics with jewels, some entrusted to pilgrims by those unable to make the journey (Fabri, *Wanderings*, p. 600). The desire for relics of the saint led, amongst other things, to theft of her remains: 'for indeed much has been taken away in past times, both by having been stolen by pilgrims, and begged by emperors, bishops, and kings, and so much has been given away in this fashion that only less than half of the sacred body is left. Now that they know of this, they guard it carefully from thieves, and neither entreaties nor bribes will induce them to give any pieces of it away' (Fabri, *Wanderings*, p. 601). Indeed, Fabri's own party were delayed leaving Saint Katherine's monastery as one of its members had chipped off a piece of the saint's coffin and the father abbot of the monastery threatened to put the matter into the hands of the Arabs if it were not returned (Fabri, *Wanderings*, p. 625). Kissing the relics is a gesture of devotion but it also renders the pilgrims themselves holy by transforming them into a (contact) relic of and memorial to the saint. They may even be said to ingest the saint's virtue, so that their mouths issue speech more devout and salvatory in its potential to convert. Saint Katherine seems to have been similarly revered by Muslims: 'After the monks we pilgrims went and worshipped the relics in the customary manner, and after us our ass-drivers did the same' (Fabri, *Wanderings*, p. 600). Pilgrimage to Saint Katherine's monastery may even have enjoyed a certain kudos because of the dangers involved: 'So the monks took up St. Catherine's body with great reverence, and bore it to the Church of St. Mary at Bush, where they placed it in a marble coffin, even as it is seen at this day, and is sought after by all Christ's faithful people scattered far and wide throughout the world, at the peril of their lives, with the greatest possible labours and expenses; wherefore a certain Pope specially forbade this pilgrimage to be made, on pain of anathema, because of the difficulty of the journey and the dangers thereof. The pilgrimage to Jerusalem was only forbidden because of the Saracens, and indeed that pilgrimage is but a holiday and pleasant excursion when compared with this one' (Fabri, *Wanderings*, pp. 606–7).

Jtem zu negst vor disem kercker sten hoche rotfarbe merbelsteinen seul peÿ xij schritten von einander. Darauff jst das rade gestanden mit schneydenden scharen, domit Sant Katherina gemartert solt sein worden, dann das es durch Gottes wunderzaichen vntterstanden ward. Vnd peÿ demselben ende hat auch Sant Katherina gar manigfaltig marter gelyden, als man das jn jrer legend eygentlichen vindet.

Jtem jn der stat Allexandria jst auch ein kirch, zu Sant Saba genant. Doselbst hat Sant Katherina, ee vnd sie gemartert ward, jr wonung gehabt. Vnd jn dieser kirchen jst der junckfrawen Maria pild einß, das Sant Lukas nach vnser lieben Fraẅen ab gecunterfet vnd gemalet hat. Die kirchen zu Sant Saba haben jnnen die krichen.

Jtem vor der stat Allexandria zu negst sind auch ij groß rot merbelsteinen seulen. Die ein jst vmbgefallen, die ander stund dieser zeyt noch. Doselbest hat man Sant Katherina jr haubt abgeschlagen, vnd, als ettlich sagen, so jst dasselb ende zu derselben zeyt jnnerhalb der stat begriffen gewesen. Wann Allexandria jst ettwen gar vil grosser vnd weyter gewest, dann es yecunt ist.[69]

[First the dungeon in which Saint Katherine was imprisoned for twelve days without bodily sustenance. It is a tiny, vaulted chamber to which a heathen living nearby holds the key. He opens it for pilgrims or other Christians whenever they want in exchange for a madin. Twenty-five madins make a ducat.

Just in front of this dungeon stand tall, red marble pillars twelve paces apart. On them stood the wheel with its sharp blades on which Saint Katherine was to have been martyred if God's miraculous intervention had not prevented it. On the same spot Saint Katherine suffered the manifold pain of martyrdom, as one finds faithfully recorded in her legend.

In the city of Alexandria there is also a church called Saint Saba's, where Saint Katherine lived before she was martyred. In this church is one of the paintings of the Virgin Mary which Saint Luke painted after the likeness of Our Blessed Lady. The Greeks have charge of the church of Saint Saba.

Just outside the city of Alexandria are two more tall, red marble pillars. One has toppled over; the other was still standing when we were there. On this spot Saint Katherine was executed and, according to some, this place then stood within the city itself, as Alexandra used to be considerably bigger and wider than it is now].

---

[69]   Tucher, '*Reise*', pp. 589–91.

This description leads the reader through the physical and temporal stages of Saint Katherine's martyrdom, from the enclosed space of a small prison cell outwards to beyond the city gates, a progression which also parallels the spread of the saint's life and cult from Alexandria to Sinai to Europe. Fasting such as that undertaken by Saint Katherine was a penitential process, part of the detachment of the self from the world; the symbolism of the 12 days, the number alluding to the disciples, may indicate how the reader is meant to view Saint Katherine, namely as a model disseminator of Christ's message and pillar of the early Church.[70] However, the need to pay entry to the prison pulls the reader back by reminding him that sacred spaces, too, are an object of trade and hence part of a real fiscal economy. The pillars outside the jail symbolize 'spiritual strength and steadfastness (Rev. 3:12) and therefore became an attribute of the allegorical figures of FORTITUDE and CONSTANCY';[71] their redness indicates the blood shed by Saint Katherine in her unwavering devotion to Christ, an allusion picked up again in the colour of the pillars at the site of her martyrdom proper.[72] As the martyrdom is linked to Alexandria's decline, the pillars mark the real impact of *Heilsgeschichte* (history of salvation) on subsequent lived history. Moreover, through these physical, tangible objects the sacred past merges with the pilgrims' present, enabling them to "live" the past in their spirit, to walk literally and imaginatively with Saint Katherine though the spaces she rendered holy. Reminders of the saint's martyrdom may trigger associations with the Heilsbronner Hof or the Sebalduskirche, so future visits to the church will merge it with the sacred sites in Alexandria.[73]

Since Saint Katherine was present throughout Nuremberg in textual, architectural, sculptural, pictorial and spiritually associative form, let us now consider how she might have been experienced – visually, emotionally and spiritually – by late-medieval residents of that city. Visual theory provides one approach into recreating their mode of apprehension, hence a brief outline of

---

[70]   Moreover, Christ Himself comes to Saint Katherine on the twelfth day of her fast, comforts her and gives her His own body, His spiritual sustenance sanctioning her resistance to the emperor (*Der Heiligen Leben*, fol. Ccliii[v]).

[71]   *Hall's Dictionary*, pp. 247–8.

[72]   In prison Saint Katherine is flagellated and fed by a white dove (*Der Heiligen Leben*, fol. Ccliii[r]). Christ was tied to a pillar during His Flagellation, so the pillars also serve as an indirect reminder of the blood He shed. An altar painted in Nuremberg c. 1490 and donated to the Katharinenkloster by Ortloph Stromer and his wife Katharina shows the Flagellation with Christ bound to a pillar of red marble.

[73]   That the pilgrims also visit Katherine's home and see Saint Luke's picture of the Virgin holding and the Infant Christ reminds them and the reader of Katherine's "bridegroom", constancy to whom ultimately caused her martyrdom. The Germanisches Nationalmuseum houses an altar (1487) by the workshop of Hans Traut which once stood in the Augustinerkirche (near the Sebalduskirche) and depicts Saint Luke painting the Virgin and Child.

the theory current in the late-fifteenth century will be given here as a means of ascertaining the impact of Saint Katherine on the viewer's psyche.[74] A widely available source was Konrad von Megenberg, author of the encyclopaedia *Das Buch der Natur*, who sums up the physical process of vision as follows:[75]

> Das gesicht ist vornen in dem haubt / wann das tier sol sehen was vor im ist Ein hohe ader geet von dem hirnn zů den augen die heysset opitus die tregt die sinnlichen geÿst zů den augen vnd wirt ÿe verstopffet so mag das aug nicht gesehen … Das aug ist geseczt in siben röck das sind siben heütlin / damit ist der cristallisch feüchtin verhüllet daran des gesichtes krafft ligt … Der augen spÿegel ist also freÿ daz das klein augäpffelin nymmpt ein ebenpild eins ganczen menschen oder eins grösseren dinges.[76]

> [The faculty of vision is in the front of the head because an animal should see what is in front of it. A main vein called the *opitus* goes from the brain to the eyes and carries the sensual spirit [the medium by which objects are apprehended by the senses] to the eyes. If it is ever blocked the eye is unable to see … The eye is constructed of seven skirts [i.e. layers], that is, seven little skins which cover the crystalline humour that possesses the actual power of sight … The mirror of the eyes is so free that the small eye ball receives a likeness of an entire person or of a very large object].

---

[74]   For theories of vision see above all David C. Lindberg, 'The Science of Optics', in David C. Lindberg (ed.), *Science in the Middle Ages*, The Chicago History of Science and Medicine (Chicago and London: University of Chicago Press, 1978), pp. 338–68; David C. Lindberg, *Theories of Vision from Al-Kindi to Kepler*, University of Chicago History of Science and Medicine (Chicago and London: University of Chicago Press, 1976). For a clear summary of different theories see also Suzanne Conklin Akbari, *Seeing through the Veil* (Toronto, Buffalo and London: University of Toronto Press, 2004), pp. 21–44. Conklin Akbari provides a useful summary: 'Whether by means of an extramitted ray or an intromitted species, the visible image makes its way through the pupil of the eye to the crystalline humour (the lens), which according to galenic theory is the principle sensitive organ of the eye. The image then is propagated along the optic nerve to the foremost *cellula* of the brain, where the *sensus communis* gathers impressions received from each of the "outer wits" of sight, hearing, smell, taste, and touch. The imaginative faculty receives the sense impression just as soft wax receives a seal; reason judges the image; finally, memory stores the image for future reference' (Conklin Akbari, *Seeing*, pp. 41–2).

[75]   The *Buch der Natur* was probably written around 1349 and had as its model Thomas of Cantimpré's *De naturis rerum*. However, Konrad's work is not a translation but an adaptation to which he adds much new material. It was first printed by Johannes Bämler in Augsburg in 1475 and at least six times before 1500.

[76]   *Buch der Natur* [fol. 4ᵛ].

Important here is the *opitus*, which transports images apprehended by the eye to the brain and the memory:

> Die hirnschal hat dreÿ kämerlin / daz ein fornen in dem haupt vnd in dem ist der
> sel krafft die do heißt fantastica oder ÿmaginaria / das ist als vil gesprochen als die
> pilderin darumb das sÿ aller bekanntlicher ding pild vnd geleichnuß in sich samlet.
> ¶ Das ander kämerlin ist zů mittelst in dem haupt vnd in dem ist der sel krafft die
> do heisset Intellectualis das ist vernunfft ¶ Das dritt kämerlin ist zů hinderst in
> dem haupt / vnd in dem ist der sel krafft die do heisset Memorialis / daz ist die
> gedächtnuß Die dreÿ krefft der sel behalten den schacz aller bekanntnuß ¶ Die erst
> wirdet schwanger wann sÿ zů gefacht die pild vnd die geleichnuß aller bekäntlicher
> ding / vnnd die pild antwurtent jr die fünff außwendig sÿnn die do heissent gesicht
> / gehör schmecken / versůchen ¶ Die ander krafft in dem anderen kämerlin die acht
> vnd schäczt die ding der vor enpfangen eben pild recht als ein wiczige ee fraw ¶ Die
> dritt krafft in dem hindersten kämerlin behůt vnd beschleüßt getrewlich die ding
> also durch brüft vnd durch merckt recht als ein sichere schlüsseltragerin / darumb
> sicht man offt das ein mensch sein gedächtnuß verleürt wenn er ser gewundet wirt
> hinden in daz haupt / oder daz es sein bescheÿdenheÿt verleürt wenn es gewundet
> wirt / oder hart geschlagen von vornen in daz haupt.[77]

[The brain has three chambers. One is at the front of the head and contains the property of the soul called *fantastica* or imagination, that is to say, the "picture-maker" as it collects within it pictures and likenesses of all known things. The other chamber is in the centre of the head and contains the property of the soul called *intellectualis*, that is, reason. The third chamber is at the back of the head and contains the property of the soul called *memorialis*, that is, memory. The three properties of the soul conserve the treasure of all knowledge. The first becomes pregnant when she receives the images and likenesses of all known things and the five external senses – sight, hearing, taste, touch [*sic*] – respond to the image. The other property in the second small chamber takes note of and treasures the objects conveyed by the previously received images just like a prudent housewife. The third property in the hindmost chamber loyally protects and locks away the objects that have been thoroughly examined and noted, just like a safe keeper of the keys. For that reason it can often be observed that a person who has been gravely injured on the back of his head loses his memory; or that he loses his judgement when wounded or hit hard on the front of the head].

---

[77]   *Buch der Natur* [fol. 2ʳ]. For medieval theories on the construction of memory and the art of memorization see Mary Carruthers, *The Book of Memory. A Study of Memory in Medieval Culture* (Cambridge: Cambridge University Press, 1990).

The brain is seen in spatial terms: one can walk through the chambers housing imagination, reason and memory the same way one can walk through a warehouse storing merchandise, the 'schacz aller beka*n*ntnuß'. Although these three powers of the soul – imagination, reason and memory – are directly acted on by external stimuli, they are themselves active: the imagination is the 'pilderin' (maker of pictures) who, impregnated by the images received through the *opitus*, gives birth in her turn. The fertile wife is matched by the prudent one, reason, the 'wiczige ee fraw', who measures the value of the images stored in her chamber. Finally, memory is the keeper of the keys, who checks, records and guards the contents of her chamber. Hence the analogy emerges of the powers of the soul as a fertile but prudent husbander of resources who, keys at her belt, polices the provisions stored in her pantry, the brain. This analogy is easily mapped onto Nuremberg, with its shrewd merchants and numerous warehouses. Thus in the same way the housewife walks through her storage chambers, so too could a person walk through the streets and churches of Nuremberg, which themselves function as a storage space for images, memories and associations like the monastery on Sinai or the site of Saint Katherine's martyrdom in Alexandria. Hence walking becomes an act of recall, a deliberate merging of memory and space that triggers associations and overlaps them in a way that may prove fertile when viewing or reading. However, just as carefully acquired and warehoused merchandise must prove profitable, so too must the use of memory in seeing and reading, in generating images of benefit to the soul. Memory – like the products of Patrician patronage in the Sebalduskirche – forms part of the economy of salvation.

If one compares the *Buch der Natur* to the *Ars memorativa* published by Johann Bämler in Augsburg in 1480, a different spatial image of the brain emerges:

> NVn wil ich sage*n* vo*n* d*er* andern stuck der küstlichen ged*ä*chtnus vn*d* pildu*n*g. Du solt wissen das die stet in d*er* kunst sint als ein wachß tauel od*er* papeir dar auff ma*n* schreÿbt also sint die pildu*n*g die gleÿchnus vn*d* die stet die s*ö*llent gleÿch d*er* geschrifft seÿn od*er* d*er* mainu*n*g die man darinen schreÿben wil Die pildu*n*g macht du also ab thŭn Vn*d* ander darein secze*n* gleÿch als in einer wachßtauel ma*n*n die pŭchstaben ab vn*d* tŭt and*er* darein secze*n*.[78]

> [Now I intend to tell you about the other part of the art of memory and imagination. You should know that in this art the locations are like a wax tablet or sheet of paper on which one writes. This is the nature of the imagination and comparisons and locations, which should be like the writing or meaning which one wants to inscribe

---

[78]   *Ars memorativa* (Augsburg: Johann Bämler, 1480), fol. 4ᵛ. The basis for this work is a treatise on the art of memorization composed by Johannes Hartlieb for the son of Duke Ludwig of Bavaria-Ingolstadt c. 1432.

in there. You can discard one image and put another one in its place, just like you can eradicate letters and put others in their place on a wax tablet].

The foremost chamber of the brain, where the *sensus communis* collects sense impressions, is soft and physically malleable, the deliberately practised art of memorization being compared to the process of writing on paper or wax.[79] Hence an alternative type of storage is envisaged, namely the brain, specifically memory, as a library full of different quasi-textual sources;[80] remembering thus becomes the act of pulling a volume from the internal library shelf, opening it and reading its contents. This second analogy has further implications. Michael Camille points out that in the fourteenth century 'seeing and reading were part of the same bodily operation, involving perception and cognition in the search for knowledge.'[81] He highlights 'the value placed upon images as ... the basis of cognition and even epistemology', since images made their way to the human soul, which was the ultimate agent of perception and knowledge.[82] In other words, seeing and reading, and their interaction in memory, have the power actively to shape the imagination of the viewer, to change his perception of the surrounding world, even to stamp on his psyche images which literally moulded his thought, behaviour and soul. Given that images and other information acquired through the senses, once actively memorized, went into the warehouse of memory, a reader-viewer would have been able to access an ever-expanding, ever richer archive of associations and imitable models, in this case Saint Katherine and representations of her in Nuremberg.[83]

Let us consider, second, the source of such associations, the late-medieval visual environment. The average late-medieval person was almost certainly more visually than textually literate, especially in devotional imagery. Images from the Bible and saints' lives were all-pervasive: in stained-glass windows, church frescoes, altar paintings, tiles, sculpture, fabrics and church plate; in the frescoes,

---

[79] Writing, then, is a form of memorization and may for the nuns in the Katharinenkloster have formed part of memorizing and reflecting on the saint's life, thus acting as a meditation exercise that helped them shape themselves in her image.

[80] Moreover, these textual sources may be erased and replaced by others, so whilst memory is about protected storage, memorization includes renewal and the overwriting of one set of images by another.

[81] Michael Camille, 'Before the Gaze. The Internal Senses and Late Medieval Practices of Seeing', in Robert S. Nelson (ed.), *Visuality before and beyond the Renaissance. Seeing as Others Saw* (Cambridge: Cambridge University Press, 2000), pp. 197–223 (p. 216).

[82] Camille, 'Before the Gaze', p. 216.

[83] However, a corollary of the comparison of memorization to writing on wax suggests that memory, like wax tablets, may easily be wiped clean, leaving it open to other influences.

sculptures and statues on houses, public buildings and fountains; on shop and house signs; in the visual pageantry of religious processions or mystery plays; in the devotional pictures on the walls at home; or on domestic objects such as doors, stoves, chests, caskets, candlesticks, glass, pewter, silver or stoneware;[84] on personal items such as shoes, belts, clothes and jewellery; and in whatever books or manuscripts a family may have owned. Practised familiarity would have enabled the reader quickly to identify iconography. This supposition is supported indirectly by the *Ars Memorativa*, which specifically cites the Katherine legend as a practice tool, a use that suggests her life and martyrdom were well-known:

> Item ob du eins heÿlgen leben oder sant Katherine wöllest außwendigen künden So secz auch an ÿedliche stat mit einem artickel Das merck eine exempel von sant Katherina die waß ein schöne junckfraw. Sÿ verschmächt jers vattre apgot. Secz in die ander stat Daz sÿ sich vmm want vnd kert von dem abgot Secz in daz drit hauß daz vater vnd mûter sÿ dar vmm strafften In daz viert daz sÿ gefangen vnd in ein kercker gelegt ward. In die .v. stat setz daz sÿ wart auß gefürt In die vj. stat setz daz rad mit scharpffen waffen In der sÿbenden stat daz der schawr. daz rad erschlûg In die viij. daz man ir daz haupt abschlûg In die ix. daz milch dar auß floß In die x. stat daz die engel sÿ fürtenn auff den perg Sÿnay. also thû allen geschriben prieffen Kronicken oder waß du lernen wild.[85]

[For example, if you want to learn a saint's life or the life of Saint Katherine by heart then put one element of it into each location. Note this example about Saint Katherine: she was a beautiful virgin. She despised her father's idol. Into the second location put the fact that she turned round and turned her back on the idol. Into the third house put the fact that her father and mother punished her for so doing. Into the fourth that she was taken prisoner and put into a dungeon. Into the fifth location put that she was led out. Into the sixth location put the wheel with its sharp blades. Into the seventh location put that the shower [of flames] shattered the wheel. Into the eighth that she was beheaded. Into the ninth that milk flowed from there [her neck]. Into the tenth that the angels carried her onto Mount Sinai. Proceed in the same way with all written documents, chronicles or whatever you want to learn].

---

[84]   For example, a door handle in the form of the Temptation or a tiled stove depicting the Annunciation, Apostles and various saints. See G. Ulrich Großmann (ed.), *Spiegel der Seligkeit. Privates Bild und Frömmigkeit im Spätmittelalter*, Ausstellungskatalog des Germanischen Nationalmuseums (Nuremberg: Verlag des Germanischen Nationalmuseums, 2000), p. 25, illustration 25 and p. 382, catalogue number 215.

[85]   *Ars memorativa*, fol. 7r. Details vary from the version in the *Legenda aurea* and Sensenschmid's *Der Heiligen Leben*.

Whilst it cannot be known whether Nuremberg Patricians practised memory exercises of this kind, let alone used Saint Katherine or any other saint as prescribed, it does suggest that a reader both visually and mnemonically versed might have employed urban space as a memory canvas, so that memory became spatial and space memorial and a walk through Nuremberg an act of calling to one's mind's eye, of re-enacting mentally and emotionally the life and martyrdom of Saint Katherine using the images of her so prevalent throughout the city. In short, memorizing the saint could have led through sculptural and pictorial reminders of her to a merging of the viewer/reader's present with the past that contained the saint, to a putting-of-the-viewer/reader's-self into Katherine's position and hence to an intensely lived and felt devotion to her, possibly to the extent of experiencing the actual bodily pain of martyrdom and "becoming" the saint in a way that transcended mere association such as that marked by the Löffelholz Altar. This possibility is confirmed by Michael Baxandall's observation that pious lay people were 'practised in spiritual exercises that demanded a high level of visualization'; he stresses the active nature of the interior visualization of holy stories, images of the same forming the basis for active religious meditation, 'a visualizing meditation,'[86] which may have been reinforced by sermons preached on the events of the Christian year and the emotions appropriate to them.[87] Buildings in a city could be given the identity of holy sites – for example, the Heilsbronner Hof that of the Katharinenkloster on Sinai – and thus used as foci of religious contemplation, so that Nuremberg could have been turned into a three-dimensional memorial to Katherine's martyrdom and become "holier" as a result. Further questions arise: what was the relationship of the envisaging body to the urban space around it? How did it *feel* to walk through ill-lit, narrow, smelly, noisy, muddy streets overhung by timber-frame buildings putting sections of Saint Katherine's legend onto architectural features and making solid stone and wood structures and the more or less narrow spaces between them into a re-enactment of her life and martyrdom? Did the practice aid a person's locking of him/herself into the meditation or was the physicality of the environment too overwhelming? Did physical and spiritual space truly merge indistinguishably into one? As Roberta Gilchrist writes: 'Space forms the arena in which social relationships are negotiated, expressed through the construction of landscapes, architecture and boundaries. The resulting spatial maps represent discourses of power based in the body.'[88] Space also forms the arena

---

[86]   Michael Baxandall, *Painting & Experience in Fifteenth-Century Italy* (Oxford and New York: Oxford University Press, 1972), pp. 45–6.

[87]   Baxandall, *Painting*, p. 49.

[88]   Roberta Gilchrist, 'Medieval Bodies in the Material World: Gender, Stigma and the Body', in Sarah Kay and Miri Rubin (eds), *Framing Medieval Bodies* (Manchester: Manchester University Press, 1994), pp. 43–61 (p. 43).

in which religious relationships are negotiated, so what power might the images of Saint Katherine in Nuremberg have given the (female) body? What relationships might the (female) devotee have formed with the saint by negotiating the spatial and spiritual boundaries imposed by mapping her legend onto the city's buildings?

In 1491 Anton Koberger, Nuremberg's leading printer and Dürer's godfather, published the *Schatzbehalter*, an illustrated didactic work on the life, suffering and death of Christ which included Old Testament analogies and was based on sermons given in the Klarissenkloster by the Franciscan Stephan Fridolin, confessor and spiritual guide to the nuns (1487–9 and 1489–98).[89] Its woodcuts are attributed to Michael Wolgemut and Wilhelm Pleydenwurff.[90] The *Schatzbehalter* includes the Old Testament story of Jephthah and his daughter (Judges 11:29–40). Jephthah delivers Israel from domination by Ammon and his forces, having vowed that if victorious in battle he would sacrifice to God the first thing to meet him on his return home. This is his only child, a daughter, whom he upbraids for the grief she causes him through her welcome; her reply is a model of quiescent submission to the paternal will:

> da zerriß er seyne kleyd. vn*d* sprach mir wee. mein tochter. du hast mich vnd dich betrogen. dann ich hab meinen mund gen gott auff gethan. vnd gott gelobt zeopfern. was mir zum ersten begegnete. vn*d* ich mag im nit anders thon. Sy sprach. Mein vater. w*az* du gelobt hast. d*az* leist. so dir der sig. wider dein feind verlihen ist. Aber das bitt ich dich. das du mich lasset zwen monet. vmb die berg geen. mit meinen gespilen. das ich mein iunckfrawnschafft beweine.[91]

> [Then he tore his clothes and said, 'Alas, my daughter, you have betrayed me and yourself, for I opened my mouth to God and swore to Him to sacrifice the first thing I encountered and I cannot break my oath to Him'. She said, 'My father, you must fulfil your vow as you have been granted victory over your enemy. However I ask you for one thing: that you permit me to go into the mountains with my companions for two months to weep for my virginity'].

---

[89]   Fridolin knew Hans Tucher, who had encouraged him to compose the *Traktat von den Kaiserangesichten* (1487) (Machilek, 'Klosterhumanismus', p. 28).

[90]   After Pleydenwurff's death in 1472, Michael Wolgemut had married his wife and taken over his studio. For a close analysis of the relationship between text, image and memory in the *Schatzbehalter* and its programmatic use by Fridolin see Ulrike Heinrichs-Schreiber, 'Sehen als Anwendung von Wissen. Aussage und Wirkung der Bilder in Stephan Fridolins *Schatzbehalter* und bei Albrecht Dürer, in Gerd Dicke and Klaus Grübmüller (eds), *Die Gleichzeitigkeit von Handschrift und Buchdruck* (Wiesbaden: Harrassowitz, 2003), pp. 49–104.

[91]   Fridolin, *Schatzbehalter*, fol. Kij^v.

In the *Schaltzbehalter* the Biblical text is given virtually verbatim, each section followed by Fridolin's exegesis.[92] Jephthah functions as a type of Christ due to his noble status, his military leadership and his office as a judge: '[C]hristus ist in dem jepte bede*ü*tet gewesen. d*er* ein f*ü*rst. ein hertzog ein f*ü*rstreitter vn*d* ein richter des volks israhels was. Wellicher wirdigkeit halben. er ein figur Christi gewesen ist'.[93] His sacrifice of his daughter prefigures Christ's sacrifice of His own virgin flesh to save mankind from its enemies: 'Diser iepte als die glos. vnd ysidorus außlege*n*. bede*ü*tet cristum. der ze*ü*berwinde*n* vnser feind zu vnserm Heil auß gel*ü*bdnus. vnd festem f*ü*rsatz. als ob er es geschworen. vn*d* gelobt het. sein iunckfrewlich fleisch geopfert hat'.[94] For Fridolin Jephthah's daughter does not even appear as a potential model of exemplary womanhood: she speaks her reinforcement of Jephthah's vow and is otherwise erased by her function as carrier of twofold meaning: first, the virtue of one particular man; second, the weak mortal flesh that caused man's downfall and must be sacrificed to achieve salvation, much as nuns subdue the flesh in their devotion to Christ.

Other medieval commentators offer various interpretations of the story.[95] First, it is seen as a parallel to the sacrifice of Isaac by Abraham, which in Christian art functions as one of the Old Testament prefigurations of God's sacrifice on the Cross of His son Christ to redeem mankind's sins.[96] Hence the

---

[92]   'And she said unto him, My father, *if* thou hast opened thy mouth unto the Lord, do to me according to that which has proceeded out of thy mouth; forasmuch as the Lord has taken vengeance for thee of thine enemies, *even* of the children of Ammon. // And she said unto her father, Let this thing be done for me: let me alone two months, that I may go up and down upon the mountains, and bewail my virginity, I and my fellows' (Judges 11:36–7).

[93]   'Christ is signified in Jephthah, who was a prince, a duke, a warrior and a judge of the People of Israel. Because of these worthy qualities he prefigured Christ' (Fridolin, *Schatzbehalter*, fol. Kij^{va}).

[94]   'As the glosses and Isidorus explain through their exegesis, Jephthah signifies Christ, who, prompted by His vow and firm intent, sacrificed His virgin flesh to overcome our enemy in order to ensure our salvation, just as if He had sworn and vowed to do so' (Fridolin, *Schatzbehalter*, fol. Kij^{vb}).

[95]   See Lois Drewer, 'Jephthah and His Daughter in Medieval Art: Ambiguities of Heroism and Sacrifice', in Colum Hourihane (ed.), *Insights and Interpretations*, Index of Christian Art Occasional Papers 5 (Princeton: Department of Art and Archaeology, Princeton University, in association with Princeton University Press, 2002), pp. 35–59. An obvious parallel is Agamemnon's sacrifice to Artemis of Iphigenia when Artemis holds up the winds needed to carry the Greek army to war against the Trojans. In Euripides' *Iphigenia in Tauris*, Artemis brings a deer as a substitute (Drewer, 'Jephthah', p. 36).

[96]   Drewer points out that the icon on the south pier of the sanctuary in the church of Saint Katherine at the monastery at Sinai depicts Jephthah's sacrifice of his daughter and is opposite the depiction of Moses about to sacrifice Isaac on the north pier. The location of this iconography of female sacrifice within the sacred space dedicated to a saint whose similar

sacrifice of Jephthah's daughter is also read as a prefiguration of the Crucifixion, as a type of the Eucharist.[97] Second, the story functions as a warning against foolish and unjustifiable actions, namely Jephthah's taking of a rash and flawed vow in the first place.[98] Third, the daughter's willing acceptance of her sacrifice transforms her from victim into "heroic Virgin" and is interpreted as the symbolic dedication of her life to God; hence she becomes a prototype Christian nun.[99] In fact, she functioned as more than that, namely as a type of the Virgin Mary, an analogy common in the fourteenth and fifteenth centuries. In the Darmstadt *Speculum humanae salvationis* (c. 1360), for example, the sacrifice of Jephthah's daughter is a type of the Presentation of Mary in the Temple, in other words, of the dedication of Mary to God.[100]

The *Schatzbehalter* concerns us here because of the two woodcuts illustrating the Jephthah chapter: the first shows Jephthah being welcomed by his daughter; the second his sacrifice of her. The method of execution has been changed: the Biblical daughter was promised as a burnt offering (Judges 11:31); here she is beheaded.[101] However, to her left (within the visual space of the woodcut) stands an altar on which burns a fire, reminding the reader of both Jephthah's original vow and of Abraham's sacrifice of Isaac:

> And they came to the place which God had told him of; and Abraham built an
> altar there, and laid the wood in order, and bound Isaac his son, and laid him on

---

martyrdom iconography is better known links the two figures and enables the iconography of each to be read in terms of the other, much as Hans Tucher may have done during his stay in Saint Katherine's monastery. This, as we shall see, in turn allows the Jezebel woodcut in the *Ritter vom Turn* to be seen as an analogy not just to Saint Katherine's martyrdom but also to the sacrifice of Jephthah's daughter, who, Drewer states, 'willingly dedicates [herself] to God's will' (Drewer, 'Jephthah', p. 39). A potential reading of the woodcut in this light further "redeems" Jezebel. Moreover, a pilgrim like Tucher may have transferred not just Katherine but also Jephthah's daughter to the Heilsbronner Hof.

[97]   Drewer, 'Jephthah', pp. 37–8.
[98]   Drewer, 'Jephthah', pp. 39–48.
[99]   Drewer, 'Jephthah', pp. 49–50.
[100]   Drewer, 'Jephthah', pp. 49–50. In a Parisian *Bible moralisée* produced for members of the Capetian court in the first half of the thirteenth century Jephthah's daughter is a type of Synagoga: 'That Jephthah returned and won the battle signifies Jesus Christ, who after His Resurrection vanquished and trampled the devil under his [*sic*] feet. The daughter who came before him with timbrels and cymbals to celebrate him signifies Synagoga, who comes before Jesus Christ and celebrates worldly things, which are money and the flesh'. The miniature depicting the daughter asking for 40 days of mourning interprets her again as Synagoga, wasting time on earthly pleasures (Drewer, 'Jephthah', p. 53).
[101]   This, however, is typical of representations of her death and in keeping with her status.

the altar upon the wood. And Abraham stretched forth his hand, and took the knife to slay his son. (Genesis 22:9–10)

Furthermore, the crossed branches from which the flames arise signal that the sacrifice is being carried out in God's name. The image, therefore, echoes the tradition of viewing Jephthah and his daughter as types, like Abraham and Isaac, of the sacrifice by God of His only son. The execution takes place inside a church-like building, framed by its Gothic vaulting and windows. Since the Bible does not specify where Jephthah's sacrifice of his daughter took place, the *Schatzbehalter* artist has chosen to locate it inside a religious space.[102] This may signify a number of things: first, that God sanctions the sacrifice (a second altar, located in a smaller chapel in the background, stands behind Jephthah's raised sword, so God "stands behind" the vow and its consequences); second; that Jephthah's daughter is so contained by the rules of her religion and obedience to her father that she has no avenue of escape from death; or, third, that she stands so firmly inside the framework of her faith that she does not question the rightness of her father's sacrifice of her life. Moreover, this representation of the execution within a closed space, the daughter kneeling in prayer and readiness, echoes images of the Annunciation and Presentation of the Virgin in the Temple, opening paths into typological readings of the scene;[103] the many windows, symbolic of Mary's purity and clarity and of God's illuminating Grace, support this reading and recall the exegesis of the daughter as a type of the Virgin and prototype nun.[104] On the second altar stand two stone tablets resembling those on which God wrote the Ten Commandments subsequently handed down to Moses. Their presence reminds the reader of the laws on which Christianity was built; the Fourth Commandment, "Honour thy father and thy mother", signalling to the nuns of the Klarissenkloster and to the young women of Nuremberg the need both to obey the paternal will – be it God's, their confessor-preacher's, or their father's – and to let their lives be shaped by the laws governing Christianity.[105] Nuns enclosed in their convent,

---

[102]   The space might be that of a private chapel, indicating the centrality of the model and, indeed, Fridolin's teaching to the nuns of the Klarissenkloster and other women readers within Nuremberg. For the architecture and function of domestic chapels see Andreas Curtius, 'Die Hauskapelle als architektonischer Rahmen der privaten Andacht', in *Spiegel der Seligkeit*, pp. 34–48.

[103]   Which resonate in the *Jezebel* woodcut yet to be discussed.

[104]   The windows illuminate the interior space in the way God's Grace illuminates His Word or Stephan Fridolin illuminates the life, suffering and death of Christ for the nuns of the Klarissenkloster and a wider readership within Nuremberg. Hence the *Schatzbehalter* itself becomes a source of illumination, a "window" onto the path to salvation.

[105]   It could, of course, be argued that the sword's slicing across the tablets echoes the tradition of disapproval for Jephthah's sacrifice as he is "shredding" the Commandments

daughters enclosed in their homes, all enclosed within the city walls of Nuremberg, lived within tenets constructed for them by more powerful men. God wrote the Commandments on stone with His finger, so they enjoy the status of written text,[106] like the *Schatzbehalter* the work of a powerful male author. Through this analogy Fridolin's text acquires greater authority as it, and the sermons forming its basis, becomes a sort of Ten Commandments for those who hear or read it. The daughter's head occupies the centre of the woodcut immediately below the tablets, which themselves are immediately below the keystone of the vaulting. Perfect obedience to the Law of God, as embodied by Jephthah's daughter, is thus presented as the keystone of the Church, monastic life and Christian society in Nuremberg.[107]

Why is the Jephthah woodcut relevant to Saint Katherine? As mentioned earlier, Michael Wolgemut, one of the artists responsible for the *Schatzbehalter* woodcuts, lived on the Bergstraße, at the foot of which stood the Sebalduskirche. The reflexions of the Löffelholz Altar in the Jephthah image are striking: the executioner and Saint Katherine kneeling in prayer under a vaulted Gothic architectural frame are found again in the sword-wielding Jephthah and his devout, submissive, kneeling daughter in their chapel. Whilst the similarity is undoubtedly due in no small part to the conventionality of execution iconography, the woodcut may have triggered memories of the Löffelholz Altar and taken the reader mentally into the Sebalduskirche, even into the monastery church on Sinai with its icon of Jephthah's daughter or to Alexandria itself. Moreover, the superimposition of Saint Katherine onto Jephthah's daughter would have reinforced the impact of the latter's sacrifice, equating it implicitly with martyrdom. Any female reader using the woodcut for meditation and putting herself into the place of Jephthah's daughter/Saint Katherine may have experienced the pain and fear of execution but also – because of the rewards granted Saint Katherine – been reinforced in her faith and her trust in God's benevolence. Any male reader viewing the woodcut may have experienced an ambivalent reaction: on the one hand, the mental substitution

---

by disobeying the Fifth, "Thou shalt not kill". Moreover, he is doing so because of his own foolishness in making the vow.

106   Much as one would inscribe text and images onto the wax slate of one's brain, the stone slate of urban space or, indeed, the type and woodcut blocks of the *Schatzbehalter*. Thus the tablets figure the function of Fridolin's work: the inscription onto the reader's memory of the immutable, God-given precepts of Christianity intended to fashion his conduct. Heinrichs-Schreiber draws attention to two woodcuts illustrating techniques of memorization that form part of the instructions for using the *Schatzbehalter* for devotional purposes (pp. 98 and 100), indicating that Fridolin's text was intended for similar mental inscription.

107   Women's position at the bottom of the spiritual-political-familial hierarchy is also made apparent by the spatial hierarchy.

of himself for Jephthah may have thrilled through the imagination of his power over young women and the obedience he could exact. On the other hand, it may have instilled in him a sense of responsibility and humility.[108] A local building – possibly the Sebalduskirche itself – might have formed the mental location for the execution. This merging of actual and remembered pictures and places may, like the comparison of the Heilsbronner Hof with Sinai, have rendered Nuremberg a more intensely spiritual space, a spatial map representing discourses of spiritual and social power based in the reader/worshipper's soul.

A further reflexion of Saint Katherine is found in quite a different quarter: in Basel in 1493 Michel Furter published the *Ritter vom Turn*.[109] A courtesy text, it was the adaptation of the *Livre du Chevalier de la Tour Landry*, written between 1370 and 1371 by the French aristocrat Geoffroy IV de la Tour Landry for his daughters. Like other courtesy texts, the *Ritter vom Turn* iterates the precepts of socially sanctioned behaviour (silence, submissiveness, modesty, piety, chastity, malleability by the dominant male) meant to rule young girls' lives; these are imparted through *exempla* of virtuous or wicked women from Biblical and other sources which, if followed, essentially erase women from the male environment by making them invisible and inaudible.[110] The Knight's recurrent exegesis ensures

---

[108]   Weakness, humility and trust in God's benevolence may also have been the result of a male reader imagining himself as Saint Katherine.

[109]   The translation into German was undertaken by the Swabian aristocrat Marquard vom Stein (1425/30–1495/6) for the benefit of his two daughters and of readers unfamiliar with French. William Caxton published an English version in 1484. For Geoffroy de la Tour Landry and Marquard vom Stein see Ruth Harvey, 'Prolegomena to an edition of "Der Ritter vom Turn"', in Peter F. Ganz and Werner Schröder (eds), *Probleme mittelalterlicher Überlieferung und Textkritik. Oxforder Colloquium 1966* (Berlin: Erich Schmidt, 1968), pp. 162–82; Hans Joachim Kreutzer, 'Marquart von Stein', in *Die deutsche Literatur des Mittelalters. Verfasserlexikon*, 2nd edn, vol. 6 (Berlin and New York: de Gruyter, 1987), col. 129–35; and the introduction to *The Book of the Knight of the Tower. Translated by William Caxton*, ed. M.Y. Offord, Early English Text Society, Supplementary Series 2 (London, New York and Toronto: Oxford University Press, 1971), pp. xi–xlv. A modern edition of the German text is Ruth Harvey (ed.), *Marquard vom Stein. Der Ritter vom Turn*, Texte des späten Mittelalters und der frühen Neuzeit 32 (Berlin: Erich Schmidt, 1988). Ruth Harvey's commentary on the *Ritter vom Turn* was published posthumously: *Marquard vom Stein: Der Ritter vom Turn. Kommentar*. Aus dem Nachlaß von Ruth Harvey herausgegeben von Peter Ganz, Nigel Palmer, Lothar Schmitt und Christopher Wells, Texte des späten Mittelalters und der frühen Neuzeit 37 (Berlin: Erich Schmidt, 1996).

[110]   For courtesy texts see Diane Bornstein, *The Lady in the Tower: Medieval Courtesy Literature for Women* (Hamden: Archon, for Shoe String Press, 1983); Susanne Barth, *Jungfrauenzucht: Literaturwissenschaftliche und pädagogische Studien zur Mädchenerziehungsliteratur zwischen 1200 und 1600* (Stuttgart: M&P, 1994; orig. Diss. Phil. Cologne, 1993); Theodor Brüggemann in Zusammenarbeit mit Otto Brunken. *Handbuch*

his daughters cannot ignore the implication for their own lives of the moral encapsulated in each *exemplum*. Nevertheless, the *Ritter vom Turn* does contain a number of individual narratives in which an assertive woman threatens to explode the bands of decorum and restraint imposed by the Knight's moralizing exegesis. A common strategy for mitigating the danger posed by unruly female behaviour is the use of violence, either awkwardly forced onto a story to twist its conclusion to the desired shape or else integral to the source.[111] As with Saint Katherine, violence can, on the surface, seem merely a blunt instrument for the fashioning of socially and dynastically desirable female behaviour, a ritual reassertion of patriarchal power aimed at restoring a threatened political and domestic hierarchy and male reputation, a socially "normative force".[112] However, it also serves to transmute female behaviour from sin to sanctity, from disruption to *exemplum*, rendering women who use their voices and bodies for their own ends into showcases and mouthpieces for the ultimate dominant male, God. One possibility for such transmutation is offered by the story and woodcut of Queen Jezebel, the latter tapping into established iconographic traditions such as that of Saint Katherine which transform Jezebel into an "exemplary virgin".

---

zur Kinder- und Jugendliteratur: Vom Beginn des Buchdrucks bis 1570 (Stuttgart, 1987), col. 739–8 and 1095–7; Jonathan Nicholls, *The Matter of Courtesy. Medieval Courtesy Books and the Gawain-Poet* (Cambridge: Brewer, 1985); Rosemary Barton Tobin, *Vincent of Beauvais' 'De Eruditione Filiorum Nobilium'. The Education of Women*, American University Studies, Series XIV Education, 5 (New York, Bern and Frankfurt am Main: Lang, 1984).

[111]   One such *exemplum* is that of the rope-maker's wife persuaded by a gift from a procuress to have an affair with a prior. One night the rope-maker spots the prior leaving his house. Though his wife denies the liaison, the rope-maker's suspicions are confirmed by the discovery of the prior's britches under the conjugal bed. When he later sees his wife continuing the affair he breaks both her calves. Upon recovery she resumes her affair with the prior, the rope-maker catches them in bed together one night and runs them both through with a sword (*Der Ritter vom Turn*, pp. 153–8). Whilst this *exemplum* resembles the *fabliau Les braies au Cordelier*, the final act of violence restores the disrupted social order by allowing the rope-maker to assert his authority over his wife and the prior, usurper of his primacy in the home and marriage bed. For the resemblance between this story and an actual event see Susanna Burghartz, 'Ehebruch und eheherrliche Gewalt. Literarische und außerliterarische Bezüge im "Ritter vom Turn"', in Hans-Jürgen Bachorski (ed.), *Ordnung und Lust. Bilder von Liebe, Ehe und Sexualität in Spätmittelalter und Früher Neuzeit*, Literatur – Imagination – Realität 1 (Trier: Wissenschaftlicher Verlag, 1991), pp. 123–40. The case is recorded in the Staatsarchiv Zürich, *Rats- und Richtbücher* B VI 209, fol. 305–6ʳ. See also Harvey, *Kommentar*, pp. 79–80 for the similarity of the story to other *fabliaux*.

[112]   Stephen D. White argues that ritual displays of anger had such a force (Stephen D. White, 'The Politics of Anger', in Barbara H. Rosenwein (ed.), *Anger's Past. The Social Uses of Emotion in the Middle Ages* (Ithaca and London: Cornell University Press, 1998), pp. 127–52 (p. 145).

The Biblical Jezebel was a ruthless, Godless, land- and power-hungry queen and active player on the political stage: she worshipped the Phoenician god Baal, supported his prophets and attempted to suppress the worship of Yahweh. In the story of Naboth the Jezreelite, Jezebel, not her husband, was the one to seize the initiative, arranging for Naboth to be falsely accused of blasphemy, tried and stoned to death so that Ahab could take possession of his vineyard (1 Kings 21). The *Ritter vom Turn* adds details such as Jezebel's cruelty to the poor (p. 162) or her persecution of hermits, the clergy and believers in the true faith (p. 162).[113] Moreover, the Queen has Naboth secretly killed and witnesses bear false testimony to his promise of the vineyard to Ahab.[114] In other words, the Queen dominates religious, political and territorial policy, modelling the very opposite of the woman the *Ritter vom Turn* sets out to create.[115] The manner of Jezebel's death is also changed: on conquering Ahab's kingdom, the Biblical Jehu orders Jezebel pushed from a tower window; when his servants go to bury the corpse nothing is left but her hands, feet and skull, the rest having been eaten by dogs (2 Kings 9:32–5).[116] In the *Ritter vom Turn*, Jezebel stands not at a window but at a town gate to watch Jehu's entry; he has her publicly executed and specifically orders her corpse *not* to be buried *so that* dogs may eat it.[117] Her body, as the site

---

[113]   Harvey argues the alterations are intended to increase the resonance for a contemporary audience (*Kommentar*, p. 88).

[114]   The Biblical Naboth is accused of blasphemy and publicly stoned to death (1 Kings 21:13).

[115]   By which is meant one who embodies the virtues previously listed: silence, submissiveness, modesty, piety, chastity, malleability by the dominant male and so forth.

[116]   God Himself ordains this fate for Jezebel: 'And of Jezebel also spake the LORD, saying, The dogs shall eat Jezebel by the walls of Jezreel' (1 Kings 22:23).

[117]   Dogs were despised by the Hebrews as scavengers and thieves; further, they could symbolize greed and the Devil as a Hound of Hell. Not only do these characteristics echo those of Jezebel herself; the evil she embodies is portrayed as literal food for the Devil. See *Harper's Bible Dictionary*, ed. Paul J. Achtemeier et al. (New York: HarperCollins, 1985), p. 224; *Hall's Dictionary*, p. 105; Murray and Murray, *The Oxford Companion to Christian Art and Architecture*, p. 139; and *Elsevier's Dictionary of Symbols and Imagery. Second, Enlarged Edition by Ad de Vries. Revised and Updated by Arthur de Vries* (Amsterdam etc.: Elsevier, 2004), p. 174. In the *Liet von Troye* Herbort von Fritslâr describes Diomedes' response when Priam requests that the body of Penthesilia (the Amazon queen responsible for killing numerous Greeks) be returned for burial: such is Diomedes' hatred of her that he wants her body eaten by dogs or dumped like a dog's in brackish water, obviously a particularly humiliating end for women who assumed masculine roles and thus defied the boundaries of their gender (Herbort von Fritslâr, *Liet von Troye*, ed. Ge. Karl Frommann (Quedlinburg and Leipzig: Basse, 1837; reprint Amsterdam: Rodopi, 1966), ll. 967–82).

of her defiance, is destroyed, the text deliberately turning her death into a public spectacle of degradation.[118]

Despite alterations two crucial elements are retained by the *Ritter vom Turn*: Jezebel's self-adornment and her scorn. The Bible says:

> And when Jehu was come to Jezreel, Jezebel heard *of it*; and she painted her face and tired her head, and looked out at a window. And as Jehu entered in at the gate, she said, *Had* Zimri peace, who slew his master? (2 Kings 9:30–1)[119]

The *Ritter vom Turn* renders the incident as follows:

> Da das die falsche böße künigin Jezabel vernam / satzt sy sich zü der porten / da der künig Jehu jn riten solte / Vnnd kleidet sich mitt guldin tüchern / vnnd edelm gestyne gar seltzsamlich vnnd anders dann andre frowenn / Vnnd als sy den künig ersach / hůb sy an zů flůchen die bösten schantlichesten flůch die sy mocht erdencken. Also begund sich der künig Jehu vmb sehen vnnd sich verwundern ab Jezabel der künigin kleydung / vnnd dem übel reden jrer zungenn. (p. 163)

> [When the false, evil queen Jezebel learnt that she placed herself at the gate through which King Jehu was to ride into the city and dressed herself in cloth of gold and precious stones in a very strange and fantastic manner quite unlike that of other women. And when she saw the king she started to curse with the wickedest, most shameful curses she could think up. And King Jehu began to look around and was amazed by Queen Jezebel's clothes and the evil speech uttered by her tongue].

Three things strike the reader. First, Jezebel deliberately positions herself in the public arena: rather than being contained within a tower she challenges from a space outwith (physical) restraint, symbolic of her mental and emotional freedom and refusal to bow to Jehu's military and political control. Second, the *Ritter vom*

---

[118]   However, according to Apostolos-Cappadona Jezebel was also 'characterized in the Old Testament as compassionate because she never permitted a funeral procession to pass without walking herself behind the bier, and clapping her hands as a sign of respect and wailing with the mourners; and she accompanied nervous bridegrooms to their wedding feasts and participated in their public joy. Thrown from the palace balcony, Jezebel was killed and her lifeless body was left for the dogs. However, her head, hands and feet were not eaten by the animals, and since these were the instruments of her good deeds they were honored with proper burial' (Apostolos-Cappadona, *Women in Religious Art*, p. 199).

[119]   Zimri was a 'commander of half the chariotry in early ninth-century BC Israel who led a successful coup against King Elah, as a result of which Zimri became an epithet for one who kills his own master' (*Harper's Bible Dictionary*, p. 1165).

Turn exaggerates the splendour, richness and otherness of Jezebel's clothes,[120] which become the costume for her performance of defiance, the translation of her speech into visible, tangible material form. Third, it changes the nature of this speech from one sarcastic remark into a torrent of obscene curses. Hence the outlandishness of Jezebel's dress and speech merge, both signs of a woman crossing the boundaries of her gender and intruding into male visual and aural space.

Visually and verbally Jezebel embodies the defiant woman: she dresses for public performance, the luxury of her dress accentuating her power, sexuality and contempt for male-imposed constrictions; her abuse of Jehu transcends mere public abuse of an individual: it is a political act, since she challenges and humiliates a king. Such politicizing of the Queen's behaviour is consonant with her portrayal in the Bible and even the *Ritter vom Turn*[121] but runs counter to the Knight's moral, which reduces the story to a lesson on charity, spousal wisdom and sartorial restraint: 'Darumb dyß eyn gůt exempel ist / gegen den armen barmhertzig zů syn / Vnnd das eyn frow jren man nit bößen rat geben sol / Sich ouch mit jren kleydüngen nit zů entschicken / Sonder sich nach stat der frommen frowen deß landes zů haltenn' (p. 164).[122] Given that a politically shrewd, disturbingly physical and spiritedly unmalleable queen constitutes a hazardous role model for maidens on the brink of matrimony, the recast moral must be intended, first, to mitigate the threatening implications of her behaviour for household harmony and, second, to emphasize the futility of resistance against the stronger male on any social, political or religious level. The other change – Jezebel's execution – corresponds not just to her royal status but also to the very public nature of her refusal to accept defeat, her public humiliation and silencing mirroring her public humiliation and slander of Jehu. The beheading of Jezebel kills speech at its source, thus enforcing the silence expected of virtuous women; the public infliction of violence on a transgressor is legitimized by reference to God. Jehu:

> GEbot synem volck das sy sy on lenger verziehen nemen vnd jr das houpt vor aller mengcklich ab schlahen sölten / Das sy also thatten dar by beuolhend / das sy nyeman vergraben solte / vnnd sy die hund vnnd thier essen wurden Das kam allein vß jrer hochfart / Als dann dick vnd vil gott der herr die straffet. (p. 164)

---

[120]   That Jezebel attires herself 'gar seltzsamlich vnnd anders dann andre frowenn' [in a very strange and fantastic manner quite like that of other women] reinforces her status as religious, political and social outsider, already indicated by her position outside the city walls.

[121]   Albeit to a lesser extent as the latter tends to foreground her religious transgression.

[122]   'For that reason this is a good example of the need to be charitable to the poor and for a woman not to give her husband evil advice and for her not to distinguish herself through her clothes but to model herself on the pious women of the country'.

[Ordered his people to seize her without any further delay and cut off her head in front of the whole crowd. They did what they were told and followed another order, namely that she should not be buried so that dogs and other animals might eat her. That was by reason of her pride alone, which God punishes frequently and severely].

Violence, specifically male violence towards women, is incorporated into the educatory, normative function of the text since by inference its use by any dominant male in the assertion of his authority is also sanctioned.

The *exemplum* is accompanied by a half-page woodcut, one of 46 cut for the German *Ritter vom Turn* and attributed to Albrecht Dürer (1471–1528).[123] By depicting the execution (one of the alterations to the Biblical story), the artist focuses on the visually most dramatic moment. Jezebel's beheading takes place outside the city walls, the gate at which she positioned herself forming its backdrop, the tower reminding the reader of her fate in the Old Testament story.[124] The location, like Jezebel's dress, symbolizes her status as outcast; the jaggedly rocky scenery reminding us she is in the political and religious wilderness.[125] She kneels

---

[123]   For the debate on the attribution of the woodcuts see: Franz Bock, *Die Werke des Matthias Grünewald*, Studien zur deutschen Kunstgeschichte 54 (Strasbourg: J.H. Ed. Heitz, 1904); Louis Poulain, *Der Ritter vom Turn von Marquart von Stein* (Diss. Phil. Basel 1906); Rudolf Kautzsch, *Die Holzschnitte zum Ritter vom Turn (Basel 1493). Mit einer Einleitung*, Studien zur deutschen Kunstgeschichte 44 (Strasbourg: J.H. Ed. Heitz, 1903); Hans Koegler, 'Die Basler Gebetholzschnitte vom Illustrator des Narrenschiffs und Ritters vom Turn', *Gutenberg-Jahrbuch* (1926): 117–31; Werner Weisbach, *Der Meister der Bergmannschen Offizin und Albrecht Dürers Beziehungen zur Basler Buchillustration. Ein Beitrag zur Geschichte des deutschen Holzschnittes*, Studien zur deutschen Kunstgeschichte 6 (Strasbourg: J.H. Ed. Heitz, 1896); and *Die Baseler Buchillustration des XV. Jahrhunderts*, Studien zur deutschen Kunstgeschichte 8 (Strasbourg: J.H. Ed. Heitz, 1896); Wilhelm Worringer, *Die altdeutsche Buchillustration* (Munich and Leipzig: R. Piper, 1912); Erwin Panofsky, *The Life and Art of Albrecht Dürer* (Princeton: Princeton University Press, 1943); Heinrich Röttinger, 'Die Holzschnitte der Druckerei des Jacob Cammerlander in Straßburg', *Gutenberg-Jahrbuch* (1936); Friedrich Winkler, *Dürer und die Illustrationen zum Narrenschiff* (Berlin: Deutscher Verein für Kunstwissenschaft, 1951).

[124]   The tower may also be an allusion to Saint Barbara, who was locked away in a tower by her possessive father, the pagan Dioscorus, to hide her beauty from potential suitors. She converted to Christianity, was tortured and eventually, in some versions of the legend, beheaded on a mountain top by her father. She became the patron saint of milliners, knights, soldiers, armourers, firemen and all those in danger of sudden, unexpected death. Barbara's attribute, a tower, is a symbol of chastity; she is frequently portrayed with Saint Katherine (Fisher, *Square Halo*, pp. 140–3; *Hall's Dictionary*, p. 306).

[125]   However, the rock is also a symbol of Saint Peter and God as well as of steadfastness and constancy.

in the front right-hand corner;[126] the hem of her gown breaches the frame of the woodcut, blurring the boundaries between her space and the reader's, drawing the reader into the image and turning her into an actual spectator. However, visually the central figure is the executioner wielding his sword; and male infliction of violence on a woman is the central theme. The image constitutes an alarming warning against self-assertion on a women's part, not least since the blurring of spatial boundaries renders the threat of male violence more immediate. The portcullis above Jehu's head forms a cross, marking him as a believer in the true faith and indicating divine sanction for his actions, whereas Jezebel is an isolated figure, her way back through the city gates into society and redemption, into a Christian community and the Kingdom of Heaven, blocked by her sins in the figure of the executioner exacting retribution. Whilst in the text Jezebel explicitly plays to the public gaze, in the woodcut she plays to no gaze but has her back turned to Jehu and the reader, a position that emphasizes her isolation. Similarly, although her crown clearly identifies her as a queen, the absence of jewels, whilst contradicting the text, renders her neck more vulnerable and her ultimate weakness in the face of male political, religious and physical power inescapably visible. Verbal/textual violence is punished by physical/visual violence, which renders a woman at the other end of the scale from Jephthah's daughter a different sort of exemplar.

However, it is the iconography and the memories activated by it that enable the Jezebel woodcut to be read differently, since it reflects the execution of both Saint Katherine of Alexandria[127] and Jephthah's daughter (and hence the Presentation of the Virgin Mary in the Temple and the dedication of herself to Christ by the Christian nun). Again, the resemblance to the Löffelholz Altar

---

126 From within the woodcut Jezebel kneels on the left, in medieval Christian art usually the locus of evil and transgression, so the ordering of space provides the reader with an aid to interpretation.

127 See, for example, Friedrich Pacher's altarpiece depicting the life of Saint Katherine (c. 1480; now in the Neustift Gallery); the Simon Marmion *Hours* (Franco-Flemish, c. 1475–81, now in the National Art Library, Victoria and Albert Museum, Saltung 1221); Lucas Cranach the Elder's *Saint Katherine* (1506, now in Dresden); and the *Belles Heures de Jean Duc de Berry* (fol. 19ᵛ; now in the Cloisters, New York). Miniatures in the *Belles Heures* depict – in iconographically very similar terms – the execution of other female saints, namely Saint Lucy (fol. 179ᵛ) and Saint Cecilia (fol. 180) as well as Maxentius's empress, Faustina (fol. 18). See Millard Meiss and Elizabeth H. Beatson (eds), *Les Belles Heures de Jean Duc de Berry. The Cloisters. The Metropolitan Museum of Art* (London: Thames and Hudson, 1974). Two examples of pious donors/Mary holding Christ Child/martyrdom of saints are Gerard David's *Virgin and Child with Saints and Donor* (c. 1510) and the *Donne Triptych* by Hans Memling (c. 1478), both in the National Gallery, London. Both depict Saints Barbara and Katherine. To a lesser extent the woodcut recalls the saint's kneeling in mystic marriage to Christ, for example, in *The Virgin and Child with Saints* by Quinten Massys (c. 1515–25; National Gallery, London).

is striking. Admittedly, the executioner's stance is conventional, just as it is unsurprising that the crowned and bearded Maxentius holding his upright sceptre resembles the crowned and bearded Jehu holding his, since this iconography traditionally represents male power and authority. Both women kneel, their hands slightly apart rather than folded together, a gesture that may be read as submission or reverence.[128] On the other hand, Saint Katherine's hair is long and loose, a sign of her virginity and a cloak for the neck's eroticism, whereas Jezebel's is elaborately tied-up, sign, as we have seen, of her vulnerability as well as her foreignness. Saint Katherine's crown functions as a symbol of her royal blood and approaching martyrdom; Jezebel's as one of status lost. Even though no wheel (Saint Katherine's attribute) is depicted in the *Ritter vom Turn* woodcut, the visual likeness is unmistakable and Dürer's familiarity with the Sebalduskirche renders the echoes of the Löffelholz Altar all the more probable. Thus Jezebel's kneeling becomes an expression not of defeat but of Katherine's piety and submission to God's Will, so ultimately of triumph through her martyrdom.[129] In the woodcut Jehu could be read as Maxentius, overseeing this martyrdom, the portcullis cross suggesting that Maxentius, too, is directed by God's Will. Jezebel's location outside the city walls represents Katherine's outside paganism, in other words, her adherence to Christianity and status as one of God's elect who go beyond normal believers in their devotion to the Lord. The location further reminds the reader that the pillars marking Saint Katherine's execution stand outside the walls of Alexandria, a further echo of the saint's legend. If a reader of the *Ritter vom Turn* knew the Löffelholz Altar, the Jezebel woodcut might have retrieved memories which took her back into the Sebalduskirche, prompting a mental tour of its sacred space and an act of devotion or meditation. Moreover, if adept at the devotional practice of visualizing meditation, such a reader may, first, instinctively have visualized the execution, possibly even imagining herself as Jezebel/Saint Katherine/Jephthah's daughter; and, second, have experienced the same sort of strong, conditioned response to the woodcut that could have been prompted by a walk through the memory canvas of Nuremberg and the use in meditation of its images of Saint Katherine. Again, the absorption of the pain, terror and shame of the execution as Jezebel combined with the salvatory

---

[128]   In the painting by Johann Koerbecke (c. 1400/1410–91) *The Virgin adoring the Child* (c. 1470–80) Joseph kneels with his hands in this position. The painting is reproduced in Henk van Os et al., *The Art of Devotion in the Late Middle Ages in Europe 1300–1500*, trans. Michael Hoyle (Princeton: Princeton University Press, 1994), p. 98.

[129]   Memories of the *Schatzbehalter* woodcut of Jephthah beheading his daughter may also inform a reading of the Jezebel woodcut, so that a double visual analogy to virtue counteracts any potential breaking of boundaries the figure of the Queen may suggest to a female reader.

grace offered by reading her as devout virgin would physically and emotionally have reinforced the desirability of internalizing the model identity offered by the text as a whole. Just as the reader becomes spectator to Jezebel's execution, she becomes witness to Katherine's martyrdom, to a potential model for her own salvation. By reflecting the iconography of a familiar female saint, the woodcut suggests the path to redemption offered by that saint: a virgin whose devotion caused her to adhere to God to the point of her own persecution and death. If this reflected image is stamped onto the reader's memory and hence her soul, she in turn has the potential to "become" the saint's reflexion and a mirror into which other women may look.

Katherine is silenced by death but her "voice" lives on, transmuted into the milk and oil that flowed from her body;[130] the miracles she performs in answer to petitioners' prayers; and her dialogue with the Nuremberg Dominican nuns and city inhabitants. A manuscript from the convent, Germanisches Nationalmuseum Hs. 1738, contains the following prayer to Saint Katherine: 'Frew dich pe: *christ*o wann nach der enthaubtung floß von dir milch fine plut von Junckfrewlicherr reinigkeit vnd erfrewest das volk vnd vil wurden bekert Eya behalt vns leib vnd sel in lauter reingkeit'.[131] God's grace converts violence into comfort and aid to those in danger or distress who petition Saint Katherine for help. Oil and milk also constitute tangible testimonies to the saint's existence that, as we have seen from Hans Tucher's account, may be taken back by the pilgrim to his home and there strengthen his personal dialogue with Saint Katherine or contribute to the civic attachment to the saint that found its expression in such artefacts as the Löffelholz Altar.

Through the reflected and refracted iconography of Saint Katherine, three women – the saint herself, Jephthah's daughter and Queen Jezebel – may be read as repositories for a range of "goods": debates on the nature of virtue, on the individual's relationship with authority, on the legitimacy of defiance and its expression (this within a strongly fortified, strictly regulated and tightly governed city); the affective intensity and need-for-physical-contact of personal piety; the intertwining of trade, financial clout, family status and devotion; the choice of and interaction between markers of Patrician identity, community and responsibility; the importance of learning and its dissemination; Nuremberg itself as collective memory, a warehouse for visual and emotive impressions

---

[130]   The milk that flows from Saint Katherine's neck on her execution expresses purity and divine mercy, since milk is associated with nurturing and motherhood. Thus her martyrdom is rendered an act of redemptive nurturing.

[131]   'Rejoice in Christ because after the execution there flowed from you milk and not blood on account of your virginal purity and you gladden people's hearts and many were converted. Hallelujah, preserve our body and soul in unblemished purity'.

imposed on, absorbed by, stored in and in their turn emitted by the very stones of the city. The Löffelholz Altar and Saint Katherine are just one example of a process of recursive reflexion repeated throughout the pages of this chapter to the eyes of the current reader.

Chapter 2

Living the Dream: The Life of
Saint Katherine of Alexandria

The story of St Katherine, with its scenes of debate and miracle, resonates with dramatic dialogue and spectacular action.[1]

Thus do Jacqueline Jenkins and Katherine J. Lewis characterize the legend of Saint Katherine of Alexandria, in the Late Middle Ages one of the most popular saints in Southern Germany and, indeed, further afield, since 'the sheer volume of material evidence produced by her cult from the eleventh to the early sixteenth centuries suggests that she was one of the most popular saints in medieval Europe'.[2] This assessment is supported by the languages into which Saint Katherine's *vita* was translated: they include English, Irish, Welsh, Anglo-Norman, Polish, Czech, Hungarian, French, German and Spanish; often several different versions existed in the one language.[3] In his entry on 'Katharina von Alexandrien' in the *Verfasserlexikon* Peter Assion comments that Saint Katherine 'dem Mittelalter als die nach Maria ranghöchste Heilige [galt]';[4] together with Barbara, Dorothy and Margaret (with whom she is often portrayed) she was one of the 'vier Hauptjungfrauen'.[5] According to Assion the core of the legend is the 'Passio', the story of Katherine's dispute with the heathen philosophers and her martyrdom under Emperor Maxentius in Alexandria. The earliest written evidence of her legend may have been in Greek and have originated in the East Roman cultural sphere in the sixth or seventh century; it is extant

---

[1]   Jacqueline Jenkins and Katherine J. Lewis, 'Introduction', in Jacqueline Jenkins and Katherine J. Lewis (eds), *St Katherine of Alexandria. Texts and Contexts in Western Medieval Europe*, Medieval Women: Texts and Contexts 8 (Turnhout: Brepols, 2003), pp. 1–18 (p. 5). Since the history of Saint Katherine's legend and its various redactions, including in *Der Heiligen Leben*, has been discussed at length in the sources given in these footnotes, it will be outlined only briefly here.

[2]   Jenkins and Lewis, 'Introduction', p. 1.

[3]   Jenkins and Lewis, 'Introduction', pp. 1–2.

[4]   'was considered the highest-ranking saint after Mary in the Middle Ages'.

[5]   'four principle virgins' (Peter Assion, 'Katharina von Alexandrien', in *Die deutsche Literatur des Mittelalters. Verfasserlexikon*, vol. 4 (Berlin and New York: de Gruyter, 1983), col. 1055–75.

in the Greek versions by Simeon Metaphrastes (early 960s)[6] and Athanasius.[7] The latter formed the basis for a Latin version by Arechis (d. c. 799);[8] from Arechis and a further translation of Athanaisus into Latin stems the standard Latin version, the 'Vulgata', which can be documented from the twelfth century onwards, was the most widespread redaction of the legend in German-speaking territories, was used by Jacobus de Voragine as one source for his *Legenda aurea* and formed the basis for the medieval German versions.[9] Another early version is found in the *Menelogium Basilianum* written for Byzantine emperor Basil II (976–1025).[10] In the West is to be found the 'Conversio', the story of Saint Katherine's conversion by a hermit and the mystic marriage, the other major component of the legend. Some manuscripts include the younger addtion of a 'Nativitas', the story of Katherine's birth.[11] The two sources, 'Passio' and 'Conversio', were fused into the version that formed the basis for the German texts. According to Bruce Beatie, the legend of Saint Katherine: 'must have existed in oral tradition as early as the eighth century: Katharine is named in eighth- and ninth-century icons in Naples and Rome, and the contents list of a Carolingian legendary in Munich refers to a "passio Ecaterine" since lost from the manuscript'.[12] It has been argued that the popularity of Saint Katherine's

---

[6]   According to Jenkins and Lewis most later Latin versions can be traced back to this one (Jenkins and Lewis, 'Introduction', p. 7).

[7]   Assion, 'Katharina von Alexandrien', col. 1056. Athanasius claims to have been the saint's slave and scribe and eyewitness to her passion and martyrdom (Assion, *Mirakel*, p. 105).

[8]   The Latin version was probably known in the West from the eighth or ninth centuries onwards (Assion, 'Katharina von Alexandrien', col. 1056–7).

[9]   Assion, 'Katharina von Alexandrien', col. 1056–7. The 'Vulgata' existed in three versions: 1) V1: the full text; 2) V2: an abbreviated version; 3) V3: an abbreviated version of V2. The full version, V1, was combined with extracts from older Latin versions to form the basis for the *Legenda Aurea*. Well over 1,000 manuscripts and 97 Latin incunabula are extant. The oldest manuscript version in German-speaking territories dates from 1282 (from Prüfening); the earliest printed edition was published by Conrad Winters de Homborch in Cologne in 1470 or possibly by Anton Koberger in Nuremberg in the same year. Koberger had published the work eight times by 1496. The content of the *Legenda Aurea* varies considerably across versions due to additions, omissions and restructuring of the text (Konrad Kunze, 'Jacobus de Voragine', *Verfasserlexikon*, vol. 4, col. 448–66).

[10]   Jenkins and Lewis, 'Introduction', p. 8; Beatie, 'Traditional Themes', pp. 788–9.

[11]   Assion, 'Katharina von Alexandrien', col. 1057. He does not date the 'Conversio'. Germanisches Nationalmuseum Hs. 15131 and Hs. 86 409 contain versions of the legend that include the story of Katherine's birth.

[12]   Beatie, 'Traditional Themes', pp. 788–9. Beatie goes into the transmission in some detail; he also discusses the "folklore" aspects of the legend. Jenkins and Lewis date the manuscript to the early ninth century ('Introduction', p. 7). Assion provides more detail: 'Als früheste Belege des Katharinenkultes gelten ein 1948 in Rom gefundenes Oratorium

legend was boosted by the "incipient Crusades",[13] the "rediscovery" of her tomb on Sinai in the 1030s and the translation of her relics to Rouen, where they were kept in the monastery of Sainte-Trinité-du-mont-de-Rouen (founded outside Rouen in 1024–33).[14] He further points to the 'wealth of textual material' about the saint: 'Hermann Knust in 1890 could already refer to 97 versions of the *Vita Katharinae*, published and unpublished in ten languages';[15] Beatie and Boykin discovered more than 50 published versions of Katherine's life in the English, French and German traditions alone; and the *Analecta Bollandiana* lists 148 texts available only in manuscript, principally Latin and Greek.[16] According to Jenkins and Lewis the mid-thirteenth century saw the composition and circulation of accounts of Saint Katherine's *vita* that included her birth and upbringing as well as her passion;[17] and Beatie records the earliest German version as being a poem of 3,452 lines dating to the second-half of thirteenth century.[18] German prose versions existed from the fourteenth century; at first only the 'Passio' was translated; later the 'Conversio'.[19] Middle High German versions include those in the *Passional* (c. 1300) and the *Märterbuch* (c. 1320) and Hermann von Fritzlar's prose rendition of around 1346. The prose versions, often supplemented by miracle stories and a 'Lobrede' (eulogy), were frequently intended as *Tischlektüre* (mealtime reading) in convents dedicated to the saint.[20] As mentioned, an account of Saint Katherine's life and miracles, based mainly on the Latin Vulgate version, was included in Jacobus de Voragine's *Legenda*

---

nördlich der Basilika S. Lorenzo als Verano mit einem Fresko von "S. Ekaterina" aus der Mitte des 8. Jahrhunderts und die Notiz im Register eines Münchner Passionars vom Ende des gleichen Jahrhunderts' [The earliest evidence for the cult of Saint Katherine is thought to be an oratory discovered in 1948 to the north of the Basilica of San Lorenzo als Verano in Rome which contains a fresco of 'S. Ekaterina' from the middle of the eighth century; and the note in the index of a Munich Passional from the same century] (Assion, *Mirakel*, p. 106).

[13]   This seems a little tenuous, given that the First Crusade was not preached until 1095, so some 60-plus years after the discovery of her tomb. Walsh argues that the spread of Saint Katherine's cult was due to its patronage by the Dukes of Normandy (Christine Walsh, *The Cult of St Katherine of Alexandria in Early Medieval Europe*, Church, Faith and Culture in the Medieval West (Aldershot: Ashgate, 2007), pp. 63–96).

[14]   Jenkins and Lewis, 'Introduction', pp. 8–9.

[15]   Beatie, 'Traditional Themes', p. 786.

[16]   Beatie, 'Traditional Themes', p. 786.

[17]   Jenkins and Lewis, 'Introduction', p. 6.

[18]   Johann Lambel (ed.), *Katharinen Martyr, Germania*, 8 (1863): 129–86; see Beatie, 'Traditional Themes', p. 790 and n. 22. Assion lists 13 rhymed and 16 prose versions of Saint Katherine's legend ('Katharina von Alexandrien', col. 1058–71).

[19]   Assion, 'Katharina von Alexandrien', col. 1058.

[20]   Assion, 'Katharina von Alexandrien', col. 1058; Assion, *Mirakel*, pp. 85–6.

Aurea (c. 1260); the oldest extant manuscript of the German translation of the *Legenda Aurea*, namely *Der Heiligen Leben* (the *Winterteil*), dates to around the end of the fourteenth century and was produced in the Katharinenkloster in Nuremberg.[21] *Der Heiligen Leben* was first published by Günther Zainer in Augsburg in 1471 and appeared in 24 editions between 1471 and 1500,[22] two of them in Nuremberg: the first was published by Hans Sensenschmid on 28 July 1475; the second by Anton Koberger in 1488. The *Winterteil* of Sensenschmid's edition contains an account of the life and miracles of Saint Katherine that accords almost verbatim with that from another Katharinenkloster manuscript, a compendium copied in 1421 by Fridricus Lenckner for Cecilia Rötin (d. 1469), who took it into the convent with her.[23] Beatie maintains that the version of Saint Katherine's life and miracles in the 1488 edition is, at some 14,400 words, roughly seven times longer than the average *vita*.[24]

---

[21]   It is now in the Stadtbibliothek Nürnberg, Cod. Cent. IV, 43, fol. 54ʳ–64ʳ (some text lost at the beginning). See Assion, *Mirakel*, pp. 66–8. A complete version from 1430 can be found in Stadtbibliothek Nürnberg, Cod. Cent. IV, 79, fol. 124ᵛ–41ʳ (Assion, 'Katharina von Alexandrien', col. 1064). The version of the legend in *Der Heiligen Leben* is not the oldest extant German version. This is the prose translation of the 'Passio' found in the *Elsässischen Legenda Aurea* (c. 1350). However, it seems to be the first German one to bring Katherine's conversion and passion together (Assion, 'Katharina von Alexandrien', col. 1063).

[22]   In 33 High German and eight Low German editions by 1521, almost all of them richly illustrated with woodcuts (Georg Steer, 'Geistliche Prosa', in *Geschichte der deutschen Literatur von den Anfängen bis zur Gegenwart*, vol. 3, *Die deutsche Literatur im Spätmittelalter 1250–1370*, Teil 2 *Reimpaargedichte, Drama, Prosa*, ed. Ingeborg Glier (Munich: Beck, 1987), Chapter 6, pp. 306–70 (p. 311)). Steer says *Der Heiligen Leben* 'läßt sich bei Weltpriestern, Adeligen und Patriziern nachweisen (vor allem in Nürnberg, Augsburg und Regensburg), diente unter anderm als ikonographisches Handbuch für Künstler, als Quelle für Meistersinger' [ownership by secular clerics, nobles and Patricians (above all in Nuremberg, Augsburg and Regensburg) can be proved. Amongst other things it served as a handbook of iconography for artists, as a source for *Meistersinger*] (p. 311). According to Kunze *Der Heiligen Leben* was the most widespread legendary in German and probably dates from between 1384 and 1400. The German version may have originated in Nuremberg and been intended either for the Patrician readership or for reformed nuns. Manuscripts of *Der Heiligen Leben* were owned by the Tucher, Holzschuher and Hartmann Schedel; Kunze calls it 'bis zur Reformation das volkssprachliche hagiographische Standardwerk schlechthin' [until the Reformation it was *the* standard hagiographical work in the vernacular] (Konrad Kunze, 'Der Heiligen Leben', *Verfasserlexikon*, vol. 3 (Berlin and New York: de Gruyter, 1981), col. 617–25.

[23]   Germanisches Nationalmuseum Hs. 877 (Assion, *Mirakel*, pp. 66–8). This is the oldest extant manuscript of the German version of the legend on its own (Assion, 'Katharina von Alexandrien', col. 1064).

[24]   Beatie, 'Traditional Themes', p. 793. Assion calculates that in the High German tradition and in the (Nuremberg manuscript version of the) *Heiligen Leben* Katherine has accumulated more posthumous miracles (29 including the *Milch- und Bestattungswunder*

However, for all Saint Katherine's popularity she may not have existed:

> The legend aside, there is no evidence of an educated Christian noblewoman named Katherine, nor of her accomplishments, persecution, and death, in sources contemporary with the fourth century. It is, in fact, unlikely she ever actually lived. St Katherine possibly originated as an amalgamated memory of the acts of defiance performed by real Christian women in Alexandria. Eusebius in *The History of the Church*, written just at the time St Katherine was supposed to have existed, describes the resistance of one woman in particular to the advances of Emperor Maximin (d. 313).[25]

Moreover, as Jenkins and Lewis point out, her legend shares with other female saints' stories:

> certain key narrative elements: the saint's beauty and virginity, the sexual/political persecution from a non-Christian figure of authority, the saint's steadfastness in her faith, her resolute defence of her virginity, her ability to endure a spectacular

---

[milk and entombment miracles]) than any saint other than the Virgin Mary (88) and Peter Damianus (30) (Assion, *Mirakel*, p. 55 and p. 59). He further points out that the *Legenda Aurea* included only three miracles by Katherine (p. 58). The miracle collection present in the Stadtbibliothek Cod. Cent. IV, 43 seems to have been transmitted unaltered in subsequent manuscripts and prints (Assion, *Mirakel*, p. 60). Apparently in the fifteenth century the Katharinenkloster itself witnessed a miracle at a side altar dedicated to the '10 tausend Rittern' [10,000 knights]. The 'kusterin nottel' written by Katharina von Mülheim in 1436 says the following: 'Man eret avch sant katerina gar fleißig auf dem altar von eines zeichens wegen, daz do pey ist geschehen' [Saint Katherine is also worshipped assiduously at that altar because of a miracle that happened there]. Nothing more is said about the miracle but a mass was celebrated at that altar on Saint Katherine's feast day, followed by two at the main Katherine altar in the choir and the main altar in the centre of the church, the *Angstaltar*. Relics of the saint were displayed on her feast day; they were otherwise kept in an altar (1359) in the sacristy and a small gold reliquary statuette. On this occasion the church was visited by inhabitants of the entire city (Assion, *Mirakel*, pp. 98–9; and citing Stadtbibliothek Nürnberg Cod. Cent. VII, 16, fol. 217[r]).

25   Jenkins and Lewis, 'Introduction', p. 6. They refer to Eusebius, *The History of the Church*, trans. G.A. Williamson (London: Penguin, 1965; rev. reprint 1989), p. 276: 'Alone amongst those whom the tyrant tried to seduce at Alexandria, a Christian woman of the greatest eminence and distinction won the victory by her heroic spirit over the lustful and wanton soul of Maximin. Famed for her wealth, birth, and education, she put everything second to modesty. In spite of his constant advances and her willingness to die, he could not put her to death, because desire was stronger than anger; but he exiled her as a punishment, and appropriated all her possessions'. The woman is identified in footnote 1 as Dorothea.

list of physical tortures, the pain of imprisonment and the joy of heavenly comfort, and, ultimately, death by execution.[26]

According to Jennifer Relvyn Bray, the 'reproduction ... of a number of stock hagiographical features is a product of the medieval hagiographer's concept of an individual saint as a manifestation, chronologically and geographically limited, of Christian virtues'.[27] Whether or not Saint Katherine existed is thus of secondary importance, since her legend serves as a showcase for specific (but not exclusively female) characteristics that resonated within the context of, in this case, Patrician mercantile Nuremberg. As Jolles puts it, the purpose of the legend as a genre is to encapsulate the 'tätige Tugend' [active virtue] of a saint, especially as demonstrated in his or her miracles.[28] He continues:

> Die Vita, die Legende überhaupt zerbricht das 'Historische' in seine Bestandteile, sie erfüllt diese Bestandteile von sich aus mit dem Wert der Imitabilität und baut sie in einer von dieser bedingten Reihenfolge wieder auf. Die Legende kennt das 'Historische' in diesem Sinne überhaupt nicht, sie kennt und erkennt nur Tugend und Wunder.[29]

> [The *vita*, the legend in general, breaks the 'historical' down into its constituent parts and fills these parts of its own accord with the quality of imitability and reconstructs them in a sequence determined by this imitability. The legend does not know the 'historical' in this sense at all; it knows and recognizes only virtue and miracle].

What matters, then, is the resonance of the virtues embodied by Katherine and their ability to generate active emulation. Taking as its basis Sensenschmid's 1475 edition of *Der Heiligen Leben*,[30] this chapter will analyse the legend, first, as a story full of 'dramatic dialogue and spectacular action'; second, with a view to establishing the key characteristics that led to the saint's popularity

---

[26]   Jenkins and Lewis, 'Introduction', pp. 9–10.

[27]   Jennifer Relvyn Bray, *The Legend of St Katherine in Later Middle English Literature* (PhD Diss. London 1984), p. 18, as cited in Jenkins and Lewis, 'Introduction', p. 9.

[28]   André Jolles, *Einfache Formen* (5th edn Tübingen: Niemeyer, 1974), p. 32.

[29]   Jolles, *Einfache Formen*, p. 40.

[30]   As the first printed and therefore more widely accessible version in Nuremberg; discussion of Saint Katherine's legend will assume, and refer to, a Nuremberg context. This version omits the story of Saint Katherine's parentage and birth, but in this civic context variants on the manuscript and printed traditions matter less as Patrician readers may not have been aware of them.

with Patrician patrons and her openness to use as an expression of Nuremberg's relationship with the Holy Roman Empire.

The opening words of her legend introduce not Saint Katherine but her father, King Costis of Cyprus: 'ES was eyn edler reycher Kung yn Cipperen land in der inselen in einer stat dy hyeß Solomina / der hyeß Costis der hett eyn tochter dye hyeß Katherina / vnd die was zu mal weiß vnd schon vnd kensch [*sic*] vnd tugentlich' (fol. cclij').[31] First, Katherine is located in terms of both lineage and geography: since her father is named and defined by his social status, power and dominion before Katherine is mentioned, she is, initially, defined by the standing of the dominant male. Moreover, as her daughterdom is the first of her qualities to be named she is identified through her family relationship to Costis as belonging to a family-based ruling elite. Identification through lineage is common in both the Bible and Arthurian romance, so echoes an authoritative cultural and literary pattern familiar to an educated urban readership.[32] It also mirrors the status-consciousness of a wealthy and powerful ruling Patrician class, the members of which were closely interconnected by blood and marriage, controlled who could sit on the all-powerful *Kleiner Rat* and recorded their lineage and history in sumptuous *Geschlechterbücher* (family histories).[33] As the nuns in the Katharinenkloster came from these Patrician families, the saint's

---

[31]   'There was once a rich king on the island of Cyprus who lived in a town called Solomina. His name was Costis and he had a daughter called Katherine who was wise and beautiful and virtuous'.

[32]   For example: 'And the names of the men *are* these: Of the tribe of Judah, Caleb the son of Jephunneh. And of the tribe of the children of Simeon, Shemul the son of Ammihud. Of the tribe of Benjamin, Elicidad the son of Chislon' (Numbers 34:19–21). In Arthurian romance Wolfram von Eschenbach's *Parzival*, Hartmann von Aue's *Gregorius* and Gottfried von Strassburg's *Tristan* provide the fullest examples.

[33]   Ulman Stromer's *Püchel von meim geslechet und abentewr* (1380/95–1407) is both the first work to chronicle Nuremberg's history and the first to record family history. Other *Geschlechterbücher* include *Das Große Tucherbuch* (1590–6) and *Das Hallerbuch* (1533) (*Stadtlexikon*, pp. 184–5 and pp. 1090–1). Karin Schneider says: 'Es lebte also praktisch im Katharinenkloster ein Teil der Nürnberger Oberschicht ... in der Heimatstadt zwar unter anderer Lebensform, aber nicht eigentlich vom weltlichen Teil der Familien abgetrennt, zumal ja die meisten Schwestern wenigstens weitläufig miteinander verwandt gewesen sein müssen' [To all intents and purposes part of the upper eschelons of Nuremberg society lived in Saint Katherine's convent ... admittedly following a different way of life in their home city but not really separated from the secular members of the family, especially since most of the sisters must have been related to one another, even if only distantly] (Schneider, 'Die Bibliothek des Katharinenklosters', p. 72). Schneider highlights the amount of intellectual and personal contact between convent and city. Similarly, from 1292–8/9 Jacobus de Voragine, author of the *Legenda aurea*, was Archbishop of Genoa, governed by consuls but also a mercantile city.

status as royal daughter may have integrated readily into their self-image as members of a governing elite. For example, in a Katharinenkloster prayer Saint Katherine is addressed as follows: 'Ave heilige kúnigin sancta katherina Costi des kunigs tochter edel gotes genadenreich ge*m*ma von allexandrina'.[34] Moreover, Katherine's royal descent means that her martyr's crown is foreshadowed by a princess's (and after her father's death a queen's);[35] and that she is a suitably high-ranking bride for the King of Heaven. Similarly, Cyprus was known to Nuremberg merchants both through trade and as a stopping point on the way to the Holy Land for those who undertook the pilgrimage to Jerusalem. Solomina may be the ancient port and capital of Cyprus, Salamis (or Constantia), destroyed by earthquakes in 332 and 342 AD. It is near Famagusta, which enjoyed an enviable reputation for the wealth of its merchants, as did the entire island:

> There are also in Cyprus exceeding rich citizens and merchants, and no wonder, seeing that Cyprus is the furthest (east) of all Christian lands, wherefore all ships both great and small, and all merchandise of whatsoever kind and from whatsoever country, must needs come first of all to Cyprus, and can in no wise pass by it.[36]

Even though location and lineage form part of the established legend, they place the narrative within the Nuremberg (convent and secular) readership's literary, economic, social and cultural comfort zone, thus rendering it immediately more accessible and more persuasive.

---

[34]   'Hail, holy Queen Saint Katherine, noble daughter of King Costis, God's merciful gem of Alexandria' (Germanisches Nationalmuseum Hs. 1738, fol. 28ʳ).

[35]   Katherine is depicted wearing a crown on, for example, the Löffelholz and Memminger Altars.

[36]   Ludolf von Sudheim, *Description of the Holy Land*, pp. 43–4. The wealth and social aspirations of Cypriot merchants (and the dangers of extravagance) find their expression in *Fortunatus*: 'Darinn [on Cyprus] ligt ein treffenliche statt / genannt Famagusta / inn wellicher ein Edler burger alts herkommens / war gesessen / dem seine Eltern groß hab vnnd gůt verlassen / also daß er fast reich / m*ä*chtig ... war ... Sein gem*ü*t war gentzlich gericht auff zeitliche ehr / freud vnd wollust des leibs / des nam er an sich ei*n* kostlichen standt / mit stechen / Thurnieren / den Künigen ghen hoff zureiten / damit er groß gůt verthet' [There lies a splendid city called Famagusta, in which a noble burgher of ancient lineage had his seat to whom his parents had left considerable property and possessions, so that he was extremely rich and powerful ... His mind was completely turned to worldly honour, pleasure and indulgence of the body, for which reason he lived in grand state with jousting, tournaments and riding to the king's court, squandering considerable sums of money in the process] (*Fortunatus* (Augsburg: Johann Otmar, 1509), fol. Aijʳ; also Hans-Gert Roloff (ed.), *Fortunatus. Studienausgabe nach der editio princeps von 1509*, Universal-Bibliothek 7721 (Stuttgart: Reclam, 1981), p. 5).

Having been introduced and situated by her lineage, Saint Katherine is, second, defined by her personal characteristics: she is 'weiß vnd schon vnd kensch [*sic*] vnd tugentlich'.[37] Beauty, virtue and chastity are prerequisites of the courtly Arthurian lady and, as Jenkins and Lewis indicate, of the female saint: Barbara, for example, also a king's daughter, is described in her legend as 'vnmeßlichen schön'.[38] Wisdom, however, is rarer in a woman; its early citation suggests it constitutes Katherine's primary virtue, one reinforced by her intelligence and facility in learning:[39]

> Vnd da sie bey sechs iaren waz da ließ man sie zu schul gen / da lernet sie gar wol / vnd da sie klug ward yn der kunst des ward sy gar volkummen darin daz man iren gleychen niedert fand / vnnd man hieß sie ein bewerte Meisterinn in den siben hochsten kunsten. (fol. cclij^r)

> [And when she was six years old she was sent to school, where she learnt easily and well and when she became clever and knowledgeable in the Arts she developed such a degree of perfection that nowhere was her equal to be found and she was called a proven Master of the Seven Liberal Arts].

Katherine starts school at the age of six, completing the entire university curriculum of the *trivium* (Grammar, Logic and Rhetoric) and more advanced *quadrivium* (Arithmetic, Geometry, Music and Astronomy), both taught in Latin; the latter was not studied by all students. That women were seldom admitted to university study in the Middle Ages only renders Katherine's learning more remarkable.[40] Whilst the emphasis on her unparalleled erudition prepares the reader for her subsequent conversion of the 50 heathen philosophers, it

---

[37] 'wise and beautiful and chaste and virtuous'.

[38] 'immeasurably beautiful'.

[39] In a prayer in a Katharinenkloster manuscript, now Germanisches Nationalmuseum Hs. 1738, Saint Katherine is addressed as follows: 'Frew dich in himelnn wann du mit deinen disputirnn die aller kunstreiche funftzig maister dieser werlt uber windst Eye lere vns kunst tugent vnd gute wicz' [Rejoice in Heaven for through your disputation you have overcome the 50 most skilful and learned masters in the world. Hallelujah, teach us skill, virtue and sharp wits] (fol. 29^r); also 'Frew dich zuhimel du künigliche iunckfraw frey kunstenreich weÿsz' [Rejoice to Heaven, you royal maiden, free, learned and wise] (fol. 31^r). Further, d'Avray point out that model sermons on Katherine privilege 'the idea of the holy woman as intellectual' (d'Avray, 'Katharine of Alexandria', p. 403).

[40] We see Katherine's public association with learning in the Lorenzkirche, where she is depicted with the four Church Fathers Augustine, Gregory, Jerome and Ambrose in the Konhofer window. The Dominicans were also known for their learning and emphasis on education. Moreover, the philosophical school of the University of Paris proclaimed Katherine the patron of philosophical studies.

also marks her out as exceptional and predestined for the "higher" wisdom that renders her loyal to Christ and rewarded by martyrdom. In fact, her learning almost masculinizes her, since other female saints are characterized only by their beauty, chastity and steadfast devotion to Christ. While not all male saints are singled out through their wisdom and learning either, Nuremberg's official patron saint, Sebaldus, is:

> vnd liessen d*az* kind czu stuhl [*sic*] da lernet es gar wol vnd was tugentlich / vnd
> da er nun groß ward da santt in seyn vater [the King of Denmark] czu Pareyß zu
> der hohen schul / da lernet er gar wol vnd was tugentlich / vnd da ward er gar wol
> gelertt.[41]

> [And allowed the child to attend school, where he learnt easily and well and was
> virtuous. When he had grown up his father sent him to the University of Paris,
> where he learnt easily and well and was virtuous and became extremely learned].

That the two most important saints in Nuremberg should both be distinguished by their education argues for the importance of learning within the city, in the late-fifteenth century also a centre of Humanism and early publishing.[42] In contrast to Saint Katherine, Sebaldus follows the standard pattern for young men by being sent abroad to enjoy a formal university education at one of the leading universities, Paris, a pattern followed by Nuremberg Patrician sons from the second half of the fifteenth century onwards.[43] Rather than Sebaldus' learning equipping him, initially at least, to convert others – as Saint Katherine does the heathen philosophers – it turns him inwards to convert himself: 'vnd gieng in sich selber vnd erkant dy vnsicherheit diser welt vnd die vnstetikeit vnsers lebens / vnd erkant auch das man gott nit wol gedynen mag in der welt' (fol. cxxxʳ).[44] Sebaldus' meditative introspection results in his leaving his bride on their wedding night and retreating into a forest to serve God, hence to action analogous to the nun's

---

[41]   *Der Heiligen Leben*, fol. cxxxʳ.

[42]   See Chapter 1.

[43]   As we have seen, from the second half of the fifteenth century onwards some Patricians sent their sons to university: for example, having attended the University of Vienna himself, Berthold IV Tucher sent his five sons to Heidelberg, where they were joined by their cousin Sixtus (Grote, *Die Tucher*, p. 65). Lorenz Tucher (1447–1503) studied in Italy for a few years before becoming Domherr in Regensburg and in 1478 Probst in Nuremberg (Biedermann, *Geschlechtsregister* [fol. Qqq 4ᵛ]); and the *Tucher-Gedächtnisbild* (1513) in the Sebalduskirche depicts Saints Katherine and Barbara on either side of the Virgin and Child.

[44]   'And he went into himself and recognized the uncertainty of this world and the inconstancy of our lives and also that man cannot serve God well whilst remaining in the world'.

oath of chastity and the taking of the veil in a closed community. Male education, then, is primarily legitimized by its contribution to male spiritual wellbeing as the only worthwhile focus, whereas female education is legitimized by its public usefulness, since what enables Saint Katherine's mystic marriage is not learning-led enlightenment but ultimately the abnegation of her beauty and her ego through pious service, physical denial and conversion. Moreover, the whole process is prompted not by recognition of the transitoriness of the world but by secular desire: Maxentius' to wed her to his son and Katherine's for a high-status bridegroom, in other words, by her vanity and standard dynastic, status-sexual concerns.[45] After conversion and baptism Saint Katherine's erudition and eloquence enable her to win the philosophers, Faustina and Porphyrius for Christ, but these qualities are imbued and activated by God in His service and to redeem others.

Saint Katherine's education seems to have belonged to an early layer of her legend, since according to Beatie she is described in Basil II's *Menologion* as follows: 'She was very lovely. And being gifted, she learned Greek grammar and became wise, also learning the languages of all nations'.[46] Furthermore, Katherine's own learning is echoed in that of the Katharinenkloster nuns, at least post-1428 reform:

> Die Durchschnittsbildung der Chorschwestern muß von einer Gediegenheit und Höhe gewesen sein, die wir uns heutzutage nur schwer vorstellen können. Ganz selbstverständlich war es, daß jede Schwester das Lateinische beherrschte ... Die Höhe der philosophischen Vorbildung spiegeln die Predigten der Mystiker wider, welche in den Frauenklöstern des Predigerordens als Tischlektüre dienten.[47]

> [The average education of the choir sisters must have been of a solidity and standard that can be imagined only with difficulty today. It was perfectly self-evident that every sister had a command of Latin ... The high standard of their

---

45   While Sebaldus does eventually go back out into the world to preach and be a model for others, he does so only after 15 years as a hermit in the forest.

46   Beatie, 'Traditional Themes', p. 789. Basil II reigned as Byzantine Emperor from 976 to 1025.

47   Fries, 'Kirche und Kloster', pp. 47–8. According to Ehrenschwendtner, 'In her correspondence with St Catherine's convent in St Gall, the Nuremberg prioress informed the Swiss nuns that each sister should spend her leisure time after lunch with spiritual reading in order to improve her spiritual life. For their private reading, the sisters were given the opportunity to borrow books from the convent's library ... There were also sisters who had small private libraries within the convent' (Ehrenschwendtner, 'A Library Collected by and for the Use of Nuns', p. 124).

education in philosophy is reflected in the sermons by the mystics which served as reading matter at mealtimes in the convents of the Dominican order].[48]

Their patron saint's wisdom identifies the convent itself as a place of learning and signals the nuns' importance as transmitters of spiritual wisdom both within their own community and outwith it, as suggested by the use of the *Der Heiligen Leben* manuscript as a basis for Sensenschmid's edition. By contrast, within the context of Nuremberg, Sebaldus' education and learning play no role and his status as the city's patron saint seems to depend on location and locally useful miracles such as changing icicles into firewood for a poor freezing carpenter (fol. cxxxj[r]).[49] Thus Saint Katherine's learning, whatever its function, renders her exceptional in terms of both male and female saints and serves as a model for, even reflexion of, the city as a whole.

The formation of the child Katherine through education and the latter's role in equipping her for future challenges echo the childhood of courtly heroes such as Tristan:

> und iedoch, dô er ir began,
> dô leite er sîn dar an
> und sînen flîz sô sere,
> daz er der buoche mere

---

[48]   Willing points out the following about the importance of communal readings: 'In den reformierten Frauenklöstern des 15. Jahrhunderts wurde die Lektio bei Tisch wieder verpflichtender Bestandteil der *vita communis*. In der "Ordinacio" für das Katharinenkloster bestimmt Bartholomeus Texerius 1429 über die gemeinschaftliche Lektio: *so wil ich, daz ir all zeit in dem refenter, wenn man da ysset oder collacion trinckt, ze tysch lest des morgens teütsch vnd ze abent einen teil latein vnd den andren ze teütsch. Des geleich sol man auch ze tysch lessen den swestren, die auser dem refender essen, die all bey ein ander sullen sein'* [In the reformed convents of the fifteenth century the practice of the nuns' being read to during meals once more became an obligatory part of communal life. In the *Ordinacio* for the Katharinenkloster Bartholomeus Texerius makes the following stipulation about the communal *lectio* in 1429: 'Thus it is my wish that whenever you are in the refectory, whether you are eating a meal or drinking a collation, you always have a reading in German in the morning and in the evening readings partly in Latin and partly in German. Similarly, you should also have mealtime readings for the sisters who eat outside the refectory and should all be gathered together for them'] (Willing, *Literatur und Ordensreform*, p. 28; quoting Theodor von Kern, 'Die Reformation des Katharinenklosters zu Nürnberg', *Jahresbericht des Historischen Vereins in Mittelfranken*, 31 (1863): 1–20 (p. 19, ll. 7–10)). Communal readings at mealtimes must have served to mould the nuns into a community and shape their communal identity.

[49]   Sebaldus missionized in the imperial forest around Nuremberg; the ox-cart bearing his body stopped of its own accord on the site of a chapel dedicated to Saint Peter where the Sebalduskirche now stands.

gelernete in sô kurzer zît
danne kein kint ê oder sît.[50]

In the case of Tristan the speed and ease of the child's mastery of material beyond his years mark him out as destined for an exceptional future.[51] A further model of wisdom is the young Christ Himself, whose precociousness means He can dispute with the masters in the Temple.[52] Again, the analogy to an established pattern signals that Katherine's effortless scholarship foreshadows an exceptional fate,[53] the next stage in which is the summons of Costis to Alexandria by the

---

[50]   Gottfried von Strassburg, *Tristan*, ed. Karl Marold (Berlin: de Gruyter, 1969), ll. 2085–90. [Yet once having started on it [his education] he applied his mind and industry to it with such vigour that he had mastered more books in that short space than any child before or after him (Gottfried von Strassburg, *Tristan*, trans. and intro. Arthur Hatto (Harmondsworth: Penguin, 1960; 7th edn 1974), pp. 68–9)]. The whole description of Tristan's education occupies ll. 2054–135. It includes manners, music, languages, jousting and sports, archery, hunting and travel. Isolde receives a similarly thorough courtly education, partly from Tristan (*Tristan*, ll. 7966–8039).

[51]   The counter-example is, of course, Parzival, whose lack of courtly education and resultant naivety similarly mark him out as exceptional (Wolfram von Eschenbach, *Parzival*, ed. Karl Lachmann (Berlin: de Gruyter, 1965), 117,7–124,16).

[52]   'And it came to pass, that after three days they found him in the temple, sitting in the midst of the doctors, both hearing them, and asking them questions. And all that heard him were astonished at his understanding and answers' (Luke 2:46–7).

[53]   Beatie argues for folk-tale elements (e.g. structure and motifs) in the narrative and even for 'the myth of the birth of the hero' à la Joseph Campbell, Otto Rank, etc. (Beatie, 'Traditional Themes', pp. 794-6). Joseph Campbell, for example, writes: '[T]he tendency has always been to endow the hero with extraordinary powers from the moment of birth, or even the moment of conception. The whole hero life is shown to have been a pageant of marvels with the great central adventure as its culmination. This accords with the view that herohood is predestined rather than simply achieved, and opens the problem of the relationship of biography to character' (Joseph Campbell, *The Hero with a Thousand Faces* (Princeton: Princeton University Press: 1949; reprint London: Fontana, 1993), p. 319). Katherine does not, however, correspond entirely to the 'Hero as Saint', being considerably feistier and more engaged with the world: '"Endowed with a pure understanding, restraining the self with firmness, turning away from sound and other objects, and abandoning love and hatred; dwelling in solitude, eating but little, controlling the speech, body, and mind, ever engaged in meditation and concentration, and cultivating freedom from passion; forsaking conceit and power, pride and lust, wrath and possessions, tranquil in heart, and free from ego"' (Campbell, *Hero*, p. 354; quoting *Bhagavad Gita*, 18:51–3). If anything, Katherine corresponds to the 'Hero as Warrior': 'For the mythological hero is the champion not of things become but of things becoming; the dragon to be slain by him is precisely the monster of the status quo: Holdfast, the keeper the past. From obscurity the hero emerges, but the enemy is great and conspicuous in the seat of power; he is enemy, dragon, tyrant … The tyrant is proud, and therein resides his doom. He is proud because

Greek Emperor Maxentius when Katherine is 13, so of marriageable age. Although Costis, his queen and daughter are received with honour and remain in Alexandria for some time, the narrative is condensed, as is Costis' death on their return to Cyprus, since these events do not in themselves contribute to Katherine's conversion and martyrdom. Subsequent developments, again related in greater detail, constitute a displaced courtship narrative in which the father woos the prospective bride in his son's stead.[54] The courtship narrative could also be read allegorically, however: as emperor of the Greeks, Maxentius enjoys the same status in the pagan world as the Holy Roman Emperor in the Christian.[55] The courting of Katherine thus becomes a battle for her soul between her pagan bridegroom Maxentius and her Christian bridegroom Christ.[56]

Maxentius wants Katherine as a bride for his son because 'sie alsz schon edel vnd reich was' (fol. cclij').[57] In other words, he sees her in the conventional dynastic-strategic terms of status, lineage and suitability for marriage defined for Katherine by her father, himself described as 'eyn edler reycher Kung'[58] at the start of the legend (fol. cclij'), and subsequently by Katherine herself. Although Katherine's mother advises her to accept, Katherine's response is one of pure vanity in which the text functions as verbal transmitter of the familiar visual icon:

> Da sach sant Katherina yn eynen spiegel / vnd da sie sach daz sy als uber
> flussyglichen schon was / da sprach sie ich sich wol das ich schoner bin dann all
> iunckfrawen in Allexandria / da von wil ich keynen man nemen er hab den vyer

---

he thinks of his strength as his own; thus he is in the clown role, as a mistaker of shadow for substance; it is his destiny to be tricked' (Campbell, *Hero*, p. 337).

[54]   This may also reflect the practice of arranged marriages, which prevailed amongst Patricians as well as the aristocracy. For Patrician marriage practices and the economic considerations influencing them see Fleischmann, *Rat und Patriziat*, 31/1, pp. 229–42.

[55]   The Byzantines inherited the Roman notion that their emperor was near-divine; Constantine and subsequent Christian emperors claimed to represent the divine.

[56]   Indeed, Jocelyn Wogan-Browne, in her comparison of hagiography to romance, describes Christ as summing up 'all the aspects of the romance hero role in himself'. She goes on to say: '[T]he virgin's opposition to her father-suitor-ruler in hagiography is an opposition that triangulates desire: the virgin is the medium of male exchange through which the hero competes with (and is bonded to) other men in order to gain the heroine', who acts 'as the medium of rivalry between Christ and the pagan' (Jocelyn Wogan-Browne, *Saints' Lives and Women's Literary Culture c. 1150–1300* (Oxford and New York: Oxford University Press, 2001), p. 97). While Christ and Maxentius do not bond, Katherine is the battleground on which rival claims to loyalty and love are played out by two dominant males. Wogen-Browne traces the structural similarities between hagiography and romance (pp. 98–9).

[57]   'was so beautiful, noble and powerful'.

[58]   'a noble, powerful king'.

ding an im / das er als edel / vnd als weyß vnd als reych sey alß ich / vnd sprach / die vyer ding find ich an des keisers sun nicht / Er furtrift mich an dem adell / so furtriff ich in ann der schone vnd an weißheit. (fol. cclij')

[Then Saint Katherine looked into a mirror; and when she saw that she was extraordinarily beautiful she said, 'I can well see that I am more beautiful than all other maidens in Alexandria. For that reason I will take no man as my husband who does not possess these four qualities: he must be as noble and as wise and as powerful as I am'. She continued, 'I do not find these qualities in the Emperor's son. He surpasses me in nobility but I surpass him in beauty and wisdom'].

A woman contemplating herself in a mirror symbolizes vanity, sub-set of pride and visually present in the Middle Ages through representations of Venus,[59] of mermaids, manuscript illustrations and church sculpture. As Susan L. Smith puts it:

> More than any other type of artwork owned by medieval women, mirrors invite the beholder to experience the act of looking as a self-conscious activity. The unique function of a mirror's reflective surface is to solicit the gaze of a beholder, whose reflected image becomes in a sense part of the object itself. In a mirror, a woman sees herself seeing, as the active possessor of the sense of sight. In a mirror, however, this identification is inherently unstable for, at the same time that she sees herself in the mirror as one who looks, she also sees herself as an image that is looked upon – as the object of a gaze that under normal conditions is that of another, whose viewing position the mirror thus encourages her to assume.[60]

Katherine's mirror performs various narrative functions. First, the concave mirrors used in the Middle Ages distort the reflected image, symbolizing the fact that by regarding herself with the gaze of the status-orientated male suitor, Katherine is misdirecting her own gaze onto superficialities which mean nothing in the eyes of God, as no earthly beauty could match His and physical beauty is in any case transitory. Second, however, a woman looking at herself in the mirror also symbolizes Prudence and Truth,[61] so even Katherine's vanity can be

---

[59] One is reminded also of the many medieval ivory mirror covers depicting lovers: cf. Michael Camille, *The Medieval Art of Love* (London: Laurence King, 1998), p. 111: the Presentation of the Heart.

[60] Susan L. Smith, 'The Gothic Mirror and the Female Gaze', in Jane L. Carroll and Alison G. Stewart (eds), *Saints, Sinners and Sisters. Gender and Northern Art in Medieval and Early Modern Europe* (Aldershot: Ashgate, 2003), pp. 73–92 (p. 74).

[61] *Hall's Dictionary*, pp. 210–11.

"rescued" as foreshadowing her redirected gaze towards, and eventual vision of, Christ. Third, when, in Katherine's first vision, Christ denies his future bride the desired sight of His face, Mary allows Katherine to see hers and instructs her in devotional practices that ultimately lead to Katherine's baptism and the mystic marriage. Since Mary is the *speculum sine macula*,[62] Katherine's mirror could be read as symbolizing what she herself will become: the image of flawless virtue and mirror-image of the Virgin herself. Fourth, for the Middle Ages external appearance expressed the soul, so Katherine's loveliness signals the exceptional piety and devotion to Christ that will be acted out in her conversion, mystic marriage and martyrdom. Fifth, Katherine's refusal of the emperor's son on the grounds that his beauty and wisdom fail to match hers continues the narrative substratum: beauty, or rather the higher wisdom and virtue it represents, are essential prerequisites for union; the emperor's son, as a pagan, is necessarily less virtuous than a future saint or God's son. Hence, sixth, Katherine's vision of herself leads to her rejection of the emperor's son and the definition of the desired spouse in terms only Christ could fulfil. Her refusal to play the marriage-alliance game, her stubbornness and defiance – otherwise presumably unwelcome characteristics in Patrician daughters destined to cement useful mercantile alliances – are thereby redeemed and defused by integration into the convent model of nuns as brides of Christ. That the narrative here changes into direct speech for the first time underlines the importance of Katherine's reasoning and its results; it also foreshadows her intelligence and eloquence in the later conversion scenes, not least since these, too, are conveyed in direct speech.[63] However, Katherine is not punished for her sin against maternal and imperial-patriarchal authority: on the contrary, her stubborn pride is ultimately rewarded with a bridegroom commensurate with her status, namely Christ.[64] However, the broken mould is carefully reassembled since in order to attain Christ as her bridegroom Katherine has to win over the Virgin Mary by subjugating the very aspect of her personality (her pride) that prompted her to reject Maxentius' son: 'da von ruff dy muter der gnaden andechtiklichen an vnd dien ir / mit beten mit fasten / mit wachen / vnd mit weinenn' ([fol. cclij^{r-v}]).[65]

---

[62]   *Hall's Dictionary*, pp. 326–8. Mary is 'the unspotted mirror of the power of God, and the image of his goodness' (Wisdom 7:26).

[63]   Structurally, the text itself resembles a set of mirrors, many episodes in the legend and martyrdom representing recursive reflexions of previous ones.

[64]   Refusal of a secular bridegroom is something of a *topos* in lives of female saints, as we see in Saints Lucy and Agnes or even Christine of Markyate.

[65]   'For that reason call on Our Mother of Grace with devotion in your heart and serve her with prayer, with fasts, with vigils and with tears'.

However, before Katherine wins her heavenly bridegroom, she has to overcome secular obstacles, the first in the form of her mother's concern. In what follows, narrative tension remains heightened by the use of direct speech in a dialogue between Katherine's mother, who is 'ser betrubt' and 'traurig' because she fears the Emperor's anger,[66] and an anonymous "herr", who advises her to seek advice from the hermit in the wood.[67] As well as simply adding interest to the narrative by varying its style and pace, the direct speech again underscores crucial steps along the road to Katherine's conversion and martyrdom, as the hermit introduces her to God. The mundane, secular speech between the queen and the "herr" foreshadows the divinely inspired salvatory speech on the part of the hermit, whose words actualize the potential grace inherent in the visit: 'Da saget er [the hermit] ir [the queen] kunfftige ding dy von der genad des heiligen geystes er wol beke*n*net / Auch daz got besunder gnad mit sand katherina wolt wnrcken [*sic*]'.[68] The hermit functions as God's mouthpiece, at the same time maintaining the reader's interest by signalling future wonders. Just as Katherine's secular identity is male-ordained (by her father's royal lineage), so her spiritual identity is male-ordained, this time by the hermit, senior to her in the hierarchy of holiness, and by God the Father.

Katherine's repetition of her refusal to marry unless her bridegroom possesses 'schone / weyßheyt / reichtum / vn*d* edel'[69] opens the door to the hermit's introduction of Christ in terms that appeal to Katherine's arrogance, sense of status and vanity; and activate the allegorical interpretation of these qualities discussed above. Christ is thus presented as the ultimate bridegroom, union with whom demands faith, service and baptism, that is, a spiritual dowry:

---

[66] 'very downcast' and 'sad' (fol. cclij'). 'Betrubt' continues the metaphor of seeing, as it means 'without light, dull, murky, overcast, dark'. In other words, Katherine's mother resembles a clouded mirror and cannot see the "truth" of God.

[67] Since the sole narrative function of the "herr" is as a vehicle for information necessary to plot-advancement, he remains anonymous, a further example of style and content being manipulated to highlight what is important in Saint Katherine's spiritual development. Hence the visit to the hermit occupies more narrative space since he is the instrument of Katherine's conversion (though as he occupies limited narrative space, disappearing from the legend once Katherine is baptized, he is not named either; in fact, besides Christ and the Virgin, who basically need no introduction, only the Archangel Michael, Costis, Maxentius, Porphyrius and Katherine herself are named in the legend).

[68] 'Then he told her about all the future events which the grace of the Holy Spirit allowed him to see, also that God intended Saint Katherine to be the recipient of an exceptional grace' (fol. cclij').

[69] 'beauty, wisdom, power and nobility' (fol. cclij').

Wiltu gelauben an vnsern herren Jhesum Cristum vnd wilt im mit fleyß dienen / vnd wurst getaufft So gewynnest du einen erwirdigen gemahel / der hat die vier gaben uberflussiklichen an im Er ist der aller weysest / wann er hat den hymell vnd die erden mit seyner weyßheit geschopfft · Er ist auch der aller edelst / wann er ist der obristen kunigs Sun vnd ist ewig vnd vntotlich Er ist auch der aller schonst / wan die Sunn vnd der Mon wundern ab seiner schon Er ist auch der aller reichest / wan waz in hymel vnd yn erde beschloffen ist des ist er eyn gewalttiger herr vnd gott / den selben schacz mugent die dieb nit gestelen. (fol. cclijʳ)

[If you will believe in Our Lord Jesus Christ and will serve Him assiduously and be baptized, then you will gain an honourable spouse who abundantly possesses the four qualities. He is wise above all others for He created Heaven and Earth with His wisdom. He is also noble above all others for He is the Son of the Lord most high and is eternal and immortal. He is also beautiful above all others for the sun and the moon marvel at His beauty. He is also powerful above all others for He is a mighty lord and God over all that is contained in Heaven and on Earth. This is a treasure thieves cannot steal].

In their repetition of certain phrases ('Wiltu'; 'Er ist auch der aller ... wan') the hermit's words constitute an easily memorable litany or creed that works intra- and extra-textually:[70] it reminds the reader of basic articles of faith at the same time as introducing Katherine to some fundamental tenets of Christianity; and it establishes the desirability of union with Christ for Saint Katherine, the nuns of the Katharinenkloster (thereby validating their vocation) and the reader, be he male or female, as Saint Katherine may have functioned as a non-gender-specific model of desire for spiritual union.[71] Since the first quality mentioned by the hermit is Christ's wisdom, a parallel to Katherine is established, although Christ's wisdom transcends hers since out of it were created Heaven and earth.[72] Divine wisdom is generative, whilst thus far Saint Katherine's has been put to no spiritually fertile use. Like Katherine, Christ is defined by His lineage since He is 'der obristen Kunigs Sun'[73] and is sold to her in terms of a conventional aristocratic marriage alliance, albeit His royal status is not secular but divine

---

[70]   'If you will; He is ... above all others for'.

[71]   In the Konhofer window, for example, the mystic marriage may symbolize Konhofer's desire for his own soul's union with God.

[72]   Moreover, the Dominican Heinrich Seuse's *Horologium Sapientiae* identifies Christ's heavenly bride as Eternal Wisdom, a parallel to Katherine that would readily have been recognized (*Stundenbuch der Weisheit*, trans. Sandra Fenten (Würzburg: Königshausen & Neumann, 2007), p. 55).

[73]   'Son of the Lord most high'.

and hence renders Him eternal, a quality Katherine herself attains only through martyrdom. Christ's beauty (and, by implication, virtue) assumes cosmic dimensions, 'wan die Sunn vnd der Mon wundern ab seiner schon'.[74] The sun and moon were created on the fourth day: 'And God made the two great lights, the greater light to rule the day, and the lesser light to rule the night'.[75] Since these planets symbolize rulership, their bedazzlement by Christ's beauty suggests their homage to Him and the superiority of His rule. Mention of sun and moon also links Creation to Christ's sacrifice on the Cross, since sun and moon avert their gaze at the Crucifixion and the world is plunged into darkness between the sixth and ninth hours.[76] In other words, they remind the reader of the moment when mankind's redemption became possible and Christ furnished a model of martyrdom subsequently emulated by Katherine and other early saints who gave their lives to establish the Christian Church. Locating Christ in the same sphere as the planets indicates His transcendence of the secular and the supremacy of His virtue, since sun and moon, the two main sources of light, symbolize virtue. Moreover, just as in courtly literature sun and moon function as symbols of beauty and of the beloved,[77] so Christ is the ultimate radiant and virtuous beloved, desire for whom transcends the physical to attain redemptive spiritual dimensions. As well as wisdom, eternal life and beauty, Christ embodies power as He rules Heaven, earth and everything in them. The hermit concludes by contrasting the transitory worldly signs of power and status sought by Katherine

---

[74]   'for the sun and the moon marvel at His beauty'. These words also echo the consecration rite for nuns, in which those present, including the maiden taking the veil, would sing an antiphon that includes the words, 'Ich bin dem verlobt, dem die Engel dienen, dessen Schönheit Sonne und Mond bewundern' [I am betrothed to Him whom the angels serve and whose beauty is marvelled at by the sun and the moon] (Nikolaus Gussone, 'Die Jungfrauenweihe in ottonischer Zeit nach dem Ritus im *Pontificale Romano-Germanicum*', in Jeffrey F. Hamburger, Carola Jäggi, Susan Marti and Hedwig Röckelein (eds), *Frauen – Kloster – Kunst. Neue Forschungen zur Kulturgeschichte des Mittelalters* (Turnhout: Brepols, 2007), pp. 25–41 (p. 30)).

[75]   Genesis 1:14–19 (1:16).

[76]   See Matthew 27:45; Mark 15:33; Luke 23:44. A well-known representation of this scene is Matthias Grünewald's Crucifixion from the Isenheim Altarpiece (1510–16), now in the Musée d'Unterlinden, Colmar.

[77]   For example, in Gottfried's *Tristan* Isolde mother and daughter are described as follows: 'Sus kam diu küniginne Îsôt / daz frôlîche morgenrôt / und fuorte ir sunnen an ir hant / daz wunder von Îrlant / die liehten maget Îsôte' (ll. 10889–93) [And so Queen Isolde, the glad Dawn, came leading by the hand her Sun, the wonder of Ireland, the resplendent maiden Isolde] (Hatto, p. 185). Isolde is further described as 'die wunne bernde sunne' (l. 11010) [[t]his joy-giving sun] (Hatto, p. 186); Isolde's maid, Brangane, as 'daz schœne volmæne' [the lovely Full Moon] (Hatto, p. 187).

to lasting spiritual values as the words 'den selbe*n* schacz muge*n*t die dieb nit gestele*n*'[78] are a reference to Matthew 6:19–21:

> Do not lay up for yourselves treasures on earth, where moth and rust consume and where thieves break in and steal, but lay up for yourselves treasures in heaven, where neither moth nor rust consumes and where thieves do not break in and steal. For where your treasure is, there will your heart be also.

If Christ becomes Katherine's treasure, then her heart will be with Him, opening the way to baptism, mystic marriage and steadfast spiritual love. Through the power of speech Katherine is transmuted from wooed to wooer: 'O wee wy eyn selige tochter wer ich / mocht ich den gemahel czu mir neyge*n*' (fol. cclij^r).[79] The word "selig" connotes spiritual bliss as well as worldly happiness, so already points forward to the joy of Katherine's union with Christ. Similarly, "tochter" could refer to her status as the daughter of Costis' queen but equally to the fact that we are all God's children, so Katherine is His daughter as well as His bride. Finally, "gemahel" echoes the Song of Songs and the soul's union with her bridegroom Christ.

The next stage in Katherine's conversion is prompted by a visual stimulus, namely a picture of the Virgin Mary with the Christ Child on her arm shown to her by the hermit.[80] This type of devotional image was extremely widespread in late-medieval homes, churches and public buildings; and hence both familiar to the readership (be it secular or convent) and easy for the reader to conjure up in his mind's eye.[81] Moreover, the Katharinenkloster in Nuremberg possessed a miraculous picture of the Virgin Mary that had become a pilgrimage shrine in the fourteenth century and may have resonated in the text at this point.[82] The presentation of the image places Saint Katherine and the reader in an analogous position, since the reader views imaginatively what the saint views actually

---

[78]   'This is a treasure thieves cannot steal'.

[79]   'Alas, what a blessed daughter I would be if I might win this spouse's affection'.

[80]   The form in which Katherine first sees Christ – as a child on His mother's arm – is the form in which she subsequently marries Him, His nature as child defusing any possible sexual overtones inherent in their union.

[81]   Apart from depictions of Mary and the Christ Child on altars such as the Krell Altar, statues of them could be found on buildings across Nuremberg. The Germanisches Nationalmuseum houses a number in stone and wood taken from houses throughout the city: Kaiserstraße 13 (1390); Weintraubengasse 2 (Wirtshaus zum Krokodil) (1420); Unschlittplatz 8 (1480). Such devotional images were also found on everyday objects such as plates, tiles, stoves, belt buckles, jewellery, etc.

[82]   Assion, *Mirakel*, p. 97; Fries, 'Kirche und Kloster', p. 16. The image was associated with various relics, including one of the Holy Lance.

(within the fiction of the text). If, in the fourteenth century, 'seeing and reading were part of the same bodily operation, involving perception and cognition in the search for knowledge' and images were considered 'the basis of cognition and even epistemology' since they found their way to the human soul, the ultimate agent of perception and knowledge,[83] then the image conjured by the reading of this passage, and the interaction in the reader's memory of text and image, may have brought to mind representations of the Virgin and Child in Nuremberg, thus serving to locate, in the reader's imagination, the events described by the text within the city itself. This is lent credence by Michael Baxandall's observation that pious lay people were 'practised in spiritual exercises that demanded a high level of visualization', the active nature of the interior visualization of holy stories forming the basis for active religious meditation, 'a visualizing meditation.'[84] Hence the reader may actively have recreated, not just in his mind's eye but in his soul, the steps to Saint Katherine's union with Christ in the mystic marriage.

Next the written word conveys a miracle of the spoken word, since the text suggests that the image of the Christ Child addresses Katherine:

> D*a*rnach bracht ir d*er* Eynsidel vnser frawe*n* bild d*a*z het eyn kind an de*n* arm /
> d*a*z sprach zu ir / du magst de*n* gemahell nit erwerbe*n* an dy hilff seiner mutter
> da vo*n* ruff dy muter d*er* gnaden andechtiklich*n* an vn*d* dien ir / mit bete*n* mit
> fasten / mit wachen / vnd mit weinenn. (fol. cclij[r-v])

> [Then the hermit brought her an image of Our Lady, who had a child in her arms
> which said to her, 'You cannot win your spouse without the aid of His mother, so
> for that reason call on Our Mother of Grace with devotion in your heart and serve
> her with prayer, with fasts, with vigils and with tears'].

Next to the sacristy in the Katharinenkirche stood an altar donated by Georg Fütterer (1438–1506) around 1500–5.[85] It consisted of nine panels, six of which depict scenes from the life of Saint Katherine, including her conversion in front of a picture of Mary and the infant Christ.[86] At its base was an almost-

---

83   Camille, 'Before the Gaze', p. 216.

84   Baxandall, *Painting & Experience*, pp. 45–6.

85   Rainer Brandl, 'Der Katharinenaltar des Georg Fütterer. Anmerkungen zu seinem wiederentdeckten Stifterbild', *Anzeiger des Germanischen Nationalmuseums* (1988): 95–115.

86   Murr says of the altar: 'Neben der Sakristey ist eine große Tafel, die sich in der Mitte öffnen lässet, da man dann das Bild der h. Katharina von Holz fast in Lebensgröße liegen sieht. Diese Tafel ist in neun Felder abgetheilet. Sie sind vortreflich gemalet, und stellen das Leben St. Katharinens vor, nebst den fabelhaften Auftritten, die sich bey ihrer Hinrichtung und Begräbniß sollen eräuget haben' [Next to the sacristy is a large picture which can be

life-size carving of the saint entombed by three angels, so the culmination of her life and martyrdom were immediately present to the viewer's eye. In the altar picture Katherine kneels in front of the devotional picture, her mother on her right and the hermit on her left pointing at the Christ Child, who reaches out towards the saint.[87] Thus from the beginning of the sixteenth century, at least, the nuns had access to an image that performs three roles: first, it models the physical gestures appropriate to the practice of devotion, demonstrated here by the saint herself; second, it renders visible to the physical eye what nuns may have seen with their spiritual eye during prayer or meditation, possibly in front of this very altar; third, this may in turn have prompted more intense reflexion on Katherine's devotion of herself to Christ, reinforcing and validating the nuns' own dedication, as the externalization through colour (itself a form of light and hence, arguably, of virtue) of an internally visualized scene on the wooden

---

opened in the middle, where the figure of Saint Katherine can be seen lying, carved out of wood and almost life-size. This picture is divided into nine fields. They are excellently executed and depict the life of Saint Katherine as well as the fantastic events reputed to have taken place at her execution and burial] (Christoph Gottlieb von Murr, *Beschreibung der vornehmsten Merkwürdigkeiten in des H. R. Reichs freyen Stadt Nürnberg und auf der hohen Schule zu Altdorf* (Nuremberg: Johann Eberhard Zeh, 1778), pp. 288–9).

[87]   In the second half of the nineteenth century the altar was moved to the Lorenzkirche, where it now stands in a side chapel in the north aisle. Two panels are missing: the *Grablegung* (Entombment) and the female donors, possibly Fütterer's two wives (Barbara Tracht (d. 1476) and Apollonia Ulstatt (d. 1506)) and five daughters from his second marriage, the eldest of whom was called Katharina (d. 1514) and married Sebastian Imhoff in 1500. The Fütterer, who died out in 1586, had been documented in Nuremberg since the early thirteenth century; conducted trade with Venice, Milan (where they maintained a permanent *Faktorei*), Frankfurt, the Netherlands and Flanders; from the mid-fourteenth century they sat on the *Großer Rat* and for a while owned the house on the Marktplatz where the *Heiltumsweisung* (display of the imperial relics) took place annually. A Heinrich Fütterer was *Losunger* from 1384 to 1392. The altar probably belonged with the wooden sculpture of the entombment of Saint Katherine by three angels mentioned by Murr and now in the Germanisches Nationalmuseum. The Fütterer also endowed a window (the East window in the South aisle) in the choir of the Katharinenkirche. It displayed the coats-of-arms of Ulrich Fütterer and Katharina Rutz; Georg Fütterer and Susanna Dörrer (1432); Georg Fütterer and Barbara Trechtin; Ulrich Fütterer (d. 1524) and Ursula Behaim (d. 1525); Jakob Fütterer and Drusiana Tucher (d. 1566); Jakob Fütterer and Helena Teztel (1568) (Fries, 'Kirche und Kloster', pp. 121–2). Together altar and window advertised family affluence, family alliances and upward mobility (the family were handworkers and represented the butchers when eight representatives of the handworkers were admitted to the *Kleiner Rat*), echoing important themes in this part of Katherine's legend. The altar also depicts Saints Andrew and Bartholomew, who with Katherine were the patron saints of mining: the Fütterer had active interests in metal-smelting works in the Upper Palatinate (Brandl, 'Der Katharinenaltar des Georg Fütterer'; Fleischmann, *Rat und Patriziat*, 31/2, pp. 404–9).

altar panel may have rendered the saint's conversion more "real" and hence more credible because communally "verifiable". Furthermore, a woman, Mary, holds the key to Katherine's salvation. The highlighting of Mary's importance resonated particularly in fifteenth-century Nuremberg: Funk postulates an intensified cult of the Virgin and saints in the fifteenth century prompted by fear of the Hussites, who rejected this form of devotion as unbiblical.[88] However, Mary is also the highest-ranking female saint and functions as divine mother, replacing Katherine's own and facilitating the marriage with her Son rather than the emperor's.[89] The rhetorical flourish of ritual service – 'mit bete*n* mit fasten / mit wachen / vnd mit weinenn'[90] – parallels the four qualities desired

---

[88]   Veit Funk, *Glasfensterkunst in St. Lorenz. Michael Wolgemut, Peter Hemmel von Andlau, Hans Baldung Grien, Albrecht Dürer* (Nuremberg: A. Hofmann, 1995), pp. 142–3. The Hussite Wars raged from 1419 to 1433, causing unrest and destruction throughout Bohemia, Germany and Poland and damaging Nuremberg trade. In 1430 the Hussites burnt and plundered their way through Franconia, coming within three miles of Nuremberg. Civic awareness of the Hussite threat may have informed the manuscript (1421) on which Sensenschmid's edition of *Der Heiligen Leben* was based. Moreover, from 1440–86 the city had also been threatened by the ambitions of the expansionist Margrave of Ansbach Albrecht Achilles and in 1474/75 supported Emperor Friedrich III in his campaign against Charles the Bold of Burgundy, so may have felt an acute need for powerful protection (Gerhard Pfeiffer (ed.), *Nürnberg. Geschichte einer europäischen Stadt* (Munich: Beck, 1982), pp. 115–20).

[89]   Mary was visible on altars, addressed in prayers and so forth. The Katharinenkloster also possessed a manuscript version of Heinrich von St. Gallen's *Marienleben*, the *Gulden puchlein*, produced in Nuremberg in 1450 by Conrad Forster, a monk in the Dominican monastery there, and illustrated by 70 woodcuts glued into the manuscript and depicting Mary's life. The particular devotion to Saint Katherine is indicated by, amongst other things, a miniature of the mystic marriage at the beginning of the main text (Peter Schmidt, 'Die Rolle der Bilder in der Kommunikation zwischen Frauen und Männern, Kloster und Welt: Schenken und Tauschen bei den Nürnberger Dominikanerinnen', in Jean-Claude Schmitt (ed.), *Femmes, art et religion au Moyen Âge* (Strasbourg: Presses Universitaires de Strasbourg, 2004), pp. 34–61 (pp. 37–8)). Also, since the prioress of the convent was addressed as "Mutter" powerful women were doubly mirrored in a nun's life.

[90]   'with prayer, with fasts, with vigils and with tears'. Tears are the outward manifestation of heartfelt remorse (*contritio cordis*), itself a product of the love for God instilled in the believer by God and the cause for God's forgiveness of sins. According to Thomas Aquinus: 'Zum Empfang des Sakramentes und seiner Wirkungen genügt ... die Furchtreue (attritio), während die Herzensreue (contritio) nicht so sehr Disposition für den Empfang der Gnade, als vielmehr kraft des Vorauswirkens des Sakramentes in seiner gläubigen Vergegenwärtigung schon Wirkung des Sakramentes selbst ist' [Remorse born of fear (*attritio*) suffices for the reception of the sacrament and its effects ... whereas the remorse experienced in one's heart (*contritio*) does not so much endow the disposition to receive grace as represent the already present effects of the sacrament itself through the power of the sacrament itself to affect the believer in adance when imagined in all faith' ('Bußwesen', in Friedrich Michael Schiele and

by Katherine in a spouse, strengthening the contrast between Katherine's initial, personal-status-affirming elevation of secular values and the physical and spiritual subjugation of the self necessary to win Christ. The tears she is expected to shed will function as baptism.[91] Tears blur physical vision yet paradoxically clarify Katherine's spiritual vision; fasting constitutes a denial of the physical body and hence of the physical beauty which prompted her vanity. The hermit's words point to sight as the means to redemption by hinting at the complex of vision denied and vision granted that results in the mystic marriage.

Katherine's response is to be 'entzundet mit grossem ernst',[92] foreshadowing the fire that later consumes the philosophers and shatters the wheel. She returns to her mother's house, so moves from one zone of maternal influence (Mary as mother of God) to another, symbolically back into the pagan world rather than forward into the Christian one. This may be one reason for her initial lack of success in seeing Christ; another may be the continued focus of her zeal on an appropriate secular rather than spiritual bridegroom since she has yet to convert to Christianity:

> vnd ruffet vnser frawen mit grosser anndacht an vnd dienet ir / mit beten mit fasten vnd mit wachen / vnd da si sich etlich tag geubet hett da ward sye in dem schlaff enczucht vnd sach vnnser frawen vnd iren lieben sun der kerett seine mynneklichen amplick vonn yr das sie in nicht gesehen mocht / darumb ward sie gar ser betrubt wan sie hett in gar geren gesehen / vnd bat vnser liebe frawen mit grosser anndacht das sie yr erwurb das sie in sehe / des bat in vnser frau gutiklichen / da wolt er es nit thun / vnd sprach sie ware im nit geleych an vyer dingen. (fol. cclij^v)

> [And she called on Our Lady with great devotion in her heart and served her with prayer, with fasts and with vigils; and after she had practised this for several days she was transported in her sleep and saw Our Lady and her dear Son, who turned His sweet face from her so that she was unable to see Him. For this reason she became very downcast for she would most gladly have seen Him; and she asked

---

Leopold Zscharnack (eds), *Die Religion in Geschichte und Gegenwart, Handwörterbuch für Theologie und Religionswissenschaft* (Tübingen: J.C.B. Mohr, 1909–13; 3rd edition ed. Kurt Galling et al. (Tübingen: Mohr Siebeck, 1957–65), vol. 1, pp. 1548–51).

[91] Tears belonged to the contemplation of one's own sinfulness and empathy with the Crucified Christ; they could also be understood 'im Sinne einer der Taufe vergleichbaren Gnade' [as a grace equivalent to baptism] ('Tränengabe', in *Lexikon des Mittelalters*, 9 vols (1st edn Lachen: Coron Verlag Monika Schoeller, 1999; reprint Frankfurt am Main: dtv, 2002), vol. 4, p. 935.

[92] 'on fire with most earnest resolve'.

Our dear Lady with great devotion to persuade her Son to let her see Him. Our Lady asked Him kindly but He refused to comply, saying Katherine was not His equal in four qualities].

That the description of Katherine's service echoes the words used earlier by the picture suggests both the internalization of its advice and a ritual form of penitential self-denial in preparation for a mystic vision.[93] Whilst following the recommended forms of religious observance does result in a dream vision, suggesting a step from the tangible towards the spiritual, Katherine is denied sight of the infant Christ's face and hence direct interaction with Him. Moreover, this fourth level of vision, the 'mystical mode, which entailed the "pure and naked seeing of divine reality"',[94] creates tension within the narrative since it constitutes a vision not of acceptance but of rejection, resulting in the paradox of a vision that denies Katherine sight of what she most wishes to see. Christ's averting of His face is the denial of what makes Him identifiable (in human terms) and enables interaction. Further, it represents the negative inversion of Katherine's contemplation of her own beauty in the mirror: the sight of ultimate (because spiritual) beauty is denied her regardless of her 'anndacht' [devotion] because she has not been baptized, that is, has not renounced secular, pagan thinking. This failure is symbolized by the absence of tears ('weinenn') in Katherine's dedication of herself to the service of Mary. The denial of vision leads to an oral response, so to a switching of senses, when Katherine asks Mary to intercede with Christ on her behalf and persuade Him to grant her sight of His face. The attempt to gain vision through speech takes place within the dream and places Mary in her traditional role as intercessor between her Son and the petitioning mortal. However, even His mother's speech cannot persuade Christ, whose refusal of Himself to Katherine echoes Katherine's rejection of Maxentius' son: 'vnd sprach sie ware im nit geleych an vyer dingen'.[95] The narrative symmetry between Christ and Katherine recalls Arthurian literature, where it serves

---

[93] The Nuremberg Katharinenkloster has been described as an 'Abschreibzentrale mystisch-aszetischer Literatur' [copyhouse central of mystical-ascetic literature], so actual devotional practices in the convent may have mirrored the text (Schmidt, 'Die Rolle der Bilder', p. 36; citing Bernhard Haage, *Der Traktat 'Von dreierlei Wesen des Menschen'* (Heidelberg, 1968), p. 216, n. 9).

[94] Compare I Corinthians 13:12: 'For now we see through a glass, darkly; but then face to face' (Michael Camille, *Gothic Art. Visions and Revelations of the Medieval World*, The Everyman Art Library (London: Weidenfeld & Nicolson, 1996), p. 17). The verse from Corinthians continues: 'now I know in part; but then shall I know even as also I am known'. This describes the process of enlightenment undergone by Saint Katherine.

[95] 'and said she was not His equal in four respects'.

two purposes: first, the mirror actions of such chivalric heroes as Gawain and Parzival underscore the transcendence of one by the other in character and destiny; second, the self-transcending actions of the same hero (for example, Erec overcoming first three robbers and then five) indicate his progress in atoning for some initial failing.[96] Hence even though Katherine may be denied sight of Christ at this point, a sophisticated reader would recognize their mirrored similarity and its implication that Katherine's wish will ultimately be granted.[97] Moreover, this whole passage instructs the reader that outward forms of devotion are meaningless without the inner dedication of the self to Christ.

Christ's rejection sparks greater observance on the part of Katherine, who, prompted by memory of the picture shown her by the hermit, attempts to recreate His image in her soul in a way that allows her conscious access to it:

> Imagination gathered the images deriving from the common sense, storing them as a prelude to further manipulation by the active fantasy. In turn, fantasy produced *phastasmata* – new images composed from the parts of old images assembled by the imagination. Finally, memory housed all these images, whether old or new, along with the reactive judgments of estimation, viewing these externally derived images and internally devised *phastasmata* as constituents of prior experience, that is, of the temporal past. The soul's action of internal sense was thus seen to liberate images from mere sense perception, allowing them to be adjusted, revised, and in effect invented, and further, preparing them for analysis and abstraction by the higher cognitive faculties of ratiocination (intellect), determination (will), and recollection (memory as thought rather than as storage). The soul, by exercising these facultative processes, could review its past operations, judge their relative merits, and aspire to improve itself, by means of engaging with the images it received, stored, altered, improved, and eventually abstracted and even transcended. In spiritual terms, the movement from external to internal sense, and the larger movement from sensation to intellection, was conceived as the soul's ascent from divinely created nature to its source in God, Creator of all things, an ascent secured by the soul's climbing of its own God-given faculties, most crucially the powers image-reception, -production, and -cognition.[98]

---

[96]   Hartmann von Aue, *Erec*, ed. Christoph Cormeau and Kurt Gärtner, Altdeutsche Textbibliothek 39 (Tübingen: Niemeyer, 1985), ll. 3106–399.

[97]   The reader/listener would presumably possess foreknowledge of Katherine's success, which would shift focus to the supplicatory process.

[98]   Walter S. Melion, 'Introduction: Meditative Images and the Psychology of Soul', in Reindert Falkenburg, Walter S. Melion and Todd M. Richardson (eds), *Image and Imagination of the Religious Self in Late Medieval and Early Modern Europe*, Proteus: Studies in Early Modern Identity Formation 1 (Turnhout: Brepols, 2007), pp. 1–36 (pp. 2–3).

Memory and imaginative reconstruction of the physically perceived image allow Saint Katherine's soul to ascend to its source in God[99] and the resultant increase in dedication leads to a second vision during her sleep, the importance of which is highlighted by Mary's addressing her in direct speech: 'vnd entschlyeff eynns nachtes / da kam vnser fraw czu ir vnd sprach du solt zu dem Einsidel gen vnd solt von im getaufft werden / vnd sollt Cristen gelauben an dich nemen So lest sich dann mein kind sehen' (fol. cclij^v).[100] Two aspects of Katherine's vision are noteworthy: first, the prominence of Mary as the channel between man and God; second, the explicit naming of Christian baptism as the sole route to the desired vision of Christ. Baptism constitutes formal acceptance of Christ by the believer and entrance into the community of the Church after the ritual cleansing of sins. Since through baptism Christ's death on Calvary becomes the believer's death, the ceremony marks the end of his alienation from God and his becoming a limb of Christ's body.[101] Whilst Katherine may desire Christ as a bridegroom, she is still "sinful" as she has yet formally to relinquish her pagan gods. On awaking Katherine relates her vision to her mother, who thus functions as the first recipient of the text that becomes the saint's legend; vision prompts redemption: 'vnd gyengen mit einauder [*sic*] czu dem Einsidel vnd empfieng den tauff von im vnd betet / vnd fur da frolichen wyder heim vnd dienet got emssigklichen' (fol. cclij^v).[102] For all the narrative build-up, the baptism is brief and its doctrinal importance unexplained, possibly because self-evident for the readership in the Katharinenkloster and the wider civic community of Nuremberg. Like Feirefiz when he accepts baptism in order to marry the Grail-bearer Repanse de schoye, Katherine is not presented as having any real understanding of her actions.[103]

The future saint's wishes are fulfilled in a third dream vision:[104]

---

[99]   It also provides a further contemplative model for nuns and the lay reader.

[100]   'And she fell asleep one night and Our Lady came to her and said, "You should visit the hermit and be baptized by him and adopt the Christian faith as your own. Then my child will let you see Him"'.

[101]   *Theologisches Begriffslexikon zum Neuen Testament*, ed. Lothar Coenen, Erich Bayreuther and Hans Bietenhard, 3 vols, vol. 2/2 (Wuppertal: Brockhaus, 1969–71), pp. 1206–8. John the Baptist baptized to effect the forgiveness of sins and in expectation of the baptism by the Holy Ghost and by fire which the Messiah would undertake. The philosophers' martyrdom by fire could thus be understood as their baptism.

[102]   'And they went together to the hermit and received baptism from him and travelled home again joyfully and served God assiduously'.

[103]   Wolfram, *Parzival*, 814 and 817–18.

[104]   Three was a highly symbolic number, associated with the Trinity, the Harrowing of Hell, the Three Marys at Christ's tomb, etc., so the third vision was bound to bring fulfilment.

da erschein yr vnser Frau mit irem Sun in kunigklicher gezird vnd klarheyt / da
sach sie ein antluczt gar klarlichen vnd recht minneklich*en* vnd redt mit yr von d*er*
gemahelschaft vnd gemahelt sich ir / vnd styeß ir ein kleines guldeins fingerlein
ann vnd sprach / O mein liebe Katherina Ich wil mich dir in d*em* gelaub*en*
gemaheln da erwachet sy vnd fand daz fingerlein an der hand vnd bekant / daz
alleß das war waz daz sie in dem schlaff gesehen hett. (fol. cclij^v)

[Then Our Lady appeared to her with her Son in royal garb and radiance and
she saw His most radiant and sweet face and He spoke to her of espousal and
He espoused her and placed a small gold ring on her finger and said, 'O, my dear
Katherine, I shall espouse you in the faith'. Then she awoke and found the ring on
her hand and realized that everything she had seen in the dream was true].

Christ's majesty, radiance and beauty reflect His status as ruler of Heaven
and earth.[105] Katherine, having purified herself physically and spiritually, has
progressed from interrupted or denied vision to its highest level, that of the
"pure and naked seeing of divine reality" – Christ's face – and to the ultimate
spouse – the Son of God rather than the son of an emperor. The two foci of
her desire merge in this vision, which is characterized by direct rather than
mediated communication when Christ pronounces the marriage vow: 'O
mein liebe Katherina Ich wil mich dir in d*en* gelaub*en* gemaheln' (fol. cclij^v).[106]
Whilst the gold ring on Katherine's hand when she awakes symbolizes royalty,
perfection, eternity (the qualities of her bridegroom), loyalty and their union, it
also functions as a guarantor of the truth of her vision, a tangible bridge between
Heaven and earth that testifies to the presence of the divine in human lives, since
Katherine literally and metaphorically carries Christ around with her for all to
see. Further, the ring signifies Christ's enduring protection of Katherine, not
least because rings were thought to fend off the Devil, evil spirits and evil (i.e.
sexual) desires.[107] Since gold rings were also worn to protect from or cure disease,

---

[105]   As rendered visible also in windows such as the Volckamer and Konhofer. Middle
High German *klâr* means "hell, lauter, glänzend schön, deutlich" [bright, pure, radiant,
shining, beautiful, clear], so light, clarity and beauty are synonymous (Georg Friedrich
Benecke, *Mittelhochdeutsches Wörterbuch*, 4 vols, vol. 1 (Leipzig: Hirzel, 1854), p. 836).

[106]   'O, my dear Katherine, I shall espouse you in the faith'.

[107]   According to the *Handwörterbuch des deutschen Aberglaubens*, 'Die erstere
[Auffassung des Ringes] scheidet nicht nur einen bestimmten Raum von der Umgebung
sichtbar ab, sondern sie ist auch die Bindung aller außerhalb von ihr befindlichen Mächte
jeglicher Art und dadurch Schutz oder Neutralisierung aller Gefährdung des eingeschlossenen
Raumes ... Der R. ist der sichtbar gemachte Zauberkreis, der als Bindung zu dienen hat' [The
former [understanding of the ring] not only visibly distinguishes a certain space from its
surroundings but also binds all sorts of forces external to it [this understanding] and thereby

Katherine's gold ring symbolizes her recovery from the "disease" of paganism or heresy and her spiritual wholeness in Christ.[108] Moreover, as Mario Klarer explains, according to medieval thought the dreamer sees:

> von einem inneren Auge Bewegungen hervorgerufen, die wiederum *imagines* nicht anwesender Objekte in der Seele erzeugen. Diese von der Seele kreierten *imagines* oder *phantasmata*, die zwar mit den von den Sinnen wahrgenommenen Bildern verwandt sind, bzw. auf analogen kinestischen Voraussetzungen beruhen, besitzen eine epistemologische Komponente, die sie über die Sinnesbilder stellt ... [Es] besteht im schlafenden Zustand die Möglichkeit, Wahrheiten in Bildern zu schauen, die den körperlichen Sinnen verborgen bleiben würden.[109]

> [movements conjured up by the inner eye, which in their turn give birth in the soul to *imagines* of objects that are not present. These *imagines* or *phantasmata* created by the soul, whilst admittedly related to pictures apprehended by the senses or based on analogous kinetic prerequisites, possess an epistomological component which renders them superior to sensory images ... In one's sleeping state it is possible to see in pictures truths which would remain hidden from the physical senses].

Katherine's dreamt marriage, then, constitutes a real experience that wakes her from the darkness of the soul which fails to recognize God into the illumination of Christian salvation, the 'klarheyt' (clarity) that characterizes the vision functioning as a 'Metapher spiritueller Wirklichkeiten' and manifestation of God.[110] The mystic marriage also furnishes a model for nuns who wed Christ on

---

functions as the protection from or neutralization of all threats to the space thus enclosed ... The ring is the magic circle made visible, the function of which is to bind] (*Handwörterbuch des deutschen Aberglaubens*, ed. Hanns Bächtold-Stäubli, 10 vols (Berlin: de Gruyter, 1927–42), vol. 7, pp. 702–24 (p. 705)).

[108] *Handwörterbuch des deutschen Aberglaubens*, p. 709. Healing properties were also ascribed to gold, as well as the ability to strengthen and purify (*Handwörterbuch des deutschen Aberglaubens*, vol. 3, pp. 918–26). Thus Christ's gold ring strengthens Katherine for her ordeal ahead and purifies her soul.

[109] Mario Klarer, 'Die mentale imago im Mittelalter: Geoffrey Chaucers Ekphrasen', in Christine Ratkowitsch (ed.), *Die poetische Ekphrasis*, Österreichische Akademie der Wissenschaften Sitzungsberichte der phil.-hist. Klasse 735 (Vienna: Österreichische Akademie der Wissenschaften, 2006), pp. 77–96.

[110] 'metaphor of spiritual reality' (Brigitte Kurmann-Schwarz, 'Fenestre vitree ... significant Sacram Scripturam. Zur Medialität mittelalterlicher Glasmalerei des 12. und 13. Jahrhunderts', in Rüdiger Becksmann (ed.), *Glasmalerei im Kontext. Bildprogramme und Raumfunktionen. Akten des XXII. Internationalen Colloquiums des Corpus Vitrearum Nürnberg, 29. August – 1. September 2004*, Wissenschaftliche Beibände zum Anzeiger des

taking the veil.[111] Indeed, Petra Seegets discusses the primacy afforded chastity and the nuns' "marriage" to Christ in the tracts and sermons written for their guidance in daily convent life, since 'die Gemahlschaft zwischen Christus und der Klosterfrau ungetrübte Freuden bereitet und schon jetzt auf die Ewigkeit hin angelegt ist'.[112] Whilst the mystical experience of marriage to Christ may have been granted very few:

> Nur in der Abgeschiedenheit des Klosters, in der Abkehr 'vo[n] allen werntlichen dingen vnd sorgen' werde Christus, den die Quelle als 'schamigen gemahel vnd gesponczen' beschreibt, zu seiner Braut sprechen, sie 'kwssen ... mit dem kuwss seins mu[n]des vnd also mit seinen arme[n] umbfahen'. Hier, abseits vom 'getümeln des volcks' und in aller 'heymlicheyt' werde der besondere Schatz, den Gott für die entbehrungswillige Nonne bereithalte, aufgetan, hier komme es zur unmittelbaren Begegnung von Gott und frommer Klosterfrau. Die unio wird mit Worten Bernhards als ein Geschehen beschrieben, das nicht nur die Seele, sondern auch das sinnenhafte Empfinden der Nonne in seinen Grundfesten so sehr erschüttert, befriedigt und beglückt, daß zusammenfassend versichert wird: 'Gar nycht nit werstu hinfure me(h)r bege(h)rn'.[113]

> [Only in the seclusion of the cloister, in the rejection of 'all worldly matters and cares', will Christ, described by the source as 'bashful spouse and bridegroom', speak to His bride, 'kiss her ... with the kiss of His mouth and embrace her with His arms'. Here, removed from the 'tumult of the people' and in all 'secrecy', the special treasure held ready by God for the nun willing to endure privation is revealed, here direct contact between God and pious nun comes about. This union is described by Bernhard [of Clairvaux] as an event which shakes, satisfies

---

Germanischen Nationalmuseums 25 (Nuremberg: Germanisches Nationalmuseum, 2005), pp. 61–73 (p. 63)).

[111]   Jeffrey Hamburger describes the consecration of nuns in the Benedictine Abbey of Saint Walburg, Eichstätt and a picture illustrating the ceremony 'in which the nun accepts Christ as her spiritual husband in a vow of eternal marriage'. Three times in the consecration liturgy the bishop offers the nuns a veil, then a ring, then a crown, saying with the latter: "'Come, O bride of Christ, accept the crown that the Lord has prepared for you in eternity'" (Jeffrey F. Hamburger, *Nuns as Artists. The Visual Culture of a Medieval Convent* (Berkeley, Los Angeles and London: University of California Press, 1997), p. 56).

[112]   'the marriage between Christ and the nun bestows unclouded joy and from the very beginning is intended for eternity'. Seegets here refers to a sermon by Johannes Diemar, *Von der geistlichen Gemahlschaft* (Ggo 406, 8ʳ-15ʳ) (Seegets, 'Leben und Streben', pp. 30–2).

[113]   Seegets, 'Leben und Streben', p. 34 (citing Stadtbibliothek Nürnberg Cod. Cent. VI, 53, fol. 61ʳᶠ, 59ᵛ–61ʳ, 61ᵛ).

and delights not just the nun's soul but also her senses to their very foundations so that in conclusion she is assured, 'You will never desire anything else ever again'].

The Dominican sisters of the Katharinenkloster, familiar with sculptures and paintings of the mystic marriage in the convent, may have used them as models for their private imagination of the narrated vision.[114] Visual associations triggered by the text thus locate the mystic marriage imaginatively within the convent or lay reader's home and the model of Katherine's devotion in stone-and-wood physicality of Nuremberg. Since Christ's union with Katherine is privileged by direct speech, the text constitutes a written (and printed) record of the "actual" words of the Son of God, making *Der Heiligen Leben* contemporary testimony to a historical truth (the marriage) that is also "true" on a spiritual plane (Christ's becoming one with the human soul). Katherine's devotion switches now from the Virgin to Christ and leads to the abandonment not only of heathen gods but of "hoffart", "vnkeusch" and "vntugent" (vanity, lasciviousness and vice), qualities thus explicitly linked to paganism. Her lack of pride in her secular status becomes the clearest signal of inner change in Katherine, who is now 'mit dem band gotlicher lieb gemahelt in einen rechten gelauben' (fol. cclijʳ).[115] This second embedding of Katherine's marriage to Christ in the Christian faith again identifies the love between Katherine and Christ as spiritual rather than literal; it also reminds both Katharinenkloster nuns and the secular reader who desires closeness to Christ of the necessity of the "rechten gelauben".

The next stage of Katherine's life is dealt with very quickly: her mother dies, she rules wisely as queen and sells all her possessions, emulating the monastic vow of poverty and an established, hence readily identifiable, pattern of sanctity.[116] Her poverty, humble service and wisdom establish an immediate contrast to Maxentius, who has ordered his subjects to sacrifice to the gods. The next step in the narrative, Katherine's first post-conversion appearance on the

---

[114]   The convent high altar, painted by Hans Pleydenwurff's circle and endowed in 1468 and 1475, depicts the mystic marriage. The remaining scenes show the Birth, Crucifixion and Resurrection of Christ. The carved depiction of the mystic marriage from an altar shrine in the convent church dates from c. 1480. Other major depictions of the mystic marriage in Nuremberg include the Konhofer window (c. 1478/9), the Volckamer window (c. 1486); and the wings of the Memminger Altar (c. 1485/90) in the Lorenzkirche; however, these post-date both the original German manuscript of *Der Heiligen Leben* and Sensenschmid's 1475 edition of it. The Löffelholz Altar (c. 1462–4) in the Sebalduskirche depicts the philosophers' martyrdom, the miraculous shattering of the wheel and Katherine's beheading.

[115]   'wedded with the band of divine love in the true faith'.

[116]   For example, Saint Martin cuts his cloak in half and gives half to a beggar.

public stage, is constructed like a theatrical performance:[117] first, Katherine is off-stage in her palace, where she hears the noise of the pagans gathering in the temple for the sacrifice. This 'geschel' (din) (fol. cclij[v]), suggestive of irreverent, meaningless pandemonium incompatible with either true piety or service of the true God, constitutes the sound effects for the performance and sets the stage for Katherine's subsequent attempt to convert Maxentius, in which her "noise" is the meaningful because redemptive Word of God.[118] Here, then, the clash of two "scripts" highlights the primacy of the Christian message. Horrified when told about the planned sacrifice, Katherine orders members of her retinue to accompany her, makes the sign of the cross, commends herself to God and goes to the temple,[119] thereby moving onstage. Her procession and gestures provide the dramatic action; her retinue contribute to the crowd scene. The sign of the cross serves three purposes: it reaffirms for Katherine and the reader the new focus of her allegiance; it functions as a protective device in a now alien context; and it acts as a visual symbol of the alternative to paganism, a sign constructed by Katherine for others to follow. Further dramatic action is provided by the reaction of the pagan population to Katherine, since when she reaches the temple they scatter from her path in a scene reminiscent of the parting of the Red Sea or Christ's expulsion of the moneylenders from the Temple.[120] Its slightly comic nature renders visible and risible the inadequacy of the pagan gods in the face of Christ. Moreover, when Katherine publicly challenges Maxentius, who sits next to and thus associates himself with these gods as if receiving the sacrifice as one of them, the text's use of direct speech introduces dramatic dialogue into the proceedings.

---

[117]   Compare, for example, *Das Katharinenspiel* ('Das Katharinenspiel', ed. Otto Beckers, *Germanistische Abhandlungen*, 24 (1905): 125–57).

[118]   "Geschel" as indicative of neglect of God's Word and association with the Devil also informs *Der Ritter vom Turn*: in one story the congregation gossip during mass; the hermit celebrating it sees a devil hopping from one shoulder to another recording their words. Even the hermit's thumping of the Bible does not silence them, so he asks God to, whereupon the gossips start screaming piteously like those possessed by the Devil (*Der Ritter vom Turn*, pp. 120–1). In the next story, Saint Brictius, during the celebration of mass by Saint Martin, sees two devils recording everything the congregation says and running out of parchment (*Der Ritter vom Turn*, pp. 121–2). The contrast of two types of word – secular, heedless, endangering versus divine, ministering, redemptive – constitutes a trope that is also a guide to the function and interpretation of *Der Heiligen Leben*.

[119]   This scene is reminiscent of Krimhilde going to Worms Minster with her retinue and quarrelling publicly with Brunhilde on the steps in front of it (*Das Nibelungenlied*, stanzas 831–43).

[120]   Exodus 14:21–2 and Luke 19:45–6 respectively.

Katherine's address to Maxentius is divided into five sections. First, she acknowledges the honour due him by virtue of his status, only to withdraw her apparent deference since he does not serve the Christian God: 'Es zympt deiner ere vnd wirdikeyt wol das ich dir zucht vn*d* ere erbute / were dein hercz als gut das du gott dientest vnd in erkantest So erest du die abgotter das sein dy bosen geyst den dienest du' (fol. cclij^v).[121] Second, her words render Maxentius' heart publicly visible, putting it on display alongside the idols he worships.[122] By identifying these as evil and reducing them to mere 'geyst' (demons), Katherine exposes their paltriness compared to the omnipotent Christian God. Third, a queen herself, she criticizes his rule: 'Du bist ein haubt an lob / du solt wissen das czam deinem gewaltt wol. So hast du das volck her geladen zu einer affen fur' (fol. cclij^v).[123] Not only does Maxentius jeopardize his own salvation, as father of his subjects he abuses his power by jeopardizing their souls as well. Apes were associated with the Devil, evil, spitefulness, frivolity, heresy and idolatry,[124] so Maxentius' summons to pagan sacrifice renders his subjects guilty of heresy and idolatry and thus of breaking the First and Second Commandments.[125] Fourth, having openly upbraided Maxentius for his wrongdoing, Katherine offers him a better path:

> wil du dynen syn zu eynem guten kerenn So sich an vnd nym war wer got sey der
> alle ding vermag vnd sich wye er alle ding wol geordnet hat sunn vnd Mon vnd
> dy Steren / den hymell vnd das firmament / vn*d* die planeten dye leuchten vn*d*

---

[121] 'It well behoves your honour and worthiness for me to offer you courtesy and deference – if your heart were virtuous enough to serve and recognize God. As it is you worship the idols, that is, the evil demons. They are the ones you serve'.

[122] In the heart a believer was, through grace, allowed the union with God that transformed him into the image of Christ. The heart was also the location of the soul's mystical union with God (*Spiegel der Seligkeit*, p. 201). Maxentius' heart thus renders him the image of the Devil, sharing a nature with the demons he worships. In the fifteenth century convent communities in particular cultivated devotion to the Heart of Jesus (*Spiegel der Seligkeit*, p. 202).

[123] 'You are a ruler who merits no praise. You should know that would well become your power. Instead you have summoned your people for a load of monkey business'.

[124] Lucia Impelluso, *Nature and Its Symbols*, trans. Stephen Sartarelli, A Guide to Imagery (Los Angeles: The J. Paul Getty Museum, 2004), p. 198.

[125] 'You shall have no other gods before me. You shall not make for yourself a graven image, or any likeness of anything that is in heaven above, or that is in the water under the earth; you shall not bow down to them or serve them; for I the LORD your God am a jealous God, visiting the iniquity of the fathers upon the children to the third and the fourth generation of those who hate me, but showing steadfast love to thousands of those who love me and keep my commandments' (Exodus 20:3–6).

vmbgehend vnd nicht stil stend / vnd das wasser vnd die erden / vnd wie daz
geweret hat von anga*n*g biß her. (fol. cclij*ᵛ*)

[If you are willing to direct your will towards the good, then regard and recognize
the nature of God, who has the power to do all things. See how well He has ordered
all things: the sun and the moon and the stars; the heavens and the firmament and
the planets that radiate and revolve and do not stand still; and the waters and the
earth; and how this has endured from Creation until today].

She directs the emperor to God in language that echoes the hermit's attempt to
win her for Christ, a tactic that, first, reinforces the hermit's teaching; and, second,
renders Katherine analogous to the hermit in her attempt to convert Maxentius.
By summarizing Genesis, running through the stages of Creation (sun, moon,
heavens, planets, waters, earth) and emphasizing God's ordering hand, Katherine
does two things: she introduces Maxentius to, and reminds the reader of, the eternal
nature of God's power; and she returns to basic teaching about the world and
man's place in it. Hence the dialogue constitutes an exposition of Christian belief
intra-textually for Maxentius and extra-textually for the reader, who is reminded
of the principles on which the Christian Holy Roman Empire was founded. The
vividness of direct speech both adds interest through a change in narrative pace
and facilitates the dramatic reading aloud, even acting out, of this episode within
the convent community or the private household.[126] Finally, Katherine concludes
by returning to her opening admonition: 'Den herren vn*d* got solt du an beten vnd
solt in eren / vn*d* saget im als vil vor das er ir nit geantwurten ku*n*t' (fol. cclij*ᵛ*).[127]
Katherine's first public display of eloquence and its success in silencing the emperor
both foreshadow her imminent conversion of the philosophers and demonstrate
the power of God's Word.

At this stage, however, Katherine's words are not yet powerful enough
to effect change and the sacrifice to the idols proceeds. Upon its conclusion,
Maxentius asks Katherine: 'Was geschlechtes bist du / dein wolgestalteß vnd
wolgeczyrtes antlutz beczeuget das / das du hochgeboren bist' (fol. cclij*ᵛ*).[128]
Maxentius' failure to recognize Katherine demonstrates that conversion has

---

[126]   Katharina M. Wilson notes the possibility of a 'dramatic reading' of the plays
of Hrotsvit of Gandersheim in her convent community as early as the tenth century (*The
Dramas of Hrotsvit of Gandersheim*, trans. and intro. Katharina M. Wilson, Matrologia
Latina (Saskatoon: Peregrina, 1985), p. 15).

[127]   '"You should worship and honour the Lord Our God"; and told him so much that
he had no response to her'.

[128]   'From what lineage are you descended? Your comely and well-adorned face bears
testimony to your high birth'.

changed her outwardly as well as inwardly. Just as Katherine wanted to see Christ's 'antlutz' (face) but was denied sight of it, so Maxentius fails to see in Katherine's face both Costis' daughter and the 'heylig Junckfraw' (holy maiden) as which she is now identified for the first time. Prior to her conversion Katherine was a heathen princess, royal like Maxentius and a practitioner of the same faith, so immediately visible to him in dynastic and religious terms; now she is a Christian woman, someone with little status or identity in the still-pagan empire and therefore unrecognizable.

Maxentius' response to Katherine's verbal onslaught is action: he summons the wisest, most learned men from his lands to dissuade Katherine from her 'vngelauben' (heresy) (fol. ccliij^r). The 50 philosophers are presented as an intellectual match for her, being 'wolgelert yn ir kunst' (fol. ccliij^r).[129] In a parallel exhortation to Katherine's earlier upbraiding of him, the Emperor exhorts the philosophers in direct speech to try to win Katherine over: 'Es ist eyn iunckfraw hye die spricht vnser gotter seyn boß geist / vnd gelaubt an einem gott' (fol. ccliij^r).[130] By repeating Katherine's own words in an effort to defeat her,[131] Maxentius inadvertently highlights a main tenet of Christianity (the one God), confirms the falseness of his own gods and sets up in advance Katherine's defeat of the philosophers who defend them. In the debate between Katherine and the philosophers two forms of (direct) speech, pagan and Christian, come into direct conflict, reflecting the pre-eminence accorded the Word in John 1:1: 'IN the beginning was the Word, and the Word was with God, and the Word was God'. The magnitude of Katherine's victory is emphasized in two ways: first, by the number of philosophers (50); second by one's amazement: 'Da sprach einer / wie ist dem das du als vil meister gesamelt hast durch einer dieren willen / das der aller mynst vnder vns woll verricht hett' (fol. ccliij^r).[132] Katherine's "one-ness" mirrors that of the God in whom she believes (in contrast to the numerous gods of the numerous philosophers); by highlighting her apparent insignificance ('dieren') the pagan philosopher highlights God's power as He triumphs through this lowly mouthpiece.[133] Before the debate Katherine prays to God, furthering the competition between different kinds of language: human speech invokes

---

[129]   'highly proficient in their field of knowledge'.

[130]   'There is a maiden here who claims our gods are demons and who believes in one god'.

[131]   'So erest du die abgotter das sein dy bosen geyst den dienest du' [Thus you worship the idols, they are evil demons, they are the ones you serve] (fol. cclij^v).

[132]   'Then one said, "How has it come about that you have gathered together here so many masters on account of a mere girl whom the least of us could have defeated?"'.

[133]   In the late-fifteenth century "diern" or "dieren" could mean "servant" or "prostitute" so the philosopher also robs Katherine of her royal status.

divine aid so that divine speech flows through Katherine's human mouth and conquers heathen speech: 'O gotliche weißheyt gesten mir bey / wann ich han dich al czeyt lieb gehabt Gib deine worten wortyn meynen mund das ich das best red wan ich vermag von mir selbs nichtz vnd gib den dy wyder mich seind das sie gelaubig werdent' (fol. ccliij^r).[134] In addressing God as 'gotliche weißheyt' (divine wisdom), Katherine appeals to that aspect of His nature that most closely corresponds to her own. Again direct speech underscores the importance of Katherine's words; it also serves to bring them closer to the reader, as if he were witnessing Katherine's prayer, which in turn provides him with a model for his own prayer. Katherine sees herself merely as the channel for divine, conversionary language, a variation on the familiar *topos* of the weak female as vessel for miracles or divine intervention.[135]

Two male authorities now clash in the text: God's response to 50 philosophers is a single Archangel, Michael (weigher of souls but also soldier angel and saint of the Church militant), sent as a messenger to Katherine; the difference in the opposing forces once more underlines God's power. Michael reassures Katherine through prophecy: 'Hab kunen mutt wann got der wil dir helffen fechten vnd gesigen / vnd dy meyster werdent all bekert vnd gemartert' (fol. ccliij^r).[136] The incipient debate is cast as a battle with Katherine as soldier, overcoming her feminine weakness to display divinely endowed male virtue. Different layers of vision are merged: the Archangel's divine status allows him sight of events still to be unfolded to human eyes whilst his visit to Katherine's prison cell is presented not as a vision but as an actual event. Through the text printed on the page and through the direct speech thus recorded the reader "witnesses" events on a higher level of truth, since the authorial intermediary between him and narrated events is "invisible". As the outcome of the debate is predicted, God's own vision is shown to allow true prophecy; hence the angel's prediction merges present and future, reassuring both saint and reader of the inevitable victory of the Christian message. Katherine's speech works on various levels: the human with her mother and Maxentius; the divine with the Archangel Michael, Mary

---

[134] 'O, divine wisdom, stand by me for I have always loved you. Place your words into my mouth so that I may speak the most inspired speech, for on my own I am unable. Grant my opponents such grace that they believe in you'.

[135] In a letter to Elisabeth of Schönau, for example, Hildegard of Bingen writes: 'I am a mere poor woman; a vessel of clay. What I say comes not from me but from the clear light: man is a vessel which God fashioned for himself, and filled with his inspiration, so that, in him, he could bring his works to perfection' (Fiona Bowie and Oliver Davies (ed. and intro.), *Hildegard of Bingen. An Anthology* (London: SPCK, 1990), p. 130).

[136] 'Be bold and unafraid for God will help you fight and win and the masters will all be converted and martyred'.

and Christ; and the salvatory when she converts the heathen philosophers, a debate reminiscent of Christ's with the masters in the Temple in Jerusalem.

When Katherine goes to deliberate with the philosophers she makes the sign of the cross three times – in front of her, on her forehead and on her breast – in an obvious allusion to the Trinity.[137] Moreover, the cross functions as a statement of her allegiance to Christ and symbol of divine protection, sacrifice and martyrdom such as she herself is about to face.[138] Her forehead alludes to her wisdom and intellectual prowess; her breast to her love for Christ. In addition, the gesture foregrounds the Cross as the central Christian icon, the focus of conversion, the centre of the Christian message and source of Katherine's eloquence. As before, Katherine's address to the philosophers amounts to a potted version of key Christian doctrine, namely Christ's humanity, Crucifixion and Resurrection: 'Dy Propheten vnd dy weyssagen haben vor geweyssagt von vnserm herren Jhesu Cristo das er mensch wordenn ist vnd geliden hat vnd tod ist vnd erstanden ist vnd ist in den hymel gefaren / vnd bewaret cristen glauben Alß wol mit der alten vnd neuen Ee' (fol. ccliijʳ).[139] Katherine's speech results in silence – the philosophers' inability to answer her. Paradoxically, lack of speech marks the triumph of speech: God's words confute mere human sophistry and effect the instant conversion of the saint's opponents. Maxentius's fury prompts him to unfruitful speech: 'Wy seyt ir all so torath worden das yr euch als ein iunge Junckfrauwen uber reden laßt' (fol. ccliijʳ).[140] Roles are reversed: Katherine's words have, in Maxentius'

---

[137]   For the significance of the Trinity in Christian thought see 'Trinität', in *Die Religion in Geschichte und Gegenwart*, vol. 6, pp. 1023–41. Augustine was crucial to the development of Christian thinking on the Trinity. He 'sah den menschlichen Geist (mens) als Ebenbild der T. an, suchte die T. nach Analogie des geistigen Lebens zu deuten, das im Zusammenspiel von memoria (als der Quelle der geistigen Inhalte), intelligentia (als dem schauenden, zur Widerspiegelung der Quelle bestimmten Organ) und voluntas (die das Organ zur Quelle hinzieht) bestehe, also auch in einer Dreifaltigkeit' [He saw the human spirit as the image of the Trinity and attempted to interpret the Trinity through analogy to spiritual life, which consists of the interplay between *memoria* (as the source of spiritual content), *intelligentia* (as the contemplative organ ordained to reflect the source) and *voluntas* (which draws the organ to the source); in other words, also consists of a Trinity] (p. 1030).

[138]   The sign of the Cross had an 'ursprünglich exorzistische[n] Charakter (s. Exorzismus); sie wird als Segnung und symbolisch als Bekenntnis zu Christus verstanden' [originally the character of an exorcism. It is understood as a blessing and symbolically as a declaration of belief in Christ] (*Die Religion in Geschichte und Gegenwart*, vol. 4, pp. 52–3).

[139]   'Prophets and soothsayers foretold of our Lord Jesus Christ that He has become man and suffered and died and risen from the dead and ascended into Heaven and proved our Christian faith to be of a true piece with the Old as with the New Covenant'.

[140]   'Why have you all become so foolish that you allow yourselves to be outargued like young girls?'

eyes, emasculated the philosophers and rendered them rather than her 'iunge Junckfrauwen' (young girls). His echoing of the philosophers' own words before the debate underscores God's might as He spoke through Katherine. Moreover, the fire ordered by Maxentius for the martyrdom of the philosophers mirrors Katherine's own state of being "entzündet" with love for Christ and renders literal, and visible, the philosophers' burning love for God.[141]

The military metaphor is continued in the philosophers' regret at their unbaptized state:

> Da sprachen dy meister czu sandt Katherina / du edel gottes braut sollen wyr nit getaufft werden das ist vns leyd / Da sprach si · Jr edelen kempfer ewr blut sol euch wol tauffen in dem fewr / da werden ir getempft vnd getaufft / Seyt nur starck an dem glauben gottes / nach dysem we get dy ewyg frewd. (fol. ccliij^r)

> [Then the masters said to Saint Katherine, 'You noble spouse of God, it would grieve us not to be baptized'. Then she said, 'You noble warriors, your blood will baptize you in the flames. There you will be tempered and baptized. Only be strong in your faith in God for after this suffering comes eternal bliss'].

First, Katherine is, for the first time, identified as the bride of Christ by a third party, her first converts to Christianity. Conversion and identification mark a significant stage in her becoming 'sandt Katherina' (Saint Katherine) since they confirm both her exulted status and the power of her own exemplary conversion. Second, the image of the philosophers as soldiers in the battle to establish Christianity echoes the Archangel Michael's message to Saint Katherine, so demonstrates the flow-through effect of sanctified speech. That, in a narrative recursive reflexion, each stage of the legend mirrors a previous one illustrates the spread of Christian exemplarity from its source in the life of Christ through

---

[141]   It also concurs with Eusebius' characterization of Maxentius: 'The whole city [Rome] cowered before him, common people and magistrates, well known and unknown, worn down by his cruel tyranny: not even when they stayed quiet and made doormats of themselves was there any escape from the tyrant's bloodthirsty cruelty. With a trivial excuse he once handed the people over to be massacred by his bodyguard, and thousands of Roman citizens were killed in the heart of the city' (Eusebius, *History*, p. 274). His successor Maximim similarly persecutes Christians: 'The [Christian] men endured fire and sword and crucifixion; wild beasts and submersion in the sea; severance of limbs and branding; stabbing and gouging out of eyes; mutilation of the entire body; and, in addition, starvation, fetters, and the mines ... As for the women, schooled by the divine word, they showed themselves as manly as the men. Some underwent the same ordeals as the men, and shared with them the prize of valour; others, when dragged away to dishonour, gave up their souls rather than their bodies to that dishonor' (Eusebius, *History*, p. 276).

the lives and miracles of the saints and eventually into the lives of contemporary readers. Membership of the Christian community is marked by baptism, hence the martyrs' blood serves as their purifying baptismal water and outward sign of their sacrifice. Fire and blood, both red, signal passion and danger, namely the intensity of the philosophers' love for God and the consequential suffering, which in its turn redeems them from the flames of Hell. Furthermore, in the *Horologium* Seuse, through Divine Wisdom, equates fire to the Eucharist:

> Doch weiß man, daß unter diesen Sakramenten vom Sakrament der Eucharistie der Strahl göttlicher Liebe und der Fluß himmlischer Gnade, der andächtige Seelen selig entflammt und süß trunken macht, auf besonders vorzügliche Art und Weise ganz speziell ausfließt. Denn wie dürres Holz einem irdischen Feuer eine geeignete Materie bietet, um seine Flammen in die Höhe wachsen und sich überall hin ausbreiten zu lassen, so bietet das Sakrament der Eucharistie den Anreiz für ein geistliches Entbrennen, Nahrung für das Feuer göttlicher Liebe, das sich selbst weiter nährt, sofern das Sakrament andächtig empfangen worden ist.[142]

> [Yet it is known that of all these sacraments it is especially from the sacrament of the Eucharist that the ray of divine love and the stream of heavenly grace, which blissfully ignite and sweetly intoxicate devout souls, flow in a particularly estimable way. For just as dried-out wood offers earthly fire suitable material to let its flames shoot into the air and spread in all directions, so the sacrament of the Eucharist offers the stimulus for spiritual ignition, nourishment for the fire of love for God that continues to nourish itself as long as the sacrament has been devoutly received].

Consumption by fire as consumption of the Eucharist and by love for God figures, then, the philosophers' taking of God into their hearts and ignites a similar passion in the soul of the reader consuming this text. Reception of the Eucharist also signals acceptance by the philosophers of the divine wisdom that transcends their earthly wisdom, since Wisdom goes on to say:

> Denn unter allen Zeichen der Liebe gibt es nichts, das den Geist des Liebenden so vollständig auf sich zieht wie die ersehnte Anwesenheit des Geliebten, der vor allem anderen der Vorzug zu geben ist. Darum habe ich beim letzten Abendmahl meinen geliebten Jüngern mich selbst sakramental dargeboten und damit ihnen und allen Dienern dieses Sakraments kraft meiner Worte die ungeheure Macht

---

[142] Seuse, *Stundenbuch*, p. 175.

gegeben, daß sie mich körperlich anwesen haben können, mich, der durch die
Anwesenheit Gottes überall ist.[143]

[For out of all the signs of love there is nothing which attracts the mind and spirit
of the lover so completely as the longed-for presence of the beloved, which is to be
desired above all else. For this reason I offered myself as sacrament to my beloved
disciples at the Last Supper and through this act bestowed on them and all
servants of this sacrament, by the might of my words, the immense power to have
me physically present, me, who thanks to the presence of God is everywhere].

Katherine's primary virtue is wisdom, so reading her legend potentially renders
the wisdom that is Christ eternally present in the reader's life; in addition, the
philosophers' martyrdom by fire as consumption of the Eucharist foreshadows
Christ's ministering of the sacrament to the imprisoned Katherine. Finally, the
image of the philosophers as steel tempered and purified in fire is a topos that
would have resonated within Nuremberg as a centre of metal-working and arms
manufacture, lived experience providing the stimulus for an actual visualization
of the process. The philosophers' martyrdom and resultant conversion of
spectators constitute the first in a series of such events that culminate in
Katherine's own death:

Da thet ytglicher Meister des heyligen creucz czeichen fur sich / vnd giengen
frolich czu dem fewr / da warff man sie all in das fewr / da thet got ein groß
wunder mit in / wann er namm yr sel von in das in ny keyn har verseret ward /
noch yr leyb / noch gewand vnd furen zu den ewigen frewden vnd ire antlutz
schinen recht alß dy roßen Von dem czeychen wurden vil menschen bekeret / vnd
die funfczig meister wurden heimlichen begrabenn. (fol. ccliij[r])

[Then every master made the sign of the Cross in front of him and they went
rejoicing into the flames and were all thrown into the fire. Then God performed
a great miracle with them, for He took their souls from them in such a way that
not a hair on their heads was harmed nor their bodies nor their clothes; and they
went to eternal bliss with their faces shining just like roses. On account of this sign
many people were converted and the 50 masters were secretly buried].

Katherine is to the philosophers what the hermit was to her. For the third time
in the narrative the sign of the cross is made, providing the ultimate evidence of
its talismanic power to protect and save as it preserves the philosophers' bodies

---

[143]   Seuse, *Stundenbuch*, p. 175.

from the flames.[144] Like Saint Katherine's ring after the mystic marriage, these bodies remain behind as visible, tangible proof of a truth normally inaccessible to human cognition.[145] In Nuremberg the textual was also translated into the visual: both the Fütterer Altar and the wings of the Löffelholz Altar in the Sebalduskirche depict the philosophers' conversion and martyrdom, so a local readership would have enjoyed readily accessible visual prompts for their mental and spiritual re-creation of this scene. The analogy of the philosophers' faces glowing like roses performs three functions: first, it facilitates visualization of their fate; second, it signals the perfection of the philosophers' sacrifice as red roses symbolized martyrdom;[146] third, it furthers the symbolism of the colour red that runs through the text, since martyrdom is painted on the philosophers' faces, paving the way for Katherine's own martyrdom.[147] Just as Katherine converted the heathen masters, this miracle leads to further conversions amongst the onlookers, confirming the powerful chain effect of an exemplary individual's own devotion. As we shall see in the discussion of Katherine's miracles, the actualization of virtue attributed by Jolles to saints flows from Christ as the fountainhead in the mystic marriage through Katherine to other actors in the theatre of her martyrdom, realizing their potential for Christian virtue. If the mystic marriage symbolizes the union of the soul with Christ, Katherine's *vita* represents a potential path for the reader: through his union with Christ he can actualize his potential for exemplary Christian virtue and realize it in his own life through his influence on others and sacrifices for their sake. Within a convent community this constitutes a strong directive for the nuns' own behaviour; within Nuremberg a web of exemplary conduct is spun out from the

---

[144] The burning of the philosophers and Katherine's earlier refusal to worship Maxentius' idols recall the story of Shadrach, Meshach and Abednego, whom Nebuchadnezzar orders thrown into a "burning fiery furnace" because they refuse to worship his gods or the golden image he has set up. They remained untouched by the flames; the king sees them in the furnace with a fourth man, whose form "is like the Son of God" and consequently commands their God be honoured (Daniel 3). The Old Testament prophet Elijah ascended to Heaven in a fiery chariot (II Kings 2:9–15), so the philosophers' martyrdom by fire signals their redemption. Elijah also promoted the worship of Yahweh rather than the more popular pagan god Baal, effectively foreshadowing John the Baptist and, at a further remove, the philosophers themselves.

[145] Christ's crucified body bore the visible, tangible evidence of His suffering, becoming the canvas for inscription of His divinity and sacrifice, whereas the very intactness of the philosophers' bodies constitutes the sign of God's protection of those who are martyred in His name.

[146] *Hall's Dictionary*, p. 268.

[147] The light emitted by the philosophers' faces ('schinen') is a further outward manifestation of their holier status.

centre, namely the text, throughout the city, binding civic space together and reinforced by associations emanating from the various representations of Saint Katherine in private chapels and public churches.

For the third time in the narrative Katherine is taken in front of Maxentius, who attempts to reassert superiority by promising her semi-divine status within paganism: 'o du schone magett deiner iugent alß auch deinen vngelouben so will ich ein bild nach dir machen lassen / vnd die leut mussen dich anbeten / vnd solt nach meyner kunginn die gewaltigest sein' (fol. ccliijʳ).[148] Not only would Maxentius' suggestion break the Second Commandment, it would make Katherine into the very type of idol she wishes to destroy and the focus of a devotion she attempts to channel towards God. Katherine, as the heathen counterpart to the image of Mary and the Christ Child that prompted her own desire to convert, has the potential to become a spectacle, the object of the wrong sort of gaze. Whilst the saint does ultimately become the object of artistic representation she does so within strict devotional and artistic conventions and within sanctioned Christian space (be it church, convent or private chapel), not the unlawful space of a pagan temple. Maxentius' repeated stress on Katherine's beauty suggests her transfiguration into a statue would cast her as the model *minnedame* worshipped on a pedestal, or even a pagan Venus alternative to the Virgin Mary; thus the image juxtaposes base, human, sexual love with pure, divine, spiritual love. Katherine rejects Maxentius' deifying sexualization of her by reaffirming her marriage vow to Christ (mirroring a nun's commitment of herself to the Lord on entering the convent): 'Da sprach sy die red ist gar verlren / ich han mir ihesum *christum* auß erleßen den will ich alzeit zu einem gemahel haben den han ich mein leben ergeben' (fol. ccliijʳ).[149] Once again direct speech highlights the import of her words, the prelude to her own martyrdom, and provides a contrast to the un-Christian and therefore wasted speech of Maxentius.

Katherine's martyrdom recalls Christ's Passion:

> Da ward der keiser zornig vnd sye ab czehen vnd ward ann ein sewl gebunden vnd
> schlug si ser mit gerten vnd mit geyseln das das blut von ir floß / vnd hyeß sie in
> einen kerker legen / Da warff man si in einenn vinstern kerker / darinnen lag si
> zwelf tag das man yr weder czu essen noch czu trincken gab / da begabt sie Gott
> vnd ir all tag ein weiße tauben vonn hymel dye bracht ir czu essen / vnd dy Engel

---

[148]   'O, you maiden, fair in your youth and your lack of faith in our gods, I shall have an image of you made and people will have to worship you and after my queen you shall be the mightiest'.

[149]   'Then she said, "You have wasted your words. I have chosen Jesus Christ as my eternal spouse. He is the one to whom I have dedicated my life."'

kamen czu ir vnd trosten si mit grosser klarheyt das dy hutter davon erschracken. (fol. ccliij')

[Then the Emperor flew into a rage and ordered her to be taken away and she was tied to a pillar and severely beaten with rods and with whips so that the blood streamed from her. She was thrown into a dark dungeon, where she lay for twelve days during which she was given nothing to eat or drink. Then God sent a white dove from heaven every day that brought her food; and angels visited her and consoled her with such great radiance that her jailers shrank back in fear].

The binding of Katherine to a pillar and her whipping clearly allude to the Flagellation of Christ,[150] the model martyr, hence to His Passion and eventual Crucifixion that made possible the redemption of mankind from Original Sin. This allusion also casts Maxentius as Pilate, clothing his obduracy and guilt in a familiar and therefore intellectually and emotionally accessible form. Blood flows like a unifying thread through the martyrdom narrative: that of the philosophers functions as baptism; Katherine's own flowing blood casts her suffering as the climatic martyrdom, baptizing her a second time and mirroring the bloodied body of Christ after His Flagellation, which, although not mentioned in the Gospels, was a popular devotional image in the affective piety of the Late Middle Ages.[151] The *Profeß* (the nun's taking of vows on entrance into the convent) was viewed by some medieval thinkers as a form of second baptism that placed the professor into a similarly sin-free state. Thus the flow of Saint Katherine's blood sets up a symbolic parallel: the nun's cleansing of her sins through the profession that allows her access to the convent community; and the cleansing of Katherine's sins through the bloody baptism that allows her access to the community of saints. Furthermore, nuns and readership alike would have known images of Christ as *ecce homo* or of the crucified Christ that could have provided a stimulus for their visualizing experience of Katherine's suffering. For example, on the south pillar of the nuns' gallery in the Katharinenkirche were painted Christ as Man

---

[150] Matthew 27:26; Mark 15:15; John 19:1.

[151] Barbara Steinke, *Paradisgarten oder Gefängnis? Das Nürnberger Katharinenkloster zwischen Klosterreform und Reformation*, Spätmittelaltar und Reformation. Neue Reihe 30 (Tübingen: Mohr Siebeck, 2006), pp. 129–32. The emphasis on blood may echo the Dominican view on self-flagellation, namely that 'blood was alive; in shedding his blood a person shed himself' (Caroline Walker Bynum, *Wonderful Blood. Theology and Practice in Late Medieval Northern Germany and Beyond* (Philadelphia: University of Pennsylvania Press, 2007), p. 129). Thus the flagellated Katherine sheds the remnants of her pagan identity in preparation for her martyrdom.

of Sorrows and Saint Katherine herself;[152] whilst a tapestry (c. 1460–5) from the Lorenzkirche, endowed by Margarete Topler in memory of her husband Martin Pessler and probably used as an antependium, depicts Christ as *ecce homo* flanked by Mary, John, John the Baptist and Saint Jerome.[153] Christ's body streams with blood which discolours His loincloth; His cloak is red and red streams decorate His halo. Finally, the flagellation of Katherine both negates the physical beauty which initially attracted Maxentius, concealing it beneath a veil of blood, and emphasizes her body, drawing attention to its – albeit suffering – physicality. The vivid mental picture of the scene conjured up by this description serves at least two purposes: first, that of sexual (even sado-masochistic) titillation in the reader (of either sex), as the male reader could imagine himself subjugating the female body and the female reader could imagine herself experiencing a pain that intensifies her awareness of that body; second, that of enabling the devout reader the better imaginatively to relive Saint Katherine's suffering and hence take a small step closer to spiritual perfection.[154] Indeed, the blood that flows from Katherine may

---

[152]   Fries, 'Kloster und Kirche', pp. 85–6.

[153]   See *Nürnberg 1350–1550. Kunst der Gothik und Renaissance* (Munich: Prestel, 1986), pp. 200–1. A miniature pasted onto the flyleaf of a Book of Hours from the Strasbourg convent of Saints Margaret and Agnes depicts a Dominican nun stretching out her arms to receive a Christ covered in streams of blood as He leans forward from the pillar to which He was bound for His flagellation (Walker Bynum, *Wonderful Blood*, plate 11). Similarly, Katherine's flagellation appears in the Tucherkapelle murals depicting her legend (Haus zur Krone, Bindergasse 26), painted in 1517 by Hans Süß von Kulmbach (Curtius, 'Die Hauskapelle als architektonischer Rahmen der privaten Andacht', in *Spiegel der Seligkeit*, p. 39).

[154]   Steinke highlights the centrality of physical suffering for the spiritual life of nuns in her following observation: 'Waren die Unterweisungstexte [used by the Dominican men responsible for the pastoral care of the nuns] wirksam, so ist unter den Nonnen mit einer christologisch begründeten, aus passionsmystischen Motiven gespeisten Leidensmentalität zu rechnen, mit einem Konzept von Leid, das negative, schmerzhafte Erfahrungen und Erniedrigung ins Positive kehrt, zumindest aber als liebevolle Prüfung Gottes interpretiert und für unausweichlich hält' [If the instructional texts were effective, then one can reckon with a mentality of suffering amongst the nuns, one justified by Christian doctrine concerning Christ and fed by motifs from the mysticism surrounding the Passion. One can reckon with a concept of suffering that transforms negative, painful experiences into something positive or, at the very least, interprets them as a loving test imposed by God and considers them unavoidable] (Steinke, *Paradisgarten oder Gefängnis?*, p. 166). Similarly, Jeffrey Hamburger comments that in the Late Middle Ages '[s]owohl Männer als auch Frauen ... sich unvorstellbaren Leiden im Namen Jesu [unterwarfen]' [both men and women subjected themselves to unimaginable suffering in the name of Christ] (Jeffrey F. Hamburger, 'Am Anfang war das Bild: Kunst und Frauenspiritualität im Spätmittelalter', in Falk Eisermann, Eva Schlotheuber and Volker Honemann (eds), *Studien und Texte zur literarischen und materiellen Kultur der Frauenklöster im späten Mittelalter*, Studies in Medieval and

be reminiscent of menstrual blood, symbolizing that Katherine, who is a bride, is fertile not in the conventional sense of giving birth to children but in creating new followers of Christ, in other words, spiritual children.

Post-flagellation Katherine is thrown into a dark dungeon where she lies for 12 days, the number symbolism putting her on a par with the Disciples of Christ.[155] Her fasting purifies her and reinforces the paradox introduced above: fasting is a denial of the body that, literally, reduces it and further destroys Katherine's seductive beauty whilst at the same time emphasizing the body's physicality by privileging its suffering. Moreover, the body becomes the parchment on which the text of Saint Katherine's martyrdom is written in her blood for spectators/ readers within and outwith the narrative. Her imprisonment and starvation constitute a symbolic death and burial which recall Christ's descent into Hell and from which she is reborn the exemplary martyr and bride who relinquishes her body to her bridegroom. If, as Steve Pile suggests, 'bodies are spaces where multiple, interrelated meanings can be mapped',[156] Katherine's becomes a site of negation and assertion, of desire and surrender, of beauty and ugliness, purification and defilement, a map of the conflict between different types of power. During Katherine's incarceration God sends a white dove, symbol of the Holy Ghost, to provide her with daily physical and spiritual nourishment, so the blood shed by Katherine may also point to the communion wine symbolic of Christ's blood.[157] His sustenance of Katherine both identifies her as elect and foreshadows one of her miracle stories, so links her life to its continuing

---

Reformation Thought 99 (Leiden and Boston: Brill, 2004), pp. 1–43 (p. 12)). He cites Dorothea von Montau (1347–94), who would stand for hours at a time with outstretched arms or hang from nails on the wall in imitation of the Crucifixion (p. 11). Descriptions of Katherine's physical torment may, for the nuns of the Katharinenkloster, have both drawn on a familiar tradition and reinforced them in their own spiritual resolve to suffer for Christ.

[155] Christ Himself was imprisoned while His Cross was being constructed, so Katherine's incarceration further heightens the parallels to Him. His imprisonment is not mentioned in the Bible but became a focus of devotion in the Late Middle Ages and was one of the sights visited by pilgrims during their procession round the Church of the Holy Sepulchre (cf. Fabri, *Wanderings*, vol. 2, 1, pp. 352–3). Copies of the prison existed in late-medieval Jerusalem landscapes such as the church of Santo Stefano in Bologna. Daniel and Paul were also imprisoned.

[156] Steve Pile, *The Body and the City: Psychoanalysis, Space and Subjectivity* (London and New York: Routledge, 1996), p. 185.

[157] This scene recalls the feeding of the Grail community in Wolfram von Eschenbach's *Parzival*: the Holy Ghost descends every Good Friday bearing a host. Similarly, Elijah was fed by ravens in the desert (I Kings 17:1–6); and comforted and sustained by an angel bringing him food and drink when he was about to die in the desert (I Kings 19:4–8).

manifestation.[158] The angels' comforting of Katherine further signals her singular status; their radiance announcing God's power over the evil symbolized by the darkness of the jail. Indeed, a prayer from a Katharinenkloster manuscript marks this radiance as a key experience by foregrounding it as a cause for joy: 'Eya frolock im her*r*n nw pistu vereinigt mit dem her*r*n ewigcliche*n* das gotlich liecht hat dich gesterckt vnd getrost tzwelf nacht'.[159] The jailers' fear parallels the shepherds' on hearing the news of Christ's birth, announcing the birth of another holy figure, a status Katherine finally achieves through her martyrdom.

The remainder of the narrative serves one overriding purpose: confirmation of Katherine's sanctity through further conversions, miracles and martyrdom. In a literary device common to both hagiography and courtly romance, the Emperor Maxentius rides out[160] and his queen, Faustina, asks his captain of the guard, Porphyrius, for access to Katherine, about whom she has dreamt. Faustina's dream is prophetic since the suffering she experiences in it because of Saint Katherine foreshadows her subsequent post-conversion martyrdom.[161] As we have seen, sleep enables the truth to be seen in pictures not normally accessible to the waking senses, so here as elsewhere the narrative plays on different levels of vision: the dream, an altered state (yet one still rooted in earthly life), allows – albeit coded

---

[158] The following miracle takes place annually on Saint Katherine's Day: 'vnd die selben gutten herren haben allwegen als gnug von sant Katherine*n* genaden wann allweg an irem abent czu vesper kommen gar vil kleyner vogelin dar vn*d* yegkliches tret ein olzweig in seine*n* schnebelin / dar*a*n sind schwar*c*ze knoplin / sam dye kriechlin dar yn ist daz ol / vnd eyn zweig ist grosser dann das ander eyns hat vier knopfllin / eyns drey / eins zwey / vn*d* werffen dy in iren creutzga*n*g d*a*z tut sy ymmer mer von einer vesper zu der andern' [and the same good gentlemen are always sufficiently provided for thanks to the grace of Saint Katherine since flocks of small birds come on the evening of Saint Katherine's Day around Vespers, each carrying in its little beak an olive branch which has little black knobs on it that look like sloes. In these is the oil. All the twigs are different sizes; one has four little knobs; another three; another two. The birds throw the twigs into the monastery cloisters and do so in ever greater numbers from one Vespers to the next] (fol. cclx*r*).

[159] 'Hallelujah, rejoice in the Lord, now you are joined with the Lord forever and ever. His divine light has strengthened and comforted you these twelve nights' (Stadtbibliothek Nürnberg, Cod. Cent. VII, 65, fol. 20*v*). This also stands for the effect of light filtering through a stained-glass window.

[160] For example, in the legend of Saint Barbara, a saint often paired with Katherine in religious art, Barbara becomes a Christian and uses her father's absence to have a third window installed in the tower in which he has imprisoned her. Similarly, Tristan and Isolde take advantage of Mark's absence from court on a hunt to meet (Gottfried, *Tristan*, ll. 14348–602; Hatto, pp. 230–4).

[161] Faustina says: 'Ich han ynn dem traum vil durch sie geleydenn' [In my dream I suffered a great deal on her account] (fol. ccliij*r*).

– access to the future and hence causes those very future events.[162] This tradition was alive in the Dominican order, since the Dominican mystic Heinrich Seuse (Suso) 'rezipierte die antike und biblische Traumdeutung, derzufolge sich gerade in Halbschlaf und Traum die jenseitige Welt kundtut, sich die himmlische Welt in das Gemüt einzuspiegeln vermag'.[163] Moreover, Faustina and Porphyrius function as prototype Katherines, their martyrdom paving the way for hers, which transcends theirs in importance and effect just as she, the bride of Christ, already transcends the merely human. The higher level of vision accessed in the dream also opens their path to yet another altered reality: the angels they see on visiting Katherine. In the prison scene the angels are, however, not merely imaginary: the heavenly is actually, physically present in the worldly; the light radiated by the angels illuminates but also contrasts with the darkness of the jail, symbolizing the difference between those who have seen the light, Jesus,[164] and those imprisoned in the darkness of pagan ignorance: 'sahen sie vill schoner Engell bey ir die hetten ir schleg geheylet mit der hymlischeuu [*sic*] salben / da schmecket sie einen gutte*n* schmack / da von wurden sie gar starck / vnd sahen auch alt herren pey yr siczen

---

[162] For example, Krimhilde's dreams about the murder of Siegfried by Günther and Hagen (at the start of the narrative she dreams of a falcon being torn apart by two eagles; just before his death she dreams of two boars chasing him and two mountains falling on him (*Das Nibelungenlied*, ed. Helmut Brackert, Bücher des Wissens (Frankfurt: Fischer, 1970), stanzas 13–17 and 920–5; cf. *The Nibelungenlied*, trans. A.T. Hatto, Penguin Classics (Harmondsworth: Penguin, 1965), p. 18 and pp. 124–5). According to *Die Religion in Geschichte und Gegenwart* dreams were seen as 'den Ort, an dem eine andere Wirklichkeit in den Menschen einbricht. Als einer Offenbarung der Gottheit kann dem T. die gleiche Wirklichkeit zukommen wie dem Wachgeschehen' [the place in which a different reality invades people. As revelation of the Godhead, the dream can be just as real as anything that happens in man's waking state] (vol. 6 (1962), p. 1001). Further, it states, 'T.offenbarungen sind also nach at. Auffassung die Weise, in der Gott mit Menschen verkehrt. Man weiß zwar, daß T.e etwas Rätselhaftes in sich tragen (Num 12, 6–8) – daher wird Mose eines unmittelbaren Gespräches mit Gott gewürdigt –, doch ist der T. sonst oft legitimes Mittel, die Gottheit zu befragen (1Sam 28, 6. 15) und ihren Willen zu erfahren (Hi 7, 13–14' [Thus, in the Old Testament understanding of them, revelations in dreams are the means by which God interacts with man. It is known that dreams are by nature somewhat mysterious – for this reason Moses is honoured by a direct conversation with God – but nonetheless dreams are often a legitimate vehicle for questioning the Godhead] (vol. 6, p. 1004).

[163] 'adapted the interpretation of dreams practised in Antiquity and the Bible according to which it was precisely in the half-asleep or dream state that the world beyond death revealed itself, that the divine world was reflected into a person's soul' (Arnold Angenendt and Kren Meiners, 'Erscheinungsformen spätmittelalterlicher Religiosität', in *Divina Officia. Liturgie und Frömmigkeit im Mittelalter*, Ausstellungskataloge der Herzog August Bibliothek 83 (Wolfenbüttel: Herzog August Bibliothek, 2000), pp. 25–35 (p. 34)).

[164] Described in John 8:12; 9:5 as the Light of the World.

der antlucz schyn als dy sunn' (fol. ccliij[r-v]).[165] The healing of Katherine's wounds marks, first, the outward manifestation of her transfigured spiritual state, itself the true beauty that comes from being nourished by God's grace (the food brought by the dove); second, the transience of human suffering compared to eternal redemption; and, third, the deliberately constructed parallels between the saint and Christ: the salve used by the angels to heal Katherine mirrors that used by Mary Magdalene to anoint Christ's feet (Luke 7:38) and the spices taken by the Three Marys to Christ's grave for the anointing of His body (Mark 16:1–2; Luke 24:1).[166] The clear symbolism of physical death and resurrection to a spiritually healed and hence more virtuous state of being informs this scene, preparing the reader for the ensuing threefold martyrdom. A sweet smell traditionally signifies sanctity, here exemplified by its restorative properties since Faustina and Porphyrius, literally given a foretaste of holiness, become physically and spiritually stronger in preparation for their own subsequent torture and death. Just as the queen's dream vision opens for her and Porphyrius a higher level of divine vision characterized by light and scent – that is, by physical stimuli that seem initially to contradict the denial of the physical represented by Maxentius' starvation of Katherine – so the reader's imaginative transformation of the text into a mental picture of the scene opens the same level of divine vision for him. Through this vision the reader could suffer in his mind and soul and be led, by God's grace, through the dark depths of his own sin to rebirth into the light of salvation. The special effects (light and smell), introduction of new characters (the angels; the old men) and change of set (the prison) further the divine drama: the reader is led through the Passion play of Katherine's martyrdom, stopping at different locations to witness the next scene.[167] The reference to the sun – symbol of Christ, His resurrection and the

---

[165] 'They saw many beautiful angels around her who had healed her blows with heavenly ointment. They smelt a sweet scent from which they grew strong; and they saw an old man sitting with her whose countenance shone like the sun'.

[166] An echo of Arthurian romance (itself probably a reference to Biblical examples) underscores the symbolism of this passage: in Hartmann von Aue's *Iwein* the Lady of Narison and two maids find the unconscious knight Iwein, naked and rendered semi-insane by remorse, at the side of the road. She sends a maid with a healing salve that awakens Iwein to new life and a new, humbler, state of mind that makes his previous life seem like a dream (Hartmann von Aue, *Iwein*, ed. G.F. Benecke and K. Lachmann, rev. Ludwig Wolff (Berlin: de Gruyter, 7th edn 1968), ll. 3359–568.

[167] Light and scent also occur as the external manifestation of healing virtue in, for example, the *vita* of Saint Walpurgis. At her burial, 'kam als ein gros licht von hymel her ab / vnd gineng als ein gutter geschmack von yrem leychnam das die mensche*n* da von krefftig wurden / dye da gegenwertig waren' [a great light descended from Heaven and such a sweet fragrance emanated from her corpse that all those present were strengthened by it] (*Der Heiligen Leben*, fol. xciiij[r]). Moreover, light and fragrance may also bring to the reader's mind

truth (as its light reveals everything)[168] – indicates the translocation of divinity to earth to overcome death.

Katherine's authority as vehicle for that translocation is symbolized by her enacting of power:

> Frewnd nempt war / gott hat euch außerwelt / daz ir euwer blut durch in vergiessen solt / vnd saget mals vil von Cristen glauben / das sie bekert wurden. Es stunden auch Engel da / dy hetten schon kron auff / da nam sand katherina der Kron eine vnd saczt sie der kungin auff / vnd sprach czw yr / Du solt dich frewen / wann von heut uber drey tag solt du mit grossen eren gen hymel faren / vnnd stercket auch Purphirium / vnd saget im von dem hymlischen lon / biß er bekert ward. (fol. ccliij^v)

> ['Friends, be aware that God has chosen you to shed your blood in His name'. She told them so much about the Christian faith that they were converted. Angels were also standing there wearing beautiful crowns. Saint Katherine took one and placed it onto the queen's head and said to her, 'You should rejoice for three days from now you will ascend into Heaven with great honour'. She also gave Porphyrius strength and told him about the reward awaiting him in Heaven until he, too, was converted].

Katherine's words both interpret the queen's dream and prophesy future events, continuing the theme of blood as baptism and emblem of sanctity since God's privileging of Faustina and Porphyrius is expressed through their shedding of blood for His sake. However, Katherine realizes her prophecy in advance of their death: her coronation of the queen with an angel's crown both anticipates Faustina's martyr's crown and echoes God's coronation of the Virgin Mary. It also echoes the ceremony in which a woman was formally admitted to a convent: after being disinvested of her secular clothes, having her hair cut off by the priest and prostrating herself in prayer, 'Wenn sie von der venig auf gestanden ist so seczt man Ir daz crönlein auf vnd Der prister singt Veni sponsa piß auf Quam tibidz singen die schuler vollen auß'.[169] Katherine's primacy amongst saints is demonstrated by

---

the candles and incense of mass, continuing and reinforcing the blood/mass imagery in this section of the text.

[168] *Hall's Dictionary*, pp. 292–3.

[169] When she has arisen from her prostration, the crown is placed onto her head and the priest sings the *Veni sponsa* as far as the *Quam tibidz* and the pupils sing it to the end (*Item hernach stet Die ordnung wie mans helt wenn eine gehorsam tut* (Germanisches Nationalmuseum Hs 7054, [fol. 3^v]). This *Ordnung* is from the convent of Pillenreuth near Nuremberg, which was, however, Augustinian. For an account of the ritual around a nun's

this extraordinary gesture of power (yet another parallel to Christ) and by her further prophecy that Faustina will ascend to Heaven in three days. The number three points both to the Trinity, actively present in structure and symbolism of the text, and to Christ's own descent into Hell and subsequent Resurrection. Conversion is effected hierarchically, with the highest-status (the queen) first, then the captain of the guard. After his conversion Porphyrius converts his 200 knights, thus continuing a chain reaction, initiated by the hermit's conversion of Katherine, that demonstrates the power of Christianity, since the number of those converted increases steadily through the text. Once more the direct speech used in this passage places the reader at the scene, turning him into a witness of the holy events, and lends the narrative the quality of a drama.

On the twelfth day of Katherine's incarceration Christ Himself visits her: 'An dem zwelff*en* tag kam vnser herr selber czu ir mit einer mannig d*er* Engell vnd Junckfrawen vnd trost sie mynniklich' (fol. ccliij^v).[170] Christ's face is described as "mynniklich" when Katherine sees it for the first time; the use of the adjective here stresses His constancy to His bride and Katherine's status as such.[171] His direct address to Katherine, which continues the martial metaphor present in the narrative, casts Katherine as a faithful warrior, much as she herself had characterized the philosophers as "kempfer":[172]

> Liebe tochter katherina / du streytest durch mich deine*n* schopfer vnd deinen erloßer / byß stet vnd furcht dir nit / ich wil dich nym*m*er gelassen / vnd alle die durch dich gelaubig werdent / der wyrt vil / vn*d* gab ir da seinen heyligen leichnam vn*d* sei*n* roßenfarbeß blut mit seinen gotlichen henden / das was eyn edle gab / vn*d* was eyn czeychen der grossen lieb dy er zu yr hett. (fol. ccliij^v)

> ['My dear daughter Katherine, you fight for the sake of me, your Lord and Redeemer. Be constant and have no fear for I shall never leave you and those who believe on account of you will be many and numerous'. Then He gave her His holy body and His rose-red blood with His divine hands. That was a noble gift and a sign of His great love for her].

---

taking of the veil see Gussone, 'Die Jungfrauenweihe in ottonischer Zeit nach dem Ritus im *Pontificale Romano-Germanicum*', pp. 25–41.

[170]   'On the twelfth day Our Lord Himself visited her with a host of angels and virgins and comforted her sweetly'.

[171]   *Minne* is the Middle High German for both the love of God for man and love of man and woman for each other.

[172]   Seuse also refers to monastic life as 'den geistlichen Soldatendienst' [spiritual military service] (Seuse, *Stundenbuch*, p. 169).

Christ's prophecy of Katherine's effecting many conversions to Christianity is realized in the miracle stories; whilst within the devotional context of Nuremberg the reader of her legend and the visual/textual testimony to Katherine combine to provide the concrete evidence of her power. Hence the reader and the city become, like Katherine's wedding ring and the objects "left behind" in her miracle stories, tangible evidence of the truth of the transcendent, salvatory events rendered accessible by the narrative.

After Christ's prophecy He functions as both ministering priest and sacrament in a celebration of the mass. According to Arnold Angenendt and Kren Meiners the Late Middle Ages witnessed the heightened importance of the mass and a craving for related miracles. The text of the liturgy was infused with layers of symbolic meaning. Moreover:

> Die an der Liturgie Beteiligten hielten aus Andachtsbüchern und Bildern in der Kirche die entsprechenden Heilsereignisse vor Augen gestellt, die sie bei den einzelnen Abschnitten der Liturgie betrachten sollten. Durch diese Kommentierung wurde die Messe zu einer rituellen Inszenierung der vergangenen Heilsgeschichte. Im Streben nach einer Verinnerlichung nahm die spätmittelalterliche Liturgie gleichzeitig Elemente auf, die das liturgische Geschehen zunehmend psychisch dramatisierten, etwa in Seufzern, Tränen und Mitleidsschreien.[173]

> [Devotional works and pictures in church conjured up before the eyes of participants in the liturgy the corresponding salvatory events that they were supposed to contemplate during the individual sections of the liturgy. This commentary rendered the mass a ritual staging of the stages in the history of salvation that had already taken place. In the striving for internalization the late-medieval liturgy simultaneously incorporated elements that increasingly created a psychological dramatization of events, for example through sighs, tears and screams of empathy].

The vividness of this passage aids internal recreation of and empathy for Christ's suffering, reinforced by its visual alignment with the Mass of Saint Gregory, the miraculous appearance over the altar of the crucified body of Christ and the instruments of the Passion during the celebration of mass by Pope Gregory the Great (c. 540–604).[174] The cult of the Mass of Saint Gregory started with the

---

173   Angenendt and Meiners, 'Erscheinungsformen', p. 31.

174   For the Mass of Saint Gregory see Andreas Gormans and Thomas Lentes (eds), *Das Bild der Erscheinung. Die Gregorsmesse im Mittelalter*, KultBild 3 (Berlin 2007); Esther Meier, *Die Gregorsmesse. Funktionen eines spätmittelalterlichen Bildtypus* (Cologne, Weimar and Vienna: Böhlau, 2006); Heike Schlie, 'Die Autoritätsmuster der "Gregorsmesse" – Umdeutungen und

erection of a new icon in the church of S. Croce in Gerusalemme in Rome in 1385/6 and grew rapidly from 1450 onwards.[175] The icon was probably given to the church by Raimondello di Orsini, who may have taken it and one of Saint Katherine's fingers from the shrine on Mount Sinai in 1380/1 and kept them in the church of Saint Katharina in Galatina, which he had built and endowed. Saint Katherine is portrayed on the reverse of the icon.[176] There is written or extant visual evidence of at least 25 representations of the Mass of Saint Gregory in Nuremberg alone, including the Tondörffer Epitaph that used to hang on the exterior north wall of the Lorenzkirche next to the Imhoff Portal; a panel (1401) inside the church itself; in the Sebalduskirche the Groland-Tucher tapestry (1410–20), donated by Leonard Groland and his wife Brigitte Tucher (d. 1424), probably as an epitaph for the latter,[177] and the Holzschuher tomb tapestry; and the epitaph for Walburg Prünsterer (d. 1434) in the Frauenkirche.[178] In the Katharinenkirche itself the Mass was depicted on the epitaph of Heinrich Wolff von Wolffsthal (1490/1500), which shows Saint Katherine standing on the right of the altar whilst mass is celebrated;[179] on the epitaph for Dorothea Schürstab;

Auflösungen eines Zeichensystems', in Frank Büttner and Gabriele Wimböck (eds), *Das Bild als Autorität. Die normierende Kraft des Bildes* (Münster: LIT, 2004), pp. 73–101; Karsten Kelberg, *Die Darstellung der Gregorsmesse in Deutschland* (Diss. Phil. Münster 1983).

[175]   Meier, *Gregorsmesse*, p. 13.

[176]   Meier, *Gregorsmesse*, p. 31.

[177]   Kelberg, Darstellung der Gregorsmesse, p. 203, no. 140.

[178]   Meier, *Gregorsmesse*, p. 13; pp. 68–70; p. 88 and plate 12; Kelberg, Darstellung der Gregorsmesse, pp. 200–1, no. 134.

[179]   Heinrich Wolff von Wolffsthal (d. 1504), originally from Nördlingen, became a citizen of Nuremberg in 1469 and member of the *Kleiner Rat* in 1499. He traded primarily in metals with Poland and Venice and c. 1500 was reputed to have a fortune of 100,000 florins that he lost in financial deals with Emperor Maximilian I. The latter ennobled him. Heinrich's son Balthasar (d. 1529) was chief treasurer to Maximilian. The family died out in 1717 (*Stadtlexikon*, pp. 1201–2). The epitaph of Heinrich Wolff von Wolffsthal is now in the Germanisches Nationalmuseum (Gm 154). Saint Katharine also witnesses the Mass of Saint Gregory on the stone epitaph for Barbara Hutten (d. 1422), wife of Peter Hutten, that used to hang on the Moritzkapelle (next to the Sebalduskirche; destroyed during the Second World War (Meier, *Gregorsmesse*, pp. 64–8 and plate 11)). Murr notes: 'Gegen über [the Fütterer Altar] an der linken Seite des Chores, ist oben die Erscheinung Gregorius, nebst mehreren alten Tafeln' [Opposite, on the left-hand side of the choir, the Mass of Saint Gregory hangs high on the wall along with several other old pictures] (p. 289). It is not possible to identify which he means. Another Gregory Mass is mentioned: 'Gegen der Kanzel über ist vor dem vorgedachten Behaimischen Altar ein anderer, auf welchem die Mutter Gottes von Bildhauerarbeit zu sehen ist. Auf dem rechten Altardeckel ist oben der heil. Andreas, unten ist die Erscheinung St. Gregorius. Auf dem linken oben, die Enthauptung der heil. Katharina, unten die Kreuzigung. Im Reliquienschranke ist inwendig in Bildhauerarbeit

and on the Volckamer Altar.[180] Epitaphs were intended to offer the visitor to a church the stimulus and opportunity for personal devotion; in other words, they acquired the function of an 'Andachtsbild' (devotional image) for nuns and Nuremberg residents: 'in besonderem Maße aber die Stifterfiguren werden zu Identifikationsfiguren, die eine angemessene Haltung vor Augen führen und zur Anbetung auffordern'.[181] Moreover, the Tucher, Groland, Volckamer, Schürstab, Prünster and von Wolffsthal were the Patrician families who sat on the *Kleiner Rat* and whose widows, mothers, daughters, nieces, sisters, aunts and cousins populated the Katharinenkloster, constituting a mobile link between Saint Katherine, the convent and the Mass of Saint Gregory that stretched throughout the city. Like the saint herself, the Mass became a medium for advertising personal piety and social prestige in the status-rich civic spaces where such advertising was bundled.[182]

---

das heilige Abendmahl, rechts aber St. Hieronymus und Gregorius, links St. Augustinus und Athanasius gemalet. Außen der heil. Christoph und Johannes, der den Segen ertheilet' [Opposite the chancel and in front of the Behaim Altar mentioned earlier is another altar on which a carved Mother of God can be seen. On the right altar wing Saint Andrew is in the upper field and the Mass of Saint Gregory in the lower. In the upper field of the left wing is the execution of Saint Katherine, in the lower one the Crucifixion. On the inside of the *predella* is a carving of the Last Supper; on the right paintings of Saints Jerome and Gregory, on the left of Saints Augustine and Athanasius. On the outside are Saints Christopher and John giving the blessing] (pp. 292–3).

[180]   Endowed in 1493 by Nikolaus V Volckamer for his parents, Peter (1431–93) and Apollonia neé Mendel.

[181]   'However, the donor figures in particular become figures with which to identify, figures that demonstrate an appropriate pose and encourage the viewer to emulation' (Meier, *Gregorsmesse*, p. 91).

[182]   Moreover, the vestments, instruments and gestures of the mass were infused with symbolism: for example, 'Der kelich bedeüt das heÿlig grab cristi Jhesu Johannis · ix' [The chalice symbolizes Christ's holy tomb (John 9)]. The host itself carries multiple symbolic meanings, which are wrapped into Christ's administration of His body to Katherine: 'Des ersten die hosti sol haben diß siben eÿgenschafften · des gelÿchen der briester vnd das volck mit jm. Des ersten soll die hosti sein weÿß vnd schön · rain vnd lautter · Also sol *der* briester vnd ein ÿegklich mensch der do empfahen wil des heÿlig sacrament des geleÿchen an jm haben. Das ist das er sol sein rain · lautter · vnd schön · vor got on all tödtlich sünde · Zů dem andern · die hosti sol gemacht werden auß waÿczem korn · vnd des natur ist *süß* · denn der herre geleÿcht sich selbs zů dem waÿczen körnlein Johannis. Ij · Es sey dann das das körnlein falle · in die erd*er*en so bringt es kein frucht · Das ist . das der herre an sich nam sein heÿlige menscheÿt · vnd die mit der gotheÿt vereinet. Die süssigkeit söll wir auch an vns haben · das ist die senfftmütigkeit wider die sünde des zorns · Zů dem dritten so sol die hosti dün*n* sein · vnd bedeüt das wir söllen sein mässig vnd bescheÿden wid*er* die sünde der vnmässigkeÿt vnd der vnbescheÿdenheÿt · Zů dem vierden so sol die hosti nit groß sein sunder klein · Also söll*en* wir vns auch diemütigen wider die sünde der hoffart · wann sÿ verstre*w*et vnd vernichtet alle tugent · Zů dem fünfften die hosti sol

The passage in *Der Heiligen Leben* presents difficulties of interpretation: it could be read as the "real" Christ functioning as priest and giving Katherine the communion host and wine that symbolize His flesh and blood; or it could be a literal interpretation of the cannibalistic elements already present in the mass since Catholic doctrine preached the real presence of Christ's flesh and blood in wafer and wine after their consecration by the ministering priest.[183] How

---

sÿnwel sein · Also *s*ö*llen wir geen von einer tuge*n*t in die andern · wider die sünde der trägheit. Z*ů dem sechßten die hosti sol gemacht sein on heffen vnd vrhab · Darumb so *s*ö*llen wir vns begeben in die liebe gottes vnnd vnsers *n*ä*chsten · wider den heffen vnd vrh*ä*b des neÿds vnd des hasses · Z*ů dem sibenden · die hosti sol gemacht sein on salcz · das ist das wir miltigkeit an vns haben *s*ö*llen · wider die sünde der geÿtigkeit · Die hosti wird geleÿchet dem auffgeopferten leÿb cristi Johannis vj · Ich bin das lebentig brot das do herab kumbt von dem hÿmel . nicht als e*w*er v*ä*ter in der *w*ü*ste etc ... vnd nicht agrest wein noch confect wein · sunder rechten lautteren vnnd klaren wein · vnd der bedeüt das sich der herre cristus Jhesus an*n* das kreücz nagelen ließ · vnd auß seinem leÿbe trucken vnd preßen ließ sein heÿliges rosenfarbes bl*ů*te Genesis · xlix' [First, the host should possess these seven characteristics, just like the priest and the congregation with him. First, the host should be white and beautiful, pure and unblemished, just like the priest and every person who wishes to receive the holy sacrament: that is, he should be pure, unblemished and beautiful and without any mortal sins in God's eyes. Second, the host should be made from wheat kernels, which are sweet by nature, since the Lord compares Himself to the wheat kernel (John 2). Unless the wheat kernel falls onto the ground it bears no fruit: that is, the Lord took upon Himself His sacred humanity and united it with His divine nature. We too should be sweet by nature: that is, we should be patient and gentle and resist the sin of Anger. Third, the host should be thin and this means we should be moderate and undemanding and resist the sins of Immoderation and Greed. Fourth, the host should not be large but small. In the same way we should be humble and resist the sin of Pride since it scatters and destroys all virtue. Fifth, the host should be round; and in the same way we should proceed from one virtue to the next and resist the sin of Sloth. Sixth, the host should be made without yeast or leavening; for this reason we should give ourselves up to the love of God and our neighbour and resist the yeast and leavening of the sins of Envy and Hatred. Seventh, the host should be made without salt; that is, we should be charitable and resist the sin of Avarice. The host symbolizes the sacrificed body of Christ (John 6): 'I am the living bread that falls from Heaven, not as your fathers in the desert etc.' ... and not sour wine nor sweet wine, but really pure, clear wine and it symbolizes that the Lord Jesus Christ allowed Himself to be nailed onto the Cross and allowed His holy rose-red blood to be squeezed and pressed out of His body] (fol. 51ᵛ–52ʳ). Thus this scene also symbolizes Katherine's vanquishment of her baser self, especially her pride, since certain characteristics of the host (its beauty, purity, sweetness, humility and love for God) are explicitly associated with her. Hence, it also signals her readiness for her own martyrdom to the greater glory of God, a sacrifice which bears fruit in her legend and her followers.

[183]   The doctrine of transubstantiation established itself in the eleventh century and became official doctrine in 1079. For the medieval understanding of the mass and the debate concerning the real presence of Christ see Willing, *Literatur und Ordensreform*, pp. 86–9; for the role of mass in Church and monastic life, pp. 89–94. In the paean to Katherine at the end of her legend this mass is identied as the twelfth sign of God's grace to the saint,

intensely and how literally the Eucharist was experienced, also by lay people, is evident in a late-fifteenth-century prayer:

> Ich *gang* hewt tzů dir als ain gewaltiger tzů ainem hailer / Vnd bitt dich das du mir hailest alle mein wunden / vnd alle die mal die mein sele ye empfieng / Ich gang heut tzů dir als ain durstiger tzů aine*m* lustigen bru*n*nen / vnd bit dich das du mich trenckest mit deiner gnad / die da fleusset vo*n* deinem vater / vnd von dem sun / vnd vo*n* de*m* hailigen gaist / Ich gang heut tzů dir / als ain hungriger zů aine*m* vollen tisch / vnd b*i*tt dich / d*a*z du mich speysest mit deine*m* hailige*n* fronlichna*m* / vnd mich trenckest mit deinem hailigen blůtt.[184]

[I go to you today as a beaten man to a healer and pray you to heal all my wounds and all the harm ever my soul was subjected to. I go to you today as a thirsty man to a pleasant fountain and pray you to quench my thirst with your grace which flows from the Father and the Son and the Holy Ghost. I go to you today as a hungry man to a laden table and prey you to succour me with your holy body and quench my thirst with your holy blood].

---

one that associates her with Saint Dionysius (Denis): 'Die zwelften genad tet vnser herr sant Dionisio do er in dem kerker lag vnd mess dar inne*n* sprach vnd die oblat gesegent het Do kum vns*er* herr zu im vnd gab im selber sein leichnam Vnd sprach zu im pis fro wan dein lon ist groß pey mir · Die genad tet vnser her*r* sant Katerina auch Do er zu ir kum in den kerker an dem zwelfte*n* tag Do gab er ir mit sein götliche*n* hende*n* sein heiligen fronleichnam vn*d* sein rosen varbes plut Daz waz ein edle gab vn*d* ein zeiche*n* der vberflüßigen lieb die er zu ir het Die gnad het sie von der große*n* hoffnu*n*g die sie zu got het' [The twelfth sign of grace was bestowed by Our Lord on Saint Dionysius, when he was in jail and celebrating mass there and had blessed the host. Then Our Lord visited him and gave him His body Himself. He said to him, 'Rejoice, for your reward from me is great'. Our Lord bestowed the same grace on Saint Katherine. When He visited her in jail on the twelfth day He gave her His holy body and His rose-red blood with His own divine hands. That was a noble gift and a sign of the abundant love He felt for her. She received this grace as a reward for the great hope she placed in God] (Germanisches Nationalmuseum Hs 86 409, [fol. 40ʳ⁻ᵛ]).

[184]   *Gebetbüchlein* (Augsburg: Günter Zainer, 1471), unfol. Prayers during the Eucharist naturally focussed on Christ's physical suffering and His blood as a source of nourishment and redemption (Germanisches Nationalmuseum Hs 1733, fol. 60ᵛ–67ʳ). Prayers were also said on the 72 wounds suffered by Christ to His head (Hs 1733, fol. 37ʳ–41ʳ). Angenendt und Meiners note the following about prayers for the laity: 'Um dem heranwachsenden Verlangen nach Verinnerlichung entgegenzukommen, schuf man für die Eucharistiefeiernden sowohl Übersetzungen liturgischer Gebete als auch volkssprachliche Begleitgebete' [In order to satisfy the growing desire for internalization [of the experience of Christ's Passion] not only were liturgical prayers translated for the celebrants, but accompanying prayers in the vernacular were composed] ('Erscheinungsformen', p. 31).

Communion was consumption, the metaphorical – or literal – ingestion of flesh and blood to still spiritual hunger and thirst; the altar the table on which the feast was laid out.[185] One image from an illustrated Upper Rhenish manuscript of Raymond of Capua's biography of the Dominican Katherine of Siena (1347–80) shows Katherine drinking blood from the wound in Christ's side until 'sy gesatte ward liplich und öch geistlich' [until she was replete in body and in soul].[186] Similarly, *Von der seligen schererin*, the record of the visions of a Basel beguine (d. 1409), describes her drinking the blood from Christ's wounds and being strengthened by it:

> Vnd sú sas dar gegen vor der marteler alter vnd sach, daz vier strolen blůtes flussent vs den fúnf minnezeichen, zwen strole vs den henden vnd einer vs den füssen vnd einer vs der siten. Vnd die vier strol blůtes flussent vornan zů sammen vnd wart vornan ein stam oder strol vnd flos ir in iren munt. Vnd sú befant befúntlich berürde vnd gesmag des blůtes in irem munde vnd wart gar ser von dem minne trang gestercket vnd erfrowet.[187]

> [And she sat opposite in front of the Martyrs' altar and saw that four streams of blood flowed out of the five signs of love: two streams from the hands and one from the feet and one from the side. And the four streams of blood flowed together in front [of the Cross] and became one stream or ray and poured into her mouth. And without the shadow of a doubt she experienced the touch and taste of the blood in her mouth and was mightily strengthened and gladdened by the love potion].

---

[185]　Elisabeth Vavra records Mechthild von Hackeborn's vision of the pietà in which Mary encourages her to approach and kiss Christ's wounds (Elisabeth Vavra, 'Bildmotiv und Frauenmystik – Funktion und Rezeption', in Peter Dinzelbacher and Dieter R. Bauer (eds), *Frauenmystik im Mittelalter* (Ostfildern: Schwabenverlag, 1985), pp. 201–30 (p. 211)).

[186]　Jeffrey F. Hamburger, *The Visual and the Visionary. Art and Female Spirituality in Late Medieval Germany* (New York: Zone, 1998), p. 460. The manuscript from which Hamburger cites is Paris, Bibliothèque Nationale, MS All. 34 (fol. 43ᵛ). The Katharinenkloster once owned two, now lost, copies of this biography. Whether or not they were illustrated is unknown (p. 462).

[187]　Hans-Jochen Schiewer, 'Auditionen und Visionen einer Begine. Die "Selige Schererin", Johannes Mulberg und der Basler Beginenstreit. Mit einem Textabdruck', in Timothy Jackson, Nigel F. Palmer and Almut Suerbaum (eds), *Die Vermittlung geistlicher Inhalte im deutschen Mittelalter. Internationales Symposium Roscrea 1994* (Tübingen: Niemeyer, 1996), pp. 289–317 (p. 308). This is just one of several such visions. These examples would suggest that in jail Katherine literally partakes of Christ's body and blood.

The Eucharist was also healing, the believer's spiritual wounds set in parallel with Christ's physical ones, out of which His healing, nurturing blood flowed. Theologically, the theme of the Mass of Saint Gregory was 'die Schau Gottes'.[188] Since no human being could stand the sight of God, He cannot be seen directly but only in His Son: 'Den Gregorsmessen liegt die Nichtsichtbarkeit Gottes zugrunde und zugleich zeigen sie Möglichkeiten auf, Gott dennoch zu schauen'.[189] This playing with vision denied and vision granted, the interweaving of different layers of privileged sight, is present in Saint Katherine's own visions of Christ, like Gregory's 'eine zeitlich beschränkte Schau Gottes, die den wenigsten Menschen in ihrem Leben zuteil wird'.[190] The text of *Der Heiligen Leben* allows such a vision, not least as light effects and colour heighten the imaginability and hence impact of the scene. Its very theatricality reflects an increasingly performative celebration of the mass:

> Es wandelte sich zunehmend vom *Officium Dei* – die vor Gott abgeleisteten Pflicht – zum *Sacrum Theatrum*, zu einer verinnerlichten Dramatik. Jede kleine Geste und jedes liturgisches Gerät und Gewand wurde bedeutungtragend und als Teil des historischen Dramas des Passionsgedächtnisses gedeutet. Was im Ritus geschah, galt fortan sowohl als Inszenierung des vergangenen Geschehens wie ebenso als dessen leibhaftige und nachzuvollziehende Vergegenwärtigung. Bei allen liturgischen Feiern sollte die Heilsgeschichte, näherhin das Leben Jehu, vor allem dessen Passion und Auferstehung, mitvollzogen werden ... Frömmigkeit bedeutete im Hoch- und Spätmittelalter die Einung mit dem 'Christus passus', das emotionale Sich-Einfühlen in die einzelnen Akte und Worte seiner Passion.[191]

> [More and more it [the liturgy] evolved from the *Officium Dei* – a divine office – into the *Sacrum Theatrum*, to an internalized drama. Every little gesture and every liturgical vessel and garment became a vehicle for symbolic meaning and interpreted as part of the historical drama that was the commemoration of the Passion. From then on what happened during the ritual was regarded as both the staging of past events and the realization of them in a form that was both a physical reconstruction and emotionally comprehensible. The history of salvation, more precisely the life of Christ, above all His Passion and Resurrection, were to be lived out emotionally

---

[188]   'the vision of God' (Meier, *Gregorsmesse*, p. 93).

[189]   'Depictions of the Mass of Saint Gregory are based on the non-visibility of God, whilst at the same time they demonstrate the possibility of seeing God nonetheless' (Meier, *Gregorsmesse*, p. 94).

[190]   'a vision of God, limited in time, but such as is granted to very few people in the course of their lives' (Meier, *Gregorsmesse*, p. 94).

[191]   Angenendt and Meiners, 'Erscheinungsformen', p. 32.

during all celebrations of the liturgy ... For the High and Late Middle Ages piety meant union with the 'Christus passus', the process of thinking one's way into and having empathy with the individual words and deeds of His Passion].

The threads of blood, redness and roses fuse here in the description of Christ's own blood: the inscription on His body of His sacrifice; His body an advertisement for the redemptive nature of suffering and imperative for emulation by the penitential Christian; the whole scene a dramatic enactment of privileged virtue and its reward. In medieval art the wounds of the crucified Christ could be painted as red roses or red flowers, so the *Der Heiligen Leben* metaphor calls on a familiar visual trigger to facilitate imagination.[192] Within the Katharinenkloster this passage (singly or combined with the epitaphs) provides a visualization model (as from a medieval pattern book) for those nuns aspiring to mystic visions of Christ; within the city as a whole it resonates with the annual *Heiltumsweisung*: the imperial relics included slivers of the True Cross, Longinus' lance, a fragment of the tablecloth used at the Last Supper and a piece of the apron worn by Christ when washing the Disciples' feet. Just as Christ displays His sacrifice by administering His body and blood to Saint Katherine in the mass as commemoration of the Last Supper, so the Crucifixion relics were ritually displayed on the main market square on the second Friday after Good Friday every year in a performance of Nuremberg's centrality to Empire. Pilgrims could even take the *Heiltumsweisung* home with them, as in 1487 and 1493 the *Kleiner Rat* published a pamphlet with a woodcut illustration of the objects on display, a summary of the accompanying ritual and a list of indulgences available at the ceremony.[193] Similarly, the Mass of Saint Gregory could have been viewed in private houses, in convent cells and in prayer books as in the second half of the fifteenth century it was increasingly reproduced in smaller panel paintings and single-sheet woodcuts intended for private devotion.[194]

---

[192]   Compare the epitaph for Abbot Friedrich Mengot von Hirschlach (c. 1350) in Heilsbronn Minster (Peter Strieder, *Tafelmalerei in Nürnberg 1350–1550* (Königstein im Taunus: Karl Robert Langewiesche Nachfolger & Hans Köster Verlagsbuchhandlung, 1993), p. 16 and p. 166). Hamburger cites the pietà in the Abbey of Saint Walburg in Eichstätt, Bavaria (Hamburger, *Nuns as Artists*, pp. 77–9).

[193]   The first pictures of the Lance were in circulation in 1425; 1458 saw the compilation of the manuscript that formed the basis of the pamphlet (*Stadtlexikon*, pp. 433–4; Josef. J. Schmid, 'Die Reichskleinodien. Objekte zwischen Liturgie, Kult und Mythos', in Bernd Heidenreich and Frank-Lothar Kroll (eds), *Wahl und Krönung* (Frankfurt: Societätsverlag, 2006), pp. 123–49 (p. 126)).

[194]   Meier, *Gregorsmesse*, p. 13 and pp. 107–19. Woodcuts could be inserted into prayer books. See Kelberg, pp. 227–39 and picture catalogue under 'Graphik'. A Nuremberg

Communion in both kinds could normally be received only by male clergy; hence Christ's offering of His flesh and blood is a sign of love for Katherine that further confirms her exceptional status. Camille argues an increased emphasis on vision, especially with regard to the display of the sacraments at mass, an emphasis which in this scene is rendered literally and authenticated by the saint herself as the ultimate source of the information. New nuns were often given a crucifix on their profession;[195] but for the nuns of the Katharinenkloster this passage, which documents the "real" 'Eindringen des Transzendenten in die unverändert gebliebene Umwelt des Schauenden',[196] may have held particular significance. Through her analysis of the convent library Antje Willing documents the focus on the Eucharist in the convent, highlighting the reading at meals of works on the Eucharist such as the *Buch von den sechs Namen des Fronleichnams* by the monk of Heilsbronn, of which the library possessed multiple copies, or the sermons of Johannes Tauler.[197] Dominican nuns were meant to take communion between nine and 15 times a year.[198] Since communion is an act of memory and commemoration for which the believer has to be prepared,[199] Christ's appearance to Katherine demonstrates the latter's absolute preparedness through penance and fasting and reinforces its importance for the nuns:

> Die biblischen Worte von der Einsetzung des Abendmahls zum Gedächtnis an Christi Leben und Leiden … und das Verständnis der Messe (deren Höhepunkt die Kommunion ist) als *memoria passionis Christi* forderten eine Passionsbetrachtung

---

manuscript prayer book of 1515 contains an illumination of the Mass of Saint Gregory by Georg Glockendon der Ältere.

[195]   Hamburger, *The Visual and the Visionary*, pp. 428–9.

[196]   'invasion by the transcendent of the viewer's environment, which remains physically unaltered' (Meier, *Gregorsmesse*, p. 94. Meier cites Peter Dinzelbacher's definition of an "Erscheinung" (Peter Dinzelbacher, 'Die Visionen des Mittelalters. Ein geschichtlicher Umriß', *Zeitschrift für Religions- und Geistesgeschichte*, 30 (1978): 116–28 (pp. 117–18)).

[197]   Willing, *Literatur und Ordensreform*, pp. 41–2; 71–4; 95–131; 133–63. The *Buch von den sechs Namen des Fronleichnams* was one of the works taken into the convent with her by the mystic Katharina Tucher. Willing also traces the overlap of texts on the Eucharist with the mystical writings that were increasingly available in the vernacular, so more accessible to a lay readership (pp. 79–84).

[198]   In his *Ordinacio* for the Katharinenkloster the Master General of the Dominicans, Bartholomeus Texerius, stipulated communion once every three weeks (Willing, *Literatur und Ordensreform*, p. 92).

[199]   Willing mentions writings on how the nuns should best prepare themselves (*Literatur und Ordensreform*, p. 76). In addition, Katherine's experience of Christ models the "correct" form of mystical vision, about which there was concern as visions could also stem from the Devil.

als Würdigung des Sakraments und als Vorbereitung auf seinen Empfang. Eine mystische Gemeinschaft mit Christus konnte im Sakramentsempfang erlebt werden oder auch schon in der Vorbereitung auf die Kommunion, in der Betrachtung des Leidens Christi.[200]

[The Biblical words on the institution of Communion in commemoration of Christ's life and suffering ... and the understanding of the mass (of which Communion forms the climax) as *memoria passionis Christi* promoted contemplation of the Passion as an acknowledgement of the importance of the sacrament and preparation for its reception. Contemplating the suffering of Christ could lead to a mystical union with Christ which could be experienced on receiving the sacrament, or even when merely preparing for communion].

Indeed, preparation for Communion and absorption in Christ's Passion could be so intense that even for lay people the Eucharist was experienced as a form of mystic marriage:

Ach siesser got her*r* ihesu criste / mein her*r* vnd mein got / ain kùnig der hymelen vnd der erden / vnd ain behalter aller der welt / O lieber herre ihesu criste / Ich lade dich in mein sele / als meinen ausserwelten lieben ewige*n* gemaheln / vnd als mein aller liebstes lieb / das du allain herre vnd wirt solt sein in meiner sel ewiglich / Vnd ich empfahe hewt deinen hailigen leib / der fùr mich an dem hailige*n* creutz gelitten hat / vn*d* empfahe dein hailiges blůt / das von / lautter myn von deinen hailigen wunden / vnd auß deinem vnschuldigen lauttern hertzen floß / tzů ainer erlösu*n*g aller der welt / Vnd empfahe hewt dein gesegnete sel / die von lautter mi*n*ne geschaiden ist / von deinem hailigen leib / vnd empfahe heut dei*n* vnmessig lautter gotthait / mit der du ain warer gott bist mit deinem hymlischen vatter.[201]

[O, sweet God, my Lord Jesus Christ, my Lord and my God, King of Heaven and Earth and guardian of the whole world, O dear Lord Jesus Christ, I invite you into my soul as my chosen, beloved and eternal spouse and as my dearest love so that you alone will be Lord and Master of my soul for ever and ever. And today I receive your holy body, which suffered for me on the holy Cross, and receive your holy blood, which out of pure love flowed from your holy wounds and from your innocent, pure heart to redeem the whole world. And today I receive your blessed soul, which is separated by pure love from your holy body and I receive

---

[200]   Willing, *Literatur und Ordensreform*, p. 84.
[201]   *Gebetbüchlein*, unfol.

today your Godhead pure beyond measure which renders you a true God with your heavenly Father].

The mystical fusion of Crucifixion, blood and flesh grants nuns physical union with Christ, who is literally absorbed into the believer; and enables them to transcend their physicality and realize their status as brides of Christ and shadow Katherines.

On his return home Maxentius is astounded to find Katherine more beautiful than ever, the outward sign of her approaching martyrdom. He takes a step towards actualizing her potential sanctity by threatening her with death should she fail to renounce her faith and by ordering the construction of the wheel that becomes her attribute:

> Da hyeß der Keyser die drey forchtsamme greuliche reder machen die waren mit schneidendenn scharsachen / die solten yren leib allen durch schneyden Vnd sie die scharpfen reder an sach / da rufft sie yren gemahel an mit grosser andacht vnd bat in das er ir czu hilff kame · Da horet sye vnser herr vnd kam ein grosser doner schlag vnd czusprach die reder das sie znfuren [*sic*] vnd totet vier tausent heyden. (fol. ccliijᵛ)

> [Then the Emperor ordered the three fearsome, horrifying wheels to be constructed with sharply severing blades that should slice her body to shreds. And when she saw the sharp wheels she called to her spouse with great reverence and asked Him to come to her aid. Then Our Lord heard her and a great clap of thunder came down and shattered the wheels so that they splintered and slaughtered 4,000 pagans].

This scene, complete with dramatic special effects, presents the clash of two competing powers: secular and divine majesty. The former is depicted as threatened and cruel; the latter as responsive and salvatory (if terrifying). Katherine's prayers for help are specifically addressed to her "gemahel" (spouse), who fulfils His promise never to abandon her. Hence the prison scene sets up not just the subsequent martyrdom but also God's demonstration of His loyalty to those who put their faith in Him. In this case God's response to prayer is aural and visual: a clap of thunder, the shattering of the wheels and the slaughter of 4,000 heathens. Martyrdom becomes *son-et-lumière* spectacle, its power raised exponentially: the 4,000 bodies echo but surpass the 50 martyred philosophers and the martyrs yet to come (Faustina, Porphyrius, his 200 soldiers and Katherine herself). These pagans' death for their faith illustrates the superior might of the Christian God. Textual narrative morphs into visual narrative since the wheel becomes Katherine's iconic attribute and the shattering of the wheel a subject of artistic representation.[202] In fact, the small woodcut at the beginning of Katherine's legend in *Der Heiligen Leben* shows the saint at prayer, whilst the wheel is shattered by flames,[203] pagans die and a rueful Maxentius looks on (fol. cclij[r]), so the whole narrative is read under the sign of this miracle, text confirming the sign given by the image. The woodcut, viewed possibly in the reader's own home, links the text to further visual models for his imaginative recreation of this scene in the rest of Nuremberg, thus binding private devotion to a more public context such as the Lorenzkirche, in which the left outside wing of the Memminger Altar depicts the shattering of the wheel and the beheading of Saint Katherine. Paintings, stained-glass windows, sculptures and altar hangings with Katherine holding her wheel may all have fed into the individual's visualization of the text at this point and with them their remembered location within Nuremberg, so that the entire city becomes the site for Katherine's martyrdom and Katherine's martyrdom sets compass points on the map of the city.

Katherine's gratitude to God, already expressed when He comforts her in jail, is iterated here like a refrain: acknowledgement of the Lord's grace is man's end of the deal. Then Maxentius' queen takes over direct speech in preparation for her role as the next authentic, (because Christian) martyr: 'Wie lang wilt du wyder den warenn Gott fechten sichst du nicht seynen grossen gewalt' (fol. ccliij[v]).[204] Verbally Faustina becomes a shadow Katherine, setting an example that will culminate in the saint herself. Physically, she functions typologically to illustrate further the struggle between two types of power and of violence, one legitimized by its Christian nature. Maxentius wreaks on his queen the vengeance he failed to achieve on Katherine: 'da styeß man ir zwen eyßnen spyeß durch ir brust vnd windet sie als lang vmb biß sie ir her ab vielen da hett sie Jhesum in yrem herczen vnd yn yrem mutt' (fol. ccliij[v]).[205] The severance of Faustina's breasts eliminates the prime markers of her femininity, reinforcing a recurrent theme: the reduction of the female body and destruction of its sexual allure as a precondition for sanctity.[206] Moreover, it "masculinizes" the queen, since the absence of breasts

---

[202]   For example, in Lucas Cranach the Elder's *The Martyrdom of St. Catherine* (c. 1505) and his *Katharinenaltar* (1506).

[203]   Fire from Heaven was a tried and tested means of dealing with enemies of the Lord as, for example, in the destruction of Sodom and Gomorrha (Genesis 19:24).

[204]   'How long will you continue to fight against the true God? Do you not see His great might?'

[205]   'Two iron spears were thrust through her breasts and turned and turned until her breasts fell off. She had Jesus in her heart and in her mind'.

[206]   In contrast, of course, to the many images of Mary as Mother offering Christ the breast. The severance of Faustina's breasts, at the same time as eliminating the primary markers

becomes the outward marker of a courage and virtue that in medieval eyes could only be masculine; and is directly linked to the presence of Christ in her heart and soul. Faustina's body is also the battleground for the combat between the two men, Maxentius and Christ, who represent two different realms, two different religions and two different claims on her. Married to one, Faustina loves the other and spiritual love easily triumphs. Jenkins and Lewis maintain that:

> the disfigurement of the specifically female body is displaced onto Maxentius's wife, so that Katherine's body remains whole (more or less) until the final beheading. One of the effects of this displacement, along with the reduced emphasis on Katherine's virginity and physical beauty (compared, say, to St Margaret), is to place a greater importance on her intellectual skills and ability to debate, and on her role as the bride of Christ.[207]

However, the German version, at least, does not support this analysis as Katherine's beauty is repeatedly mentioned and her body emphasized by her flagellation. Moreover, Katherine does not lose her primary gender markers, so her physical beauty, as well as being highlighted, remains unimpaired. Indeed, even after her beheading her body is reconstituted by the angels who translate it to Sinai, so her beauty remains undamaged posthumously as well and transcends the merely physical to become a sign of sanctity. Rather, Faustina functions as a foil, an object for transcendence that throws Katherine's exceptionality into even sharper relief – hence Maxentius' order that Faustina be beheaded, as Katherine is subsequently, and the dialogue between the saint and the queen:

> Da sprach die keyserin czu Katherina / bitt Gott das er mein sel empfach / da sprach si Laß dir deinen leyb durch gott neme*n* So wirt dir heutt vmb eynen armen tod ein reyches leben vn*d* wirt dir heut Got geben fur einen ewigen breuttigam · Da wardt sie gar fro / vn*d* sprach czu dem schergenn daz er alles daz an ir thet das

---

of her sexuality, focusses attention on them and recalls depictions of the martyrdom of Saint Barbara such as that by the Dominican Meister Francke discussed by Bob Mills in 'Invincible Virgins', Chapter 4 of *Suspended Animation. Pain, Pleasure & Punishment in Medieval Culture* (London: Reaktion, 2005), pp. 106–44. Saint Agatha also had her breasts cut off. Faustina's martyrdom plays to sadistic sexual fantasy whilst simultaneously rendering her body a 'pained entity as a focal point for desire and spiritual transcendence' (Mills, *Suspended Animation*, p. 106). Wogan-Browne, on the other hand, argues against torture as 'the fulfilment of clerical sexual fantasy', seeing it instead as 'the articulation of transcendence' and as the means to 'distinguish revenge and sacrifice, earth and heaven, pagan and Christian' (*Saints' Lives*, p. 108).

[207]   Jenkins and Lewis, 'Introduction', p. 11.

er wolt / da schlug man ir das haubt ab vnd ließ sie vor den hun̄den ligen / da fur
ir sel czu den ewygen frewdenn. (fol. ccliij^v)[208]

[Then the Empress said to Saint Katherine, 'Ask God to receive my soul'. To this
she replied, 'Let go of your body for the sake of God and today you will be given
a rich life in return for a poor death and today you will be given God as your
spouse for eternity'. Then the Empress's mood turned to utter joy and she told the
executioner to do to her what he would. Then she was beheaded and her body was
left lying for the dogs. Her soul then ascended to eternal joy].

Three things stand out here: first, Katherine's function as an intermediary
between the petitioning human in need and God, a role she subsequently
assumes as one of the *Vierzehn Heiligen*, the group of helper saints particularly
popular in Southern Germany;[209] second, Faustina's future status as a bride of
Christ;[210] and, third, the queen's joyful, even eager, acceptance of martyrdom, an
attitude that validates her suffering intra- and extra-textually.

The next stage towards Katherine's martyrdom is Porphyrius, who buries the
queen's body at night.[211] In his fury and a gesture reminiscent of King Herod,
Maxentius causes innocent blood to be shed in trying to discover the culprit.
Porphyrius' confession that he not only interred the queen but is himself a
Christian leads to his martyrdom and that of his knights:

Da sprachen sye all Vnser herr vnd wir haben einen rechten glauben an vns
genomen vnd glauben an vnser herren Jhesum Cristum / wann es ist der war gott
/ von dem wollen wir nit kum̄men / was wir darumb leyden sullenn Da ward der
keyser gar czornig vnd hyeß die zwey hundert ritter enthaubten das liden sie geren
durch gott / vnd furen ir selen czu den ewigen frewden Da gab in got der marter
lon. (fol. ccliiij^r)

[Then they all said, 'We and our lord have accepted the true faith and we believe
in Our Lord Jesus Christ, for He is the true God. We shall not forsake Him,
whatever we may suffer for His sake'. On hearing this the Emperor was enraged
and ordered the two hundred knights to be beheaded. They suffered this gladly

---

[208]   This is a clear echo of the story of Jezebel. See Chapter 1, this volume.

[209]   Funk, *Glasfensterkunst*, p. 39; Vera Schauber and Hanns Michael Schindler,
Bildlexikon der Heiligen (Munich, 1999), p. 416.

[210]   This could also echo the nun's "death" to the secular world and resurrection to
spiritual life in the convent on taking the veil.

[211]   This may be reminiscent of Joseph of Arimathea's burial of Christ's body, which he,
however, does beg from Pilate and obtain permission to bury (Mark 15:43–6).

for the sake of God and their souls ascended to eternal joy. Then God gave them the martyrs' reward].

The use of direct speech for the knights' profession of faith both makes it more convincing, as if the reader were actually witnessing the scene, and encourages the reader to profess his own belief in God. Two hundred severed heads illustrate the pagan Maxentius' weakness as the execution creates martyrs who swell the ranks of God's elect and strengthen His forces. Finally, it "wraps up" the fate of the minor characters before the heroine, Katherine, takes centre stage for her big scene; and indicates the glory that awaits her, namely "der marter lon".

The final scene of Saint Katherine's legend, and the transcendent counterpart to the mystic marriage, is the most dramatic in the narrative, since Katherine conducts a dialogue with the disembodied voice of Christ:

> Da bracht ma*n* si an dy stat da man sie enthaubten wolt / da bat sie den schergen das er ir frist gebe / byst das sie yr gebet gesprach / das thet er / Da hub sie ire augen auff in den hymell vn*d* sprach · O herr Jhesu Criste ein czird vn*d* eyn heyl aller Cristen O gutter Jhesu ein ere vnd ein hoffnu*n*g aller iu*n*ckfrauen ich sag dyr genad vnd danck das du mich außerwelet hast / das ich durch deynen willen leyden sol / Vnd bitt dich auch durch alle dein gut / alle die menschen dy mich anruffen vnd mein leyden eren / das du den czu hilff kummest in allen iren noten. Da kam ein stymm von hymel vn*d* dye sprach · Kum meyn lyebe tochter vnd mein gemahel / des hymels thur stet die [*sic*] offen · Kum in d*a*z brautbet deynes gemahels / vnd alle die menschen dye dein marter erent vnd dich anruffent in iren notten den wil ich czu hilff ku*m*men in allem irem leyden. (fol. ccliiij^r)

[Then she was taken to the place where they wanted to behead her. Then she asked the executioner to give her time to say her prayers. He granted her request. Then she raised her eyes to Heaven and said, 'O Lord Jesus Christ, an ornament and salvation to all Christians, O, good Jesus, an honour and hope to all maidens, I give you grace and thanks that you have chosen me to suffer for your sake; and ask you through your supreme goodness to come to the aid of those who in their dire need call on me and honour my suffering'. Then a voice came down from Heaven and said, 'Come, my dear daughter and my spouse. Heaven's door stands open for you. Come to the bridal bed of your spouse; and all those people who honour your martyrdom and call on you in their dire need will I aid in all their tribulations'].

Faustina, Porphyrius, the knights and Katherine all profess their faith immediately prior to their execution, a ritual repetition reminiscent of the

Creed. Just as Faustina turns to Katherine with her request for God's grace, so Katherine turns to God Himself, her raising of her eyes to Heaven indicating the direction for the reader's physical and spiritual gaze. As her prayer is relayed in direct speech, it provides an actual model for emulation. Whereas at the start of the narrative Katherine's awareness of her exceptional nature focusses on her beauty, wisdom and secular royalty, here it focusses on her status as God's elect and channel of God's grace to those in need, explicitly as one of the *Vierzehn Heiligen*, with whom she is depicted in the Konhofer window and Memminger Altar and who, before their martyrdom, supposedly asked God to grant aid to anyone asking for it in their name. Thus a Nuremberg reader experiences, in a volume published in Nuremberg, Katherine assuming one of her main functions in not just the city but the entire region. In the Konhofer window Katherine's role as intercessor is illuminated by a light that symbolizes God's grace not just towards Katherine but towards the worshipper in the Lorenzkirche as well, so the pious reader may actually or imaginatively place himself beneath the Konhofer window and receive God's mercy. If Katherine's blood (from her flagellation and execution) is indeed fertile in producing new believers and strengthening the faith of old, then she has given birth as Christ's spouse in a manner that might also be emulated by Patrician women and the nuns of the Katharinenkloster, not as active martyrs but as models of devotion and support to others.

Christ's direct response stresses the filial and the spousal relationship, associating martyrdom and the bridal bed in language reminiscent of the Song of Songs.[212] Death becomes the consummation of Katherine's marriage to Christ in an image that recalls the language and visions of the mystics;[213] here

---

[212]   Whilst it is hard to find an exact parallel, the echo is unmistakable: e.g. 'My beloved spake, and said unto me, Rise up my love, my fair one, and come away' (Song of Songs 2:10).

[213]   For example, in Seuse's *Stundenbuch* the soul which has lost its bridegroom says: 'Da jener himmlische Bräutigam mir doch in seiner Liebe zuvorgekommen war, mich zu seiner Braut erwählt hat, sich mir mit seinem Ring verlobt und mich geschmückt hatte mit vielem. Honig und Milch habe ich oft aus seinem honigfließenden Mund empfangen. Hie und da kam ich in den Genuß eines Kusses von seinem Mund. Manchmal tröstete jener geistliche Bräutigam, Geliebter der Lilien, mich mit einer geistlichen Umarmung und erfüllte mich mit viel Gutem' [Since that heavenly bridegroom had anticipated me in His love, chosen me as His bride, betrothed me with His ring and adorned me with many things. I have often received honey and milk from His mouth from which honey flows. Now and then I have experienced the joy of a kiss from His mouth. Sometimes that spiritual bridegroom, lover of the lilies, comforted me with a spiritual embrace and filled me with much goodness] (Seuse, *Stundenbuch*, pp. 31–2). Katherine, like the Virgin, is frequently addressed in prayers as "rose" or "lily", so the linguistic resonances of this Dominican text contribute to the fusion of Katherine with her bridegroom Christ and of the believer's soul with the Godhead; and reprise the milk that flows from the saint's neck on her execution and spiritually nurtures her followers.

Christ's marriage vow becomes the promise to help those who ask for aid in her name. Her actual martyrdom mirrors Faustina's assumption: 'Da wardt sie gar fro / vnd neyget da ir kelen czu der erden Da schlug man ir / ir haubtt ab / vnd ir sel fur czu den ewigen frewden czu irem gemahel Jhesu Cristo da sie dy ymmerwerenden frewd vn*d* wu*n* hat' (ccliiij*r*).[214] The joy of martyrdom for Christ is iterated every time someone is killed in His name, a narrative device that manipulates and intensifies the reader's response. Even if he cannot assume the mantle of martyrdom, he can gladly tolerate, even seek out, suffering and hardship in *imitatio Christi*, strengthened by the knowledge of the bliss that awaits him. As with Faustina, Katherine's courage in accepting the pain of her execution masculinizes her (as did her wisdom and learning); the execution ensures her eternal union with her bridegroom Christ, thereby turning the vision of the mystic marriage into an eternal reality in a realm beyond human vision.

The account of Katherine's life ends on two miracles that signal to Maxentius and to the reader her already-saintly status:

> da geschahen czu hannd czwey grosse zeiche*n* D*a*z erst d*a*z schone millich von yr kelen flos / vnd machett das ertreich als feucht als begosse*n* ware / d*a*z was eyn zeichen irer magtlichen vnschuld · Das ander das dye Engell da waren / vnd huben iren leychna*m* hoch auff in den lufft / vnd furten in biß auff den perg Sinay da got die czehen gebot gab / wann es was niemant wirdig der dy heyligen Junckfrawen begrub / dann dy Engel / darumb bereitten sie ir ein czierlichs grab in eynem Marmelsteyn / vnd begrubent sie gar wirdigklichen. (fol. ccliiij*r*)

> [Then straightaway two great miracles happened. The first was that sweet milk flowed from her throat and made the earth as moist as if it had been watered. That was a sign of her virginal innocence. The second was that angels were present and lifted her body high into the air and carried it to the top of Mount Sinai, where God handed down the Ten Commandments, for no one was worthy of burying the holy maiden but the angels. Hence they prepared for her a finely wrought marble tomb and buried her with great honour].

Whilst the milk that flows from Katherine's neck may symbolize her innocence and purity, it also recalls the Virgin Mary and the latter's role as nurturing mother. Katherine, then, is the nurturing mother of her nuns and of all those who call on her for aid. In addition, her milk acts as a libation, watering the earth to make it fertile for other miracles and conversions – or for the text to which it has already

---

[214] 'Then she was filled with joy and bent her neck to the ground. Then she was beheaded and her soul ascended to eternal joy and to her spouse Jesus Christ, in whom she has everlasting joy and bliss'.

given rise. Her legend in the *Legenda Aurea* and *Der Heilgien Leben* could be seen as Katherine's child or the first fruit of her sacrifice. The transmutation of Katherine's blood – first shed during her flagellation – into milk echoes the transmutation of Christ's blood into wine during the mass but also symbolizes her transcendence of her earthly, fragile, pain-ridden body into redemption.[215] Miracles are, then, crucial as a demonstration of sanctity. Moreover, as Assion states: 'Von dem schon zu Lebzeiten und gerade bei der Passion durch Wunder verherrlichten Heiligen durfte daher in besonderem Maße auch nach seinem Tod Wunder bzw. wunderbare Hilfe erwartet werden'.[216] This first miracle, then, promises continuing miraculous intervention on behalf of those who invoke the saint's aid. That only angels are fit to bury her again marks her superiority over her shadow parallel, Faustina (buried by the mere mortal Porphyrius); whilst the parallels to Christ are resumed in the angels who place her in the marble tomb and mirror those guarding Christ's resting place. Katherine's burial on Mount Sinai, where God handed down the Ten Commandments to Moses, links the saint with the very foundations of Christianity and the laws governing it; with an earlier portentous dialogue between God and a mortal; and with the persecution and return home of a chosen people.[217] Through the association with Moses Katherine's authority is increased and her importance as a leader of the believer's soul to Christ asserted.[218] Katherine's burial in a site redolent of salvation and God's covenant with man is foregrounded in Katharinenkloster prayers that explicitly link Katherine, Mount Sinai and the pinnacle of virtue: 'du hast auch iren ersammen leichnam die engel heißen begraben · auf die höhe

---

[215]   According to Jenkins and Lewis, the milk that flows from Katherine's neck links her to 'grace given to St Paul on account of his virginity and not to any specifically female function of her physical body' (Jenkins and Lewis, 'Introduction', p. 10).

[216]   'From the martyr already exulted by miracles during his life and particularly during his martyrdom one could expect *post mortem* miracles and miraculous aid to a greater than usual extent' (Assion, *Mirakel*, pp. 107–8). Even before her death the miraculous shattering of the wheel marks Katherine out as particularly holy.

[217]   Lewis observes that the 'monastery on Mount Sinai became the focal point of the cult of St Katherine from the late tenth century onwards' (Katherine J. Lewis, 'Pilgrimage and the Cult of Saint Katherine in Late Medieval England', in *St Katherine of Alexandria. Texts and Contexts*, pp. 37–52 (p. 38)).

[218]   As earlier through Costis and Christ, her status is determined through the dominant male.

des perges synai / also verleihe vns genediglich · das wir gefürt werden zu der höhe der tugent'.[219] In addition, it is the sixth of her 'siben freud' (seven joys):[220]

FRew dich vor den andern wann von sunder vor gab hat dir got bereit ein wirdiges begrebtnuß auf dem perg synay in der hohe da dich vil menschen besuchen vnd von dem ölfluß von deinen gepeinen werden vil kranckheit geheilt Eia begrab vnß hertz in got vnd pit vns gesuntheit vnd parmhertzigkeit.[221]

[Rejoice above all others since as a special sign of favour God has prepared for you a worthy burial on the pinnacle of Mount Sinai. Many people will visit you there and the oil that flows from your bones will heal many illnesses. Hallelujah, bury our hearts in God and pray for [spiritual] health and mercy for us].

A Nuremberg reader, if a wealthy member of the ruling Patrician elite, might well have visited Katherine's grave on top of Mount Sinai as well as the Greek Orthodox monastery at its foot where her bones now lie and which had changed its original patron from the Virgin Mary to Katherine, possibly at the end of the tenth century.[222] Nuns in the Katharinenkloster unable to travel could

---

[219]   'You also commanded the angels to bury her worthy body on the pinnacle of Mount Sinai. In the same way mercifully grant us that we may be led to the pinnacle of virtue' (Stadtbibliothek Nürnberg, Cod. Cent. V, App. 81, fol. 104ʳ).

[220]   These, of course, recall the Seven Joys of the Virgin, another instance of Katherine being set up as a recursive reflexion of Mary (and, indeed, Christ).

[221]   Stadtbibliothek Nürnberg Cod. Cent. VII, 65, fol. 26ʳ⁻ᵛ. A similar wish is expressed in the *Gebetbuch* for Graf Ulrich VII von Montfort: 'Allmächtiger ewiger gott der du hast gegeben die gesaczte moysi jnn der hoche des bergs Synai vnd an der selbenn statt den lib der seligenn iungkfrowenn vnnd marterin Sannt Katherina durch din hailigenn enngeln wunderbarlichen gelegt hast wir bittenn dich gib vnns durch ir fürbitt vnd verdienen das mir wirdigklichenn zů dem berge der da cristus ist mügenn komen Durch den selbigenn vnnsern herren jhesum cristum dinen sun. Amen' [Almighty, eternal God, who passed down the Commandments of Moses on the pinnacle of Mount Sinai and miraculously had the body of the blessed virgin and martyr Saint Katherine placed on the same spot by your holy angels, we pray to you to give us, for the sake of her intercession and merit, that we be worthy to ascend the mountain on whose pinnacle sits Christ. In the name of the same, Our Lord Jesus Christ your Son. Amen] (Germanisches Nationalmuseum Hs. 1737, fol. 96ᵛ).

[222]   Jenkins and Lewis, 'Introduction', pp. 7–9. Hans Tucher and Sebald Rieter visited the monastery. Fabri has the following to say about its foundation and name: 'Now, in the reign of the Emperor Justinian, in the year of our Lord's Incarnation 1528 [*sic*], this same emperor was moved by the prayers of holy men to found on the place of the bush a church and monastery, in honour of the Blessed Virgin Mary, which he named the Church of St. Mary at Bush; and in the East it is so called to this day, but we, since the transition thither of St. Catharine, call it the Church and Monastery of St. Catherine' (Fabri, *Wanderings*, p. 611).

have visited the saint's resting place in their imagination: a tapestry now in the Germanisches Nationalmuseum and possibly woven in the Katharinenkloster c. 1440/50 depicts six angels placing the saint's body in an ornate marble tomb.[223] The decapitation wound in Katherine's neck is clearly visible, the red of the blood dripping from it being the same shade as her robe, the red panels and the red base of the tomb on which stands the angel holding her head. The resultant impression of a tomb overflowing with the saint's blood echoes the textual depiction of Katherine's body and tomb as an overflowing fountain pouring grace over her devotees. However, a more prominent *locus* of imaginative re-creation and devotion still was the altar endowed by Georg Fütterer in the sacristy of the convent church. Whilst painted panels show scenes from Saint Katherine's legend, its base is a slightly-less-than-life-sized limewood carving of the saint's body guarded by three angels.[224] The miracle which generated text is here rendered tangible, the word made wooden flesh. For nuns into whose spiritual flesh the text of the saint's legend was woven, the altar, as a possible site of physical pilgrimage within the convent, may have prompted a visualization of Katherine's translation and entombment as well as provided a substitute for an actual pilgrimage to Sinai.

Two further explicit analogies to Christ provide the transition into the account of miracles performed by the saint, the first being to His Flagellation:

> Auff dem perg da sand Katherina begraben ligt da seyen gar vil stein vnd ist in einem yeglichen stein ein zeichen als ein rutt / vnd wann man dy steyn auff einander schlecht / vnd als vil stuck darausz werdent So hat ein yeglichs stuck ein rutten Daz bedeut tet dy lieb in der sie die grossen schleg gedultigklichen leid an der seul mit den rutten. (fol. ccliiij')

---

[223]   This tapestry is one of a number woven either for the nuns' own use or on commission (Fries, 'Kloster und Kirche', pp. 59–61). Jane L. Carroll sees the weaving of tapestries in the convent as the desire of the reform movement to 'return the Dominican sisters to practical work', arguing that 'the production of tapestries, woodcuts, and illuminated manuscripts was deemed fitting labor for the patricians' daughters' (Jane L. Carroll, 'Woven Devotions. Reform and Piety in Tapestries by Dominican Nuns', in Jane L. Carroll and Alison G. Stewart (eds), *Saints, Sinners and Sisters. Gender and Northern Art in Medieval and Early Modern Europe* (Aldershot: Ashgate, 2003), pp. 182–201 (p. 185)). Weaving of scenes from saints' lives would also have been a form of contemplative devotion; even 'gifts to the glory of God' like those offered by the Magi (p. 195).

[224]   The painted panels are now in a side chapel off the north aisle of the Lorenzkirche; the carving is in the Germanisches Nationalmuseum. For an account of the altar and its donor, see Brandl, 'Der Katharinenaltar des Georg Fütterer'.

[On the mountain where Saint Katherine lies buried are many stones and in every stone is a symbol like a rod and when you hit one stone with another so that they shatter into many pieces, each stone has a rod inside it. That signifies the love in which she patiently endured the grievous blows from the rods when tied to the pillar].

Just as the wedding ring remains on Katherine's hand after the mystic marriage as visible witness to events in a reality beyond human vision, so the stones act as a tangible witness to events in human time but outwith the reader's own temporal reach and experience. Katherine's martyrdom is embodied in the physical landscape; geography and geology confirm the truth of divine history. Moreover, the pilgrim to Sinai could not only see these stones for himself but also bring one back to Nuremberg, a "relic" of the saint and physical link to the stages of her martyrdom. Nature itself, in the very fabric of the mountain, provides proof of Katherine's holiness and may thus be read as a witness to salvatory events.[225] Life and legend of the saint form the rod inside the stone of *Der Heiligen Leben*, which, no matter how many times it is reprinted, can be opened to reveal them and can be incorporated into the individual's devotional and temporal landscape: it is, finally, explicitly pointed out that Katherine died on a Friday, as did Christ. However, Christ was, according to the text, born on a Friday as well, so Katherine dies to be reborn to eternal life as Christ's bride. The date of her death is given as the year 315, an embedding within the chronology of remembered human experience and its documentation that situates the Christian reader in the direct line of descent from the saint, much as Katherine herself is located, in the Volckamer Tree of Jesse, in the direct line of descent from God.

---

[225]   The story of the stones echoes one reported in pilgrimage reports about the banana (also known as Adam's apple): the seeds that become visible when a banana is sliced open form the shape of a cross thought to symbolize that on which Christ was crucified.

1   Löffelholz Altar, Sebalduskirche: Saint Katherine and the Wheel

2   Löffelholz Altar, Sebalduskirche: Execution of Saint Katherine

3   Volckamer Window, Lorenzkirche

4   Konhofer Window (detail: Mystic Marriage), Lorenzkirche

5   Kaiserfenster (Imperial Window), Lorenzkirche

6   Memminger Altar, Lorenzkirche

7   Fütterer Altar, Lorenzkirche (formerly Katharinenkloster). Detail: Saint Katherine kneeling before the image of the Virgin Mary and Christ

8　　　　　Fütterer Altar, Lorenzkirche (formerly Katharinenkloster). Detail:
Saint Katherine debating with the philosophers before Maxentius

9   Fütterer Altar, Lorenzkirche (formerly Katharinenkloster). Detail: Empress Faustina and Porphyrius visiting Saint Katherine in jail

10   Fütterer Altar, Lorenzkirche (formerly Katharinenkloster).
Detail: the burning of the philosophers

11   Fütterer Altar, Lorenzkirche (formerly Katharinenkloster).
              Detail: the destruction of the wheel

12   Fütterer Altar, Lorenzkirche (formerly Katharinenkloster).
Detail: the execution of Saint Katherine

13   Fütterer Altar, Lorenzkirche (formerly Katharinenkloster).
Detail: Georg Fütterer and sons with Saint Andrew

Chapter 3

Manifesting Martyrdom: The Miracles of Saint Katherine

The miracles attributed to a saint, no matter how far removed in time, constitute, along with the physical relics, what is "left over", a less tangible link than bone, hair or clothes but one that nevertheless opens for the believer a conduit into a realm of the spiritual imagination where human anxiety and hope for redemption may merge with the divine promise of salvation as preached by the clergy and embodied in the physicality of church and monastic buildings.[1] Through the sanctity of their content, the manuscripts and printed books that transmit miracle stories themselves become paler relics, shadows, ever-smaller images reflected in multiple mirrors in a process of holy recursive reflexion reminiscent of that observed by the Lady of Shalott:

> And moving thro' a mirror clear
> That hangs before her all the year
> Shadows of the world appear.[2]

The text of Katherine's miracle stories is the 'web' into which the 'mirror's magic sights' are woven (Stanza 8, ll. 1–2). Looking into the mirror – by reading the miracle stories – enables the believer to witness divine power manifested in the physical realm; to imagine himself as recipient of God's grace in the form of a miracle performed through the conduit of a favourite saint; and to anchor into his own life hope of salvation as long as he remains faithful to that saint. Indeed, like the Virgin, Katherine herself is compared to a mirror: 'O lauter spiegel den die heiligen engel an wider glantz ·so lüsticlich schawent'.[3] Looking into

---

[1]   Goodich also sees miracles as a source of 'continuing solace against the disorder and violence of the world' (Michael E. Goodich, *Violence and Miracle in the Fourteenth Century. Private Grief and Public Salvation* (Chicago and London: University of Chicago Press, 1995), p. 1).

[2]   Alfred, Lord Tennyson, 'The Lady of Shalott', Stanza 6, ll. 1–3.

[3]   'O flawless mirror into which the holy angels look so joyfully without reflexion' (Stadtbibliothek Nürnberg, Cod. Cent. V, App. 81, fol. 133ᵛ).

the mirror may even enable the reader to become integrated into the recursive reflection itself:

> More than any other type of artwork ... mirrors invite the beholder to experience the act of looking as a self-conscious activity. The unique function of a mirror's reflective surface is to solicit the gaze of a beholder, whose reflected image becomes in a sense part of the object itself.[4]

Mirrors symbolize self-knowledge, so the reader may read Katherine's miracle stories, recognize himself in their fallible sinners and repent. As Susan L. Smith continues:

> In a mirror, a woman sees herself seeing, as the active possessor of the sense of sight. In a mirror, however, this identification is inherently unstable for, at the same time that she sees herself in the mirror as one who looks, she also sees herself as an image that is looked upon – as the object of a gaze that under normal conditions is that of another, whose viewing position the mirror thus encourages her to assume.[5]

Reading the miracle stories may thus have encouraged the reader to view himself as an object regarded by God as in need of stabilizing through penance and the constant exercise of virtue. Manifestation of divine power may be geographically and temporally dislocated, appearing in a place and time other than the reader's own, but – in the case of Saint Katherine – the light emitted by the saint herself radiates through the physical object that is the book to illuminate the reader's present, bathing him in redemptory grace in the same way as light streaming through stained-glass windows in a church.[6] Miracle stories thus become the windows into grace.

Like the woman beholder's self-identification in the mirror, however, medieval miracle stories are inherently unstable in that they can wander from saint to saint: although a collection of Katherine miracle stories had been known in Germany since the *Dialogus miraculorum* (1223/4) by Caesarius von Heisterbach, it was expanded in the fourteenth century by the addition of reworked Marian miracles. Other sources include Thietmar's *Peregrinatio* (1217), which contains stories brought back by pilgrims from Saint Katherine's

---

4   Smith, 'The Gothic Mirror', p. 74.
5   Smith, 'The Gothic Mirror', p. 74.
6   Theologically, light symbolizes life, the soul, salvation, bliss and emanation, virtue, the Law, justice, the glory or presence of God, Christ Himself (John 8:12) and the illumination of the world through Christianity.

tomb on Sinai; and another miracle tale, *Lúpold von Wiltingen*.[7] According to Assion, Latin versions of the legend already included an appendix with miracle stories, some of which were used as sermon *exempla* by Johannes Herolt.[8] The oldest extant German version of the appendix dates from the late-fourteenth century.[9] However, the fact that the miracles of Saint Katherine are adapted from various oral and written sources, including the miracles of the Virgin Mary, is less

---

[7]   Assion, 'Katharina von Alexandrien', col. 1070–1. Assion identifies nine Marian miracles.

[8]   Johannes Herolt (d. 1468) was a Dominican confessor, preacher and from 1451 *Generalvikar* at the Katharinenkloster in Nuremberg. Boundaries between genres were fluid: whilst miracle stories could be used as sermon *exempla*, sermon *exempla* functioned as the basis for secular literature: the courtesy text *Le livre du chevalier de la Tour Landry* (1370–1) includes a number of stories adapted from a collection of sermon tales from the latter half of the thirteenth century, the *Miroir des bonnes femmes*. See J.L. Grigsby, 'Miroir des bonnes femmes', *Romania*, 82 (1961): 458–81 and *Romania*, 83 (1962): 30–51; and 'A New Source of the *Livre du Chevalier de la Tour Landry*', *Romania*, 84 (1963): 171–208. The Strasbourg preacher Johann Geiler von Kaisersberg (1445–1510) preached a series of sermons in the cathedral based on Sebastian Brant's *Das Narrenschiff* (Basel: Johann Bergmann von Olpe, 1494). Geiler's sermons were published in Strasbourg in 1511 under the title *Navicula sive speculum fatuorum praestantissimi sacrarum literarum doctoris Joannis Geiler Keysersbergii*. Campana points out that from the thirteenth century onwards popular preachers such as Jacques de Vitry included saints' legends such as those found in the *Legenda aurea* as illustrative examples in their sermons (Luc Campana, *Die 14 Heiligen Nothelfer* (Lauerz: Theresia, 2008), p. 37).

[9]   It is is found in Stadtbibliothek Nürnberg, Cod. Cent. IV, 43 (Assion, *Mirakel*, pp. 55–6). Assion's is the fullest account of the sources, development and transmission of the miracles attached to Saint Katherine and includes a list of sources for the additional miracle stories (p. 481). He postulates that the miracles were included in *Der Heiligen Leben* between 1363 and the end of the fourteenth century (Assion, *Mirakel*, p. 58); the collection of miracle stories found in Stadtbibliothek Nürnberg, Cod. Cent. IV, 43 seems to remain unchanged in all later versions of *Der Heiligen Leben* (Assion, *Mirakel*, p. 60). Only the Virgin Mary (88) and Petrus Damianus (30) boast more than Katherine (29, including the *Milch- und Bestattungswunder*). Saint Elisabeth of Thuringia comes next with 27; Sebaldus, the patron saint of Nuremberg, only has six miracles to his name (Assion, *Mirakel*, pp. 59–60). Whilst the attribution of posthumous miracles to saints is not uncommon, Katherine's are remarkable for the richness and variety of the material (Assion, *Mirakel*, p. 60). Eis divides the miracle stories surrounding Saint Katherine into three groups: 1) those about Sinai and Saint Katherine's Monastery there; 2) those taken over from other saints, especially the Virgin Mary; 3) sagas connected to certain places and found in other collections such as Caesarius von Heisterbach (Gerhard Eis, 'Lupold von Wiltingen. Eine Studie zum Wunderanhang der Katharinenlegende', in *Festschrift für Wolfgang Stammler zu seinem 65. Geburtstag*, ed. Wolfgang Stammler, Gerhard Eis, Johannes Hansel and Richard Kienast (Berlin: Erich Schmidt, 1953), pp. 81–3).

important for four reasons: first, this was a not uncommon practice;[10] second, a reader may or may not have been aware of the source narratives; third, even if he were, any confluence with, say, the miracles of the Virgin may only have served to reinforce the authority and prestige of Saint Katherine, who acts as a "shadow" Mary imbued with similar concern for her devotees and similar powers of advocacy with God; fourth, the incorporation of oral sources in the form of pilgrims' reports from Saint Katherine's grave and of miracles attributed also to

---

[10]   For example, even the healing oil that flows from Saint Katherine's bones is not peculiar to her: when Saint Walpurgis, sister to Saint Wunbold, was exhumed prior to the translation of her remains to Eichstätt, healing oil dripped from her fragrant bones and, unlike Katherine's, continued to flow. Prior to exhumation a great light from heaven had illuminated and sweet scent radiated from her bones; these manifestations of sanctity also possessed healing powers. Saint Walpurgis' speciality seems to have been the cure of lameness and malformed limbs (*Der Heiligen Leben*, fol. xciiij^(r-v)). Similarly, Saint Dominic's legend shares a number of features with Saint Katherine's: just as her star lights the way to her tomb for Hans Tucher and his companions, so a woman dreams Saint Dominic was born with a shining star on his forehead that symbolizes his victory over heresy. His learning is emphasized, especially his mastery of Christian doctrine. In a challenge to heretics to establish whose beliefs are truer, Dominic has Christian and heretical writings burnt; and, just as the philosophers burnt by Maxentius go to Heaven, so do the Christian books jump out of the fire whilst the heretical ones are consumed. He even has similar visions: for example, in one Mary appears with two virgin saints and salves the body of Riwalt, a fatally ill Dean of Rome, upon which he recovers and becomes 'an tugent vn*d* an heylikeyt vn*d* an golticher lere eyn liechter spigel' [a shining mirror of virtue and holiness and God's teaching] (*Der Heiligen Leben*, fol. c^r) (cf. Saint Katherine's salving of the poisoned count in the Holy Land, which she carries out with the help of Saints Margaret, Cecelia and Thecla (*Der Heiligen Leben*, fol. cclix^v)). In another three beautiful maidens appear to him in the dormitorium. Dominic recognizes the particularly lovely one in the middle as Mary and kneels down to worship her; she then declares that Christ has made her a special protector of the Dominican Order. The other two are Saints Katherine and Cecilia. Dominic then enjoys a further vision in which he sees Heaven and his fellow monks sheltered under Mary's cloak (*Der Heiligen Leben*, fol. c^v–cj^r). The echoes reinforce Dominic's own status as Christian saint; anchor the Virgin Mary and Saint Katherine more firmly in the Dominican Order as its protectors; and illustrate that order's tradition of privileged (visionary) access to God. The male Dominic outstrips the female Katherine, however, in that, through prayer and in Christ's name, he manages to instigate miracles whilst still alive, a number of which echo Christ's own: he drives out evil spirits (*Der Heiligen Leben*, fol. c^v and fol. cj^v); saves men from shipwreck (*Der Heiligen Leben*, fol. cj^r); raises a man from (near-) death (*Der Heiligen Leben*, fol. cj^v); multiplies loaves and turns water into wine (*Der Heiligen Leben*, fol. cij^v); he even translocates (*Der Heiligen Leben*, fol. cij^v). Such parallels signal Dominic's exceptional status, earned through the battle against heretics documented in his *vita*, which in turn reassures the reader that membership of the Dominican order and devotion to Saint Katherine are doctrinally unimpeachable, guaranteeing him the Virgin's favour and protection and the ability to resist evil.

other saints weaves Katherine firmly into a web of sanctity that stretched across and beyond medieval Europe into the Holy Land and Egypt. In Nuremberg, that web was enmeshed with the fabric of the city: in the mid-fifteenth century a Katherine miracle was recorded at a side altar in the Katharinenkirche actually dedicated to the Ten Thousand Knights.[11] For the Nuremberg reader, who may have himself have undertaken the pilgrimage to Sinai and heard the miracle reports on the site of their generation, this larger web was mirrored in the microcosm of his own context, not just in text but also in the local miracle, sign of the saint's active presence in the city and God's grace at work; and in 'magic sights', that is, the many images of Saint Katherine in the churches, monastic foundations, public and private buildings in Nuremberg, all of which images had the potential to come alive as they do in the miracle stories. Through inhabiting this marked-out space, the reader himself becomes woven into the web and his potential as a recipient of the divine grace mediated by Katherine is realized. Much the same could be claimed for the nuns in the Katharinenkloster, where in 1455–61 a list was compiled of literature suitable for reading aloud during meals on Sundays and feast days. It included a manuscript compiled by Kunigund Niklasin that contained the legend and miracles of Saint Katherine; these were read out at meals on the feast of the discovery of Saint Katherine's body (13 May) and on her actual feast day (25 November).[12] Katherine's *vita* and miracles thus helped shape the liturgical year and lives of the cloistered nuns, for whom their foundation may, as site of the German translation of the *Legenda aurea* and other versions of her life and miracles, have become *lux*, a mirroring source of the light radiated by the saint and illuminating the stones of convent and city.[13] This light, like that transmitted through the Volckamer window, did not just bathe nuns in redemption: it actualized their potential as brides of

---

[11]   This unspecified miracle was recorded by Katharina von Mühlheim (the first sextoness after the reform of 1428) in a list of feast days and their ceremonies from 1436. The altar was the seventh, but '[m]an eret avch sant katerina gar fleißig auf dem alter von eines zeichens wegen, daz do pey ist geschehen' [Saint Katherine is also honoured assiduously at that altar because of a miracle that happened there]. Assion points out that no other mention of this miracle exists and that it was not included in any of the miracle collections in the convent. However, on Saint Katherine's feast day the first mass of the day was celebrated at this altar rather than the main one (Assion, *Mirakel*, pp. 98–9). The Sensenschmid edition of *Der Heiligen Leben* includes the legend of 'zehen tauset martrern' (fol. xlviij^r–lj^r), who are referred to as knights. According to the *Handwörterbuch des deutschen Aberglaubens*, during Hadrian's reign the 10,000 knights were thrown off Mount Ararat and pierced through by thorns on landing. Their feast day is 22 June (vol. 5, p. 1726).

[12]   Assion, *Mirakel*, pp. 95–6.

[13]   See Camille, *Gothic Art*, p. 42.

Christ to be shadow Katherines and recipients of visions in their turn.[14] Saint Katherine, incarnated in the codex in which her miracles are copied, leaves the convent to move through the streets of Nuremberg, fixing it at the heart of the web of associations, influences and sanctity spun by the German translation of *Der Heiligen Leben*. In this chapter her miracle stories will be analysed, first, as testimonies to the saint's continued impact on and importance for Nuremberg; second, as documents of her wider European context.

In *Der Heiligen Leben* Katherine's martyrdom and translation to Sinai are located within the early history of the Christian Church: Silvester is Pope and Mayencius is Emperor (fol. ccliiij^r).[15] The consequent welding of martyrdom and miracles into what is recognizably the reader's own recorded and hence accessible time locates him in the history of salvation that continues to shape his world. Since these stages in the construction of Katherine's literal and literary corpus preface the account of miracles on Sinai, the power of Katherine's miracles is appropriated to the service of the early and the contemporary Church: 'Es geschahen auch gar vil czeychen auff dem perg da dy heylig Juckfraw begraben ist / vnd fleusset alle tag oll auß irem grab vnd von iren gelidern oder wo irs gepeins ist da tropfet oll herauß' (fol. ccliiij^r).[16] Thus the miracles constitute the positive current of her martyrdom: they are the oil flowing from her coffin, as are the prayers directed to the saint. As we have seen in the *Gebetbuch* for Graf Ulrich

---

[14]   However, the prior of the Katharinenkloster from 1425 to 1428, Eberhard Mardach, expressed grave reservations about visions in his 'Sendbrief' of 1422: 'solche andacht und innikeit, solche süssikeit und offenbarunge, solche züge und gesichte, soch [*sic*] ingezogenheit und mangel der speiß, und des geleicht vil; Die sint wol gut wen sie von got sint und von genaden und wen sie demütiglichen enpfahen kan, nutzlichen brauchen, und weißlichen halten. Aber es sint nicht ... ware zaichen der heilikeit, noch rechter warer sicher andacht, wan sie sint oft und dik gar unsicher, ungewise, und betrögelichen' [such devotion and such transports, such sweetness and such revelations, such witness and visions, such introversion and renunciation of food and much more of the same – these things are good when they come from God and His grace and when they can be received with a humble heart, put to good use and wisely observed. However, they are not true signs of holiness or proper, true and certain devotion, for they are often and frequently very unsure, uncertain and deceptive] (Jeffrey Hamburger's transcription of a passage from Stadtbibliothek Nürnberg MS Cent. VI 43m, fols. 2^r–2^v (Hamburger, *The Visual and the Visionary*, p. 586, n. 99)).

[15]   The following analysis will discuss the miracle stories individually and sequentially. Whilst this methodology may seem cumbersome, it mirrors the structure of the narrative, allows continuities and links to be thrown into sharper relief and suggests the cumulative effect of reading the stories sequentially (whilst recognizing that they may have been dipped into at random). However, only selected stories will be discussed.

[16]   'Numerous miracles happened on the mountain where the holy virgin lies buried; and oil flows from her tomb every day and wherever her limbs are or her bones oil drips out from them'.

VII von Montfort, Katherine's burial on Sinai and association with Moses and the Law signal her particularly favoured status at the heart of Christian history and doctrine, a status important not just to the nuns in the Katharinenkloster but to lay people as well. This is confirmed by the *Gebetbuch* (1460 and 1550) of Katharina Peutinger, wife of Christoff Peutinger, *Stadtpfleger* in Augsburg. It contains the following antiphon:

> Gegrüsset seyest du heilige iunckfraw zart / entsprunge*n* vnd geboren von hoher küniglicher art / übertreffenlichen hoch vnd wol gelert / durch dich seint die fünfftzig kü*n*streicher bekert. Du nun selige marterin Katharina / rastest auff dem hohe*n* berg Syna, auff dem Moyses von gott / hat empfange*n* die zehe*n* gebott. do hin bist du gefüret mitt engelischer handt, do bey wirt dein besonder heiligkeit erka*n*t, heylsam öle trüffet von deine*m* gebein / machet vil krancken gesunt vnd rein. Eya ich dein armer diener vnd knecht / wölst mir vnd alle*n* meine*n* geschlecht, wan*n* du ye ein besondere grosse nothelfferin bist / erwerbe*n* von deine*n* liebste*n* gemahel Jesu Christ / auch gesunthait gnad vnd barmhertzigkait / vnd ain seliges von hinne*n* abschaidt. Das bitt ich auß hertze*n* demütigklich / o Junckfraw*n* rain / wöllest erhöre*n* mich. Ame*n*.[17]

> [Hail, you holy and tender virgin, descended and born from high royal lineage, excellently and immensely learned, on whose account the 50 wise and skilful philosophers converted. Now, holy martyr Katharine, you rest on high Mount Sinai, on which Moses received the Ten Commandments from God. Angelic hands bore you there and your particular sanctity was thus recognized; healing oil drips from your bones and makes many sick people healthy and pure again. Alas, I am your poor servant and slave: please be so gracious as to win, from your dearest spouse Jesus Christ, health, grace, mercy and a blessed end for me and all my lineage, for you are a helper great beyond all others. I ask you this with a humble heart. O pure virgin, hear my prayer. Amen].

The flowing of oil acts as a metaphor for the course and effect of the narrative: just as the oil flows out of Katherine's bones and grave to heal, so the story of her martyrdom flows into the miracle stories, actualizing her virtue in the service of those who call on her for help. Hence a Katharinenkloster prayer states: 'Vber all genad ist das ein wunderlichst das dein gelider im grab flißen in öl vnd auß in entspringt von *christ*i guttigkeit zu meru*n*g cristenlichs glawbe*n*s vn*d* zu meru*n*g deins verdiene*n*s'.[18] The structure imposed by the narrative is the river bed guiding

---

[17]   Germanisches Nationalmuseum Hs. 117 254, fol. 294–5.

[18]   'It is a most wondrous mercy above all mercies that in your tomb your limbs flow in oil which springs from them by the goodness of Christ so that the Christian faith may be

the course of oil and grace. Further, the flowing of oil functions as a metaphor for the effect of the miracles on the lives of recipients and readers: the beneficiaries of the miracles experienced divine grace flooding into their lives; readers of the miracle stories, depending on reading practice, feel reflected grace flowing into theirs.[19] Indeed, a Katharinenkloster prayer makes the analogy explicit in its reference to the 'prunen *der* gotlichen gutwilligkeit'.[20] This flow continued in contemporary Europe: as suggested by the phrase, 'wo irs gepeins ist da tropfet oll herauß',[21] Katherine's bones had been dispersed as relics and with them the grace brought by her martyrdom and manifested in her miracles.[22] As we have seen in 'Saint and the City', pilgrims to Sinai were both given cotton wool in which the saint's bones had lain and permitted to dip cotton wool into the oil that flowed from them. By taking these contact relics home with them, they aided this dispersion and became, like Hans Tucher and Felix Fabri, active conduits of grace themselves. Felix Fabri, who travelled in 1483–4, sheds further light on the practice:

> The sacred bones seem to have lain in oil, because they are not white, but are of the colour which a bone or piece of wood contracts by lying in oil. It is the belief of the holy church that the virgin's limbs once sweated forth oil; but this miracle has now ceased for a long while, and the holy limbs are swathed in silk, pieces of which are now given to pilgrims instead of oil. They soak these pieces of silk in the lamps which hang in the chapel of St. Mary at Bush, and so take them home as St. Catherine's oil. I had a little glass bottle, which I filled with this same oil, and

---

spread and your merits be multiplied' (Stadtbibliothek Nürnberg, Cod. Cent. VII, 65, fol. 19ᵛ–20ʳ).

[19]   That is, depending on whether they read the miracle stories in one sitting or one or two at a time; sequentially or randomly.

[20]   'fountain of divine benevolence' (Stadtbibliothek Nürnberg, Cod. Cent. VII, 65, fol. 5ᵛ).

[21]   'wherever her bones are, oil drips from them' (fol. ccliiijʳ).

[22]   There were relics (three small bones) in the monastery of the Holy Trinity in Rouen (Walsh, *The Cult of St Katherine*, p. 63). Moreover, in the eleventh century a monk called Simeon is meant to have brought one of Katherine's fingers to Rouen, where the Bishop of Rouen commanded a church (now destroyed) be built for it on Saint Katherine's Hill (La Côte Sainte Catherine). Both the Frauenkirche and the Katharinenkloster in Nuremberg possessed a Katherine relic. That in the Katharinenkloster was kept in a small gold reliquary statuette in the sacristy and displayed on her feast day, when the church was visited by inhabitants of the entire city (Assion, *Mirakel*, pp. 98–9). Hans Tucher mentions the right arm and a hand of Saint Katherine in the chapel of the Grand Master of the Hospitallers on Rhodes (Tucher, *'Reise'*, p. 365).

soaked much wool therewith; yet it is known that the oil taken from the aforesaid place is very efficacious on silk.[23]

Such "relics" of Saint Katherine in Patrician homes brought Sinai to Nuremberg (or, in Fabri's case, to Ulm) and interacted with the relics in the Katharinenkloster and Frauenkirche to potentize the saint's presence there. Indeed, a small hollow in the chest of the wooden sculpture of the saint's body at the base of the Fütterer Altar in the convent sacristy may once have contained relics of the saint. Thus the altar literally housed Sinai and the saint in Nuremberg and the reality of her physical presence in the city may have confirmed, in the worshipper's mind, the reality of the miracles recorded in her legend.

Establishing the physical context for the miracles frames the ensuing narrative, which starts by recording miracles related to Sinai itself, leaving the primacy of its claim on the saint in no doubt. The first miracle story relates the pilgrimage to the Holy Land and Sinai of Saint Diemer,[24] so the validity of pilgrimage to Katherine's tomb is immediately affirmed by a male saint who provides an authoritative role model for the reader and authoritative witness for the splendour of Katherine's coffin, a splendour which functions as both an outward manifestation of her elect status and as proof of God's miraculous powers, since it hovers in mid-air:[25]

> sach das grab vnd den sarch Sanndt Katherinen / der was so adelich bereittet von den Engeln in einem Marmelstein vnd schwebt vnd waz erhebt von dem erttreych / vnd sach das man daz grab da auff vnd czu thet vnd sach daz oll darinnen flyessen / Da gyenng der Bischoff mit ym / vnd beteten gar mit grossem fleyß vnd andacht / Vnd der Bischoff thet ym das grab der heyligen Junckfrawen sant Katherina auff vnd hyeß in hin einsehen / da sach diemer gar ein schonß heyliges antlutz vnd kusset es mit grosser andacht / vnnd ire gelider an einander hangen vnnd sach sy ob dem oll schwymmen vnd sach das oll flyessen von allen yren gelidern. (fol. ccliiij^{r-v})

---

[23]   Fabri, *Wanderings*, p. 601.

[24]   According to Assion, the Diemer story is taken from stories pilgrim brought back with them from Sinai. Diemar became confused with Thietmar/Ditmar/Thiemo, an Archbishop of Salzburg, who wrote a travel report himself in which he lists Katherine's miracles (Assion, *Mirakel*, pp. 205–9).

[25]   Mohammed's sepulchre at Mecca also hovered in mid-air. According to the Dean of Mainz Cathedral Bernhard von Breidenbach this was an irreverent parody of the Ascension and further example of the Prophet's fraudulence, since the elevation is achieved by the cunning use of magnets (Bernhard von Breidenbach, *Die heyligen reyssen gen Jherusalem* (Mainz: Erhard Reuwich, 1486), fol. 65^v–66^r). In Muslim-controlled Egypt the genuine sanctity of Christianity triumphs implicitly over the fake sanctity of Islam.

[He saw the grave and the sarcophagus of Saint Katherine, which was so nobly wrought by the angels in marble and hovered and was raised from the ground. He saw the grave being opened and closed and saw the oil flowing within it. Then the bishop went with him and they prayed with great dedication and devotion; and the bishop opened the grave of Saint Katherine for him and told him to look inside; and Diemer saw a lovely, holy countenance and kissed it with great devotion. He saw her limbs joined together and saw them swimming on top of the oil and saw the oil flowing from all her limbs].

First, Katherine's nobility (actual and metaphorical) is displayed by her tomb.[26] Second, that the tomb was prepared for her by angels further signals her sanctity and status as one of God's chosen elite; the use of marble recalls the tomb monuments of aristocrats and royalty throughout Europe, so establishes the saint in a familiar memorial and hierarchical landscape.[27] Sepulchral hovering locates the tomb between heaven and earth, symbolizing Katherine's status as an intermediary between mankind and God. Within the narrative Diemer acts as an eyewitness to Katherine's still-active miraculousness as transformed into flowing oil, his own sanctity rendering him an unimpeachable guarantor. Moreover, the sixfold repetition of "sach" [saw] within a relatively short passage, combined with the infinitive "einsehen" [look into], emphasizes sight as the conduit to divine truths behind the fabric of earthly existence. In Katherine's legend we have seen the game of vision denied and vision granted. Here, after the saint's martyrdom, her virtue is unquestionable and sight of her is immediately granted the pilgrim. Her sanctity is on public display; and Diemer resembles a news journalist reporting live from the scene, the repetition of "sach" replacing the seeing lens of the camera. Diemer also serves to confirm ritual practice in the monastery at the foot of Mount Sinai (the opening and shutting of the coffin in the presence of pilgrims).[28] This acts as a double assurance to a reader either sceptical of oil flowing from bones or afraid he might be denied sight of the body if he visits Sinai; it also illustrates the first flowing of Katherine's martyrdom into an admittedly unusual, because saintly and therefore particularly exemplary, pilgrim-devotee's life.[29] Intense prayer and devotion are also presented as channels to privileged vision, since they

---

[26]   Fabri describes the coffin as follows: 'The coffin stands on the right-hand side of the choir, in a high place. It is made of white polished marble, and on its surface all round there are carved figures and plants with leaves' (Fabri, *Wanderings*, p. 602).

[27]   See also Paul Binski, *Medieval Death. Ritual and Representation* (London: British Museum Press, 1996).

[28]   See also Fabri, *Wanderings*, pp. 599–602.

[29]   Sensenschmid's *Der Heiligen Leben* contains no stories of Diemer but Assion refers to some in a Berlin manuscript.

precede the bishop's opening of the coffin to allow Diemer sight of Katherine's face. Her uncorrupted beauty (her face is "schonß" [lovely]) suggests a further miracle, namely the preservation of the corporeal remains (a reverse Pygmalion-like transformation of marble statues into flesh that echoes, yet transcends, the unchanging figures on tomb monuments) as an external sign of her everlasting life in God and the continuing power of her virtue. The freezing of decay also symbolizes the eternal, incorruptible mercy and love of God; and Katherine's body functions as an advertising billboard for God's power that prompts more intense devotion in pilgrims anxious for a sign of His grace. Moreover, the face-to-face encounter with an individual identifiable through her appearance suggests a "real", potentially reciprocal, relationship between devotee and saint that is actively expressed in Diemer's kissing of Katherine's face, an act of devotion that mirrors the love of a suitor for his sweetheart.[30] Katherine thereby assumes a status in death – that of desired lover – rejected by her in life but foreshadowing her relationship to her male admirers in the miracle stories, in which she at times conducts herself like a jealous sweetheart.[31] This relationship reflects the intensity of her followers' desire (possibly focussed on one image of the saint that comes alive in the imagination – or, in the miracle stories, actually). Dietmar's witnessing of the integrity of Katherine's body confirms the miraculous angelic reconstitution of remains on Sinai and God's power; it could also be read as symbolic of the believer's being healed and whole in God.[32] Since the body hovers above the oil

---

[30] Hence the kissing of Katherine's bones by Tucher and his companions may have constituted an authorized, traditional devotional practice. However, Fabri records that when his party went to see Saint Katherine's relics, the sacristan had trouble opening the tomb 'because both the locks and the keys were altogether covered with rust and out of order' (Fabri, *Wanderings*, vol. 2, part 2, p. 600). When the monks finally succeeded in wrenching open the coffin, the abbot 'plunged his head into the coffin, kissed that treasure house of heavenly wisdom, the virgin's sacred head, and then raising himself up again, remained standing beside the head of the coffin. After him all the monks drew near, beginning with the eldest, and kissed the holy relics in the same manner as the Abbot. After the monks we pilgrims went and worshipped the relics in the customary manner, and after us our ass-drivers did the same' (Fabri, *Wanderings*, vol. 2, part 2, p. 600). Fabri then touches the saint's head with the jewels given him by the noblemen in his party and entrusted to him in Ulm, thereby creating contact relics. The base of the Fütterer Altar may thus have acted as a substitute for the entombed body of Saint Katherine and opportunity to act out this devotion in Nuremberg.

[31] This relationship is most clearly evident in the story of the Graf's wife who commits suicide in the belief her husband is having an affair with the saint (fol. cclviij[r]–cclix[r]).

[32] By the time of Felix Fabri's second pilgrimage (1483–4) Saint Katherine's body was somewhat less intact as over half had been either stolen or given away. However, the 'greater part is still there' that is to say, the entire head of the holy virgin, covered with a golden crown adorned with many gems and with the symbol of sanctity; and the left hand, whose fingers are covered with exceedingly costly rings set with precious stones. The other hand, the monks told

and oil pours from its limbs, it becomes a fountain of divine grace, which flows – like the narrative – through the eyes into the reader's life and heart. The saint's body could even be seen as a baptismal font, the flowing oil as the water of baptism; by analogy the text also functions as a font since its words "baptize" the reader into a world of divine might, truth and promise beyond corporeal vision.[33] Like so much in the miracle stories, the events of Diemer's visit to the tomb are inherently spectacular, lending themselves to dramatic staging in the reader's imagination; they also recall the Three Marys' visit to Christ's tomb, continuing the fusion of Katherine and Christ begun in her *vita*.

Diemer's enquiry as to how the body came to the church allows the story of its translation from the top of Mount Sinai to be related within a natural context and fuses three layers of time: that of the translation; that of the account; and that of the fifteenth-century Nuremberg reader.[34] Through Diemer the reader accesses the miraculous past in a sort of narrative flashback much like a film: a hermit living by Mount Sinai saw radiance ("klarheyt") there day and night. This light may represent a continuation of the Biblical tradition surrounding the mountain and further cement Katherine into Old Testament authority:

> its especial praise and its holiness may be more distinctly gathered from many places in the canonical books of Scripture, such as Exod. iii., xix., xx., and Deut. v., where we are told that the mountain did burn with fire even up to the heavens, and throughout the Pentateuch, the Psalms, and the Prophets. In all these places we are taught that the Mount Horeb of Sinai is a most excellent and lofty mount ; a mount inhabited by God and frequented by angels ; a mount of light, fire, and burning ; a mount of dreadful clouds and darkness ; a mount of wisdom and learning ; a mount of pity and promise, of righteousness and cursing ; a mount of lightning and flashing fire ; a mount of trumpets and noise ; a mount of kindness and alliance ; a mount of clemency and propitiation ; a mount of sacrifice and prayer ; a mount of fatness ; and a mount of visions and contemplation.[35]

---

us, is in Georgia; but they of Rhodes boast that they possess it, and show it to pilgrims. We saw some of the ribs, shin-bones, and many other members of the holy virgin lying in the coffin' (Fabri, *Wanderings*, p. 601).

[33]   According to Yvonne Northemann, on 11 June 1359 an altar was consecrated in the sacristy of the Katharinenkirche that, in addition to such relics as a piece of the pillar on which Christ was flagellated and some of Saint Peter's hair, contained some of the oil from Saint Katherine's bones (Yvonne Northemann, *Zwischen Vergessen und Erinnern. Die Nürnberger Klöster im medialen Geflecht* (Petersberg: Michael Imhof, 2011), p. 75). Thus the fountain of grace flowed for the nuns within the very walls of the Nuremberg convent.

[34]   A fourth layer is, of course, that of the contemporary reader.

[35]   Fabri, *Wanderings*, vol. 2, part 2, p. 560.

The light emanating from Saint Katherine's resting place, created by the candles brought by angels honouring her tomb,[36] serves three purposes: it functions as a neon advertisement for the martyrdom narrative and divine presence on the mountain; it constitutes literal enlightenment of those ignorant of the saint's presence; and it serves as a symbol of God's power to illuminate the life of the contemporary reader through the power of His saints. Since the hermit who discovers the body mirrors the one who baptized Katherine, he symbolizes the culmination of Saint Katherine's path to Christ; he also enables future pilgrims to find their path to her. In their devotion to Katherine the angels function as models for Diemar and the reader; whilst the light of the candles constitutes the visible manifestation of Katherine's sanctity, the saint as *lumen*, part of Christ multiplied as the Light of the World. The candlelight belongs to a chain of recursive reflexions: much as the Burning Bush guided Moses to God, the candlelight acts as a beacon guiding people to the saint's body in a narrative parallel to the radiance emanating from Katherine's prison that drew Faustina and Porphyrius to the saint. The candlelight fuses further layers of devotional time by reflecting the Star that guides the Magi to the stable in Bethlehem and Saint Katherine's star that 15 centuries later guides Tucher and his companions to the monastery at Sinai.[37] God's signposting of Katherine's body continues the theme of Katherine as a mirror-image of Christ Himself, not least since the angels worshipping at Katherine's coffin recall the angels guarding Christ's sepulchre. As we have seen in the previous chapter, for the nuns in the Katharinenkloster at least this textual mirroring was rendered visible and tangible in the tapestry depicting the saint's entombment and on the Fütterer Altar. Life, legend, miracles, their textual and artistic renditions set up a series of images that continually reflect each other, a spiritual Hall of Mirrors that surrounds and traps the believer on all sides, continually confronting him with images of the holy and ensuring he cannot escape contemplation of himself and his sinfulness in contrast to the exemplar that is Katherine.

The hermit functions as messenger, descending the mountain – in a first step in the literary translation of her legend that mirrors the oil flowing from Katherine's bones – to tell the monks and bishop about 'das gesicht das er teglich sehe' (fol. ccliiij').[38] Even before their own sight of the body, monks and bishop are 'gar fro'

---

[36]   Candles lit the soul's way to God.

[37]   Tucher, 'Reise', p. 523. See Chapter 1 for a discussion of Saint Katherine's Star.

[38]   'the vision he has every day'. Fabri provides a slightly different version of the discovery of Saint Katherine's body: 'Now, in the monastery beneath Mount Horeb, the Father of the monks, a good man, often thought of going forth with his monks to seek for saints in the wilderness, but he always put off doing so. But one night he received a command in a dream to set out on the morrow with his monks and find a treasure which would be coveted by Easterns and Westerns alike. On the morrow he called all his monks together, and having told them of

[very happy], though on discovering the body in the coffin they fail to recognize it. Their puzzlement engenders mystery and awe that set the stage for the dramatic inner-narrative revelation. At this point the already-enlightened reader knows more than the participants in the intra-narrative drama, who occupy the spiritual darkness that is ignorance of divine presence. The response of the assembled men is recourse to the highest male authority, God, for an explanation. Katherine may be female, but nonetheless it is again men – ignorant though they may be – who steer her destiny and her afterlife as a saint:

> vnd rufften vnsern herren mit grosser andachtt an / vnd baten in das er in kund thet
> weß der leichnam were / Da erhort sie gott vnd sanndt einen Einsidel dar bey einnen
> Engel / den furten dy engel durch den lufft wol czweinczig tagweid von Allexandria
> da die lieb iunckfraw sant Katherina gemartert war biß zu dem perg Synai vnd der
> Einsidel saget yn das / das es der lieben Junckfrawen Sand Katherina leychnam were
> / der wirdigen martrerin / vnd saget in auch das sie in Allexandria gemartert wer
> vnd das nyemant wirdig were der sie begrube dann die heyligen Engel / dy hetten
> sie auff den perg gebracht mit grossem lob gesang vnd mit saytten spil. (fol. ccliiij^v)

> [and called upon our Lord with great devotion and asked Him to reveal to them
> whose corpse it was. Then God heard them and sent a hermit there by an angel.
> The angels bore him through the air a good 20 days' journey from Alexandria,
> where the dear virgin Saint Katherine had been martyred, as far as Mount Sinai.
> The hermit told them [the monks] that the corpse was that of the dear virgin Saint
> Katherine, the worthy martyr; and also told them that she had been martyred in
> Alexandria and that no one other than the holy angels was worthy of burying her.
> They had brought her to Mount Sinai with great songs of praise and music].

Again the appropriate devotional attitude is emphasized ("mit grosser andachtt")[39] as the prerequisite for access to the divine, prayer allowing knowledge and clarity (the "klarheyt" around Katherine's body). Prayer also instigates a dialogue with God, whose response is to send an angel to Alexandria to fetch a third hermit, the culmination of the trinity since he sheds light on Katherine's identity. Angels transport him back to Sinai through the air, echoing the translation of the

---

his vow, he kindled a vehement desire of finding this treasure in their hearts' (Fabri, *Wanderings*, p. 605). Father and monks are led by God to a cave where they encounter the hermit who relates his visions of light on top of the mountain. Together they climb the mountain and discover Saint Katherine's body at the top, only for a second aged anchorite suddenly to appear and tell them about her life and martyrdom. The monks then take the body down to the monastery, then known as "St. Mary at Bush" (Fabri, *Wanderings*, pp. 605–6).

[39]   'with great devotion'.

saint's body. In the legend hermits function as flying facilitators and channels of information, a divine Internet (or pigeon post) *avant la lettre*. Moreover, since the legend records God speaking directly only to Katherine, hermits – as (iconographically, at least) bearded elderly men – act, in the web of recursive reflexion that binds the text, as smaller mirror images of, and mouthpieces for, God. As Alexandria is 20 days' journey away, the speed and means of transportation accentuate God's power, collapsing time and space into the eternal present of the text and of God's superior view of human history. The Alexandrian hermit provides, first, a tangible link between the site of Katherine's martyrdom and that of her discovered body; second, an inner-textually credible eyewitness[40] who reinforces yet again the primacy of vision as confirmation of divine truth. The recognition (for the reader the reminder) of the saint's martyrdom fuses the account of her life with that of her miracles; one flows into the other like the oil from her bones; whilst the fact that only angels are worthy of burying Katherine again stresses her exceptional status as bride of Christ.[41] The angelic music and song that accompany the translation of the saint's body to the mountain top (itself symbolic of her spiritual elevation above ordinary mortals) both add sound effects to what has essentially been constructed as a dramatic performance[42] and echo the music of the spheres as expression of the harmony and perfection of God's Creation, here incarnated in the perfection of His saint. As so often in Katherine's life and miracles, place and time collapse and fuse, like a black star, into a single

---

[40]   The text does not specify whether the hermit is the same one who converted Katherine to Christianity in the first place.

[41]   Katherine's particular status is even more evident in Fabri: 'The hollow [on the plateau at the top of Mount Sinai] is not made by any iron tools of human workmen, but is impressed in the rock by a miracle; for when the angels bore the virgin's body hither from Alexandria, and placed it upon this exceeding hard and smooth rock, presently the rock by the action of angelic power yielded to the saint's body, even as soft wax yields to anything hard and heavy that is laid upon it, and so the saint's body pressed out a coffin for itself fitting its shape, wherein it lay at rest for thirty years unknown to mankind, guarded by the angels. A proof of this guardianship is given by hollow places on either side suitable to sit in, as though someone had sat there. Indeed, the angels who watched over her body are said to have sat there, perhaps in material bodies' (Fabri, *Wanderings*, pp. 570–1). Katherine permanently inscribes herself upon the otherwise unyielding landscape, moulding it to her shape and purpose, leaving a lasting testimony to the truth of her miraculous translation. Again, an analogy to her legend and to *Der Heiligen Leben* itself could be seen here.

[42]   Nuns sang during the divine office and Passion plays could contain songs, so the mention of music in the text may have served as an auditory stimulus, prompting memories of actual performances. See also Peter Macardle, 'Die Gesänge des "St. Galler Mittelrheinischen Passionsspiels". Ein Beitrag zur Rekonstruktion und Lokalisierung', in *Die Vermittlung geistlicher Inhalte*, pp. 255–70.

dense point that carries within itself layers of location, history and interpretational possibilities. Thus, in a secular re-enactment of the divine translation, Katherine's body and tomb are taken to the monastery church to be guarded by monks rather than angels and to become the locus of frequent visions of Christ and His mother. The light of Katherine's original vision is herewith multiplied into the present to be seen by visitors to her tomb and transmitted through their oral retelling into the heart of Nuremberg itself.

The next miracle concerns a monk in the monastery at Sinai, the continued focus on location reinforcing Sinai's centrality to the cult. This story documents the first dispersal of Katherine's miraculous oil, since the monk carries some from the grave in a small vessel. The oil, then, becomes a symbol for both the fertile sanctity of the saint herself (as a physical product of her bones that generates miracles in its turn) and for the spread of her cult beyond Sinai, as on leaving the monastery the monk enters the desert and is robbed of the oil and all his possessions.[43] This may well reflect actual pilgrim experience: Hans Tucher, for example, expresses anxiety about attacks by the Bedouins, a fear echoed in other pilgrimage reports.[44] The theft of her relic prompts Katherine's first posthumous miracle: the robbers 'gyengen da von ym / vnd thetten das veßlein auff mit dem oll / vnd verkaufften das ein teyl / da ward es czu blutt' (fol. ccliiij').[45] This transmutation of the oil into Katherine's blood foregrounds three salvatory events: first, Katherine's own blood-streaming flagellation and martyrdom as the prerequisites for the posthumously miraculous; second, Christ's transformation of water into wine during the Marriage at Cana; third, transubstantiation during the mass. Whilst, strictly speaking, this miracle represents a "reverse" transubstantiation since the oil from Katherine's body turns into blood rather than her blood turning into wine, more than any other parallel between Katherine and Christ it marks the exceptional nature of their bond as the blurring of sanguinary boundaries suggests the merging of bodies in the marriage symbolic of the union of the soul with Christ. So amazed are the robbers by the transformation that they return the vessel to the monk, who 'thett das veßleyn auff / Da geschach ein grosses wunder / das vor blutt was gewesen daz ward wyder

---

[43]   The monk is robbed by 'dy schacher vnd dye rauber' [thieves and robbers], 'schacher' being the word used in Middle High German for the thieves crucified next to Christ. Whilst normal usage, it does serve further to reinforce the parallels between Katherine and Christ.

[44]   For example, he writes: 'Vnd auff beyd seytten von weitten hat es grosse sandtpirg, darauff auch arben wonen, die die lewt do berauben vnd die offt mit gutten zennen vbell essen. Vnd wo die lewt doselbst furzÿehen, die lauffen sie an' [And for a very long way on both sides there are large sand dunes on which the Arabs live who rob people there and often eat bad food with good teeth. And when people travel through, the Arabs attack them] (*'Reise'*, p. 515).

[45]   'left him and opened the small vessel containing the oil and when they sold some of it, it turned into blood'.

oll / Da schyeden dye schacher mit schanden von dannen'.[46] This further reverse transubstantiation, a divine thwarting of the robbers' evil intent, both effects and symbolizes the spiritual transformation within them, since they depart "mit schanden". Just as the wine that is Christ's blood is displayed to the congregation during mass, so the oil that was Saint Katherine's blood is displayed to the robbers. As outlined in Chapter 1, seeing has the power actively to stamp on the viewer's psyche images which mould his thought, behaviour and soul. Like the soul of the 'schacher' (thief) on the right of the crucified Christ, the robbers' souls have been re-formed into an awareness of sin and repentance which serves also to signal Katherine's redemptive power.

Theft provides continuity with the next miracle story, which deals with a nobleman from Stopach who wishes to steal Saint Katherine's body and house it in a different church. Both stories thus narrate the illicit attempt to wrest Katherine from her context by transferring her physical remains to an alien location, thereby rewriting the text that is the history of salvation. Whilst the attempted robbery expresses a desire to be closer to the saint, it also represents an attempt both to dispose of her body in ways not authorized by God (who relocated her to Sinai) or her Greek Orthodox guardians; and to appropriate the power and prestige resident in her relics. Illicit attempts to control the saint's remains and their miraculous power thus weave these stories together and throw into relief the licit, because sanctioned, relic-gathering of Tucher, Fabri et al. Thus the text channels and safely defuses illicit desires, pointing the way to appropriate forms of devotion. The nobleman and his retinue encounter:

> die gottlich krafft / vnd kam ein groß vinster wind / das man kom gesehen mocht / vnd eyn grosser erdbidem / der warff dye grossen perg vnd velßenn nyder / das man es noch heutt auff dysen tag sicht. (fol. ccliiij')[47]

---

[46] 'who opened the little vessel. Then a great miracle happened: the blood turned back into oil. Then the robbers departed from there disgraced'.

[47] 'divine power; and such a fierce, dark wind blew up that they could hardly see. Then a great earthquake caused high mountains and cliffs to tumble and the damage can be seen to this day'. Colin J. Humphreys postulates volcanic activity in Mount Sinai at the time of the Exodus, ascribing to it the pillar of fire and smoke seen by the Israelites (cf. Exodus 13:21–2: 'And the LORD went before them by day in a pillar of a cloud, to lead them the way; and by night in a pillar of fire, to give them light; to go by day and night: / He took not away the pillar of cloud by day, nor the pillar of fire by night, *from* before the people'). Cloud and ash could account for the darkness experienced by the nobleman and his retinue. Moreover, there are records of earthquake activity in Egypt, Arabia and the Red Sea and a volcanic eruption near Medina in June 1256. The ash and flames thrown out by erupting volcanoes could be seen for miles (Colin J. Humphreys, *The Miracles of Exodus. A Scientist's Discovery of the Extraordinary Natural Causes of the Biblical Stories* (London: Continuum, 2003), pp. 168–71). The earthquakes

Divine protection of Katherine is rendered visibly and audibly explicit through further special effects. Vision-obscuring wind and earthquake may reflect actual natural phenomena such as desert storms that shift sand dunes, thereby changing the physical landscape, or earthquakes that cause rock slides.[48] However, these are more than merely natural events: the darkness symbolizes the spiritual blindness of the sinner who contravenes God's Will; the wind and earthquake His wrath and vengeance. The physically rent, jumbled landscape delivers current, verifiable testimony to God's determination to protect His bride that links the divine past with the reader's present since the latter, too, can visit Saint Katherine's monastery and observe the physical traces of the earthquake with his own eyes.[49] Moreover, the recasting of physical terrain also symbolizes the spiritual change effected in the nobleman since, in a parallel to the previous story, God's revenge prompts repentance on the part of the sinner:

> Da kam der selb Edelman kom in dye kirchen / Da der heylig innen lag vnd gewan rew vnd leyd uber seynn sund / vnd gelobet Gott vnd der liebe*n* heyligen Junckfrawen Sand katherina besserung / vn*d* gab den Muniche*n* vnd der kirchen groß gutt. (fol. ccliiij*ᵛ*)[50]

The nobleman is reshaped into a model for the reader: chastened by his experience he enters the church and, in the presence of the saint, repents

---

in the miracle stories (and Fabri's description of Mount Sinai) could therefore echo actual seismic events. Indeed, earthquake activity on the Sinai Peninsula continues to this day. See N. Hurukawa, N. Seto, H. Inoue, K. Nishigami, I. Marzouk, A. Megahed, E.M. Ibrahim, H. Murakami, M. Nakamura, T. Haneda, S. Sugiyama, T. Ohkura, Y. Fujii, H.M. Hussein, A.S. Megahed, H.F. Mohammed, R. Abdel-Fattah, M. Mizoue, S. Hashimoto, M. Kobayasi and D. Suetsugu, 'Seismological Observations in and around the Southern Part of the Gulf of Suez, Egypt', *Bulletin of the Seismological Society of America*, 91 (2001), 4: 708–17.

[48]   Earthquake and wind also echo Revelation: 'And I beheld when he had opened the sixth seal, and, lo, there was a great earthquake; and the sun became black as sackcloth of hair; and the moon became as blood; And the stars of heaven fell unto the earth, even as a fig tree casteth her untimely figs, when she is shaken of a might wind. And the heaven departed as a scroll when it is rolled together; and every mountain and island were moved out of their places' (Revelation 6:12–14); and the opening of the Seventh Seal by the Lamb: 'And the angel took the censer, and filled it with fire of the altar, and cast *it* into the earth: and there were voices, and thunderings, and lightenings, and an earthquake' (Revelation 8:5).

[49]   When imprisoned at Philippi, Paul and his companion Silas were saved by an earthquake that shattered their chains and burst open the doors to the prison (Acts 16:25–34).

[50]   'The same nobleman went into the church in which the saint was lying and was overcome by remorse and sorrow for his sins and promised God and dear Saint Katherine to mend his ways and made a sizable donation to the monks and the church'.

and donates property as the externalization of his altered spiritual landscape. Katherine is thus portrayed as a source of enlightenment and salvation, her body as the physical source of spiritual grace for the sinner and financial bounty for the monks at Sinai. Moreover, the nobleman's desire to possess Katherine's body foreshadows the later story of Katherine's "lover", a young count thought by his wife to be conducting an affair, the saint being the "other woman". In accordance with the emphasis on Katherine's royal status noted by Walsh,[51] the nobleman belongs to the appropriate social class; whereas the lower-class robbers are not redeemed in the same way but leave 'in schanden'.

Elements of the first two stories recur in the next one, fusing all three into a single homily on the wrong sort of acquisitiveness, namely the desire for worldly goods (oil, body, cloth) rather than spiritual benefits:

> ei*n* geistlicher man der hett dye heyligen iu*n*ckfrawen Sand Katherina gar lieb / de*r* furet eynes mals tuch / das gehorett den Mumchen [*sic*] czu kleydern dye yres grabs hutten / vud [*sic*] kam da mit in eyn statt / Da kamen dye Rauber an in vn*d* Namen [*sic*] ym das tuch / Da klaget es de*r* gutt man dem Richter / yn der selben weyl da verhenget Gott vnd sein liebe*r* Gemahel dye heylig Junckfraw sant Katherina das dye rauber erblinten Vnd czytterten vnd bidmetenn gar ser / Vnd weßtenn nicht wa sy waren Vnnd wa sye hyn woltenn. (fol. ccliiij^v)

> [A cleric loved the holy virgin Saint Katherine very much. One day he was taking cloth for the monks who watch over her grave to make clothes and came with it to a town where robbers came and took the cloth away from him. The good man made a complaint to the judge and at the same time God and His dear spouse, the holy virgin Saint Katherine, caused the robbers to go blind. They shivered and shook mightily and did not know where they were and where they were going].

Since this story is not located in any named place it resonates with any number of cities, especially those involved, like Nuremberg, in the cloth trade.[52] Familiar elements shape the narrative: the monk devoted to Saint Katherine; an object (cloth) stolen from the guardians of her tomb; the transition from monastery to city, resonant for an urban readership. Whilst this third story reflects the danger of travel and trade, even the lived experience of merchant readers of *Der Heiligen Leben*, for whom acquisition formed the foundation of life and status, its main

---

[51]   Walsh, *The Cult of St Katherine*, p. 147.

[52]   Nuremberg's desire to promote exports determined the acquisition of whole new branches of trade: for example, in 1489 the weavers of *Barchent* (a textile made of linen and cotton) were lured en masse from Augsburg to Nuremberg; the small workers' houses known as the *Sieben Zeilen* were built for them by the Council.

message is the inevitability of justice: although the judge to whom the victim complains is unidentified (city judge or supreme judge, the Lord Himself), God and Katherine (whose spousal status is identified as the source of her power) extract revenge. The robbers re-enact, on their very bodies, the disruption of landscape in the previous story: they go blind in an embodiment of the dark wind that prevents vision, their loss of sight signalling their spiritual blindness;[53] they tremble and shake like the earthquake;[54] they lose orientation completely. Their condition symbolizes a wandering through the emotional landscape of sin and distance from God.[55] The same end result – repentance – is expressed in similar language, the ritual repetition of progress from penance to restitution to joy: 'Da gewunnen sye rew uber yr groß sund vnd gaben dem gutten man sein tuch wider da wurden

---

[53]   Physical blindness as a sign of spiritual blindness is replicated in a later story: a priest in Tralot loves Saint Katherine, invites many poor priests for a meal in her honour and gives everyone alms. Once, when everyone is at church celebrating mass on Saint Katherine's Day, four thieves break in to steal the priest's money. When a small dog barks loudly at them, they cut off its head, force open the rooms and take the priest's money and jewels from the chests in which they are stored. Katherine, who wishes to keep her servant's possessions for him, 'verhenget daz dy dieb mit offen augen vnd bey hellem tag dy kammer tur nye kunden gefinden vnd giengen ymmer mer yn der kamer vmb vnd ball das hawbt ymmer mer das si dem hundlein heten abgeschlagen' [prevented the thieves, with open eyes and in broad daylight, from being able to find the door out of the room. They went round and round the room and the head they had cut off the little dog barked louder and louder]. Further evidence of miraculous intervention is the dog's continued barking. Cutting off his head, far from depriving him of voice, transforms him into the soundtrack to the miraculous, audible proof of Saint Katherine's powerful loyalty. The priest's servants come running, take the thieves prisoner and recover their master's possessions (fol. cclviij'). According to *Hall's Dictionary*, 'a black and white dog with a flaming torch in its mouth alludes to the story that his [Saint Dominic's] mother dreamed she gave birth to such a creature; it is more likely explained as a pun on his name: "Domini canis"' (p. 106). In *Der Heiligen Leben* the flames, symbolic of the Word of God, set the world alight (fol. xcviij'). It is attractive to think that this miraculous dog symbolizes the spiritual wakefulness of the Dominican Order. Thieves being deprived of their sight for stealing from or damaging the saint's devotees occurs in a miracle story of Our Lady of Rocamadour, who deprives three thieves who rob pilgrims on their way to her shrine of their sight and the power of movement and only restores them in answer to the pilgrims' prayers for mercy (Marcus Bull (intro. and trans.), *The Miracles of Our Lady of Rocamadour* (Woodbridge: Boydell, 1999), pp. 146–7).

[54]   This sounds like epilepsy, especially as the robbers also suffer emotional disorientation. Saints Valentine and Vitus (the latter one of the *Vierzehn Heiligen*) were patron saints of epilepsy sufferers.

[55]   Just as Parzival's alienation from God is symbolized by snow on Good Friday (Wolfram von Eschenbach, *Parzival*, ed. Karl Lachmann (Berlin and Leipzig: de Gruyter, 6th edn 1926; repr. 1965), 446, 6–448, 9; and *Parzival*, trans. A.T. Hatto (Harmondsworth: Penguin, 1980), pp. 228–9).

sie gesehent vnd wurde*n* ga*r* fro' (fol. ccliiij*ᵛ*–cclv*ʳ*).⁵⁶ The narrative encodes the restoration of moral, legal and physical order, the necessary sequence underlined by restoration of sight only after the thieves have "seen" the error of their ways, returned the cloth and visibly demonstrated virtue. The first three stories relate the physicality of a miraculousness written onto sinners' bodies. However, they also affirm rightful ownership and power; cement Katherine into Sinai; consolidate the monks' claim to her remains; and warn off those coveting illicit possession of the saint since Katherine and God gang up like a pair of holy bully-boys to scare away the competition. Simultaneously, the narrative web of Katherine's sanctity and protective power is spun wider to incorporate places away from Sinai.

Such narrative opening is reflected in the next story, set in an unspecified location. A prostitute who loves Saint Katherine:

> vn*d* tet d*a*z gancz iar nimmer keyn gutt / dann an irem abent so fastet si / vn*d* betet andechtiglichen ann yrem tag / vnd hett rew vber yr sund die si das gancz iar getan hett / vnd bat si mit grossem ernst / daz si yr ein gutt end vmb gott erwurbe / vnd daz si von got nimmer gescheyde*n* wurde. (fol. cclv*ʳ*)⁵⁷

> [and performed no good deeds throughout the year apart from fasting on Saint Katherine's Eve and praying devoutly on Saint Katherine's Day and repenting the sins she had committed throughout the year and asking the saint most earnestly to ensure her a good death for God's sake and that she never be separated from God].

As prostitutes feature primarily in urban life, the story resonates for any city and follows a typical pattern: the sinner who boasts one redeeming trait, namely devotion to a given saint who aids the sinner as reward for his devotion. This textual mould forms an empty vessel into which any saint could be poured. The prostitute's fasting and praying constitute denial of the body she otherwise uses illicitly to earn her living; they also replicate Katherine's denial of her own body prior to baptism. Lack of corporeal nourishment leads demonstrably to spiritual nourishment; but at the same time fasting, as denial of the body, privileges it by negatively focussing on its physical needs. In either case the body is objectified as a

---

⁵⁶ 'They were filled with remorse for their grievous sins and gave the good man back his cloth, upon which their sight was restored and they rejoiced'.

⁵⁷ Assion identifies this as one of the miracle stories taken over from the Virgin. Goodich notes that the twelfth and thirteenth centuries saw a 'continuing change in favor of posthumous miracles, often performed at some distance from the site of the relics, in which the themes of deliverance and protection predominate' (Goodich, *Violence and Miracle*, p. 2). This is the first of the Katherine miracles that falls into this category, in that the prostitute is delivered from potential damnation by the saint.

target of lust or chatisement. The prostitute observes her routine for 20 years, then follows her practice of visiting Saint Katherine's church to pray on the saint's feast day: 'In der selben kirche*n* wa*z* ein groß bild sa*nt* Katherin hoch auff gemacht da fiel si nider vnd betet mit grosser andacht vnd rew / vn*d* het einen gute*n* fursacz si wolt sich bessern In der weil fiel das groß bild herab vnd fiel auff si d*az* si starb' (fol. cclv*r*).[58] Saint Katherine literally crushes sin out of the prostitute by crushing her to death, the ultimate denial of the body, so the concrete image of Katherine becomes the literal embodiment of the grace she bestows on the devoted believer, who dies in a moment of inner transformation effected by a genuine desire to reform.[59]

The prostitute's body is discovered by the *Meßner* (sacristan) on his way to ring the bell for vespers:

> Da gebot der kirchen Priester dem volck allem das sie gott anruffeten vnd yn beten das er si erkucket / d*az* teten si mit ernst da ward si wider lebentig vnd sprach O heylige sa*nt* Katherin wy groß gnaden erwirbst du den dy dich eren vn*d* lieb haben vnd hyeß yr einen einen beychtiger bringen vnd beychtet all yr sundt vnd enpfie*ng* vnsers herren fronleychnam vnd dy heyligen olung. (fol. cclv*r*)[60]

> [Then the priest of that church told all the people gathered there that they should pray to God and ask Him to revive her. They did that most earnestly and she [the prostitute] came back to life and said, 'O, holy Saint Katherine, what great grace

---

[58]   'In the same church, high up on a wall, was a large image of Saint Katherine. She [the prostitute] fell down in front of it and prayed with great devoutness and remorse and made the virtuous resolution to mend her ways. At that point the large image fell off the wall and onto her, causing her death'.

[59]   Images of saints that come to life belong to the typical pattern of miracle stories: for example, the crucifix that leans forward to embrace the praying Bernard of Clairvaux.

[60]   A later story echoes this one: a man who loves Saint Katherine (this is the formalistic beginning to every story) 'ließ alle iar etwas durch iren willen vnd betet yr all tag funff Pater noster' [gave something every year for her sake and prayed five Our Fathers to her every day]. As with the prostitute, prayer, so communication with the saint, plays a prominent role in devotion and salvation. The man falls ill; has received the last rites (in the unction we once more have oil as the link to Katherine since it recalls that which flows from her body); lies still for a long time; then praises God for all His grace. When those present ask him what is going on, he says, 'frewet euch wann ich bin vor gottes gericht gewesen vnd han gesigt wann dye lieb iunckfraw sant Katherin hatt mir geholffen vnd hatt mir vmb gott erworben d*as* er mir gnediglichen geta*n* hat' [Rejoice, for I have stood before God's judgement and have triumphed for the dear virgin Saint Katherine helped me and interceded with God so that He treated me mercifully] (fol. cclvj*r*). Katherine's power to intervene positively on her devotee's behalf increases her status; and since the dying man has, like Katherine, been granted sight of something beyond the normal human power of vision, his vision parallels hers, only is of her. He thus becomes a documented eyewitness to her power in heaven. After giving witness he receives the host and dies.

you obtain for those who revere you and love you'. She asked for a priest to be brought to hear her confession and confessed all her sins and received Our Lord's body and the last unction].

If Christ is the Word made Flesh, this miracle (which recalls Christ's raising of Nazarus from the dead) is the literalization of new life in the Word and by the Word, here prayer. The prostitute is a living miracle whose previous resolution to reform is then acted out through her renewal of that Word in her confession, communion and the last rights, the oil of unction replicating the oil from Katherine's bones in perpetuation of the saint's body as fountain of grace. On being asked by the priest what had happened the prostitute responds in direct speech, as always the signal for important salvatory content:

> ich han yn czweinczig iaren nye als guten fursacz gehabt das ich mein leben bessern wolt als heutt Vnd da ich yn dem gutten willen was da forcht sant Katherin ich verlor den guten willen vnd volbrecht yn nicht vnd verhenget daz ir bild auff mich fiel vnd mich ertotet das ich an meinem guten willen bleib also stirb ich anderweid yn vnserm herren ihesu cristo yn dem ich mich ewig frew / vnd starb also / da fur yr sel zu den ewigen frewden. (fol. cclvʳ)

> [In 20 years I had never made such a firm resolution to change my life as today. And when that virtuous will had hold of me, Saint Katherine was afraid I would lose it again and fail to act on it, so she caused the image to fall on top of me and kill me so that I might hold fast to my virtuous resolution. Thus I die again in Our Lord Jesus Christ in Whom I rejoice forever. With this she died and her soul went to eternal bliss].

The prostitute functions as eyewitness to and direct channel for verification of the miraculous, simultaneously confirming Katherine's loyalty towards her followers. Furthermore, her death and rebirth occur within a church, a consecrated space where the believer is surrounded by previous testimony to God's might. It is a small step for the reader to substitute a church in his home town and imagine animated salvatory images; a Patrician might appropriate for the story a statue or painting endowed by himself or an ancestor.

From the prostitute the narrative moves to a possible client, a wicked judge who on Saint Katherine's Day swears to desist from 'etlich heimlich' for her sake.[61] The judge attracts the first of Katherine's posthumous visitations: 'Da kam si eins mals zu ym yn einem bosen rock als ob si gar eyn armes mensch were vnd bat yn

---

61   'various secret activities'. By this is almost certainly meant his visiting of prostitutes.

daz er yr etwas geb durch Sant Katherinen wille*n*' (fol. cclv^r).[62] Katherine's actual (rather than dream) presence introduces oscillation between divine and earthly planes that threads the narrative together by reactivating the reader's memory of the saint's own visions. Her occupation, and hence bridging, of both spheres mirrors her coffin hovering in space, which thus serves as a metaphor for her status as one of the Fourteen Holy Helpers who bridge the gap between human sin on the one hand and divine redemption on the other. It serves also as a metaphor for the text, even for the printed volume itself, a tangible object that mediates for its reader the intangible but potent truth that is God's power actualized in His saints and their intervention on behalf of their servants. To return to the narrative. Saint Katherine tests the sincerity of the judge's devotion by disguising herself: her initial denial of herself through concealment of her identity becomes a recurrent theme in the miracle stories that parallels her own thwarted pre-baptism visions of Christ. Katherine's followers are transformed into shadow-Katherines in their attempts to win her mercy, Katherine being cast as the demanding mistress: 'Da sprach der Richter w*az* hettest du gern da sprach si ich hett geren dein rechte hanndt da gieng er hyn vnd nam eyn beyhel vn*d* schlug ym selber sein rechte hannd ab vn*d* gab si der frawen / da verschwandt sie' (fol. cclv^r).[63] As right is the side of virtue and justice – Christ sits on right hand of God to judge the quick and the dead – the judge's loss of his right hand and subsequent physical imperfection visibly represent his emotional imperfection as he lacks virtue and justice.[64] By cutting off his sword hand, the sword being symbolic of power and the exercise of justice, the judge renders himself powerless and functionless in the public sphere. His absent hand becomes the present manifestation of his absent virtue. However, it also becomes the present manifestation of the constancy and devotion which save him: as Katherine vanishes without explanation or self-revelation, the judge is left to sustain dedication to her without her help or reward. His friends, ashamed of him, advise him to enter a monastery, so embody the evil from which the judge has literally severed himself in the saint's name. His retreat to a monastery constitutes concealment of his public shame – he disguises it by assuming different clothes and a different identity, much as Katherine does – but his "death" to public life also constitutes rebirth to the life of the soul and, ultimately, salvation:

---

[62]   'One day she visited him dressed in threadbare clothes as if she were a very poor person and asked him to give her something for Saint Katherine's sake'.

[63]   'Then the judge said, "What would you like?". To this she replied, "I would like your right hand". Then he went and took an axe and cut off his own right hand and gave it to the lady, upon which she disappeared'.

[64]   As well as being a civic functionary, the judge is an inverted shadow of the final judge, God the Father.

Vn*d* da er siben iar yn dem Closter was gewese*n* da erschein ym die heylig
Junckfraw sand Katherin vnd sprach czu ym Ich byn dy die dich deiner hannd
beraubt hat das thet ich darumb das ich dich bey gott behub / wann ich mocht
dich yn keiner anderen weyße czu got bringe*n* da mit verschwa*n*d si. (fol. cclv[r])

[And when he had been in the monastery for seven years the holy virgin Saint
Katherine appeared to him and said, 'I am the one who robbed you of your hand.
I did that in order to gain you favour with God as I was unable to bring you to
God's mercy in any other way'. With that she disappeared].

The judge's loss of his hand is symbolically inverted as his physical deformity
ultimately expresses moral integrity, rewarded by Katherine's revelation of her
identity to her servant after his seven years of penance in the monastery.[65] Katherine,
in acting as the judge's judge, has mediated on his behalf by punishing him and
ensuring his elevation in God's eyes: 'Da frewet er sich des trostes den er von yr
gegenwertikeyt enpfangen het / vnd dancket ir d*er* grossen gnaden vnd dyenet
yr furbas mit grossem fleiß vn*d* starb da selig' (fol. cclv[r]).[66] However, this story
represents a thwarted narrative of miraculous healing since the expected ending,
the regrowth of the judge's hand as reward for his devotion, fails to materialize.
Thus the reader himself is thwarted, denied a neat, rounded conclusion in the same
way as sinful or lapsed devotees of Katherine may initially be denied sight of her; in
this sense the narrative remains as imperfect as the judge's body. On the one hand,
this absence demonstrates particularly sincere devotion on the judge's part in that
the grace of Katherine's presence suffices to sustain him in his physical deformity
because he has healed spiritually. On the other, it reminds the reader that his own
hope for redemption may be thwarted if he considers devotion to the saint an easy
path requiring no sacrifice or effort. The reader has the potential to remain the
physically and spiritually crippled judge.

From an unspecified location the reader is transferred in the next story to
the centre of the Christian world – Jerusalem – and of the saint's cult – Sinai.
Sabinus, Bishop of Milan, adores Katherine and 'eret si mit seinem andechtigen

---

[65]   Seven is so significant a number because it a) represents the seven days of Creation;
b) symbolizes earthly time (because seven days make a week); c) is the number of the
Old Covenant and the time of the Law; d) is the number of man (made up of the four
elements plus three spiritual powers) (Heinz Meyer and Rudolf Suntrup, *Lexikon der
mittelalterlichen Zahlenbedeutungen*, Münstersche Mittelalter-Schriften 56 (Munich:
Fink, 1987), col. 450).

[66]   'Then he rejoiced in the consolation he had gained from her presence and thanked
her for her great mercy and served her henceforth most assiduously and died in bliss'.

gebet vnd mit allem das er vermocht' (fol. cclv^r).[67] Following medieval practice he undertakes a pilgrimage to the Holy Sepulchre with Abbot Theodorus, two chaplains, six knights and 30 servants 'durch ablas vnd gotlicher gnaden willen' (fol. cclv^r).[68] From Jerusalem the party proceeds to Saint Katherine's grave: 'vnd da si all vnden an den Berg kame*n* da begegnet ynn zumal ein greulicher heydenischer man der kamm gare mit vil gewapneten mannen von dem soldan Vnd da er nur Sabinu*m* sach mit seinem gesind / da ertodtet er ym alles sein gesinnd' (fol. cclv^r).[69] This encounter reflects the real danger of travelling through the Sinai Desert to Saint Katherine's monastery, above all the threat posed by hostile Arabs. The vocabulary used to describe the attacker ('ein greulicher heydenischer man')[70] emphasizes the vulnerability felt by Christian travellers in the face of the heathen enemy, threatening embodiment of everything alien and disruptive of Christian certitude. The murder of Sabinus' retinue is, then, qualitatively different from the Katherine-inspired chopping-off of his hand by the judge: sight leads here not to salvation but to death since it prompts the heathen to kill the Christians.[71] Sabinus and Theodorus are identified by their offices (Bishop and Abbot), focussing attention on the affront to God's Church rather than their fate as individuals. However, their response stresses

---

[67]   'and honours her with his devout prayer and with everything that lay within his power'. According to Assion, the source for this story is pilgrimage literature, although it is not genuine and there is no trace of a miracle in pilgrimage reports. Its core (the mutilation and restoration of Sabinus and Theodorus) is taken from a Marian miracle first recorded by Caesarius von Heisterbach. Bishop Sabinus of Milan and Abbot Theodorus of Monte Cassino were not historical personages, although Monte Cassino may, according to Assion, have been the source of the story as since the eleventh century it had been one of the main European centres of the cult of Saint Katherine. Theodorus has a feast day (13 November) in the local hagiography. The story in included in the *Legenda aurea* but in an appendix compiled only in the fourteenth century to scoop up locally revered saints in Germany. Saints' lives such as those of Adrian and James provide the model for the hacking off of limbs (Assion, *Mirakel*, pp. 234–55). For a discussion of this story and the 'Wunderanhang' to the *vita* of Saint Katherine see Gerhard Eis, 'Lupold von Wiltingen. Eine Studie zum Wunderanhang der Katharinenlegende', in *Festschrift für Wolfgang Stammler*, pp. 78–91. Saint Adrian was a Roman officer at Nicomedia who converted to Christianity after seeing the suffering of persecuted Christians; at his execution his hands and head were cut off (*Hall's Dictionary*, p. 7).

[68]   'for the sake of indulgences and God's grace'.

[69]   'And when they all reached the foot of the mountain, they were met by a hideous and terrifying heathen who came from the sultan and was accompanied by many armed men. When he saw Sabinus with his retinue, he killed all his retinue'.

[70]   'a hideous and terrifying heathen'.

[71]   Sabinus and Theodorus are described as hearing about the slaughter, which oddly implies their absence from the scene.

their devotion: 'Latt vns nur die liebenn heyligenn iunckfrawenn vnd gar getreulichen uothelfferin [*sic*] Sandt Katherinem vor sehenn was yr dann mit vns tut / das wollen wir gedultiglichen leiden' (fol. cclvʳ).⁷² The two Christians line themselves up for martyrdom as models of patient suffering, allowing the heathen duke's insistence on the primacy of Saracen will to be read as the stubbornness of those who fail to recognize Christ.⁷³ The next act confirms Islam as barbaric "Other": 'vnd schnitten yn czuhanndt dy augen / vberlid / zungen / oren / hand vnd fuß ab / vnd verbrantten da dye ab geschnitten glieder alle / vnd furten sie da also verwund czu sant Katherinen grab auff yren turen' (fol. cclvᵛ).⁷⁴ The treatment of Sabinus and Theodorus corresponds to Islamic practice:

> The punishment of those who wage war against Allah and His messenger and strive to make mischief in the land is only this, that they should be murdered or crucified or their hands and their feet should be cut off on opposite sides or they should be imprisoned; this shall be as a disgrace for them in this world, and in the hereafter they shall have a grievous chastisement. (Qur'an 5:33)

Thus their mutilation marks them publicly as soldiers of Christ in the battle against heresy (though as heretics themselves from the Islamic point of view). Moreover, their blinding and the severing of their eyelids constitute the physical enactment, the rendering visible, of the denial of the Christians' request to see Saint Katherine, although, as with the judge, absence signifies presence: corporeal deformity becomes the outward manifestation of true virtue and the Churchmen remain spiritually sighted whilst the Saracens remain spiritually blind.⁷⁵ Furthermore, the excision of their tongues renders them incapable of the audible expression of their faith through spoken prayer.⁷⁶ Since Katherine, famed for her eloquence, is

---

⁷² 'Let us just see the dear holy virgin and most loyal helper Saint Katherine first and then we shall suffer patiently whatever you want to do with us'.

⁷³ The duke says: 'wyr wollen daz vnser will vor gee vnd nit der euwer' [We wish our will to take precedence and not yours] (fol. cclvʳ⁻ᵛ).

⁷⁴ 'And immediately cut out their eyes, eyelids, tongues, ears, hand and feet and burnt all the body parts they had cut off and led them in their wounded state to the doors of Saint Katherine's tomb'.

⁷⁵ Theoretically their blinding denies Sabinus and Theodorus the chance of seeing a "physical" visitation by Saint Katherine; they are left with only their imagination or the possibility of a dream vision.

⁷⁶ It also recalls Proverbs 10:31 'The mouth of the just bringeth forth wisdom: but the froward tongue shall be cut out'. Excision of the tongue was an ancient punishment for slander, perjury, bearing false witness and preaching forbidden doctrine that was still used by the Inquisition. Hence familiar Christian practices are being appropriated and ascribed to Islam to characterize it as barbaric and cruel in an ironic cultural crossover, since from

also patron saint of those with diseases of the tongue, denial of speech refers to her patronage as well as signalling heathen contempt for Christian sanctity. In addition, the severance of the pilgrims' ears means they can hear neither prayer nor God's message. The heathens' action renders the two Christians less than human since the removal of identifying features reduces them to mere lumps of semi-sentient flesh incapable of lifting their hands in prayer or, in a parodic inversion of pilgrimage to the Holy Land that requires motion across vast distances, of unassisted movement.[77] The burning of the two men's limbs recalls the flames of martyrdom experienced by the 50 philosophers so functions as the symbolic martyrdom of bishop and abbot, the apparently ineradicable destruction of the limbs throwing the subsequent miracle into even sharper relief.[78]

The heathen duke taunts the Christians by casting doubt on the saint's power to help: 'vnd wan euch euwer gelider wider wachssen *daz* vnmuglich ist an czweyffel so wil ich euweren glauben an mich nemen' (fol. cclv[v]).[79] The death of bishop and abbot at Saint Katherine's tomb heightens the subsequent shock as the miraculous now seems closed down. In the ensuing narrative elements familiar from previous

---

the Islamic point of view Sabinus and Theodorus are unbelievers who preach false doctrine; whilst from a Christian point of view it is Muslims who are heretical.

[77]   This literal rendition of the proverbial "See no evil, hear no evil, speak no evil" may save the two Christians from the temptation of conversion and therefore mortal sin (since the desert was the place where Christ was tempted by Satan). The story may also contain faint traces of an actual martyrdom narrative of a Saint Sabinus (of whom a number exist). When the edicts of Diocletian and Maximin Hercules against the Christians were promulgated in 303, Saint Sabinus, Bishop of Spoleto, his deacons, and several other members of his clergy were caught in Assisi and thrown into prison by Venustianus, Governor of Etruria and Umbria, as a punishment for their revolt. A few days later they were summoned and ordered to worship his statue of Jupiter. Sabinus threw down the idol, breaking it into pieces. The governor had his hands cut off and his deacons tortured on the rack and burnt with torches until they died. Saint Sabinus was thrown back into prison, where he was helped by a Christian widow, Serena, who brought him her blind nephew to be cured. Fifteen prisoners who witnessed this miracle were converted to Christianity. Venustianus, himself suffering from a painful eye problem, heard of the miracle and visited the bishop in prison with his wife and two sons to ask for his help. Saint Sabinus agreed on condition that Venustianus, his wife and children be baptized. The governor consented and threw his broken statue into the river. Soon after Lucius, whom Maximus Hercules had sent to Spoleto after hearing of the conversions, had Saint Sabinus so cruelly beaten that on 7 December 303 he expired under the blows. Serena, after having him buried near the city, was also martyred. A basilica was later built at the site of the bishop's tomb and a number of monasteries in Italy were consecrated in his name.

[78]   It may also refer indirectly to the flames of the Holy Ghost that fell from the sky to destroy the wheel built for Katherine's martyrdom.

[79]   'and if your limbs grow again – although that is utterly impossible – then I shall convert to your faith'.

tales merge in a medieval horror story worthy of Hollywood dramatization: at midnight an earthquake, again the manifestation of God's wrath, shakes the whole mountain and terrifies the heathens; subsequently a mysterious light is seen: 'vnd darnach vber drey stund da erschein gar ein groß liecht da wolten si wenen es wer der licht tag' (fol. cclv[v]).[80] Rather than a new day, however, the light – which recalls the angelic glow that guides the hermit to Katherine's resting place on Sinai – signals the emergence of Katherine from her grave: 'Vnder dem da gieng die Edel iunckfraw sant Katherin auß dem grab / salbet dem Bischoff Sabino alle seine gelider / Oren / Augen / Nasen Czungen / hend vnd fuß / vnd machet yn wol gesund' (fol. cclv[v]).[81] The list of severed body parts recalls the original mutilation, foreshadowing its reversal; but also contributes to the gruesome, otherworldly nature of the scene with its detached limbs, uncanny light and ambulatory corpse. Two parallel miracles take place: first, Katherine's resurrection from her tomb mirrors Christ's from His;[82] and, second, is mirrored in turn by that of the bishop, not merely healed but awakened from the dead. Katherine's affinity with the Virgin is also activated, since her emergence from her tomb to salve the bishop, representative of God and the Church, mirrors in reverse the Three Marys' visit to Christ's tomb to salve His body.[83] Her salve symbolizes the literal and metaphorical healing power of Christianity, experienced by the saint on her own body when angels visit her in prison to salve her flagellation wounds. Just as Katherine is made physically whole again when translated to Sinai after her execution, so the bishop, in the fountain effect already encountered in the text, is rendered whole again by Katherine. Light, woven via the saint and angels into fabric of the narrative, heralds the miraculous since it presages not only the bishop's resurrection (and

---

[80]   'and over three hours later a very great light appeared and they started to think that it might be the light of day'.

[81]   'In the meantime the noble virgin Saint Katherine emerged from her grave, anointed all Bishop Sabinus's limbs, ears, eyes, nose, tongue, hands and feet and restored him to full health'.

[82]   The three hours between the start of the earthquake and the light appearing being a reference to the three days before Christ arose from the dead.

[83]   John 20:1; Matthew 28:1; Luke 23:5; Mark 16:1. Balsam was cultivated in Egypt, just outside Cairo, so here again may be a trace of its importance not just biblically but also economically (See *'Reise'*, pp. 557–8). This story resembles a Marian miracle in the life of Saint Dominic: a learned deacon, Riwalt, turns his back on the world and becomes a Dominican monk. When he falls ill and doctors are unable to help him, Dominic's prayers cause Mary (described as more radiant than the sunshine) to appear with two virgins and salve Riwalt's eyes, ears and limbs, repeating the words uttered by the priest when performing the last unction. The monk is cured and becomes 'an tugent vnd an heylikeyt vnd an gotlicher lere eyn liechter spigel' [a shining mirror of virtue and sanctity and divine teaching] (*Der Heiligen Leben*, fol. c[r]).

subsequently the abbot's) but also the duke's conversion and rebirth into a new life of the soul as a Christian.[84]

The next stage in the narrative contrasts types of blindness: blindness due to the putting out of one's eyes versus blinding by the light of sanctity, as the bishop, in a Pauline moment, 'mocht den glancz yr schone nit geleyden vnd fiel fur si da stunden czwen Engel bey ir dy huben yn wider auff' (fol. cclv').[85] Katherine, whose angelic retinue highlights her elect status, now functions as Christ's mouthpiece:

> du solt wissen daz dich mein herr Jhesus Christus hie vnd dort eren will / dich vnd
> alle menschen dy mich eren du hast dein zungen durch meinen willen verloren / du
> kundt nur ein sprach / so han ich dir mein zungen gelihen dye kan wol krichisch
> vnd welsch vnd solt auch wissen das deines gesindes selen alle bey gott seind / vnd
> wan es nur tag wird so solt du dem Ewangelier alle seine glider vnder dem Ewangelio
> salben mit dem oll daz von meynen glidern fleusset so wirt er wider lebentig vnd ee
> dy meß auß kumpt so ist er gesundt vnd alß starck vor. (fol. cclv')

> [You should know that my Lord Jesus Christ wishes to honour you in this world
> and the next, you and all the people who honour me. You have lost your tongue
> on my account. Previously you were able to speak only one language; now I have
> lent you my tongue that can speak Greek and Italian. You should also know that
> the souls of your entire retinue are with God and when day dawns you should,
> during the reading of the Gospel, anoint all the limbs of this servant of the Gospel
> with the oil that flows from my limbs and if you do this he will come to life again
> and before mass is over he will be well and as strong as before].

Katherine's body is the site of the martyrdom through which she gains access to divine might which she channels back through her body in the form of miracles for the follower in need. Fragile, sinful, female physicality thus figures the transforming power of faith and Katherine's distribution of her body parts signals the spread of both her importance and that faith. She infuses her devotees to the very core of their being as she embeds herself into their physicality (tongue) or possesses it as her own (abbess's body), redeeming her followers as a result.[86] In a reprise of the

---

[84]   In addition, the 'groß liecht' [great light] may be another reminder of the Burning Bush and the Patriarch Moses, revered by Islam as well.

[85]   'was unable to bear the brightness of her beauty and fell to his knees in front of her and the two angels standing by her lifted him to his feet again'.

[86]   Further, Katherine's donation of her body echoes Christ's administering of His own body and blood to Katherine when she is in jail. Katherine's distribution of her body parts continues in the next miracle story but one: a monk on Sinai loves Katherine, serves her for 12 years 'vnd het stete begird vnd liebe zu yrem heyltumb' [and always carried in his heart

Whitsun miracle the bishop goes from being speechless, *a-lingual*, to multi-lingual, suggesting a multiplication in his potency thanks to the incorporation into him of Katherine as both tongue and language (Greek; presumably the Bishop of Milan spoke Latin and Italian).[87] This actualization of the virtue present in the saint suggests transcendence of linguistic boundaries by the cult of Saint Katherine: like the 12 Disciples the bishop can now speak miraculously to convert non-believers to Christianity. In addition, Katherine's tongue as a symbol for the salvific power of the "right" (i.e. Catholic-Christian) sort of speech is given concrete form in the *Legenda aurea*, translated into many languages and tangibly accessible in a codex or printed volume. Sabinus is constructed as a shadow-Katherine: just as she has raised him from the dead, so will he raise Theodorus from the dead, so that the latter, too, becomes a recursive reflexion of the saint. Resurrection of the abbot

---

great desire and love for her relics]. The length, constancy and strength of devotion are then rewarded: 'czu einem mal da betet er mit grossem ernst vnd *a*ndacht auff irem grab / da sach er dort her flissen yn dem ol ein finger glid da nam er daz heiltumb mit grossen frewden vn*d* andacht vn*d* dancket vnserm herrn ihesu cristo vnd auch yr des lones vnd d*az* heiltumb nam er mit ym / vnd fur frolich*en* heym czu seinen brudern' [one day he was praying at her tomb with great earnestness and devotion when he saw a finger flowing out in the oil. He took the relic with great joy and devotion and thanked Our Lord Jesus Christ and her as well for his reward and took the relic with him and travelled home to his brothers rejoicing] (fol. cclvj[r]). Katherine's liberality with her body parts (the monk is rewarded with his own personal relic, her finger) may perpetuate the foregrounding of the body (starvation, flagellation, beheading) in the saint's martyrdom. The finger reminds the reader of Christ's placing of a ring on Katherine's finger in the mystic marriage, which is mirrored throughout the text in small details (like smaller recursive reflexions in mirrors the greater the degree of mirroring). The flowing oil takes the reader back to the oil flowing from the saint's bones at the beginning of the miracle stories, a fountain that brings grace into the life of the individual devotee. The trigger is prayer, something every reader can practise at home, so a model is established of individual devotion that might lead to a similar miracle. A finger features in the penultimate miracle story as a relic in a Cologne church, where it is visited on Saint Katherine's Day by a usurer, leaps out of its locked reliquary in front of everyone's eyes and only returns once the usurer has realized his sinfulness, confessed and returned all his ill-gotten gains – a case of the saint literally pointing the finger of blame (fol. cclix[r]). Cologne recurs as part of a discussion about the decline in miracles at saints' tombs, though Fabri hurriedly assures the reader of Saint Katherine's continuing activity: 'Great miracles are wrought at this day by St. Catharine in many places—for instance, in the monastery of nuns of the Order of Canons Regular at Reuenroth in the Diocese of Cologne, at which place unheard-of miracles have come to pass, seeing that it is said that oil, milk, balsam, and manna all flow from one small bone of St. Catharine; and other astounding things are said to have happened there on the testimony of truthful witnesses' (Fabri, *Wanderings*, vol. 2, part 2, pp. 603–4). Unfortunately it has not proved possible to find out anything more about Reuenroth except that its church, dedicated to Saint Katherine, dates from the twelfth century.

[87]   'And they were all filled with the Holy Ghost, and began to speak with other tongues, as the Spirit gave them utterance' (The Acts 2:4).

at dawn, symbolic of Christ's own resurrection, again highlights the triumph of (Christian) life over death promised by the Crucifixion, itself commemorated in the mass and echoed by Katherine's administering of her own body (the oil from her bones) to revive Theodorus.[88]

The bishop's identity as a shadow Katherine (in parallel to Katherine's presentation as a shadow Christ) is reinforced by her gift to him of a ring and a letter written in golden letters. Since gold symbolizes majesty and eternity (it does not rust), her words are marked as transmitting eternal truth and *Der Heiligen Leben*, as a vessel for that truth, morphs into a shadow letter.[89] Letter, ring and the fragrance she leaves behind reinforce the trail of "left-over" objects scattered throughout the legend and miracle stories as reinforcement of the latter's authenticity. With their noses cut off, Sabinus and Theodorus were unable to smell her scent, so it marks not just Saint Katherine's virtue but also their restoration to wholeness and her triumph over evil. Sabinus (identified by his Christian name now he has been restored to recognizable individuality) reads the three-line letter: 'Sabine du solt wissen / dye buchstaben sollen czwischen

---

[88]   A Katharinenkloster prayer specifically addresses this quality: 'Gegrusset seistu die noch deinem tod rast auff dem perg sÿna du heilsame ertzneÿ der die dich an ruffnn vnd dich von hertzen suchn Gegrussett seistü von der grab ol rinet das da heilet die seüchen aller der die do siech sein' [Hail to you, who after your death rested on Mount Sinai, you healing medicine for those who call on you and seek you with their hearts. Hail to you, from whose grave oil flows that heals the illnesses of all those who are sick] ('Von sancta katherina', in Germanisches Nationalmuseum Sammelhandschrift 114 263b, [fol. 70ʳ–72ʳ]).

[89]   Golden letters as signifiers of the divine occur in a later story: in Canterbury a virtuous young scholar who serves Saint Katherine assiduously is entrusted with the education of the king's son. The prince is a bad pupil; the master threatens to beat him; the prince runs away and jumps off a bridge into a river. The master calls on Saint Katherine to protect his pupil: 'da wolt sant Katherin yren diener nit yn notten lassen vnd kam czuhand vnd behyelt des kuniges sun auff ynn dem wasser daz ym nie nichts geschach / vnd beleib frisch vnd wolgesund von tercz czeyt biß an den anndern tag czu tercz zeit vnd was yn dem wasser recht sam er yn einem lustigen hawß were' [Then Saint Katherine did not want to abandon her servant in his distress and came straightaway and kept the king's son afloat in the water so that nothing happened to him and he stayed fresh and well from terce that day until terce the next day; and even though he was in the water he felt as though he was in a pleasant, well-appointed house] (fol. cclvijᵛ). When she brings the child to the river bank 'vornen an dem hembd ob dem herczen da stund ein vers auß dem Psalter mit gulden buchstaben der sprach Herre gib mir sinn vnd vernunfft das ich deyne gebot lerne' [on the front of his shirt, just above his heart, was inscribed in letters of gold a verse from the Psalter. It said: 'Lord, give me wit and reason so that I may learn Your Commandments']. In other words, the immersion in the river acts as a baptism; the gold letters, symbolic of transfiguration, serve as visible proof of the miracle that has happened, so the miracle can be read on the prince's body, as if he were a billboard for the marvellous. The prince is a walking text, a self-displaying relic.

mir vnd dir sein ein czeichen der ewigen lieb'.[90] Effectively, this is a "love letter" that, combined with the ring, makes Sabinus into a "bridegroom" of Katherine. Next Katherine writes: 'An d*er* anderen zeyl stu*n*d dein grosser schmercz vnd dye lieb die du zu mir hast dy bereyt dir dye ewige*n* frewd' (fol. cclv^v).[91] Physical suffering for and emotional constancy to Katherine have ensured Sabinus eternal life. He has replicated her martyrdom and receives a parallel, if lesser, reward (because neither the bride of Christ nor bridegroom of Mary). Finally, '[a]n der drite*n* czeyl stund geschriben du solt den Herczogen tauffen vn*d* solt noch czehe*n* iar leben / darnach kummest du zu mir auff de*n* Palast des ewigen kuniges' (fol. cclv^v).[92] Just as Katherine converted the previously heathen Faustina and Porphyrius, so Sabinus will baptize the heathen duke.

The following day the duke witnesses the miraculous realization of Katherine's intervention: Sabinus, alive and whole, salves the abbot's limbs and restores him to life by the end of the mass. Paradoxically, the heathen duke becomes the Christian reader's eyewitness guarantor of the veracity of these events. Eyes as the channel to the soul for (divine, salvatory) truth effect the repentance and conversion of the spiritually blind duke and his men, who are baptized by the bishop. Conversion leads to exemplary charity, that is, to financial gain for the Church: the heirless duke sells his land, donating part of the proceeds to the Sinai monastery.[93] The

---

[90] 'Sabinus, you should know that these letters shall be a sign of eternal love between you and me'.

[91] 'On the next line stood your great pain; and the love you feel for me bestows on you eternal bliss'.

[92] 'On the third line was written that you shall baptize the duke and live for another ten years, after which you will join me in the palace of the eternal King'.

[93] This corresponds to the Western feudal model as Bedouins were nomads who did not own land. Moreover, the duke's actions align with the familiar strategy of presenting Muslims as more pious and respectful of holy places than Christians. Even Bernhard von Breidenbach, whose pilgrimage report is notable for its anti-Islamic vitriol, admits this: 'Item die Sarracen halten Salomons tempel in grosser ere · vn*d* lyden kein vnreynigkeit dar ynn · sye gen mit blossen fußen dar ynn · vnd nennen ynen den heiligen velsen vnd eyn tempel des herren · vn*d* das vß sollicher vrsach · wann mitten dar yn ist eyn kleyner velß mit eym yssin gitter zů ring vmbgeben · vnd als vns die ma*m*malucken · das ist die verlaugetten cristen sagetten · keyn sarracen oder heyd vermißet sich de*n* selben velsen ynn eynigen weg zů nahen · vnd ko*m*men doch von verren landen den velsen andechtiglichen an zů betten · wan vil gar grosser wu*n*der zeychen leset man vff dem selben velsen geschehen syn' [The Saracens hold Solomon's Temple in great reverence and tolerate no uncleanliness in it. They walk round inside it with bare feet and call it the holy rock and a temple of the Lord. They do so because in its centre there is a small rock surrounded by iron railings and the Mamelukes – that is, the Christians who deny their faith – told us that no Saracen or heathen presumes to go anywhere near it. Yet they come from distant lands in order to worship the rock devoutly for we read that many great miracles took place on that rock] (*Die heyligen reyssen*, [fol. 32^r]). Moreover, alms-giving is one of the five pillars of Islam.

duke accompanies Sabinus and Theodorus to Rome, travelling literally and metaphorically from the physical margins of the Catholic world to its centre to gain indulgences; once in Rome he gives more money to the poor. The converted heathen becomes a model of Christian charity and piety: 'Darnach stifftet er ein Closter yn sant Katherinen ere d*az* heist der sal gottes vnd gab vil erbs vn*d* eygens darein vnd wird ein Munich yn dem Closter vnd dienet vnserm herre*n* vnd seiner lieben Mutter Marie vn*d* sa*n*t Katherin mit fleyß biß an sein end' (fol. cclv^v).[94] The whole story testifies to Katherine's power: her actions integrate a previous enemy of the faith into the heart of Christendom. She defuses, textually at least, the threat that is Islam by catalysing its submission to Christianity. The tale then ties up loose ends so that no element of Katherine's miracle is lost: thanks to his borrowed tongue Sabinus speaks both Latin and Greek until his death 10 years later. An inversion of the original miracle confirms it posthumously:

> da sucht man dy czungen yn seine*n* mund / da fand man keine darin da vo*n* sol niemant zweyfeln Sant Katherin hab ir czungen wider genumen die si ym vor zehe*n* iare*n* gelihe*n* het vn*d* d*az* fingerlein vn*d* de*n* brieff behelt man noch zu meila*n*d zu einer gedechtnuß des zeiche*n*s. (fol. cclv^v)

> [They looked for the tongue in his mouth and found none, which should leave no one in any doubt whatsoever that Saint Katherine reclaimed the tongue she

---

Breidenbach notes: 'Do [sancti Abrahe castel] ist gar eyn richer vnd herlicher spytall vnder gewalt der sarracenen vnd herschung deß Soldans vnd allen denen menschen waz sect sie joch syen die dar ko*m*men vnd das almusen begeren gibt man brodt vnd öll vnnd eyn gemüse · Da beckt man all tag tusent vnd zwey hundert brodt daz den armen wurdt vß geben · vnd durch eyn gantz jar wurdt so groß almusen do vßgeben daz die summ der expenß oder vßgebung kommet vff · xxiiij · hundert ducaten · ... Vnder wegen als wir ritten kamen wir zů vil cisternen dar vß die sarraceni mit grosser erbeyt wasser schopffen vnnd reychen eß den pilgern vmb gottes willen' [There can be found an eminently rich and magnificent hospice under the power of the Saracens and rule of the Sultan. Bread, oil and vegetables are given to everyone who comes there desiring alms, regardless of their religion. Twelve hundred loaves are baked there every day and distributed to the poor. Throughout the course of one year so many alms are distributed that the total expense or outlay amounts to 24 hundred ducats ... As we were riding on our road we came to a large number of wells from which the Saracens draw water with considerable effort and give it to pilgrims for the sake of God] (*Die heyligen reyssen* [fol. 113^r]).

[94]   'After all this he founded a monastery dedicated to Saint Katherine; it is called the Chamber of God. He endowed it with much of his heritage and property and became a monk in that monastery and served Our Lord and His dear Mother and Saint Katherine assiduously until the day he died'. The *Mirabilia Romae* lists a church and convent dedicated to Saint Katherine in the vicinity of Saint Peter's 'am stein wege' (I have been unable to identify this church). It contained relics in the form of the oil and milk that flowed from her body (*Mirabilia Romae* (Nuremberg: [Peter Wagner], 1491), [fol. 53^v]).

had lent him ten years previously. The ring and the letter are kept in Milan in commemoration of the miracle].

Absence of the tangible (the tongue) paradoxically confirms the presence of the miraculous, which now reverts from the human plane to the divine. The tongue functions as a transmitter of the miraculous because it can speak an eyewitness account of the physically improbable; now the narrator intervenes to become guarantor of the seemingly incredible. Just as Christ's ring remains on Katherine's finger after the mystic marriage, the ring and letter she gives the bishop remain as tangible, accessible evidence of salvatory events, relics the reader may see for himself in Milan. The letter, preserved inside the reliquary shrine of *Der Heiligen Leben*, lends this text authority as a "genuine" historical document.[95]

In a subsequent story Katherine's own vision is replicated in another of the self-referential echoes that bind the narrative: a good man slackens in his devotion to Katherine, who proves her loyalty to her servants by seeking him out (fol. cclvj[r]). The man's dream parallels Katherine's pre-conversion vision of Christ: 'da sach er vil schoner iunckfrawen fur yn gen vnder den gieng eyn schone iunckfraw die verhielt ir antlitz vor ym dy het er gern gesehen wann sie leuchtet mit schonheit vber die andern all / da wolt si sich nit lassen sehen' (fol. cclvj[r]).[96] Katherine's denial of sight of herself to her follower and the radiant beauty of the desired object (as badge of its virtue) form a deliberate analogy to Christ's denial of His face to Katherine. As in her conversionary sequence, vision is denied in

---

[95]   The story, one of the longest, reads like an attempt to promote relics at Milan, but it has not proved possible to establish whether Milan possesses a letter and ring attributed to Saint Katherine. In addition, this story prefigures a later one in which Saint Katherine stands in for the miscreant abbess of a convent dedicated to her.

[96]   'Then he saw many beautiful maidens processing in front of him amongst whom walked a beautiful maiden who kept her face hidden from him. He would gladly have seen her as her beauty was even more radiant than all the others' but she did not want to allow herself to be seen'. The dream as sight of an alternative reality or more perfect world has a long tradition: 'Seit Menschengedenken übt der T. eine fast numinose Anziehungskraft aus. Da er anders als die Tageswirklichkeit ist, zugleich aber auch Bildelemente aus dem Tagesleben bietet, sah man in ihm oft den Ort, an dem eine andere Wirklichkeit in den Menschen einbricht. Als einer Offenbarung der Gottheit kann dem T. die gleiche Wirklichkeit zukommen wie dem Wachgeschehen. In vielen Kulturen findet sich die Meinung, die Seele verlasse den Körper während des Schlafes' [Since time immemorial the dream has exercised an almost luminous attraction. As it is different from the reality experienced during the day, while at the same time incorporating images from the day, the dream is often seen as the place in which a different reality invades people. As divine revelation the dream may be just as real as events experienced while awake. Many cultures believe the soul leaves the body during sleep] (*Die Religion in Geschichte und Gegenwart*, vol. 6, pp. 1001–4 (p. 1001)).

a state which itself constitutes an altered form of vision closer to divine truth. However, in the context of Katherine's life and miracles even denied vision suggests unrealized potential for virtue. Whilst withholding sight of one's face is tantamount to refusing the beholder a personal relationship, it also signals that one should never lose sight of the saints' importance as intermediaries between God and the individual in need. Moreover, Katherine's interaction with the Christ Child, who ultimately grants her not just sight of His face but the mystic marriage, becomes the ultimate model for the individual's relationship to the Lord: constant service and union of one's soul with the Godhead.[97] In the dream, one of the saint's companions, when asked the identity of the maiden concealing herself, performs the hermit's role in identifying the devotee's transgression:

> Es ist sant Katherin die dir lieb was vnd du yr nun vergessen hast darumb will sie sich nit lassen sehen da erschrack er gar sere vnd fur auff vor grossem leid in dem schlaff vnd het gar grosse rew darumb daz er si ausz dem sinn het gelassen / vnd keret furbas sein gemut mit gannczer liebe wider czu yr vnd dyenet yr mit ganczen ernst vncz an sein end / vnd starb da seliglich daz erwarb ym sant Katherin vmm got. (fol. cclvj^r)

> ['It is Saint Katherine, whom you loved and whom you have now forgotten. For that reason she does not wish to allow herself to be seen'. He was completely horrified by this and, stricken with immense pain, started in his sleep and was filled with remorse for having let her slip his mind. Thenceforth he turned his whole heart and soul to loving her absolutely and served her with great dedication until the end of his days and died a blessed death, which Saint Katherine obtained for him from God].

Denial of vision leads to repentance to renewed devotion to a blessed end, although Katherine's servant is not allowed sight of her face even after he renews his devotion to her, much as the judge is not allowed regrowth of his hand. What is striking is the vocabulary used to express realization and remorse: sudden physical movement ("erschrack"; "fur auff") signals emotional movement as pain replaces

---

[97]   This model would have been particularly pertinent within a convent; and the procession of Katherine and her female companions may reflect the procession of nuns to service in their church, where they would have seen and prayed to images of the saint. It may also have simultaneously reflected and provided a model for the civic procession of a saint's relics, events which 'reflected the social relationship between governed and governor, between church and state, between class, gender, and age cohorts' and the route of which defined the 'geography of the sacred' (Goodich, *Violence and Miracle*, p. 18).

indifference ("gar sere"; "vor grossem leid"; "gar grosse rew").[98] The light, sound, procession and gestures also contribute to the theatricality of the vision, which unfolds like a staged performance of punishment and reconciliation. Katherine acts like a jilted girlfriend, a *minnedame* who rewards constant service as her servant eventually dies a good death. The vision foreshadows a later one in which Katherine's role as the "other woman" in a devotee's life prompts his wife's suicide.

The theme of vision as the road to redemption is continued in two other miracle stories, both of which concern canons. In the first, the canon, who, unusually, is named, dated (1226) and located near Nuremberg,[99] does not experience the vision himself but is saved by that of his chaplain, whose loyalty mirrors Saint Katherine's own:

> d*er* hett eine*n* tugentliche*n* Capplan / d*er* sach eines nachtes yn einem gesicht das vnser herr Jhes*us* crist*us* zu gericht sasß vnd sein herr der von Wiltingen wa*r*d fur gericht bracht / vn*d* eyn Priester d*er* gie*ng* mit seinem herren all tag zu tisch dy wurden beyd zu dem tod vervrteilet. (fol. cclvj[v])

> [He had a virtuous chaplain who one night had a vision of Our Lord Christ sitting in judgement; and his master, the Lord of Wiltingen, was brought to judgement, as well as a priest who dined with him every day. They were both condemned to death].

The fact that the self-indulgent canon's devotion to Saint Katherine is not in itself enough to prevent his eternal damnation echoes the satire directed against the clergy in the German *Schwank* and French *fabliau* traditions; and warns against taking the saint's favour for granted. The contrast between actual and ideal is all the more pointed for the model of self-abnegation demonstrated in previous story

---

[98] The rhetoric of pain parallels the rhetoric of diminishing love ("ließ er ab an der liebe"; "gedacht ga*r* selten an si"; "ließ si auß dem mut"), thereby stressing the strength of the remorse.

[99] He is described as 'ein reycher Korherr zu Wirczburg der hieß der von Wiltinge*n*' [a rich canon from Würzburg called von Wiltingen] (fol. cclvj[v]). For a discussion of the origins, adaption and context of this story see Eis, 'Lupold von Wiltingen', pp. 83–91. Eis sees a connexion to both the Klarissenkloster (which he claims is dedicated to Katherine; however, according to Fehring and Ress, *Die Stadt Nürnberg*, it was dedicated first to Mary Magdalene, then to Saint Clare) and the Katharinenkloster in Nuremberg, since one source for the story is the Dominican Johann Herolt (d. 1468), who preached in German, especially in the Klarissenkloster. Eis seems postulates a German source for Herolt's sermons in the collections of legends, sermons and devotional literature produced in the Katharinenkloster and points to one of its manuscripts, copied by Kunigund Niklasin, which contains exclusively Katherine material in German and was lent to the Klarissenkloster.

by a mere handworker who impoverishes himself, such is his desire to give alms to Saint Katherine. That the virtuous chaplain has the vision is a further indication of the distance between his superior, whose sin is explicitly identified as gluttony, and salvation. Privileging of the body through overindulgence offers a grotesque inversion of Katherine's privileging of her body through fasting. The chaplain's vision performs multiple functions: it parallels Saint Katherine's own; it binds the narrative together through association with other visions in the text; and it pre-empts Judgement Day since Christ sits in judgement on Herr von Wiltingen. In it Saint Katherine intervenes for her servant and wins him one year's grace in which to improve his conduct. His partner in vice has no one to intervene on his behalf and, in a reflexion of Saint Katherine's martyrdom and foreshadowing of the canon's fate, is executed in the vision. When, the next day at table, site of transgression, the chaplain tells the canon about his dream-vision they together seek out the priest, only to discover him dead in bed. The priest's corpse, translated not through the air but across the barrier separating human and divine realities, functions like the wedding ring, the physical object left behind, relic-like, that bears witness to the reality of the dream; it also represents a dramatic negation of the body as a source of pleasure in its consumption of food. Herr von Wiltingen, shocked into restoring to the priests everything he has unjustly taken from them, gives away his worldly goods (like Katherine herself after the mystic marriage) and becomes a monk at Heilbronn, where he dies a good death. Through his complete withdrawal from worldly pleasure into ascetic service he functions as a living relic, the tangible proof of a divine truth that activates potential virtue. Contained monastic ritual provides the inverted mirror image of his initial uncontained, disorderly indulgence.[100] The

---

[100]   The next story reinforces the first, since it features another canon who routinely commits three Deadly Sins (Vanity, Avarice, Lust). God's proposed punishment is revealed to him in a vision of judgement and Hell. That the canon himself has the vision highlights the gravity of his obstinate sinning. Saint Katherine does not intervene until he repents, calling on her in his heart. Fear is used as the means to redemption; and Katherine appears in her role as Holy Helper, persuading God to lengthen the canon's life so that he may do penance for his sins. God accedes for Saint Katherine's sake, so her servant's transgressions function as a vehicle for emphasis of her particular prestige and loyalty even to sinners condemned by other saints. On awakening the canon reinforces the message of the previous story by mirroring the actions of his narrative predecessor: he becomes a monk, renounces his living and all his worldly goods 'vnd busset sein sund vnd gedacht alle zeyt es were besser er peyniget seinen leyb hye vnd hett dort ewige frewd / dann das er hye wol lebet vnd dort ewige peyn hett' [and performed penance for his sins and thought all the time that it was better for him to chastize his body here on earth and to have eternal bliss there in Heaven than to live a life of indulgence here and suffer an eternity of pain after death] (fol. cclvij[r]). This more explicit moral is in keeping with the extreme ends of the behavioural spectrum illustrated by the text, which runs from sin to piety and renunciation. The pain inflicted by the canon

dream-vision provides the sight of a potential reality that it subsequently negates by prompting the action necessary to evade that reality, a function performed by the text itself.

Katherine's loan of her tongue is transcended by her loan of her entire body in the next story. At its core lies a debate about "right" and "wrong" forms of love that thematizes the issue of chastity in the religious orders and its precariousness in non-enclosed communities. The location of the narrative in a named town, Kameratten,[101] lends it the authority of an actual case study. Kameratten boasts a large convent whose abbess is noble, rich and virtuous. Her brother visits the convent in the company of another knight, who is forced by illness to remain there. At her brother's behest the abbess tends the sick knight assiduously; the latter falls in love with her and:

> thett sein hercz gen yr auff / vnd sprach solt er seinen willen nit mit ir habe*n* so must er ye sterben / da was der frawen gar leyd / vn*d* nam yn da vo*n* so si best mocht das halff alles nit wann der vei*n*d hett yn vberwunden dem dy kewscheyt alweg wyd*er* ist. (fol. cclvij*r*)

> [opened his heart to her and said that if he did not have his way with her he would inevitably die. This troubled the lady deeply and she tried to divert him from these thoughts as best she might. However, her efforts were to no avail, since he had been conquered by the enemy to whom all chastity is repugnant].

In this first stage of the narrative *caritas* – the nun's duty of charitable love towards the sick and needy – battles against *luxuria* or lust. Driven by the Devil, the knight chooses spiritual death over the physical death he claims will ensue if he does not have his way with the abbess. Although initially she remains virtuous, her duty as a nun and to her brother ensures continued exposure to temptation, prolonging the conflict. Eventually lust triumphs: the abbess 'gieng eines nachtes vo*n* altar czu altar nach yrer gewonheyt mit grosser andacht vnd het si der boß geyst gar vberwunden da*z* si ye mit de*m* ritter wolt vnd wolt vrlaub vo*n* de*n* heiligen nemen' (fol. cclvij*r*).[102] Despite succumbing to lust (the spiritual blindness caused

---

on his body through renunciation and penance is a pale shadow of the torment he would have experienced in Hell, only it serves as salvation rather than the penalty for salvation lost. The dream-vision provides the sight of a potential reality that it subsequently negates by prompting the action necessary to evade that reality, a function performed by the text itself.

101 It has not proved possible to identify this town.

102 'went from altar to altar one night with great devotion, as she was accustomed to do; and the evil spirit had overcome her so completely that she wanted to run away with the knight and wanted to say goodbye to the saints'.

by sexual desire is symbolized by the night),[103] the abbess is still locked into habits of devotion which eventually save her: she does not desecrate the convent by sinning but departs it; she visits each altar in turn 'nach yrer gewonheyt'; she takes her leave of the saints, suggesting an intensely felt personal relationship to them which expresses itself in a direct address to Mary: 'lyebe muter vnser fraw ich byn czu vast anczundt mit vngeorneter lieb mit dem Ritter vnd mag nit lennger bleyben' (fol. cclvijʳ).[104] The story coalesces into the struggle between worldly love, here represented by sexual desire, and spiritual love, represented by the abbess's relationship to the saints. She recognizes but stops resisting her sin, her use of "anczundt" suggesting the flames of both passion and the Hell that awaits her for breaking her vows. The conflict between different types of love takes visible form in the conflict between different types of light; the lack of accompanying radiance when the Virgin and Katherine, models of "correct" chaste marital love, appear to the abbess indicates the dimming of the latter's virtue by lust. The spiritual love (*caritas*) still present in her soul is expressed by her recommendation of the convent to Mary's care. On the Virgin's appearance, the reader, conditioned by the miracle stories to this point, expects vision of

---

[103]   It is also the opposite of the radiance emitted by Katherine.

[104]   'Dear Mother, Our Lady, I am much too inflamed with illicit love for the knight and cannot stay here any longer'. Elisabeth Vavra discusses both the animation of saints' images (statues, pictures, crucifixes) recorded in such sources as Caesarius von Heisterbach, German nuns' *vitae* and visions from the fourteenth century; and nuns' visions that were influenced by works of art. Mary and the Christ Child feature particularly frequently in these visions. One aspect they share is the particularly intense, intimate relationship nuns have to particular works of art, as if they were living people. Vavra suggests images were used for personal meditation; for the instruction of nuns and the laity; and for facilitating the empathic experience by the believer of Christ's own suffering (to the point of *imitatio*) (Elisabeth Vavra, 'Bildmotiv und Frauenmystik – Funktion und Rezeption', in Peter Dinzelbacher and Dieter R. Bauer (eds), *Frauenmystik im Mittelalter* (Ostfildern: Schwabenverlag, 1985), pp. 201–30). Carola Jäggi makes a similar point in her discussion of convent cloisters and the use of the images they housed, citing an image of the Virgin that seeks to comfort a distressed nun by laying her hand on the latter's head; and of a crucifix in the cloisters at St. Katharinenthal that reminds the sick nun Richmut von Winterthur that even Christ had to suffer to regain His own Kingdom (Carola Jäggi, *Frauenklöster im Spätmittelalter. Die Kirchen der Klarissen und Dominikanerinnen im 13. und 14. Jahrhundert*, Studien zur internationalen Architektur- und Kunstgeschichte 34 (Petersberg: Michael Imhof, 2006), pp. 293 and 302 respectively (citing Ruth Meyer, *Das 'St. Katharinentaler Schwesternbuch'. Untersuchung, Edition, Kommentar*, Münchener Texte und Untersuchungen zur deutschen Literatur des Mittelalters 104 (Tübingen: Niemeyer, 1995), pp. 123 and 98 respectively)). Visions of Katherine and other saints in these stories therefore express a familiar pattern of convent spiritual life and (especially Dominican) nuns' personal devotion.

the sacred to result in realization, penance and redemption.[105] Mary reminds the abbess of her oath to Christ, who, as 'ein blum ... aller iunckfrawen vnd eyn spyegel aller reinikeyt',[106] is the model of the virginal purity she abandons (fol. cclvij^r). Further, Christ is the abbess's true bridegroom, whom she wed on taking the veil, so she commits (spiritual) adultery by leaving Him for the knight.[107] Curiously unbothered, the abbess proceeds to the altar of the Holy Cross and addresses Christ Himself: 'Mich hatt leiblich begird als gar vberwunden das ich nit beleyben mag' (fol. cclvij^r).[108] The narrative presents the subsequent miracle of Christ's image coming alive not as a vision but as fact:

> Da ließ vnser herr sein wunden vor ir fliessen / vnd sprach zu ir Liebe tochter
> kere dich nit von mir / ich han dich herttiglichen gekaufft mit meyner marter
> vnd mit meinem tod / vnd bin durch dich gecreuzigt worden da von laß dich dy
> anfechtunge nit vber winden das halff alles nit an yr. (fol. cclvij^r)[109]

[Then Our Lord caused blood to flow from His wounds before her eyes and said to her, 'Dear daughter, do not turn away from me. I have paid a heavy price for you with my martyrdom and my death and have been crucified for your sake. For

---

[105]   If, of course, he has read the text sequentially. The appearance of Mary is in itself a further disjuncture as the reader would expect Saint Katherine; it may reflect the gravity of the abbess's sin.

[106]   'a flower ... of all virgins and a mirror of all purity'.

[107]   Events thus constitute the inverse reflexion of Katherine's life so characteristic of both her *vita* and the miracle stories: the abbess mirrors Katherine as bride of Christ, yet reverses Katherine's rejection of human, sexual love and charts its consequences, the path Katherine might have trodden away from sanctity to sin.

[108]   'I have been so overcome by physical desire that I cannot stay'.

[109]   In 'Living the Dream' we have seen the image from an illustrated Upper Rhenish manuscript of Raymond of Capua's biography of Katherine of Siena (1347–80) which depicts Katherine drinking blood from the wound in Christ's side until 'she was replete in body and in soul' (Hamburger, *The Visual and the Visionary*, p. 460); and Mechthild von Hackeborn's vision of the pietà in which she is urged by Mary to kiss Christ's wounds (Vavra, 'Bildmotiv und Frauenmystik', p. 211). Steinke reproduces an image from Katharina Muffel's copy of the *Breviarium Romanum* that depicts a nun kneeling before an altar on which an altarpiece depicts the Crucifixion with Mary and John at the foot of the Cross and on the right-hand wing (from viewer's perspective) an unidentifiable saint. The nun's hands are folded in prayer; in the air in front of her four angels carry the crucified Christ, His hands crossed and bound in front of Him (the bindings also make a cross-shape), His wound on His right foot visible, His hands, feet and legs streaming with blood. He looks down at nun; she looks up at Him (Munich, Bayerische Staatsbibliothek, Cgm 177, fol. XII^r; Steinke, *Paradiesgarten*, p. 167). Thus a visual example of Christ's display of His bloody suffering to a nun was readily accessible to those in the Katharinenkloster.

this reason do not allow yourself to be overcome by temptation'. However, none of that had the slightest effect on her].

In a miracle that transcends all others in the Katherine stories, Christ inhabits His image, animating it in a re-creation of the Crucifixion as His wounds start to bleed. A theologically versed reader could retrieve various wax tablets from the storehouse of his memory: first, Katherine's own bloody wounds after flagellation; second, the transmutation of her stolen oil into blood in her first miracle (fol. ccliiij^v); third, the miraculous transformation into the body of the crucified Christ displaying His wounds of a host during celebration of mass by Pope Gregory; fourth, Saint Bernhard's experience while praying in front of the crucified Christ of the latter bending forward from the Cross to embrace him;[110] fifth, Christ's ministering of the Eucharist to Saint Katherine with His own hands. This layering of the miraculous is reinforced by Christ's direct appeal to the abbess: the flow of His blood morphs into the flow of His words, becoming a metaphor for the salvific intention of both the printed text and the words spoken by the priest during mass. Christ reminds the abbess of the salvational history being re-enacted before her eyes, His martyrdom on the Cross for her sake, to which she becomes an actual eyewitness. That the abbess ignores Christ's words indicates the strength of her lust and through lust of sin generally. Sexuality entered the world with the Fall; like Eve the abbess is acting out the sinfulness inherent in all women.

Indeed, the whole narrative stages a drama of thwarted redemption complete with scenery (the interior of the convent church); stage lighting (night; the light of visions); props (altars, paintings); costume (the nun's habit, no longer the tangible outward manifestation of her inner state but a disguise for it); dialogue; special effects (Christ's flowing blood) and action (the procession round the altars). The performance (one can imagine a dramatized reading-aloud of the story) culminates in the nun's visit to Saint Katherine's altar:

> vnd gieng czu leczt fur sant Katherin altar dy was yr gar lieb / vnd was hawbtfraw
> yn dem Closter vnd sprach Junckfraw sant Katherin ich bin aller ding yn der
> anfechtung vberwunden / vnd mag nicht yn dem Closter bleyben Da erscheyn
> yr die lieb heylig iunckfraw sant Katherin vnd sprach / liebe tochter gedenck
> darann / das ich eines edelen kuniges tochter bin gewesen vnd het gar groß gutt
> vnd ere / vnd mocht gar wol vil lustes haben gehabt yn czeytlichen dingen / das
> verschmechet ich alles vnd gab allen zeytlichen lust auff durch meinen herren

---

110   This resonates with both the believer's reception of the body of Christ during mass and the bridal mysticism of the Song of Songs (*Spiegel der Seligkeit*, p. 207). Saint Bernard of Clairvaux also has a vision of suckling on the Virgin's breast.

Jhesum Christum vnd leyd gar grosse marter vnd peyn vnd einen herten tod von seinet wege*n* vberwindt dich yn der anfechtung. (fol. cclvij^r)

[And went last of all to Saint Katherine's altar. The abbess loved Saint Katherine, to whom the convent was dedicated, and said to her, 'Virgin Saint Katherine, I have been completely overwhelmed by temptation and cannot remain in the convent'. Then the beloved holy virgin Saint Katherine appeared to her and said, 'Dear daughter, remember that I was the daughter of a noble king and possessed great wealth and honour and could have enjoyed all worldly pleasures to the full; yet I scorned all that and renounced all worldly pleasure in the name of my Lord Jesus Christ and suffered great martyrdom and tribulation and a hard death for His sake. Overcome your temptation'].

In the trinity of farewells the culmination is Saint Katherine, patron saint of the convent, who, in her appeal to the abbess to renounce temptation, establishes a hierarchy of suffering that highlights the paltriness of renouncing sexual love by comparison to the pain of martyrdom: 'Nun leydest du doch wid*er* schleg noch stoß vnd vergeust dein blutt nicht' (fol. cclvij^r).[111] The abbess's threefold visit to three altars (the symbolism of the Trinity is obvious) without being diverted from her course indicates her distance from God and entrapment in sin. It also effects a serial thwarting of reader expectation: two failures (Mary and Christ) would normally pave the way for the success of Saint Katherine as the abbess's favourite saint, as patron saint of the convent and as culmination of the sequence. Thwarting throws open the narrative: the reader might anticipate punishment for sin, yet another established pattern is Katherine's loyalty to those devoted to her, no matter how heinous their behaviour.

Finally the abbess commends the convent to Saint Katherine and departs with the knight, having given Katherine's image the key in another act that suggests an intensely felt, personal relationship to the saint experienced as a "real" person. Literally as well as metaphorically Katherine becomes the guardian of the foundation dedicated to her, whilst the abbess not only remains unpunished but appears rewarded: she and the knight spend many years together and have lovely children. Only when the knight dies and the source of temptation is removed does the abbess reconsider her life and decide to return to her convent and confess her sins. The path is opened by her realization of God's mercy: 'vnd gedacht ... daz dy barmherczikeyt gottes also grossz ist das er keynen

---

[111]   'Now you suffer neither blows nor punches nor do you shed your blood'. On becoming the bride of Christ Saint Katherine renounces the possibility of sexual relations ('allen zeytliche*n* lust' [all worldly pleasure] (fol. cclvij^r)), as the abbess did on taking the veil.

sund*er* ve*r*schmechet' (fol. cclvij*^r*).[112] On her arrival she finds Saint Katherine at the window:[113] 'dy hymelische*n* edelen Abtesin dy hett si dy iar alle an aller leut wissen yn dem Closter ve*r*wesen da erkannt si yr nicht' (fol. cclvij*^v*).[114] The abbess's failure to recognize Saint Katherine symbolizes her distance from God and monastic virtue after many years of living 'wyder yr sel heyl' (fol. cclvij*^r*).[115] As Katherine has assumed the abbess's appearance during her absence, it also indicates the latter's alienation from her true self. The story acts as validation of nuns' choice of a monastic life, particularly as Katherine has done more than lend a single individual, a bishop, her tongue so that he may continue office (cclv*^v*): she has lent an entire religious community her body,[116] ensuring the convent's continuing function and the spiritual wellbeing of its members:

> da sprach si zu yr es ist czeyt das du auß d*er* welt kummest vnd das ich czu hymel far vn*d* laß dich wissen das ich dich dy czeyt alle verwesen hann an allem dem d*az* an dein ampt czu tun w*az* da von leg dein geistlich gewannd an vn*d* verwiß dein ampt alß vor wann es weiß niemant d*az* du ausen bist gewesen. (fol. cclvij*^v*)

> [Then she said to her, 'It is time for you to leave the world and me to return to Heaven. I want to let you know that I have governed in your stead all this time and performed all the duties incumbent on your office, so don your spiritual

---

[112]   'and thought that God's mercy is so great that He does not turn His back on any sinner'.

[113]   This reflects actual medieval practice of a supervised window as the only interface with the world outside the convent walls. The Katharinenkloster had two: one with a wheel contraption for taking in goods from outside without seeing the donor; the other was double-barred or had nails to prevent physical contact (Fries, 'Kirche und Kloster', p. 44). Moreover, post-reform nuns observed enclosure strictly: when in 1487 Emperor Friedrich requested from the Council a Corpus Christi procession round the market square and Frauenkirche in which children and teachers from all four schools as well as priests, monks and nuns were to participate, the nuns from the convents of Saint Katherine and Saint Clare and the Carthusian monks successfully petitioned for exemption 'weil solchs der Regel ihrer Orden und ihrer Gewonheit zuwider were' [because such a thing contravened the rules of their order and their custom] (Müllner, *Annalen*, vol. 3, pp. 84–5). Civic processions took place mainly to celebrate the entrance into the city of the ruling emperor (cf. Müllner, *Annalen*, vol. 2, pp. 179–80 and pp. 354–6; vol. 3, pp. 10–13, pp. 102–5 and pp. 461–3); or the advent in Nuremberg of the *Reichskleinodien* (Müllner, *Annalen*, p. 247).

[114]   'the divine, noble abbess had governed the convent all those years without other people knowing. She did not recognize her'.

[115]   'contrary to the salvation of her soul'.

[116]   This echoes the metaphor of the Church as the body of Christ.

garments and take up your office as before, for no one knows that you have lived outside the convent'].

The saint literally embodies loyalty to the community that serves her: by disguising herself as the abbess, that is, by inhabiting a body separated from its soul by sin, she has both purified that body and preserved the spiritual health of the convent body innocent of the failings of its head.[117] The end of the story forms the reverse parallel of its beginning: the abbess rejoices, dons her habit, reclaims the key from Saint Katherine and resumes her office. Her habit is no longer a disguise for the lustful sinner but the true outward manifestation of her changed soul, so she re-inhabits her purified body and her office without any disjunction. As well as a model of loyalty, the saint serves as a model of humility, since a queen and true bride of Christ stoops to aid an errant devotee: 'daran merck wir ir grosse demutikeyt / das si sich *der* mue alß vil jare vnd*er*wannd vnd yn einem geistlichen schein gieng vnd tet alles das dy abtesin tun solt' (fol. cclvij*v*).[118] The abbess reveals the miracle – to which the nuns have been unwitting eyewitnesses – to the convent chapter:[119] like the oil flowing from the saint's bones, word of her miracles flows outwards to the convent community within the text to the convent community (initially the Katharinenkloster Nuremberg) outwith the text and through the printed edition of *Der Heiligen Leben* into Patrician homes and the city beyond the convent walls. Due the abbess's life-long performance of penance for her sins she dies blessed and the anticipated salvation of her soul is eventually realized. The story's length emphasizes the importance of its content for a convent community: the unceasing possibility of repentance and redemption; and the absolute value of love-as-*caritas*. Moreover, the animation of sacred images and their dialogue with mortals suggest that saints genuinely inhabit their images and are actually present – and active – within the convent community, a source of comfort, of moral pressure (above all on the abbess to emulate Saint Katherine) and miraculous potential that may have bound a community more tightly to the saints and through them to God.

---

[117] In this story the saint's whole body is the physical object that remains behind in a marked contrast to her denial of sight of her face to the man who slackened in his devotion. Katherine's "incarnation" parallels Christ's; symbolizes her "real presence" amongst her followers and embodies the potential for redemption present in all mankind.

[118] 'Let this show you her great humility as she subjected herself to that toil for all those years and pretended to be a member of the convent community and did everything the abbess should have done'.

[119] In the Katharinenkloster the chapter was held after mass; the reader announced the business for the day and a prayer was said. At the end of the chapter meeting nuns guilty of transgression confessed and were punished (Fries, 'Kirche und Kloster', p. 45).

One of the most striking miracle stories in the collection is that of Saint Katherine as the "other woman", cast in the role of the adored in this world rather than the next and hence a shadow abbess (fol. cclviijʳ–cclixʳ). The young son of a count is devoted to Saint Katherine and frequently prays in the church near his castle, which is dedicated to the saint. One day, however, he falls asleep in front of the altar and three beautiful maidens appear to him in a dream.[120] Katherine is frequently portrayed with two other female saints (apart from the Virgin), usually Barbara and either Agnes or Dorothy.[121] In language recalling Katherine's early self-assessment, the third maiden is described as 'vberflussiglichen schon', as wearing 'eyn czyerliche kron', as 'ein kunigin vbᵉr dy andern' and 'so wil schon vber dy andern alsz der moʳgen stern vber dye tag sterne scheynet' (fol. cclviijʳ).[122] These attributes immediately identify her as a martyr and as the bride of Christ, Himself described as the 'bright and morning star' (Revelation 22:16). Further, they echo both Marian poetry and *Minnesang*, expressing secular-sexual as well as spiritual love since the Morning Star is Venus.[123] Katherine the adored saint in Heaven is fused with Katherine the adored mistress on earth. In his dream the young man is too startled to look at her, covering his eyes with his hands and thereby simultaneously receiving and blocking physical and metaphysical vision

---

[120]   This resembles a vision Saint Dominic has of Mary accompanied by two virgins, Cecilia and Katherine herself, in which the former identifies herself as protector of the Dominican Order. In the vision Dominic is taken up to Heaven and sees the Trinity, all the angels and his fellow monks sheltering under the Virgin's cloak (*Der Heiligen Leben*, fol. cᵛ–cjʳ).

[121]   For example, in the Lorenzkirche a sandstone sculpture (c. 1410) on a pillar in the north aisle shows three virgin saints with their conventional attributes: Saint Katherine, Saint Agnes and Saint Barbara.

[122]   'extraordinarily beautiful'; 'a finely wrought crown'; 'a queen above all others'; 'her beauty outshone the others' as the morning star does the day stars'.

[123]   According to *Hall's Dictionary*, the star is usually seen on the Virgin's cloak. It derives from her title 'Star of the Sea' (Lat. *Stella Maris*), the meaning of the Jewish form of her name, Miriam (*Hall's Dictionary*, p. 330). The star was also associated with Saint Dominic, founder of the Dominican Order: '[A]ccording to one contemporary account his brow radiated a kind of supernatural light; another tells that his godmother saw a star descend on his brow at his baptism' (*Hall's Dictionary*, p. 106). In *Der Heiligen Leben* a blessed woman dreams, at the time of Dominic's birth, that he has a star on his forehead which illuminates the entire world and symbolizes his eradication of heresy through his teaching (fol. xcviijᵛ). In another story a master of Holy Scripture in Toulouse dreams of seven beautiful stars brought to his school; their radiance grows and illuminates the whole of Christendom. These stars symbolize Dominic, his six companions and their papal permission to preach, hear confession and eradicate heresy (fol. cjᵛ). This may partly explain the emphasis on radiance in the miracle stories of Katherine.

of the holy.[124] In his altered state he denies himself what in his waking state he desires. As with the discovery of Saint Katherine's body on Sinai, light serves as a guide to the believer and a signal of the miraculous. The altar (where the count falls asleep) was, in a medieval church, a particular focus of light in the form of candles illuminating both the altar as physical object and its central role in the liturgy. Whilst the altar is not specifically identified as dedicated to Katherine, it still forms the *locus* of the encounter between saint and devotee that transforms his love for her into a spousal relationship, since when Katherine upbraids him she says: 'wy tust du alsz gar beuerischen nun bist du doch edel Nun seyen wyr czu dir kummen vnd sehen dich so wil du vns nit sehen vnd verhabst dein augen Begerst du einer gesponsenn So nym vnser eine welhe du wilt' (fol. cclviij[r]).[125] The accusation of peasant behaviour discards the count from the courtly frame; his redemption, i.e. being spiritually as well as socially 'edel', is to look at the three maidens and choose one as his wife. Until he chooses, sight is not reciprocal: the count, who mirrors Christ's turning of his face from the unbaptized Katherine, is merely an object of the saints' vision rather than an active viewer in search of spiritual enlightenment. Katherine's demand recalls the Judgement of Paris, casting the count as a Christian Paris, the saints as Classical goddesses and Katherine as Helen, the most beautiful woman in the world: 'Da der Graff das sach vnd hort da sach er auff vnd ward sein hercz begossen mit einer hymelischen liebe' (fol. cclviij[r]).[126] Sight generates a love, flowing like Katherine's oil, that is carefully distinguished from the carnal form enjoyed by Paris and Helen.

The count requires prompting to choose the saint: 'wann als vil si schoner ist wan vnser eine / als vil ist si wirdiger mechtiger vnd gewaltiger bey got / vnd mag dir vnd allen den dy si anruffen basz gehelffen gegen got' (fol. cclviij[r]).[127] These words, which recall Katherine's reasons for rejecting Maxentius' son and the hermit's advocacy of Christ, foreground power as the basis for preference. Hierarchies of power are, then, built into the fabric of devotion and its textual embodiment, reinforcing and advertising the wisdom of Nuremberg's cultivation of Saint Katherine as a strategy for the maintenance of its own political and

---

[124] Being blinded by divine light marks a pivotal moment of transformation: cf. the Annunciation to the shepherds or Saint Paul on the road to Damascus.

[125] 'Why are you acting like a peasant when you are noble? Now we have come to you and are looking at you but you refuse to look at us and cover your eyes. If you wish a spouse, then choose one of us, whichever you want'.

[126] 'When the count saw and heard that he looked up and a divine love flowed into his heart'.

[127] 'For in the same way as she is more beautiful than any of us, so is she worthier, mightier and has more sway with God and is in a better position to intercede with God on behalf of all those who call on her'.

economic might. In addition to reinforcing the parallels between Christ and Katherine that identify her as superior to other saints, the narrative suggests the primacy of her bond with the count, whose failure to recognize her serves mainly to build up suspense before the dramatic revelation of her identity. The cleansing of his eyes with baptismal tears of joy introduces a motif familiar from the saint's life: baptism as clarifying clouded early vision and enabling recognition of the divine. His appeal, *Minnesänger*-like, for mercy results in a tangible sign of the saint's favour:

> Da seczett ymm die lieb heylig Junckfraw Sanndt Katherin gar eyn schonen Rosenkrancz auff sein hawbt der was von roten Rosen vnd sprach czu ym / Nym vnd behalt den krancz der sol ein zeichen sein einer rechten lieb zwischen mir vnd dir vnd hut dich daz du kein anndere fur mich nemest. (fol. cclviij^r)

> [Then the beloved holy virgin Saint Katherine placed a beautiful garland of roses onto his head. It was made of red roses. She said to him, 'Take and keep this garland as the sign of a true and proper love between you and me and beware of taking any other woman in my place'].

This act can be interpreted in a number of ways. First, in crowning her servant with a symbol of love, the garland of roses, Katherine performs the gesture of a courtly lady rewarding her lover with a symbol of her affection: in the *Große Heidelberger Liederhandschrift* images of poets crowned with a garland of roses include, for example, Kraft von Toggenburg (fol. xj^r), Jakob von Warte (fol. xviij^r) and Neidhart von Reuental (fol. Lxxxi^r). Second, since Katherine herself is compared to roses and lilies, the gift of roses could be read as the saint's gift of herself.[128] Third, crowning is a gesture of (feudal) power, as Katherine is obviously socially and spiritually superior to the count, but at the same time it acknowledges his devotion. Fourth, red roses symbolize the blood of Christ, whose wounds could be represented as roses.[129] Fifth, they symbolize martyrdom, so commemorate the

---

[128]   For example, a Katharinenkloster prayer starts 'Gegrusset seistu ... du lawtre ros vnd lilg' [Hail ... you pure rose and lily] (Stadtbibliothek Nürnberg, Cod. Cent. VII, 65, fol. 11^{r-v}). Lilies and roses also form the comparison for the beauty of the beloved in courtly romance: 'der wunsch was an ir garwe/ als der rôsen varwe/ under wîze liljen güzze/ und daz zesamene vlüzze/ und daz der munt begarwe/ wære von rôsen varwe/ dem gelîchete sich ir lîp' [She was the height of perfection / If someone wanted to pour rose red into lily white and mix it together so that the mouth was entirely rose red, that is what her appearance would resemble] (Hartmann von Aue, *Erec*, ll. 1700–3).

[129]   For example, on the Diptych with the Virgin and Child facing the Man of Sorrows (c. 1350) currently in the Kunsthalle, Karlsruhe (cf. Camille, *Gothic Art*, p. 117) or the roses

suffering of Katherine and the philosophers, externalized in the metaphorical roses in their cheeks since 'ire antlutz schinen recht alß dy roßen'.[130] Once more, layered symbolism condenses into a single object: at the altar where Christ's sacrifice for mankind is commemorated Katherine binds the count to her with a garland redolent of the Crown of Thorns, sign of Christ's martyrdom and ultimately of the love for man that moved God to sacrifice His son.[131] Katherine's words – 'Nym vnd behalt den krancz der sol ein zeiche*n* sein einer rechten lieb zwischen mir vnd dir'[132] – echo those of Christ at the Last Supper: 'Take, eat; this is my body' (Matthew 26:26); and 'This is my body which is given for you: this do in remembrance of me' (Luke 22:19). Katherine's gesture and speech encapsulate the conflict at the core of this story (as of the previous one), namely the privileging of the love for God over the love for man and the necessary sacrifice in living out loyalty to that love.

However, this story also fuses a debate on the balance between different types of love with a more specific concern. As Jeffrey Hamburger points out, roses were particularly significant in Dominican devotion, since the mystic Heinrich Seuse (c. 1295–1366) chose the rose for his attribute and a leitmotif in his autobiography:

> In almost all the images, which were integral to Suso's design for the book, the Dominican friar appears in the guise of a bride, crowned with a garland of red and white roses, bearing his other "attribute", the monogram of Christ, on his chest. Both symbols are written in blood, for the roses represent the stigmata on the friar's hands and shoes (his feet remain covered). In one of the visions recorded in the narrative, the noblewoman Anna, who asks an angel the meaning of the flowers, is told that the white roses signify his purity and the red roses his patience in the various kinds of suffering he must endure. And just as the golden halo that one usually paints around the head of saints signifies the eternal happiness which they possess in God,

---

carved on the wooden frame of Meister Francke's *Man of Sorrows* (c. 1420) currently in the Museum der bildenden Künste, Leipzig (cf. Camille, *Gothic Art*, p. 102). Further, Jeffrey Hamburger points out that '[i]n a *Sendbrief* from the Katharinenkloster (first half C15[th]), "Von Jhesus pettlein", Christ Himself is likened to a rose bush; each drop of His blood is like one of its blossoms' (Hamburger, *Nuns as Artists*, p. 77; the *Sendbrief* is in Stadtbibliothek Nürnberg Ms. Cent. VI 43[b], fol. 83[v]-92[v]).

[130]   'their faces radiating just like roses' (fol. ccliij[r]).

[131]   Hence the garland becomes a symbol for the fact that in Christ the power hierarchy is reversed as the Mightiest humbles Himself for the sake of the humble, just as Katherine does whenever she aids her servants. At the same time, however, humility is a marker of power.

[132]   'Take and keep this garland as the sign of a true and proper love between you and me'.

so this bright crown of roses signifies the various sufferings the dear friends of God
have to bear as long as they are serving God with knightly endeavour.[133]

Thus, the garland of roses hints at the suffering the count will endure on account
of his love for the saint. Just as Seuse, who serves as the visionary model for the
Dominican Order, is the bride of Christ, so the count is the bride of Katherine,
herself "masculinized" by her martyr's virtue. Further, the garland, like the ring
Christ gives Katherine in the mystic marriage, provides a concrete symbol of
their bond which remains present even after the vision, a physical object which
transcends the divide between this world and the next, thus providing a visible
link to the latter. Finally, Katherine casts herself as the jealous woman who denies
her servant any relationship with a "real" bride, an aspect of the saint we have
encountered previously: Katherine as flirtatious, capricious *minnedame* who
admits no rivals to her affection and reacts badly to neglect, another example
of the intense personalization of the relationship between saint and devotee.
Mutuality suggests the saint is as invested as her follower. When the Graf wakes,
a further reminder of the vision is the sweet scent of the garland, traditional
attribute of sanctity: 'vnd der Jungling hett das schone krenczeleyn das schmecket
gar vberflussiglichen vnnd ausdermassen wol vnd ist noch heut bey dem Closter
also frisch vnd wolscwmeckent / wann er stifft da selbs ein Closter / daz heyst
zu dem Rosenkrancz / von des selben rosenkrenczeleins wegen' (fol. cclviij[r-v]).[134]
The garland becomes a relic, a tangible, olfactory guarantor of the veracity of the
monastery's foundation legend and of Katherine's enduring, active presence on
earth, hence a visible, graspable guarantor of a vision of the ungraspable divine
and the unchanging nature of God's love for man (the roses do not wilt nor does
their scent fade).[135] The rosary fuses memory, prayer and Passion, since it is 'itself

---

[133]   Hamburger, *Nuns as Artists*, p. 64.

[134]   'And the young man had the beautiful garland, which smells extraordinarily and
immeasurably fragrant and can still be seen in the monastery today, just as fresh and fragrant,
for he founded a monastery on that spot called "Of the Rosary" after that very same garland
of roses'.

[135]   Dominic also emits a sweet scent after his death (*Der Heiligen Leben*, fol. ciij[v]). As
well as interweaving Katherine and the Virgin, the text intertwines Katherine and Dominic.
Compare this story to a previous one which paves the way for it: a young man, devoted to
Saint Katherine, 'macht im all tag eyn krenczlein von rosen oder von blummen wann er
sie gehaben mocht das trug er dan yn der liebe der heyligen iunckfrawen Sant Katherinen'
[made himself a garland of roses or whatever flowers he could find every day and wore
it out of love for the holy virgin Saint Katherine]. Roses, as symbol of love, still act as an
outward manifestation of an inner state and the young man's crowning of himself with roses
constitutes a gesture of homage, since it was customary for a serf to present his master with
a chaplet of roses as a token of his homage. A rich man, jealous of this young man, ruins him

an instrument of memory, in which each bead stood for a single blossom and enumerated a prayer evoking an event in the history of salvation'.[136] Hamburger points out that on some rosaries beads 'culminated in a hollowed-out ball or "nut" containing an extraordinarily detailed depiction of the Passion', so this particular miracle story stands for monastic devotional practice focussed on the mass and Christ's salvation-enabling suffering as ritually commemorated in prayer.[137]

The rose garland, then, functions as a mnemonic device on various levels: within the text it reminds the count of Saint Katherine; outwith the text it reminds the Dominican reader of the founder of his order and one of that order's most prominent mystics; finally, it reminds the lay reader of the story itself, of Mary, of Christ, of the rosary and the potency of prayer. As Arnold Angenendt and Kren Meiners state: 'Jedes Gebet setzt durch seine Rezitation eine gewisse Wirkung frei, die einen Wert besitzt. Dieser Wert kann man durch wiederholte Rezitation steigern. Je größer die Anzahl der Wiederholungen, desto höher die Wirkung'.[138] This constitutes 'ein heiliges Zählen' and a 'Technik zur Schulung des inneren Menschen; Hilfe, Tugende einzuüben, Affekte zu regulieren und sich selbst zu disziplinieren'.[139] However, prayer was not mechanical, for '[m]an wollte aber auch verstehen; Verstehen machte das Gebet inniger; darauf kam es an'.[140] Moreover, Hamburger points out that: 'in the tradition of prayers known as *Handwerkliches Beten* that was common in, if not exclusive to, convents, supplicants offered up make-believe gifts fashioned, not from gold, silk, or beads, but from prayer formulas reiterated so often that the words took on the character of an incantation'.[141] The monastery subsequently endowed by the Graf, as well as representing a model of pious endowment, is an even more tangible, visible

---

financially. God causes the rich man to go blind in both eyes. The latter realizes he has sinned towards the young man, humbles himself before him, recompenses him for all the damage done and has his sight restored by the grace of Saint Katherine (fol. cclv^v–cclvj^r).

[136]   Hamburger, *Nuns as Artists*, pp. 68–9.

[137]   For pendants on rosaries see *Spiegel der Seligkeit*, pp. 299–306.

[138]   'Through recitation each prayer achieves a certain effect which has a specific value. This value can be increased by repeated recitation. The greater the number of repetitions, the greater the effect' (Arnold Angenendt and Kren Meiners, 'Erscheinungsformen spätmittelalterlicher Religiosität', in *Divina Officia. Liturgie und Frömmigkeit im Mittelalter*, Ausstellungskataloge der Herzog August Bibliothek 83 (Wolfenbüttel: Herzog August Bibliothek, 2000), pp. 25–35 (p. 29)).

[139]   'holy counting'; 'a technique for training the inner person; help in practising virtue, controlling emotions and disciplining oneself' (Angenendt and Meiners, 'Erscheinungsformen', p. 29).

[140]   'people also wanted to understand since understanding made prayer more fervent and that was crucial' (Angenendt and Meiners, 'Erscheinungsformen', p. 30).

[141]   Hamburger, *Nuns as Artists*, p. 75.

reminder of his bond to the saint, a thing-left-over magnified, the miraculous petrified for generations. Moreover, since the monastery is named after the garland, its physical fabric is a memorial not just to the vision but to the rosary itself, as the German word "Rosenkranz" means both "rosary" and "garland of roses". The monastery, then, constitutes a prayer in stone, part of a string of foundations stretched, like the numerous versions of the *Legenda aurea* itself, across Europe to commemorate and render concrete the bond between man, saint and God. Indeed, the reader, if so minded, could visit the monastery to confirm the presence of the relic, an object that, like Saint Katherine's tomb, occupies a space between this world and the next.

Not long after his vision the count is married against his will to a beautiful noblewoman who conceives his child. However, his frequent visits to Saint Katherine's church lead his wife to suspect him of seeing another woman. When she asks a maid, 'da neidet dy magt den Graffen vmb seine gute werck vnd sprach / er get czu der kirchen da siczt ein man d*er* hat ein schone tochter czu der get er' (fol. cclviij^v).[142] In the sense that we are all, including the saints, God's children, the maid's statement is true; however, the count's wife takes it literally and challenges her husband who, thinking it is a joke, responds: 'Nein es ist des mannes tocht*er* nit dye ich lieb hab vn*d* zu der ich gee / sie ist noch tausend stunndt schoner' (fol. cclviij^v).[143] The next morning his wife, not realizing he means Saint Katherine, 'wa*r*t si ser betrubt vnd stund auff vnd nam ein schwert vnd rach sich darann vn starb' (fol. cclviij^v).[144] The instrument of the saint's martyrdom becomes that of the wife's death, Katherine assuming the role of the "other woman" in an adulterous triangle.[145] She also makes the wife into a sinner, guilty of despair, suicide (particularly heinous because they express doubt in God's mercy) and the murder of the unborn child, an act which destroys not only a potentially Christian soul but also the family bloodline.[146] The wife's blood mirrors the redness of the roses

---

[142]   'The maid envied the count because of the good works he performed and said, "He goes to the church because a man is there who has a beautiful daughter and he visits the daughter"'.

[143]   'No, it is not the man's daughter whom I love and visit but a woman a thousand times more beautiful'.

[144]   'became very downcast and stood up and took a sword and threw herself on it and died'. This story echoes a miracle attributed to Our Lady of Rocamadour, who restores to life the pregnant wife of a count who stabs herself because her husband pretends jokingly that he enjoys many mistresses (Bull, *Miracles*, pp. 106–7).

[145]   It could be argued that from Katherine's point of view the wife occupies that role.

[146]   About suicide *Die Religion in Geschichte und Gegenwart* states: '[D]er Mensch hat sich das Leben nicht gegeben und darf es sich deshalb auch nicht nehmen. S. ist deshalb eine Versündigung gegen Gott und verdient Strafe. Nach dem kirchlichen und weltlichen Recht des MA war sogar der bloße Versuch des S.s strafbar, Selbstmördern wurde ein kirchliches

in the garland given to the count by Katherine, identifying the causal connexion between saint, gift and suicide and suggesting a shadow "martyrdom" on the wife's part. The count loses consciousness for an hour in a symbolic parallel to both his wife's death and his visionary slumber at the altar. However, he experiences no further vision and, unlike Iwein, awakes to neither a new identity nor a life of atonement. The count's ritual mourning gestures enact a public performance of guilt-induced grief: 'da weynet er iemerlich vnd schrey vnd klagt vnd raufft sein har ausz vnd schrey laut ... ich bin leyder deines todes ein vrsach / darum das ich dir nit saget waz mein geschefft des morgens were wann ich von dyr gieng' (fol. cclviij^v).[147] Remorse leads to confession, penance and prayer: 'O heylige iunckfrau sant Katherin / wolt got daz ich fur si tot were / vnd das ich nur ann mir nit schuldig were darumb daz ich dich han gelassen So ist mir daz geschehen / wann ich han eyn andere fur dich genummen' (fol. cclviij^v).[148] The count recognizes his guilt as twofold: his dishonesty towards his wife, whose death is advanced as punishment for his disloyalty, and, above all, his infidelity to Katherine, his treatment of her constituting the opposite of Katherine's primary virtue.

The count's solution is to realize the rosary in prayer, turning the symbolic potential into the salvific actual: 'Vnd da er lanng gebetet hett vnd wyder wachett noch schlieff / da erschein ym sant Katherin mit czweyen iunckfrawen alsz vor vnd

---

Begräbnis verweigert' [Man did not give himself life and for that reason may not take his own. Suicide thus constitutes a sin against God and deserves to be punished. According to medieval canon and civil law, even the mere attempt at suicide was punishable and those who committed suicide were denied a church burial] (vol. 5, p. 1675). It continues: 'Die Verwerflichkeit des S.s kann nicht von irgendeinem Gesetz her begründet werden, auch nicht von dem Glauben an irgendeinen Schöpfergott, sondern nur von der Botschaft von der Gnade Gottes in Jesus Christus. Freigemacht von der Knechtschaft unter den Schicksalsmächten dieser Welt und unter der Last unserer eigenen Schuld gehören wir demjenigen, der uns erlöst hat' [The reason for the reprehensible nature of suicide cannot be found in any law or in the belief in any creator God but only in the message of God's grace in Jesus Christ. Liberated from servitude to the forces of destiny at work in this world and to the burden of our own guilt, we belong to Him who redeemed us'] (pp. 1676–7). According to Thomas Aquinus, 'since we are by nature members of a community, it [suicide] is damaging to the interests of society' (Goodich, *Violence and Miracle*, p. 80).

[147]   'Then he wept piteously and screamed and wailed and tore out his hair and screamed loudly ... "Alas, I am the cause of your death because I did not tell you what I was busy doing in the morning whenever I left you"'. Laudine performs a similar ritual when her husband is killed by Iwein: 'Von jâmer sî vürder brach/ ir hâr und diu cleider' [For grief she tore her hair and her clothes] (Hartmann, *Iwein*, ll. 1310–11. The entire description of Laudine's grief runs from ll. 1310–1402 and ll. 1454–77).

[148]   'O holy virgin Saint Katherine, I wish to God that I were dead in her place and that I did not bear the burden of guilt for having left you. This has all happened to me because I took another woman in your place'.

gieng aber yn der mitte vnd w*a*z gekronet mit einer schonen kron' (fol. cclviij^v).[149] The "in-betweenness" of the count's state suggests that, much like Katherine, he has prayed himself into a trance, into an altered (i.e. divinely inspired) state that permits a genuine vision, not a dream. His repeated visions of Katherine bring to mind her repeated visions of Christ, only now with the saint occupying the role of the desired, her crown the symbol of her status as queen, martyr and true mistress of his heart. Katherine wipes the count's tears from his eyes and cheeks. We have seen before that tears represent baptism, the cleansing of (earthbound) vision and consequent ability to see events on a different level of reality, so the count's recognition of his double guilt is reinforced by Katherine's admonition: 'Du hast nit recht getan das du ein andern gemahel fur mich genummen hast aber syet du mich lieb gehabt hast vn*d* mir alsz fleyssiglichen dienest vn*d* alsz offt in dye kirche*n* gast vnd mich lobest da*r*um*m* will ich dich ymmer gelassen hie vnd dort' (fol. cclviij^v).[150] Her speech, the rhetorical structure of which parallels the count's performance of grief, constitutes a checklist of the way to a saint's heart and to forgiveness for transgression and infidelity, a model for the reader. Katherine resurrects the count's wife as Christ resurrects Lazarus or God resurrects Christ Himself:

> Stee auff vn*d* gee heym du findest dein frawen lebentig vn*d* hat ein tocht*er* gewunne*n* dy solt du nach mir Katherin heyssen dy wirt gott alsz genem d*a*z sy deines vaters sele yn einem iar ausz dem fegfewer erloset mit yrem gebet der wer vmb sein sund ewiglichen verdampnet dy er mit rauben vn*d* mit bre*n*nen beganngen hatt dann d*a*z ich im an seinen letsten czeytten rew vn*d* bussz vn*d* beicht erwa*r*b / vn*d* solt yn de*n* fegfeuwer brinnen bisz an de*n* Jungsten tag Dy gnad geschach ym darumb d*a*z er dy kirchen yn meiner ere gebawet hett. (fol. cclviij^v)[151]

---

[149]   'And when he had prayed for a long time and was neither awake nor asleep, then Saint Katherine appeared to him with two maidens just like before and once again walked between them and wore a beautiful crown'.

[150]   'You have done wrong in taking another spouse in my place but because you have loved me and serve me assiduously and go to church and praise me so often, I will never forsake you either in this life or the next'.

[151]   Through God's grace and Katherine's favour this recursive reflexion of Katherine will enjoy a power over Purgatory similar to Christ's victory over and release of souls from Hell (taken mainly from the Gospel of Nicodemus; cf. also Matthew 27:51–3; 1 Peter 3:19–20). Christ's Harrowing of Hell was also the subject of Easter and Passion plays so readers may have been able to imagine a concrete, animated setting for the father's Purgatory. See Gerhard Wolf, 'Zur Hölle mit dem Teufel! Die Höllenfahrt Christi in den Passions- und Osterspielen des Mittelalters', in Timothy Jackson, Nigel F. Palmer and Almut Suerbaum (eds), *Die Vermittlung geistlicher Inhalte im deutschen Mittelalter. Internationales Symposium Roscrea 1994* (Tübingen: Niemeyer, 1996), pp. 271–88. One widespread vision of Heaven and Hell was the *Visio*

[Rise and go home. You will find your wife alive and she has given birth to a daughter whom you shall name Katherine after me. She will be so pleasing unto God that in a year her prayers will free your father's soul from Purgatory. He would have been eternally condemned because of the sins he committed by robbing and burning had I not brought him to remorse, penance and confession towards the end of his life; and he would have burnt in Purgatory until Judgement Day. He was awarded this grace because he had built this church in my honour].

Just as the garland persists from the vision into secular reality, so Katherine herself is transferred into the physicality of the count's baby daughter: the divine object of his affection becomes the earthly object of his affection and concrete proof of his second vision.[152] Katherine's virtue translates itself as well, if the daughter's exemplarity is to effect the release of the count's father from Purgatory.

News now comes from the castle that the count's wife is alive and has given birth to a daughter, as if Katherine had spoken the event into being, just as God spoke Creation. The power of the divine Word is thus encapsulated in the very text in front of the reader.[153] As the count tells his wife and child about Katherine, he becomes the first textual source for the miracle, relaying promise and prophecy to those who are the concrete evidence of its realization. Reminiscent of the earlier miracle stories is the wife's account of her own vision: 'Da saget im dy fraw alsz bald wye dye bosen geist zu yrem end kummen weren vnd hetten yr sel hyn geczuck vn*d* wie Sant Katherin kummen wer vnd si von den bosen geysten erloset

---

Tnugdali by a Brother Marcus (Regensburg, c. 1148–9) (Harald Spilling, *Die Visio Tnugdali. Eigenart und Stellung in der mittelalterlichen Visionsliteratur bis zum Ende des 12. Jahrhunderts*, Münchener Beiträge zur Mediävistik und Renaissance-Forschung, 21 (Munich: Bei der Arbeo-Gesellschaft, 1975)). Spilling states: 'Mittelalterlicher Überzeugung nach bestand nun eine Art göttlicher Stärkung und Ermunterung darin, den Menschen vorzeitig das Ziel schauen zu lassen, das er für seine Seele erkämpfte, sowie ihm den Untergang zu zeigen, den seine Niederlage seiner Seele bereiten würde' [According to medieval conviction, allowing man prematurely to see the goal which he was struggling to achieve for his soul, as well as the doom which would be caused by the defeat of his soul, constituted a sort of divine strengthening and encouragement] (p. 1). Visions of Purgatory were similarly found in didactic and popular literature: in *Der Ritter vom Turn* a hermit has a vision of the suffering in Purgatory of a knight's wife, whose sin had been to spend too much money on her appearance (pp. 144–5); whilst Fortunatus visits Saint Patrick's Purgatory in Ireland (*Fortunatus*, pp. 61–3).

[152]   In one of the many parallels in the miracle stories, a twist on the maid's lie turns the count from a man visiting a father on account of the latter's daughter to a man with a daughter himself.

[153]   It contrasts, too, with the ambiguity of human speech that prompted the suicide in the first place.

hett vnd bracht si wid*er* czu dem leybe' (fol. cclxviij^v–cclix^r).[154] Katherine's rescue of the countess's soul, while pointing to Christ's Harrowing of Hell, also conjures up woodcuts of the bad death found in contemporary *Ars moriendi* depicting devils seizing the dead person's soul: because the wife committed suicide hers is condemned.[155] Hence, this scene contributes further dramatic action to the horror film that is distance from God. That story concludes on general praise of the Lord leaves the reader in no doubt as to the dominant male source of power and of Katherine as a mere vehicle for God's might.

However, the garland of roses as bridge between two worlds is not confined to miracles by Saint Katherine but belongs to a broader, mystic tradition: a fourteenth-century anonymous treatise, *Von zwei bayerischen Klosterfrauen Leben*, tells the story of two nuns, Katherine and Magrede, so desperate to see Christ that on Shrove Tuesday they remain in their cell, flagellate themselves and eventually experience an ecstatic vision. Their fellow nuns, who notice them missing, 'fundent die zwo heiligen frowen rehte ufreht bigenander sitzende und fundent zwei schöne rote rosenschappel uf iren höbeten'.[156] These garlands, too, are preserved in that convent as relics. Hamburger comments: 'In these and other stories the rose emerges as the consummate emblem and instrument of prayer, both an image and the means by which images are honoured'.[157] The clear parallels to the story of the count allow his roses also to be read as emblematic

---

[154]   'Now his wife told him how the evil spirits had gathered round her at her end and had grabbed her soul and how Saint Katherine had come and rescued her from the evil spirits and had restored her to her body'.

[155]   The Latin *Ars moriendi* (*The Art of Dying*) dates from 1415/50; was written by a Dominican; translated into most Western European languages and became one of the earliest printed books, circulating in nearly 100 editions before 1500. It was especially popular in Germany. A guide to the correct way to die a good, Christian death, it was originally intended as an aid for priests at the bedside of the dying but soon became popular amongst lay people. The *artes moriendi* were illustrated by a series of woodcuts depicting the temptations facing the dying man and the way to overcome them (*Spiegel der Seligkeit*, pp. 339–40). The iconography of these woodcuts percolated into popular didactic literature as well: *Der Ritter vom Turn* contains a story about a woman who spent all her money on her dogs rather than charity to her fellow men. The accompanying woodcut shows her lying in bed dying with small dogs (symbols of the Devil) licking her face (fol. Bvj^r). Of course, the scene also, as a counterbalance, prompts memory of the exemplary Dormition of the Virgin, a popular motif in medieval art which shows Mary's soul in the arms of either God in Heaven or Christ standing by her bed.

[156]   'found the two holy women sitting bolt upright side-by-side and found two beautiful garlands of red roses on their heads' (*Schriften aus der Gottesfreund-Literatur*, 1. Heft, *Sieben bisher unveröffentlichte Traktate und Lektionen*, ed. Philipp Strauch, Altdeutsche Textbibliothek 22 (Halle: Niemeyer, 1927), pp. x–xii and pp. 1–21 (p. 5)).

[157]   Hamburger, *Nuns as Artists*, p. 75.

of the prayer that led to his vision. Love (both secular-sexual and divine)[158] that leads to sacrifice, martyrdom, devotion, prayer and vision manifests here in the physical object that is the chaplet. Moreover, roses resonated for the Dominicans not just because of Seuse but also because of Saint Dominic (1170–1221), who in 1208 himself had a vision of the Virgin and Child in the church of Prouille in which either Mary or Christ gave him a rosary; indeed, early Dominican historians claimed he invented the rosary,[159] the cult of which spread from the late-fifteenth century onwards. According to Ludwig Grote, it was introduced into Nuremberg by the Katharinenkloster nuns in 1490.[160] A convent prayer book contains an account of indulgences granted the nuns for reciting the rosary:

Von dem krönlin maria der wirdigen mütter gottz

Es ist gewesen Ein Erwirdiger andechtiger vatter barfüsser ordens Jn güter kuntschafft der erwirdigen mütterpriorin zü sant katherina zü nürnberg prediger ordens Jn dem xvC vnd ij jar ist er gewesen zü Rom vnd hat gebetten den aller heiligsten vattre den babst vmm besundern applas von dem bett das man heisst die kron Der junckfräwen maria Des hat Jn der Heilig vatter der babst gewert vnd hat geben Jm vnd seijnem Couent xxiiij tusent jar applas so dick jr einer die kron spricht vnd hat jm auch geben ettwen vil tusent menschen nach seinen willen vnd geuallen – vnd nach den hat er den heiligen vatter den babst gebetten mer vnd mütlichen das er den applas auch wöll geben der Erwirdigen mütter priorin vnd Jrem couent vor bestimpt da hat jn der babst aber erhört vnd noch mer dar zü thon Das sie auch söllichen applas geben mög vnd verkünden · sol tusent menschen wern / wenn sie wöll sie seint weltlich oder geistlich das die selben

---

[158]   In the scene of Mark's discovery of Tristan and Isolde sleeping in the *minnegrotte* (lovers' cave), Gottfried's *Tristan* coyly (but unmistakably) links Isolde's rose-red cheeks to sexual exertion: 'Ine weiz von welher arbeit/ diz mære spellet unde seit/ von ders erhitzet solte sîn/ und lûhte ir varwe unde ir schîn/ als suoze und alse lôse/ als ein gemischet rôse hin ûf wider den man' (ll. 17565–71) [Heaven knows of what exertions the tale romances here that might have flushed her cheeks, whose radiance glowed up at the man with the sweet freshness of a rose in which red and white are mingled (Hatto, *Tristan*, p. 272)].

[159]   *Hall's Dictionary*, pp. 333–4. However, it 'was subsequently maintained on the contrary that the use of the rosary as an aid to devotion was first propagated by a Dominican friar towards the end of the 15th cent'.

[160]   Fries notes that in 1490 the nuns wanted to celebrate the new Feast of the Rosary and in conjunction with this a fresco of a rosary was painted on the north wall of the Katharinenkirche nave (Fries, 'Kloster und Kirche', p. 32). The nuns could thus relate this story directly to a readily available image, one connected to an important ritual in daily worship. The image would also have been visible to lay people who prayed in the church.

auch sollen haben vsß seine*n* bebstlichen gewalt xxiiij m jar applas so offt vnd dick Jr eins spricht Ein krönlin.[161]

[Of the crown of Mary, the worthy Mother of God

Once there lived an honourable, devout father of the Franciscan Order, a good friend of the honourable mother prioress of Saint Katherine's in Nuremberg of the Dominican Order. In 1502 he went to Rome and begged our most blessed Father the Pope for special indulgences for the prayer known as the Crown of the Virgin Mary. Our blessed Father the Pope granted him this and gave him and his convent 24,000 years' worth of indulgences for every time someone recited the Crown. He also gave him many thousands of people according to his will and pleasure. Then he bravely asked our blessed Father the Pope for more, namely that he grant the indulgences to the prioress and her convent mentioned above. The Pope granted him that and even more: that she should be permitted to grant and announce such indulgences; and should there be a thousand people, whether laymen or members of a monastic order, they should have by his papal authority 24,000 years' worth of indulgences as often and as frequently as they said a Crown].

Telling the rosary occupied an important place in the salvational ritual of Dominican nuns and Franciscan friars in Nuremberg and may be linked to a revived cult of the Virgin in that city.[162] The practice of telling the rosary had been given an impulse by Cologne's military victory over Charles the Bold in 1474, when Jakob Sprenger, the Prior of the Dominican Order in Cologne, had praised it as an effective weapon in battle. Membership of the Cologne Brotherhood of the Rosary rose from around 5,000 in 1475 to around 50,000 in 1478 and 100,000 in 1481. Due to the announcement on 8 December 1476 of the dogma of the Immaculate Conception under Pope Sixtus IV, veneration of the Virgin increased generally in the late-fifteenth century. Peter Ochsenbein points to the devotional works on the rosary that started appearing from around 1479/80.[163] In fact, the Dominicans were known as the Brothers of Mary because they sung the *Salve Regina* after compline and, according to legend, Mary herself encouraged Dominic to enter monastery life and taught him how to say the rosary. From

---

[161]   *Gebetbuch* [fol. 122ʳ–123ʳ] (Germanisches Nationalmuseum, Hs 1733).

[162]   Compare Funk's suggestion that the Konhofer window reflected the intensified cult of the Virgin and saints prompted by fear of the Hussites, who rejected such cults as unbiblical (Funk, *Glasfensterkunst*, pp. 142–3).

[163]   Peter Ochsenbein, 'Handschrift und Druck in der Gebetbuchliteratur zwischen 1470 und 1520', in Gerd Dicke und Klaus Grubmüller (eds), *Die Gleichzeitigkeit von Handschrift und Buchdruck* (Wiesbaden: Harrassowitz, 2003), pp. 113–27 (p. 114).

the end of the thirteenth century indulgences were granted to promote the practice of saying "Gegrüßt seist Du Maria" (Hail Mary) after every recitation of the Lord's Prayer. In 1499 Kaspar Hochfeder published in Nuremberg the *Verkundung des englischen grus mit einem andechtigen gepet*; its woodcut of the Annunciation had already appeared in Koberger's 1488 edition of the *Legenda Aurea*. The beginning of the sixteenth century saw a Brotherhood of the Rosary in Nuremberg for which the city doctor, Ulrich Pindar, published *Den beschlossen gart des rosenkranz Mariae* in 1501; it contained numerous woodcuts by Hans Baldung Grien, Hans Schäufelein, Wolf Traut and Hans Süß von Kulmbach. A year later Albrecht Dürer painted the Feast of the Rosary for the church of the German merchant community in Venice.[164] In 1503 an indulgence sermon on the rosary was preached in the Lorenzkirche and an associated woodcut published. Garlands of roses hung in city churches, rendering visible and tangible the abstraction of prayer and enabling the public performance of personal piety: 'Aus dem Haushaltsbuch von Anton Tucher erfahren wir, daß es in der Dominikaner- und Frauenkirche und in St. Clara Rosenkränze gab, die wie Kronleuchter aufgehängt waren, für die er alljährlich weiße, aus Venedig bezogene Wachskerzen schenkte'.[165] Within Nuremberg this story may have served to promote the cult of the rosary, the garlands in city churches serving as substitute relics redolent of the possibility of a local rosary miracle. The boundaries between human and divine are blurred in these churches as miracle story and ecclesiastical space become enmeshed, rendering the city itself a visionary and "envisioned" space. The cult of the rosary in Nuremberg reached its culmination in the *Englischer Gruß*, a wooden carving of the Annunciation within a rosary, and accompanying candelabra commissioned in 1517 by Anton II Tucher from Nuremberg sculptor Veit Stoß for the Lorenzkirche, where it has hung in the choir ever since.[166]

The final miracle story takes place in the arch-diocese of Salzburg. A powerful count undertakes a pilgrimage to the Holy Sepulchre and Sinai. He arrives at an inn by the sea whose landlord is poor but learned and whose daughter 'was czumal schon vnd hyeß Katherina vnnd was frum vnd erber vnd hett sant

---

Grote, *Die Tucher*, p. 70.

165   'From Anton Tucher's household accounts we learn that garlands of roses were hung up like candelabra in the Dominican and Franciscan churches and in Saint Clara's; and that he made an annual gift of white wax candles that were sent for these from Venice' (Grote, *Die Tucher*, p. 70). Peter Ochsenbein also points to the growth in the cult of the rosary from the 1470s onwards (Peter Ochsenbein, 'Handschrift und Druck', pp. 113–27).

166   In the same year Anton II Tucher also commissioned Hans Süß von Kulmbach to paint murals of the life of Empress Faustina in the chapel of the Haus zur Krone, the ancestral house of the principal Tucher line.

Katherine*n* yre reinikeyt gelobt czu halten dyweil sy lebet'.[167] Thus a second shadow-Katherine enters the narrative: it is no longer the oil emanating from the saint's body but the body itself which multiplies and flows though the text. Moreover, two of Katherine's patronages are activated: of scholars (the father) and maidens (the daughter). Sight of the daughter's beauty fires the count's heart with Devil-driven lust. At the same inn lodges an old woman whom the count engages as a go-between. In a *fabliau* twist, the procuress dangles the count's promise of enrichment in front of the parents and convinces them to pimp their daughter: 'Wir sein erber leut vn*d* sein doch gar nottig wir sollen ym vnser tochter heinnacht zu legen so macht er vns reych / vn*d* tund das heimlich das seyn niemant ynne*n* werd' (fol. cclix^r).[168] Casting both mother and old woman as procuresses illustrates the power of money and, above all, female greed, since the daughter is handled as an object of trade.[169] Moreover, night, which may be intended to conceal parental and filial shame, symbolizes sin, deception and spiritual blindness (the parents are "verblendt" [blinded]),[170] so renders visible the evil of the proposed betrayal of not just the daughter but also the saint to whom she has pledged her virginity. Narrative expectation now shifts to Saint Katherine's intervention to save her namesake, who refuses her parents' wish: 'ich hann d*er* heylgen iunckfrawen Sannt Katherinen mein reinikeyt gelobt dy weyl ich leb vnd ward ser weynen' (fol. cclix^r).[171] The formulaic repetition of her vow to Saint Katherine turns the narrative into the conflict between two types of "gut" [possessions, riches], material and spiritual: 'Da hett vater vnd mutter boß gir czu dem czeytliche*n* gut gewunnen wann d*er* boß geyst het yn yr hercz verblendt ynn d*er* begird die si czu dem czeytlichen gutt hetten' (fol. cclix^r).[172] Avarice, as one of the Seven Deadly Sins, is laid directly at the Devil's door, as is the lust that prompted the attempted transaction. Force prevails:

---

[167]   'was beautiful and was called Katherine and was pious and honourable and had pledged her chastity to Saint Katherine for as long as she lived' (fol. cclix^r).

[168]   'We are honourable people and yet we are very poor, so we should give him our daughter to lie with tonight and he may make us rich and we should do so secretly so that no one finds out about it'.

[169]   The tale could reflect economic circumstances c. 1260 or even in late-fifteenth-century Nuremberg.

[170]   As were the robbers in an earlier miracle story.

[171]   '"I have pledged my virginity to Saint Katherine for as long as I live"; and started to shed bitter tears'.

[172]   'Both mother and father had been seized with an evil desire for transient worldly possessions for the Devil (lit.: evil spirit) had blinded their hearts in their desire for transient worldly possessions'. In their lust for money the parents echo the usurer in the previous story, so the concentration on this theme may be intended to sharpen readers' thinking in a city grown enormously wealthy on trade. For the social and economic problems caused by avarice

the daughter, fearing for her "schacz d*er* reynikeyt", is coerced into lying with the Graf, who, thwarted of his anticipated 'gar vil grosser frewde*n* vn*d* trost' asks why she weeps.[173] She replies: 'Ich wein darumb das vater vnd muter alß vntrewlich an mir getan haben wan*n* ich ha*n* mein reinikeit vnd mein dienst Sandt Katheri*n* gelobt di weil ich leb' (fol. cclix^v).[174] On this, the third utterance of this phrase, the reader expects either a change of heart on the part of the count or a miraculous rescue by the saint, especially as the daughter, whose loyalty provides a foil to the parents' treachery, is set up as a pious mirror of the saint she worships. However, just as in the judge and abbess stories, reader expectation is destabilized as Saint Katherine does not intervene personally. However, her name is enough to rescue a devotee, since the count repents and promises 'ich will dy sund gern ve*r*meiden durch dy lieben iunckfrawe*n* Sand Katherin / vnd will dich heynnach zu einer tochter nemen vnd will dir ynn das Closter helffen' (fol. cclix^v).[175] Hence the count, his vision cleansed not by his own tears but by the daughter's, moves from the night of sin into spiritual enlightenment and, by taking the young girl as his daughter[176] and facilitating her entry into a convent, becomes a better father to her than her own: 'vnd gewan ir des morgens sein pfrundt / vnd gab yr gar vil gutz dar czu yn daz Closter / vn*d* tet si erlichen darein / vnd befal si gott vnd Sant Katherin vnd / gab dem vat*er* vn*d* der muter auch vil gutz vnd czoch vb*er* mer' (fol. cclix^v).[177] The sinful riches intended by the count for the parents become spiritual riches for both himself and the girl since he performs a charitable deed by endowing the girl as a bride of Christ who preserves the virtue he had threatened. His gift to the poor parents constitutes further charity. There is still no sign of Saint Katherine so the narrative plays on thwarted reader expectation that heightens anticipation of the saint.

The count continues his pilgrimage to the Holy Land: 'Da kam eins nachtes ein vergiffter wurm vnd vervnreinet ym sein beyn vnd stach yn darein das ym gar wee geschach / wan*n* es sein ga*r* schedlich wurm yn demselben land' (fol.

---

in Nuremberg see Sharon J. Baker, *Sachs and the City: Staged Avarice as a Barometer for Civic Confusion* (MA Diss. Bristol 2009).

[173]   'treasure of virginity'; 'great joy and pleasure'.

[174]   'I am crying because my father and my mother have betrayed my trust in them because I had pledged my virginity and my service to Saint Katherine for as long as I live'.

[175]   'For the sake of the dear virgin Saint Katherine I shall gladly avoid sinning and from now on shall treat you as a daughter and help you to enter a convent'.

[176]   The parallels to Saint Katherine are obvious as Christ calls her "lyebe tochter" when He summons her to Him.

[177]   'And in the morning he organized a benefice in her name and in addition gave her a considerable sum of money to enable her to enter the convent. In this he behaved honourably towards her and commended her to the care of God and Saint Katherine. He also gave a considerable sum of money to her father and mother and then travelled overseas'.

cclix^v).¹⁷⁸ The poisonous snake performs multiple roles: first, it signifies the threat posed by the Oriental, non-Christian Other and hence the fear experienced by European travellers in their encounters with it. Second, it symbolizes the Devil, the evil to which the count initially succumbs and which poisons him spiritually. Finally, thwarted reader expectation is unexpectedly fulfilled:

> vn*d* in d*er* selbe*n* nacht da sein diener von ym kamen vnd sein kammer verspert
> w*az* / da sach er ga*r* eyn minniglich gesicht d*az* vier schone engel eingiengen dy
> truge*n* vier brinnet kerczen vnd giengen vier schon iu*n*ckfrawen nach yn / vnd
> dy letst was die allerschonst dy trug ein hubsch buchsleyn mit edler hymlischer
> salben yn yr hand. (fol. cclix^v)

> [And in the same night, when his servants had left him and his chamber was
> locked, he saw a delightful vision of four angels entering his chamber carrying
> four lighted candles. Four beautiful maidens followed them, the last of which was
> the most beautiful and carried in her hand a pretty little casket containing noble
> divine ointment].

Various familiar threads are drawn together in the theatrical culmination to all the miracle stories: the devotee's vision that parallels Katherine's own; the angels;¹⁷⁹ the light; the procession of beautiful maidens, the most beautiful of whom is Saint Katherine;¹⁸⁰ the (potentially) detached body part, whether the

---

178   'One night a poisonous snake came and polluted his leg and bit him on it, causing him a great deal of pain for the snakes in this country are extremely dangerous'. Poison as a motif for the Otherness, even evil, of the foreign and the fear it inspired can be found in Ludolf von Sudheim, where it is condensed above all in the snake, the symbol of Satan: 'In this country the serpent called *tyrus* is found and taken, whence what is called tyriac (treacle) gets its name, for it is chiefly made thereof. This is a serpent not half an ell long, as thick as a man's finger, of a yellow colour mixed with red, and it is blind. No cure for its poison is known except cutting off the bitten limb. When it is angry it puts out its tongue like a flame of fire, and one would think that it was fire indeed, save that it does not burn the creature; it sets up the hair on its face like an angry boar, and its head at such times grows bigger. Were it not blind I believe that no man could escape from it, for I have heard from those whose trade it is to catch these serpents that if they bit a man's horse, they would kill the rider' (Ludolf, *Description of the Holy Land*, p. 117). (The thyriac is a viper and is caught near Sodom and Gomorrah.)

179   Their number, four, could symbolize the four corners of the earth to which the light of God's Word spreads; or the four Gospels that carry that Word. The light of their burning candles represents goodness, virtue, God's grace; they guide man's passage to the afterlife and illuminate the darkness in the same way that Katherine brings physical and spiritual salvation.

180   The three saints accompanying her are Margaret, Cecelia and Thecla. Saint Margaret was the daughter of a pagan priest of Antioch (Turkey) who was rejected by her father when

saint's or the devotee's; the healing salve (with its allusion to the Three Marys) as symbolic of the healing powers of the Christian faith. The performative elements seal the acting-out of redemption before the reader's eyes, the narrative of *Der Heiligen Leben* constituting stage directions and script:

> Vnd da si czu dem bett komen da sprach Sant Katherin czu sant Margrethen was wiltu tun / da sprach si ich wil den fuß haben / da sprach si czu sant Cecilia waz wilt du tun / da sprach si ich wil in vmb halten / da sprach sandt Tecla ich will mich auff yn legen daz er nit auff stet biß er gesalbet wirt / da nam Sant Katherin der hymelischen salben auß dem buchslein / vnd salbet irem diener seinen fuß / da ward er czu hanndt gesund alß ob ym nichts geschehen were. (fol. cclix^v)[181]

> [And when they reached the bed Saint Katherine said to Saint Margaret, 'What do you want to do?'. She said, 'I shall hold his feet'. Then she said to Saint Cecelia, 'What do you want to do?'. She said, 'I shall hold him round the middle'. Then Saint Thecla said, 'I shall lie down on top of him so that he does not get up until he has been covered in ointment'. Then Saint Katherine took the divine ointment out of the little casket and with it anointed her servant's feet. He immediately became completely well, just as if nothing had ever happened to him].

The ritually repetitive nature of the dialogue, like the saying of rosary beads, leads into a miracle of healing before the reader's eyes. The restoration of the count's

---

she converted to Christianity and became a shepherdess. She refused to marry the governor of Antioch, was denounced by him as a Christian and tortured. In prison she was swallowed alive by a dragon that subsequently burst open and released her. Having converted many to Christianity, Margaret was eventually martyred under Diocletian at the beginning of fourth century. Her attribute is a dragon (which may explain her appearance here as "wurm" is Middle High German for dragon) and she is also one of the *Vierzehn Heiligen*, so is regionally significant for Nuremberg. Saint Cecilia was a third-century Christian virgin who, despite having dedicated her virginity to Christ, was given in marriage to a pagan, Valarian (echoes of the innkeeper's daughter). Valerian was so moved by Cecilia's vow of virginity that he and his brother converted and were martyred. Cecilia herself was first boiled in water, then beheaded; from the sixteenth century onwards she was the patron saint of music. Saint Thecla was a pupil and companion of Paul. She went from Iconium (present-day Konya in Turkey) to Seleucia, where she excelled as a philosopher, speaker and worker of miracles. Fleeing from jealous doctors she hid in a cave, which closed behind her, leaving only her veil. She was celebrated as one of the early martyrs of the Church. Her feast day is 23 September; she is the patron saint of the dying and those suffering from eye problems (*Handwörterbuch des deutschen Aberglaubens*, vol. 8, p. 754). She was popular amongst ascetic women in fourth-century Alexandria. Her legend is included in *Der Heiligen Leben*, fol. clxxij^r–clxxiij^r.

[181]   Compare Saint Dominic's vision (*Der Heiligen Leben*, fol. c^r).

physical intactness mirrors – and rewards – his preservation of his "daughter's" virgin intactness: 'du solt wissen das dye genad von der leiblichen gesuntheyt / dyr dye heylig Junckfraw Sant Katherin des dienstes da mit gelonet hatt / den du yr tet an deiner tochter das du yr aller scho*n*test durch durch yren willen / vnd sie yn das kloster tet' (fol. cclix[v]).[182] Saint Katherine is again shown as honouring loyalty in her servants. In the morning the Graf awakes healthy, his sound body the material object left over from the vision since his foot signals presence where there might, as with the judge, have been physical and spiritual absence. Since the count relates the entire story to those surrounding him, he becomes tangible proof for and oral source of the text that feeds into *Der Heiligen Leben*. His account of his miraculous vision becomes a narrative for those endowed with physical sight only, so that they, who have had only mediated experience of the vision, have it imprinted on their brain (the reader by this means sees it twice). Predictably, the tale concludes on praise for the saint that indicates a mutually obliging contract: 'darumb sollen wir sye eren vnd sollen ir auch mit allem fleiß dienen / wann sie lett mit nichten keynes dienstes vngelonnet' (fol. cclix[v]).[183]

In the end the narrative returns to its source at Mount Sinai, to the monastery and to Saint Katherine's tomb. In coming full circle, the text replicates the wedding ring on Katherine's finger: it has been left behind to inform a Christian readership of the miracle of Saint Katherine's life and to provide a focus for contemplation and emulation. The ensuing praise of monastery[184] and monks merges layers of sacred time: their chapter house stands on the location of the Burning Bush (fol. cclx[r]), so the present of the narrative is overlaid onto Old Testament time while Saint Katherine is linked to Moses and thus to God's command to lead the Children of Israel from exile in Egypt back to the Promised Land (Exodus 3:2–4:17).[185] Her role as guide and saviour is confirmed in a Katharinenkloster prayer:

---

[182]   'You should know that the gracious gift of physical health bestowed on you by the holy virgin Saint Katherine is a reward for the service you did her by not inflicting harm on her daughter for her sake and by helping her to enter a convent'.

[183]   'For that reason we should honour her and serve her assiduously for she never leaves any act of service unrewarded'.

[184]   The text states that the monastery was 'gestyfftet in vnser frawe*n* ere' [endowed in honour of Our Lady] (fol. cclix[v]–cclx[r]). According to Walsh, the monastery was founded by Emperor Justinian (527–65) in the mid-sixth century, probably around 548–65. From its foundation until the translation there of Saint Katherine's relics, probably in the late-twelfth century, from Jebel Katrin (a neighbouring mountain) the monastery was known as St. Mary's. After that a gradual change in dedication took place (Walsh, *The Cult of St Katherine*, pp. 39–40).

[185]   The chapter house is site of decision-making and law-giving within the monastic community, so building it on the site of the Burning Bush physically incorporates one of the

Pit fur vns heillige katerina Das wir wirdig werden *christi* genaden Got der du orom host gegeben das gesetz moysi in der hoh des pergs synay vnd in der selben stat host wunderlichen gesetzt den leichnam durch dein heillig engel der seligen junckfrawen vnd deiner martrerin katerina verleich vns gnedigclich das wir mit irem verdienen vnd pittungen mugen kumen zu dem perg der da ist *christus*.[186]

[Pray for us, Saint Katherine, that we may become worthy of Christ's grace. God, you who handed down the Law of Moses on the top of Mount Sinai and has miraculously caused the body of your blessed virgin and martyr Katherine to be placed on the same spot by angels, grant us through your grace that, thanks to her merit and her intercession on our behalf, we may come to the mountain that is Christ].

Guided by Saint Katherine's legend to this site, the Christian pilgrim comes closer to his home in God, as does the nun who has followed the journey in her imagination and prayer. The above prayer finds its recursive reflexion in those left by pilgrims in the Latin church at Sinai:

The walls of this church [the Latin church inside the monastery compound at Sinai] are of mud, but they are covered with mats of divers colours, woven of plaited palm-leaves, whereon beauteous prayers addressed to St. Catherine are written by pilgrims; for it is custom that every company of pilgrims should write a poem on the blessed Catherine and hang it on the wall, in which poem the blessed Catherine must be praised and every one of the pilgrims in that company must be named, provided always that the company has among its members one who knows how to write such verses.[187]

In their written prayers pilgrims are, then, creating further versions of Saint Katherine's legend and martyrdom, miniature *Der Heiligen Leben*, documenting key aspects of the life that drew them to Sinai. By inscribing their presence at the monastery, whence the saint's cult radiated outwards, pilgrims are completing the ring of legend by returning full-circle to its source. Moreover, just as pilgrims believed that burial in the Valley of Jehosaphat meant speedier access to Heaven on Judgement Day, so prayers left close to Saint Katherine's relics may have been judged particularly efficacious. Indeed, for nuns forbidden to travel, an antiphon to the saint requests the following: 'du hast auch iren

---

most sacred sites in Christendom into the very physical fabric and holy space of the building and into its governance. The Burning Bush was also thought to prefigure the Annunciation.

186   Stadtbibliothek Nürnberg, Cod. Cent. VII, 65, fol. 4ʳ.
187   Fabri, *Wanderings*, vol. 2, part 2, p. 613.

ersammen leichnam die engel heißen begraben · auf die höhe des perges synai / also verleihe vns genediglich · das wir gefürt werden zu der höhe der tugent · vnd in den sal des himellischen hofes an end gesetzt werden Durch vnsern herren'.[188] Reading *Der Heiligen Leben* is a spiritual pilgrimage for those unable to undertake a real one and the Sinai monastery forms its logical culmination.[189] Moreover, the Burning Bush symbolizes Mary: just as it remained unconsumed by the fire, so her virginity remained intact despite the birth of Christ.[190] The Virgin and Katherine are thus united in the sacred shrine, underpinning an association initiated by the mystic marriage and depicted by the windows in the Lorenzkirche.[191] Saint Katherine may not have given birth to the Son of God, but her exemplary life and martyrdom have given birth to a cult which, as the miracle stories demonstrate, saves those dedicated to her. The light and fire emitted by the Burning Bush reinforce the thread that has bound the narrative from Saint Katherine's first vision of Christ and the philosophers' martyrdom. Linked to vision of the divine, light and fire represent the consumption by passion for God of the believer who has been illuminated by God's grace and the glimpse of salvation. Potential and limits of human vision are both highlighted here, since Moses sees the Burning Bush but turns his face away from the sight of God: 'And Moses hid his face; for he was afraid to look upon God' (Exodus 3:6).[192] This may be due to his not being a Christian and therefore denied sight of the Godhead; or it may be that no human being is permitted

---

[188]   'You also ordered the angels to bury her worthy body on the pinnacle of Mount Sinai. Therefore grant us graciously that we may be led to the pinnacle of virtue and ultimately take our places in the eternal court of Heaven for the sake of Our Lord' (Stadtbibliothek Nürnberg Cod. Cent. V, App. 81, fol. 104ʳ).

[189]   Moreover, although Acre, the last Christian stronghold in the Holy Land, did not fall to the Saracens until 1291, at the time of writing of the *Legenda aurea* (c. 1260), Christian presence in the Holy Land had been severely reduced, so the reference to the Burning Bush may constitute gentle encouragement to Christian princes to launch a new Crusade and return Christians to their true spiritual home in Jerusalem and the Holy Land.

[190]   *Hall's Dictionary*, p. 214. The passage reads: 'And the angel of the LORD appeared unto him in a flame of fire out of the midst of a bush: and he looked, and, behold, the bush burned with fire, and the bush *was* not consumed' (Exodus 3:2).

[191]   Fabri makes the Marian symbolism of the Burning Bush particularly clear (though it locates it in a chapel adjoining one dedicated to Saint John the Baptist): 'This is the place where stood that miraculous bush of Moses, which he saw burning, and the flames rising aloft from out of it ; yet was it not hurt by any fire, as we read in Exod. Iii. But even more wondrous was the fulfilment of this vision, when Mary, that ever-green bush, ever-flowering and sweet-scented, was kindled and impregnated by the Divine fire, while nevertheless her virginity suffered no hurt' (Fabri, *Wanderings*, vol. 2. part 2, p. 607).

[192]   The turning away from sight of the divine is echoed by the young count in the story of Saint Katherine as the "other woman" (fol. cclviijʳ).

sight of God until he sees Him face to face on Judgement Day. In either case, Saint Katherine's privileged status is highlighted as she does see Christ face-to-face, albeit in a dream.

The merging of temporal strata continues: Old Testament time embodied in Moses blends into the time of Katherine's translation to Sinai and thence into the monastery church; into the time of composition of the *Legenda Aurea*; into the fifteenth-century reader's present; into the contemporary reader's present, since for God time has no beginning and no end. In His eyes the whole history of salvation is eternally, co-temporally present, a vision granted the reader of *Der Heiligen Leben* at the moment of his reading of this passage, since he, too, is permitted a – textually transmitted – vision of the Burning Bush which fuses temporal strata: 'wann man hat eyn guldynn busch dar [in the chapter house] gemachtt nach dem busch den moyses sach / vnnd vnsers herren bild ist auff dem busch / vnnd Moses knyet also barfus vor dem busch' (fol. cclxʳ).[193] Old Testament time is tangibly, visibly present; the pilgrim to Sinai and the reader of the text may see both Moses seeing and what Moses himself saw, thereby becoming a witness to God's recorded presence on earth and a "reflected" Moses, just as figures within the mirror of Katherine's miracle stories become reflexions of the saint.[194] However, whereas Moses hides his face and does not look at God, the pilgrim or reader is vouchsafed a vision from which even the Lord's elected saviour of His chosen people withdrew. If sight of God was the fourth and highest level of vision, textually the pilgrim/reader is granted a foresight of the joy that awaits him if saved through his virtue and piety.[195] Gold symbolizes transfiguration, majesty and eternity, so the Golden Bush represents

---

[193] 'For in the chapter house a golden bush has been created like the one which Moses saw and the image of Our Lord is in the bush and Moses kneels barefoot in front of the bush'. Fabri's description highlights the sanctity of the site for Muslims as well as Christians: 'Beneath the altar is the place where the bush is believed to have stood, and in the pavement there is a brazen plate, whereon is carved the figure of the burning bush, and of Moses sitting down putting off his shoes. Many lamps hang above the place, for it is held in great respect by all men. Saracens, Arabs, and Turks beg earnestly to be admitted to this place, and when they are admitted do not enter it save barefoot. Jews would be exceedingly glad to enter it, but are not suffered so to do' (Fabri, *Wanderings*, vol. 2. part 2, pp. 607–8). Muslims had a mosque within the monastery compound (Fabri, *Wanderings*, vol. 2. part 2, p. 614).

[194] The reader is prompted to draw on his knowledge of the Biblical text, to use his imagination and the detail provided by the text to recreate in his own mind's eye the scene in the chapter house. The reader's mind becomes a library of images for visualizing devotion.

[195] According to Camille, citing Richard of Saint-Victor (d. 1173; prior of the Abbey of Saint-Victor in Paris), the fourth level of vision was 'the mystical mode, which entailed the "pure and naked seeing of divine reality" as described in 1Corinthians 13:12: "for now we see through a glass, darkly ; but then face to face"' (*Gothic Art*, p. 17).

God's everlasting might and its power to transform the base metal of the unredeemed sinner into the purified gold of virtue, a thread that runs through the history of salvation and fuses together Creation, mankind and eternal bliss after Judgement Day. Moreover, if seen by candlelight the Golden Bush would reflect the flickering flames, throwing off shafts of light as if on fire and thereby reconstructing Moses' privileged vision for the pilgrim/reader, who could thus witness his own "miracle", just as he was co-witness to the visions and miracles in Saint Katherine's legend. The sacred, transformative nature of the vision is reinforced by its location since, just as Moses was not allowed to approach the Burning Bush because the ground was hallowed, so no one is allowed inside the chapter house.[196] Together Katherine's tomb and the chapter house form the sacred heart of the exemplary community at Sinai: the monks are 'gar selig' and 'eins heiligen tugentlichen lebens';[197] they fast nearly all year on bread and water; on feast days they celebrate together in the refectory by eating fish and oil; they rarely drink wine (fol. cclx^r). Their denial of the body by constant fasting echoes Saint Katherine's self-abnegation in jail; the oil they consume alludes to that which flows from Katherine's bones; whilst their communal feasts echo the Last Supper, rendering them an ideal community of believers.

The next stage in the narrative is Saint Katherine's connexion to this site of ideal community and sacred past:

> vnd die selben gutten herren haben allwegen als gnug von sant Katherinen genaden wann allweg an irem abent czu vesper kommen gar vil kleyner vogelin dar vnd yegkliches tret ein olzweig in seinem schnebelin / daran sind schwarcze knoplin / sam dye kriechlin dar yn ist daz ol / vnd eyn zweig ist grosser dann das ander eyns hat vier knopfllin / eyns drey / eins zwey / vnd werffen dy in iren creutzgang daz tut sy ymmer mer von einer vesper zu der andern. (fol. cclx^r)

> [And the same good men constantly enjoy Saint Katherine's grace to the full for every year at vespers on Saint Katherine's Day flocks of small birds descend on the monastery, each one carrying in its beak a olive twig on which there are small black knobs like sloes in which is the oil. The twigs vary in size: some have four knobs, others three, others two and others one. The birds drop them in the cloisters and do so in ever greater numbers from one vespers to the next].

---

[196]   Potentially, however, the Katharinenkloster nuns could have imagined their own chapter house as the location of the Burning Bush, a further relocating of the divine within the walls of Nuremberg.

[197]   'most blessed'; 'lead a holy, virtuous life'.

The annual miracle of Saint Katherine's grace on her feast day activates a number of associations.[198] First, the small birds with olive branches recall Noah's dove: 'And the dove came in to him in the evening; and, lo, in her mouth *was* an olive leaf pluckt off; so Noah knew that the waters were abated from off the earth' (Genesis 8:11). This particular olive twig 'symbolized to Christians the making of God's peace with man', so the miracle identifies Sinai as a place of peace and hope.[199] Second, the birds recall the dove that every Good Friday descends to the Grail community with a miraculous host that nourishes the community throughout the year:

> Ez ist hiute der karfrîtac,
> daz man für wâr dâ warten mac,
> ein tûb von himel swinget:
> ûf den stein diu bringet
> ein kleine wîze oblât
> [...]
> dâ von der stein enpfæhet
> swaz guots ûf erden dræhet
> von trinken unt von spîse,
> als den wunsch von pardîse.[200]

The monks on Sinai are, then, in God's direct care. Moreover, the Grail community, like the Templar, Hospitaller and Teutonic Orders, is both

---

[198]   Felix Fabri includes this miracle in his pilgrimage account: 'Every year on the virgin's feast-day there flew thither certain most beauteous birds of an unknown kind, bearing in their beaks green boughs of olive-trees covered with fruit. These birds settled on the roof of the church, and threw the boughs down below, where the brethren took them up, and pressed from them fine and pleasant-tasted [*sic*] oil in such abundance that they had enough for their table and their lamps throughout the year' (Fabri, *Wanderings*, vol. 2, part 2, p. 602). Tucher, however, notes: 'Auch haben manche jar jerlichen an Sant Katherina tag die vogel vil olczweig jn jren schnebelen zu dem closter vnd der kirchen pracht, von dem oll nachuolgend dasselbig jar die bruder gelebt, das auch pey kurczen jaren auffgehort hat, als die bruder deß alles bericht haben' [For many years birds brought olive twigs to the monastery and the church in their beaks annually on Saint Katherine's Day and the monks lived on the oil during the whole of the following year. That ceased a few years ago, as the brothers reported to us] ('*Reise*', p. 527).

[199]   *Hall's Dictionary*, p. 228.

[200]   *Parzival*, 470, 1–14. '[F]or today is Good Friday, when one can infallibly see a Dove wing its way down from Heaven. It brings a small white Wafer to the Stone … from which the Stone receives all that is good on earth of food and drink, of paradisal excellence' (Hatto, *Parzival*, p. 240).

monastic and military,[201] so the merging of the Sinai community with that other ideal recipient of divine grace bestows upon the former the status of warriors for God's Word in a hostile, heathen environment.[202] Saint Katherine's care for her community is rendered visible by the birds' dropping of the olive twigs into the cloisters in a public performance of divine grace. The monks put the buds into a "kuffen" [press], press the oil out, eat it (a reference back to feast days) and burn it in their lamps, so Saint Katherine nourishes and illuminates them literally as well as metaphorically, sending them the light of spiritual grace and salvation. Moreover, the oil press brings to mind the grape press and production of communion wine, so the whole process provides an analogy for the text's purpose and effect: distilling and condensing wisdom for the reader, nourishing him spiritually and directing him towards perpetual grace, here symbolized by the monks' receiving enough oil to last them an entire year.[203] To encourage the reader, the following story furnishes an inner-textual eyewitness for the theatre of grace: a sick knight who loves Saint Katherine begs her to intervene with God to cure him, promising to visit her grave if he recovers:

> Nun het der Ritter wol gehort daz die vogel in daz ol dar brachten / darumb kam er mit andern herren dar / auff iren tag / vnd sach das schön zeychen selber / das ist in kurczen iarn geschehen / da lobten sye alle gott vmb das schön zeychen das er durch seiner gemaheln willen sant Katherinen tut. (cclx͏ʳ)

> [Now the knight had heard that birds brought the oil there to them and for that reason he went there with other lords on Saint Katherine's Day and saw the beautiful miracle for himself. That happened only a few years ago and they all praised God for the beautiful miracle He had performed for the sake of His spouse Saint Katherine].

The knight's status renders him an unimpeachable witness, so the reader is reassured of God's continuing, indeed recent, intervention at Sinai and the

---

[201] In Book 9 of *Parzival* the Grail community knights are referred to as 'templeise' (468, 28).

[202] The text mentions that 'heydenn' [heathens] visit the chapter house too (fol. cclxʳ).

[203] If the oil fails to materialize one year the birds bring more for the following two years so that the monks have enough, provision that rather contradicts the notion of the oil being an annual event. The text may reveal actual circumstances prevailing underneath the veil of the miraculous in that the monks may have grown their own olives that were then converted into olive oil. That the birds are not seen much throughout the year suggests the annual bringing of tribute at harvest time. The text may display an inadvertent crack in the edifice of the miraculous that allows sight of the process of creating the miracles pilgrims wanted to experience.

possibility of viewing the miraculous during a pilgrimage there.[204] This final story, although brief, combines and imprints on the reader's mind Saint Katherine's essential attributes, qualities iterated throughout the miracle collection: her loyalty to her devotees; her role as one of the *Vierzehn Heiligen*;[205] her status as bride of Christ and His continuing loyalty to her that manifests itself in aid to those pray for help in her name. For the nuns in the Katharinenkloster, who not only read and listened to the miracle stories but from 1500/1505 could see, at the base of the Fütterer Altar, the entombed Katherine guarded by three angels on Mount Sinai, the last two miracle stories merged their convent with the one at Sinai, promising enduring protection and provision and rendering their physical and spiritual home a more intensely holy place.

After this concluding miracle story the narrative completes an even bigger circle by returning to the beginning of Saint Katherine's legend and offering a condensed recapitulation of her life that highlights further principal attributes in handy *aide-mémoire* form for both the nun and the lay devotee. Just as Katherine's sanctity flows beyond the boundaries of the monastery at Sinai, so it flows beyond the text into convent and city, manifesting itself in the many tangible witnesses to her cult. Through the merging of textual and (reactivated memories of) the visual (such as the Volckamer window) Katherine steps out of the pages of the narrative into the reader's actual physical space, illuminating him spiritually as a window through which divine light is transmitted. Both text and saint become windows onto salvation.

Only it is not that straightforward. Whether one understands the miracle stories as illuminating windows onto salvation; as the fountain of grace flowing from the saint's martyrdom like the oil from her bones; or as individual beads on the rosary of redemption, to be rehearsed, like prayer, in ritual repetition and reflexion – they embody reticence as much as communication of divine mercy. The stories are patterned by Katherine's refusal of herself as much as by her granting, by absence, silence and disguise that transmit the ultimate incomprehensibility of the divine. The holy is staged, the performativity of the stories[206] a dramatic enactment of man's

---

204 No matter when this miracle story was written or included in the *Wunderanhang*, a reader of, say, *Der Heiligen Leben* could have understood his own time as the referent for the phrase 'in kurczen iarn'.

205 The defining characteristic of this group is God's promise to grant any prayer made to Him in their name: the knight 'bat sy [Saint Katherine] daz sy vmb got erwurbe daz er gesund wurde' [asked her to intercede with God on his behalf so that he might recover] (fol. cclxʳ).

206 Dramatic elements include dialogue, costume, disguise, sound and lighting effects, changing identities, props, landscape, stage sets, falling images, horror (headless barking dogs, walking corpses), special effects (earthquakes, wind, flying hermits), visions that open a parallel reality much like a dream sequence or flashback in a film.

attempts to grasp the nature of God and His saints, to present the unpresentable in ways that scare or encourage believers into piety, submission – and the financial generosity towards the Church that translates into furnishing its physical fabric with advertisements for the power of the ultimately unknowable. Actors within the stories function as eyewitnesses to – and hence guarantors of – the truth of the miraculous, but simultaneously destabilize it by creating multiple narrative layers between reader and narrated event. Miracles may, in Jolles' terms, encapsulate the "active virtue" of a saint, but such virtue is unreassuring unless rendered material, tangible in objects-left-behind. Ultimately, grace is unpredictable; saints are capricious über-egos that must be wooed and won; and the object-left-behind that is the text of Katherine's life and miracles leaves the reader in a state of constantly propitiating uncertainty.

Chapter 4

Showcasing a Saint: Saint Katherine of Alexandria, Patrician Patronage and Empire in Fifteenth-Century Nuremberg

To the south of the River Pegnitz that runs through the centre of Nuremberg, on the road from the Königstor to the Hauptmarkt, stands the Lorenzkirche,[1] one of the city's two main parish churches. A chapel dedicated to Saint Laurence at the Holy Sepulchre on this spot is mentioned in papal records from 1235 and 1258.[2] Building on the present Gothic church started between 1243 and 1315; work was finally completed in 1477. The Nuremberg *Rat* oversaw the building of the church, the construction of which was funded by donations, endowments in wills and the sale of indulgences.[3] The construction of the choir was largely funded by voluntary donations from the residents of Nuremberg and those visiting the city for the *Heiltumsweisung*, the annual display on the Hauptmarkt every second Friday after Easter of the imperial relics, brought to Nuremberg in 1424 from Burg Karlstein (Hrad Karlštejn) near Prague by order of Sigismund, King of the Germans, to protect them from Hussite advances.[4] The hall choir

---

[1]   *Stadtlexikon*, p. 651. The cult of Saint Laurence increased in popularity in Germany from the thirteenth century onwards. Saint Laurence, deacon to Pope Sixtus II, was martyred by being roasted alive during the persecution of the Christians under Emperor Valerian (253–260) in 258, the Pope having ordered him to give away the Church's treasures to the poor. On refusing to surrender these treasures to the Roman prefect, Laurence, who identified the poor as the Church's true treasures, was martyred (Funk, *Glasfensterkunst*, p. 37; *Hall's Dictionary*, pp. 190–1).

[2]   According to Müllner, Emperor Heinrich II was responsible for the dedication to Saint Laurence (Müllner, *Annalen*, vol. 1, p. 47).

[3]   See Gerhardt Weiland, 'Heiligen-Konjunktur. Reliquienpräsentation, Reliquienverehrung und wirtschaftliche Situation an der Nürnberger Lorenzkirche im Spätmittelalter', in Markus Mayr (ed.), *Von Goldenen Gebeinen. Wirtschaft und Reliquie im Mittelalter*, Geschichte und Ökonomie 9 (Innsbruck, Vienna and Munich: Studien-Verlag, 2001), pp. 186–220 (pp. 188–9).

[4]   Sigismund (1368–1437), son of Emperor Karl IV, was crowned King of the Germans on 10 September 1410 and Holy Roman Emperor on 31 May 1433. On 31 December 1424 Pope Martin V approved the transfer of the *Reichskleinodien* to Nuremberg. They entered Nuremberg in a solemn procession on 24 March 1424 and included the imperial crown, sceptre, orb, swords, coronation garments and various relics: namely, the imperial cross with relics of the True Cross in its shaft; a splinter of Christ's crib from Bethlehem; a tooth of John the Baptist; a piece of John the Evangelist's robe; the chains of Saints John the

was built between 1439 and 1477 as a result of the increased veneration of Saint Deocarus (d. 832), confessor to Charlemagne and first abbot of the Benedictine monastery in Herrieden (near Ansbach), whose skull had been given to Nuremberg by Ludwig of Bavaria in 1316 as a reward for military assistance against Duke Friedrich der Schöne of Austria, a rival claimant to the imperial throne in whose territories Herrieden stood.[5]

Amongst the many testimonies to Patrician patronage of the Lorenzkirche the East choir boasts the Volckamer window, donated circa 1486 by the Patrician Peter II Volckamer (1431–93)[6] in memory of his wife Apollonia

---

Baptist, Peter and Paul; a piece of the tablecloth used at the Last Supper; the Holy Lance with which the Roman soldier Longinus pierced Christ's side and which also had bound into its shaft one of the nails with which Christ was nailed to the Cross; and a piece of Christ's apron from His washing of the Disciples' feet (*Stadtlexikon*, p. 874; Müllner, *Annalen*, vol. 2, pp. 244–50). In 1518 Anton Tucher, Hieronymus Ebner and Martin Gander commissioned reliquaries by Hans Krug for the fragments of tablecloth and apron (Grote, *Die Tucher*, pp. 51–2; plate 56).

[5]   Friedrich der Schöne (1289–13 January 1330) was elected German King by four Electoral Princes in Sachsenhausen on 19 October 1314; Ludwig of Bavaria was elected German King by four Electoral Princes on 20 October 1314. Pope John XXII refused to recognize either candidate; eventually a decisive battle was fought on 28 September 1322 at Mühldorf, where Friedrich was taken prisoner. In March 1325 Ludwig released him; on 5 September 1325 they signed a treaty agreeing joint kingship and joint rule, although Johannes XXII still refused to recognize Friedrich. (*Lexikon des Mittelalters*, vol. 4 (1st edn Lachen: Coron Verlag Monika Schoeller, 1999; reprint Frankfurt am Main: dtv, 2002), p. 939; *Stadtlexikon*, p. 204; Georg Stolz, 'Die zwei Schwestern. Gedanken zum Bau des Lorenzer Hallenchors 1439–77', in Herbert Bauer, Gerhard Hirschmann and Georg Stolz (eds), *500 Jahre Hallenchor St. Lorenz zu Nürnberg 1477–1977*, Nürnberger Forschungen 20 (Nuremberg: Selbstverlag des Vereins für Geschichte der Stadt Nürnberg, 1977), pp. 1–21 (pp. 3–6); Müllner, *Annalen*, vol. 1, pp. 372–3). The Deocarus Altar, now in the north aisle of the choir, shows Ludwig's donation of the relics.

[6]   The Volckamer are documented for the first time in Neumarkt in 1278; Hertel (Hartwig I) Volkmar (d. 1375) came to Nuremberg in 1337 and became a *Genannter* in the *Großer Rat* in 1339 (a *Genannter* signed official documents on behalf of the city) (Fleischmann, *Rat und Patriziat*, 31/2, p. 1043). The family dealt in spices and cloth. By 1362 they were already represented on the *Kleiner Rat*; they also functioned as representatives of Nuremberg on diplomatic missions: for example, Peter I Volckamer represented the city's interests at the Council of Konstanz in 1414/15 (*Stadtlexikon*, p. 1144; Fleischmann, *Rat und Patriziat*, 31/2, p. 1046) and in 1414 was sent by the *Rat* to Cadolzburg to negotiate with Graf Wilhelm von Montfort, who was hostile to the city (Müllner, *Annalen*, vol. 2, pp. 217–18). He also led Nuremberg's troops in the campaign against the Hussites in 1421 and played a decisive role in the *Rat's* illegal political and economic contacts with them in 1429–30 (Fleischmann, *Rat und Patriziat*, 31/2, p. 1046). Andreas II Volckamer was *Ratsbaumeister* (Master of Buildings and Works) for 30 years and in charge of extending the city fortifications in the 1420s (Fleischmann, *Rat und Patriziat*, 31/2, p. 1045). Berthold Volckamer (1397–1451) was appointed 'zweiter von fünf Kriegsherren' (second of five military commanders) by the *Rat* in 1449 in the First *Markgrafenkrieg* (Margrave's War) and led negotiations with Margrave Albrecht Achilles and the latter's chancellor in Heidelberg in 1450 (Fleischmann, *Rat und Patriziat*, 31/2, p. 1046). In 1457 Endres Volckamer and in 1470 Hannß Volckamer were *Pfleger* of the church and *Pilgerspital* St. Martha, endowed c. 1360 by Conrad Waldstromer (Müllner, *Annalen*, vol. 2, p. 28). According to Carbach, Andreas Volckamer was *Kirchenpfleger* of the Lorenzkirche from 1398–1428 and Hans Volckamer from

Mendel.[7] The window depicts the Tree of Jesse: Jesse, father of King David and first in the genealogy of Christ, is shown sleeping; the family tree that culminates in Christ grows out of his chest. The Tree of Jesse is the visual realization of the prophecy from Isaiah:

1464–70 (Carbach, *Nürnbergisches Zion*, p. 21). Paul I Volckamer (1448–1505) was married to Margarete Mendel (d. 1495) c. 1464 and after her death to Apollonia Haller. In 1489 he became *Kirchenpfleger* of the Sebalduskirche and was responsible for commissioning Veit Stoß to do a *Passionsrelief* (relief sculpture of Christ's Passion) there in 1499, the 'Volckamersche Gedächtnisstiftung' (Fleischmann, *Rat und Patriziat*, 31/2, pp. 1049–50). According to Fleischmann, Peter III Volckamer (1431–93) was responsible for commissioning the window (Fleischmann, *Rat und Patriziat*, p. 1051). Peter III Volckamer was a merchant, appointed *Genannter* in 1449 and *Jüngerer Bürgermeister* in 1485, but there is little information on him in documentary sources. Fleischmann neither mentions a Peter II nor includes him in the family tree. Biedermann lists a Peter Volckamer, son of Peter Volckamer and Anna Hallerin, who died in 1418 and lies buried in the Sebalduskirche (*Geschlechtsregister*, table DXXXII (p. Xxx2ʳ).

    [7]   Apollonia Mendel, the daughter of Peter Mendel and Apollonia Waldstromerin, died on 24 December 1485 (Funk, *Glasfensterkunst*, p. 56). The Mendel, one of the *älteste Geschlechter*, are first mentioned in 1305 as *Hammerherren* and armourers; in 1313 as founders of the Moritzkapelle, the rebuilding of which in the Sebalduskirche cemetery was financed by Eberhard Mendel; in 1430 Marquardt Mendel endowed a small organ; in 1454 Peter Mendel's son had the chapel and altars decorated with paintings; various members of the family endowed masses (Müllner, *Annalen*, vol. 1, pp. 311–12). By 1354 at the latest the Mendel served on the *Kleiner Rat*, Heinrich Mendel being mentioned in the *Ratsverzeichnis* in 1354 (Müllner, *Annalen*, vol. 2, p. 8). By 1377 at the latest the Mendel owned one of the 56 chambers in the Fondaco dei Tedeschi in Venice. In the second half of the fourteenth and first half of the fifteenth centuries they played a crucial role in trade with Italy and the Levant, though the firm went bankrupt in 1448. In 1380 Marquard I Mendel founded the Carthusian monastery to the south of the city, outside the then walls and between the Klarissenkloster and Sankt Jakob, church of the Teutonic Knights (See also Müllner, *Annalen*, vol. 2, pp. 77–8). The monastery is now occupied by the Germanisches Nationalmuseum. In 1388 Marquard's brother Konrad I founded the Zwölfbrüderhausstiftung, dedicated to the care of elderly Nuremberg artisans who could no longer work or support themselves (Müllner, *Annalen*, vol. 2, pp. 147–8 (who has 1382 as the date of foundation); (*Stadtlexikon*, p. 688). After Konrad Mendel's death his brother Peter was to be *Pfleger* of the Zwölfbrüderhaus (from 1414) and after the latter's death the founder's son Konrad was to assume that role before power to name a *Pfleger* fell to the *Rat*. However, members of the Mendel family continued to be appointed: Wilhelm in 1423; Marquard in 1425; Peter in 1438; Marquard in 1486. The Mendel are associated through the Zwölfbrüderhaus with the Volckamer, as Paulus Volckamer became *Pfleger* in 1473 and Hannß Volckamer in 1522 (Müllner, *Annalen*, vol. 2, pp. 148–9). Before 1392 Konrad I and his younger brother, Peter I, founded the *Seelhaus am Paniersberg* (*Stadtlexikon*, p. 688; Fleischmann, *Rat und Patriziat*, pp. 701–2). The *Seelhäuser* were established by wealthy families as residences for Beguines or *Seelnonnen*, impoverished elderly women who lived in monastic-like communities and dedicated themselves to the care of the sick, dying and imprisoned (*Stadtlexikon*, p. 971). In 1400 Conrad Mendel was *Pfleger* of the church and *Pilgerspital* St. Martha (Müllner, *Annalen*, vol. 2, p. 27); in 1401 Peter Mendel a *Pfleger* of the Egidienkloster (Müllner, *Annalen*, vol. 1, p. 116). A Peter Mendel celebrated his *Jahrtage* there as well (Müllner, *Annalen*, vol. 1, p. 117). This was not the first alliance between the families: in 1455 Cunegunda Volckamerin (1435–63?), daughter of Hans Volckamer (1409–87), had married Sartel Mendel. A Katharina Mendel had been prioress of the Katharinenkloster in 1394 (Fries, 'Kirche und Kloster', p. 43); and Peter Mentel was *Pfleger* of the Katharinenkloster 1420–30 (Carbach, *Nürnbergisches Zion*, p. 67), a possible link to the subject of the window.

And there shall come forth a rod out of the stem of Jesse, and a Branch shall grow out of his roots:

And the spirit of the Lord shall rest upon him, the spirit of wisdom and understanding, the spirit of counsel and might, the spirit of knowledge and of the fear of the Lord. (Isaiah 11:1–2)[8]

What is striking about this rendition is the image at its centre: the mystic marriage between the infant Christ and Saint Katherine of Alexandria.[9] The depiction of Saint Katherine is in itself nothing unusual: in the fifteenth century she was one of the most popular saints in Southern Germany;[10] 1293 had seen the endowment in Nuremberg by the Patrician Konrad von Neumarkt and his wife Adelheid, née Pfinzing, of the Dominican convent dedicated to her; and representations of her were found across the city in churches and private chapels.[11] Her particularly high status in Nuremberg may be due in part to its excellent trade links with Alexandria and personal ties to the resident Venetian merchants involved in the spice

---

[8]   See also Isaiah 11:10: 'And in that day there shall be a root of Jesse, which shall stand as an ensign for the people; to it shall the Gentiles seek: and his rest shall be glorious'. In Matthew (1:5–6) and Luke (3:23) Jesse is expressly named as an ancestor of Christ. According to Otto Kaiser, Isaiah 11 directs attention to 'the coming time of salvation', 'renewal of kingship' and 'righteousness of the rule of the one to come'; also to the 'idea that the king ultimately needs the support of the spirit of Yahweh for his rule' (Otto Kaiser, *Isaiah 1-12. A Commentary*, trans. John Bowden, Old Testament Library (1st edn London: SMC, 1972; new edn 1983), pp. 254–6; original German: Otto Kaiser, *Das Buch des Propheten Jesaja*, Das alte Testament Deutsch 17 (Göttingen: Vandenhoeck & Ruprecht, 1981)). Typologically, Jesse refers to the sleeping Adam (who sleeps during his creation), to the Tree of Knowledge of Good and Evil and hence to the Cross. Patricians appropriated the iconology of the Tree of Jesse for their own genealogy, as the *Tuchersches Geschlechterbuch* demonstrates, e.g. the picture of Lienhard Tucher (1487–1568) and his two wives, Magdalena Stromerin and Katharina Nützlin, each of whom has a tree growing out of her side.

[9]   This is not the only depiction of Saint Katherine associated with the Volckamer family: an antiphonar commissioned by Agnes Volckamer (d. 1468) for her niece Magdalena Holzschuher in the Dominican monastery of Heilig Kreuz and completed in 1491 boasts a full-page illumination of the mystic marriage now pasted inside the front cover of the summer volume (Corine Schleif, 'Forgotten Roles of Women as Donors: Sister Katerina Lemmel's Negotiated Exchanges in the Care for the Here and the Hereafter', in Truus van Bueren in collaboration with Andrea van Leerdam (eds), *Care for the Here and the Hereafter: Memoria, Art and Ritual in the Middle Ages* (Turnhout: Brepols, 2005), pp. 137–54 (p. 137)).

[10]   The Ulm Dominican Felix Fabri provides most eloquent testimony to this: he regards Saint Katherine as his 'sweetest spouse', 'betrothed' to him in his youth and 'chosen' by him 'from among all the most precious maidens of the Kingdom of Heaven' (*Wanderings*, vol. 2, p. 564).

[11]   For example, the Tucher chapel in Sixtus Tucher's *Gartenhaus* in the Grasersgasse, near the Carthusian monastery (Grote, *Die Tucher*, plate 49). Moreover, the Haus zur Krone, the *Stammhaus* of the *älteste Linie*, on the corner of the Bindergasse and Neumarkt (Bindergasse 26), had a chapel that boasted pictures of the legend of Empress Faustina by Hans Süß von Kulmbach, commissioned by Anton II Tucher around 1511, the time he received papal permission for an annual celebration of mass in the chapel (Grote, *Die Tucher*, p. 22; plate 50).

trade there.[12] Moreover, Nuremberg Patricians cultivated an active tradition of pilgrimage to the Holy Land[13] and Mount Sinai, where Saint Katherine's bones lie, having been translated by angels from the site of her martyrdom in Alexandria. In 1482 one, Hans VI Tucher, published the *Reise zum Heiligen Grab*, an account of his journey that became one of the most popular late-medieval pilgrimage reports and included not just a description of the Greek Orthodox monastery at Sinai but a comparison of it to the Heilsbronner Hof in Nuremberg.[14] Furthermore, Katherine's presence in Nuremberg was textual as well as visual: on 28 July 1475 *Der Heiligen Leben*, the augmented German translation and adaptation of Jacobus de Voragine's *Legenda aurea*, was published in Nuremberg by Hans Sensenschmid, the first Nuremberg printer. Its winter volume contains a life of Saint Katherine of Alexandria taken almost verbatim from a Katharinenkloster manuscript of 1421 and, at some 14,400 words, roughly seven times longer than the average saint's life in the work. Saint Katherine was, then, textually and visually rooted in the spiritual and cultural consciousness of Nuremberg. Indeed, she was so popular that she enjoyed the status of an unofficial patron saint to the city.[15]

---

[12] On his pilgrimage to the Holy Land and Egypt Hans Tucher and his companions stayed with the Venetians in Alexandria, some of whom they knew personally since within the family trading company Tucher and his sons were responsible for trade with the Venetians. From 1440 to 1575 the Tucher family rented chambers and storage ('Kammer und Gewölbe') in the Fondaco dei Tedeschi on a permanent basis and young male members of the Tucher family were sent to Venice to learn the family business (Grote, *Die Tucher*, pp. 32–3). Through Venice the Tuchers imported spices, drugs and fruit such as pepper, saffron, ginger, raisins, almonds, Seville oranges, cinnamon, dates, canella, cloves, galingale and sugar (Grote, *Die Tucher*, p. 35). Trade relations between Nuremberg and Venice probably began in the second half of the thirteenth century and flourished, as in 1347 the *Signoria* remarked that trade with Venice had enabled Nuremberg to go from rags to riches (Veit, *Handel*, p. 11). Trade was so prosperous that Nuremberg disobeyed Emperor Sigismund's trade prohibition when he was at war with Venice; the lion of St. Mark was mounted on the houses of Nuremberg merchants who traded mainly with that city and Nuremberg's constitution was modelled on that of Venice (Veit, *Handel*, p. 11).

[13] Nuremberg pilgrims to the Holy Land include: Hans Rieter 1384; Heinrich Ketzel (knighted) 1389; Hans Lochner (dr. med.), Sebastian Volckamer, Hans Stromer 1435; Hans Bart, Berthold Deichsler, Gabriel Fütterer, Peter Harsdörfer, Konrad Haller, Erhard Haller, Paulus Haller, Georg Pfinzing, Peter Rieter, Gabriel Tetzel 1436; Georg Ketzel 1453; Ulrich Ketzel 1462; Sebald Rieter; Sigismund and Alexius Haller 1463; Gabriel Muffel 1465; Nikolaus Muffel senior with his two sons Nikolaus and Gabriel 1467; Martin Ketzel 1468; Andreas Rieter 1475; Martin Ketzel 1476; Hans Tucher, Sebald Rieter, Dr Otto Spiegel (Chancellor of Herzog Albrecht von Sachsen) and his servant Peter Pyres, 'der Lesemeister vom St. Marienkloster in Nürnberg' and a 'junger Gesell aus Breslau', Valentin Scheurl 1479; Martin Ketzel 1488; Wilhelm Rieter 1490; Wolf Ketzel 1493; Georg and Sebald Ketzel 1498; Wenk aus Nürnberg 1500; Michael Ketzel 1503. See also Arnold, 'Wallfahrten als Nürnberger Familientradition um 1500'. The votive picture endowed by the Jerusalem pilgrim Hans VI for the family tomb in the Sebalduskirche in 1485 includes the Katherine wheel of the monastery at Sinai (Grote, *Die Tucher*, p. 63).

[14] See Chapter 1 for a discussion of this text.

[15] Eichhorn, 'Sebalder Engelschor', p. 113, fn. 126. The "real" patron saint was Saint Sebaldus, whose relics were kept in a shrine in the church bearing his name.

However, this alone is not enough to explain her explicit inclusion as Christ's bride in His family tree. The Lorenzkirche possessed no relics of Saint Katherine,[16] so the Volckamer window raises questions that go beyond any potential liturgical or cult function.[17] Indeed, the prominent showcasing of Saint Katherine in endowments to the Lorenzkirche – windows, altars, altar hangings, epitaphs – not only reflects her popularity but suggests, in a church worshipped in and endowed not just by the Patrician rulers of Nuremberg but also by the Holy Roman Emperor Friedrich III, an agenda that went beyond the spiritual into the political. This chapter will consider these endowments in an attempt to ascertain the following: first, the aspects of the saint's life that held particular significance for Nuremberg and helped to shape devotion in the Lorenzkirche; second, Katherine's role in marking and reflecting Patrician identity, alliances and politics; third, Katherine's status as a sign not only of Nuremberg's self-image but also of its prominence within and relationship to the Holy Roman Empire itself.

As one looks at the high altar at the East end of the church the Volckamer window is the second on the right in the south aisle. Endowment of the main East window was reserved for emperors and kings; of the windows on either side for

---

[16]   According to Gerhardt Weilandt the Katharinenkloster possessed one that was kept in the eastern choir of the convent church. However, he does not specify the nature of the relic (Gerhardt Weilandt, 'Pilgrimage in the Medieval City. The Example of Nuremberg in the 15th Century', *Peregrinationes*, 1, 4, 20 at http://peregrinations.kenyon.edu/vol1-4/articles/weilandt.pdf). Corinne Schleif and Volker Schier mention that in 1516 Peter Imhoff commissioned for the Lorenzkirche a gilt silver reliquary in the form of Saint Katherine that housed pieces of her gown and one of Saint Peter's fingers (Corine Schleif and Volker Schier, *Katerina's Windows* (Philadelphia: Pennsylvania State University Press, 2009), p. 47). This was obviously some 30 years after the donation of the Volckamer window. According to Müllner, relics of Saint Katherine were placed in the Frauenkirche (the imperial church) in the altar of Saint Barbara, consecrated by the papal *nuncio* Brother Johannes of the Franciscans in 1358. Saint Barbara's altar is also known as Saint Wenczel's altar (Müllner, *Annalen*, vol. 2, p. 12). Fries mentions an altar dedicated to Saint Katherine in the sacristy of the Katharinenkirche that contained a relic and a gilded silver reliquary statue; both already missing (Fries, 'Kirche und Kloster', pp. 117–18). Pilgrims to the Holy Land may have seen Saint Katherine's hand on Rhodes, as did Steffan Paumgartner: 'Inn derselbigen [the city of Rhodes] ist manncherlei glauben vnnd volckh auss allen ländern. Auch liess man vns daz Heilthum sehen Sant Katharina hanndt vndt vonn S. Georgen vndt der Pfenning einer, da Christus umb verkaufft ist worden, vnd einen Dornen von der rechten Kron Christi, vnd derselbige Dorn pluet noch alle Jar am Kharfreitag' [In the same city you find many different faiths and people from all countries. We were also allowed to see relics, namely Saint Katherine's hand, a piece of Saint George and one of the pieces of silver for which Christ was sold and a thorn from the genuine Crown of Thorns and that same thorn blossoms every year on Good Friday] (Steffan Paumgartner, 'Die Jerusalemfahrt des Herzogs Heinrich des Frommen von Sachsen (1498)', ed. Reinhold Röhricht, *Zeitschrift des deutschen Palästina-Vereins*, 24 (1901): 1–25 (p. 7)).

[17]   Madeline H. Caviness asks to what extent stained-glass windows catered 'to the rhythms of the popular cult, that is to people coming to pray at the saint's altar or reliquary, regardless of the liturgical feasts' (Madeline H. Caviness, 'Stained Glass Windows in Gothic Chapels, and the Feasts of the Saints', in *Kunst und Liturgie im Mittelalter. Akten des internationalen Kongresses der Bibliotheca Hertziana und des Nederlands Instituut te Rome. Rom, 28.–30. September 1997, Römisches Jahrbuch der Bibliotheca Hertziana*, Beiheft zu Band 33 (1999/2000) (Munich: Hirmer, 2000), pp. 135–48 (p. 135)).

high-ranking clergy; of the windows immediately to the left and right of those for the highest-ranking noble or Patrician families.[18] Hence the very position of the Volckamer window indicates the spiritual and social prestige of both the family and the subject matter. That the window was imported from Strasbourg and is the product of the leading stained-glass workshop in Southern Germany further signals the wealth of the donors and the importance of Saint Katherine to Nuremberg and the family:[19] Strasbourg windows were known for their quality and even in cities with their own significant tradition of stained-glass production, such as Nuremberg, Ulm, Augsburg or Munich, patrons would commission windows from Strasbourg.[20] Moreover, the window was one of a number of family donations to the Lorenzkirche: circa 1360 the rose window in the west façade had been donated by Hartwig I Volckamer, the first of the family to come to Nuremberg (1337) and a member of the *Kleiner Rat* from 1362; it already bears the Katherine wheel in the family coat-of-arms.[21] In 1436/7 Andreas II Volckamer and his wife Margaretha Haller had endowed the altar for the relics of Deocarus, Charlemagne's confessor,[22] having already brought the corpse of Saint Eucharius from Herrieden

---

[18]   Funk, *Glasfensterkunst*, p. 16.

[19]   For example, Kungundt, Hertwig Volckamer's daughter, was a nun in the Katharinenkloster in 1359 (Müllner, *Annalen*, vol. 1, p. 274) and a Margretha Volckamerin an abbess or prioress there in 1391 (Müllner, *Annalen*, vol. 1, p. 273). Moreover, in 1493 Nikolaus V Volckamer, Peter Volckamer's son, endowed an altar in the Katharinenkirche in memory of Peter II Volckamer, Apollonia Mendel and two Dominican nuns from the Volckamer family (possibly Gertrud V and Klara (d. 1525)). The central panel depicts Saint Gregory's Mass; the inside wings Mary with the Fourteen Holy Helpers and the Mystic Marriage (*Kataloge des Germanischen Nationalmuseums zu Nürnberg. Die Gemälde des 13. bis 16. Jahrhunderts*, ed. Eberhard Lutze and Eberhard Weigand, 2 vols (Leipzig: Koehler, 1937), vol. 1 *Kataloge des Germanischen Nationalmuseums zu Nürnberg. Die Gemälde des 13. bis 16. Jahrhunderts*, ed. Eberhard Lutze und Eberhard Weigand, 2 vols (Leipzig: Koehler, 1937), vol. 1 *Textband*, p. 130). In the mid-fifteenth century Gottlieb Volckamer (d. 1475) and his second wife Margareta Schürstab commissioned from the Katharinenkloster a tapestry of the Last Judgement; it depicts both coats-of-arms. Margareta Schürstab died in the Katharinenkloster in 1496 (Fries, 'Kirche und Kloster, pp. 59–60).

[20]   The Katherine workshop was in existence 1477–81 and consisted of five glass painters: Peter Hemmel von Andlau, Lienhart Spitznagel, Hans von Maursmünster, Theobald von Lixheim and Werner Störe. See Hartmut Scholz, 'Aktuelle Forschung zur Glasmalerei in St. Lorenz', in Christian Schmidt and Georg Stolz (eds), *Hundert Jahre Verein zur Erhaltung 1903–2003*, Schriftenreihe des Vereins zur Erhaltung der St. Lorenzkirche in Nürnberg 2 (Nuremberg, 2004), pp. 52–9. Peter Hemmel had done two previous Jesse windows: one in the Stiftskirche in Tübingen (1478) and the Kramer window in Ulm Minster (1479/80). For the Volckamer window see Funk, *Glasfensterkunst*, pp. 55–63 and pp. 156–69.

[21]   Fehring and Ress, *Die Stadt Nürnberg*, 2, p. 88; and Funk, *Glasfensterkunst*, p. 125. The west façade between the towers can be dated by the coats-of-arms of Emperor Karl IV and Anna von Schweidnitz, who married in 1353. In 1363 Hartwig I Volckamer bought a farm (*Hof*) from Graf Johann von Nassau; he died in 1377.

[22]   Müllner records the following: 'Endreß Volckamer, Heinrich Volckamers und Anna Schürstäbin Sohn, hat mit Bischof Johann zu Eystatt, geborn von Haideckh, bei dem er in sondern Gnaden gewest, Bewilligung S. Eucharii oder Deocarii Leichnamb, welcher bei Kaiser Ludovici IV. Zeiten mit Bewilligung

to Nuremberg in 1419 and endowed it and an altar to the Lorenzkirche.[23] The
donor of the Saint Katherine window, Peter II Volckamer, was born in Nuremberg
in 1431 and died there in 1493.[24] Bursar (*Kirchenmeister*) of the Lorenzkirche, in
1471 and 1485 he served on the *Kleiner Rat*; in 1486 he acted as Nuremberg's
deputy at the election in Frankfurt by the Seven Electoral Princes of Friedrich
III's son Archduke Maximilian as *Deutscher König*.[25] He was not the first member
of his family to be involved in the administration of the Lorenzkirche, however:
Endres Volckamer had been *Kirchenpfleger* of the Lorenzkirche in 1404 and
Hanß Volckamer in 1464.

The Volckamer window, then, serves the policy of announcing the family's
status in Nuremberg by linking them, in one of the main showcases of Patrician
patronage, explicitly to governance of city and church[26] and to the Holy Roman

---

des Papsts und Kapituls zu Herieden, von dannen gen Nurnberg gebracht und in S. Laurentzen Kirch
geführet worden, in einen silbern Sarg legen lassen, und erstlich auf den Altar der Zwölf Boten praesentiert,
nachmals eine sonderbare Kapell darzu bauen und einen Altar darzu aufrichten lassen. // Der ist geweihet
Anno 1406 in der Ehr Herr Philippi und Jacobi, auch S. Deocarii und aller anderer Apostel den 5. Junii
durch Euringum Anavensem Archiepiscopum, sonst Weihbischof zu Bamberg' [Andreas Volckamer, the
son of Heinrich Volckamer and Anna Schürstab, had, with the permission of Bishop Johannes of Eichstätt,
né von Haideck, whose special favour he enjoyed, the corpse of Saint Eucharius or Saint Deocarus put into
a silver sarcophagus and first displayed on the Altar of the Twelve Apostles and then a special chapel built
for it and an altar erected for it in there. The corpse had been brought from Herrieden to Nuremberg at the
time of Ludwig IV with the permission of the Pope and the monastery Chapter at Herrieden and taken
into the Lorenzkirche. The altar was consecrated by Archbishop Euringus Anavenses, formerly Suffragan
Bishop of Bamberg, on 5th June in the year 1406 in honour of Phillip and Jakob, also of Saint Deocarus and
all other Apostles] (Müllner, *Annalen*, vol. 1, p. 50). The silver coffin was made in 1437 and was carried in
a festive procession round the church on the last day of Whitsun every year (Müllner, *Annalen*, vol. 1, p.
50). Andreas II Volckamer also endowed a Deocaruskapelle in the church of the Kartäuserkloster, where
two of his sons were monks (Fleischmann, *Rat und Patriziat*, 31/2, p. 1045).

23   Biedermann, *Geschlechtsregister*, fol. Xxxr.

24   After his death Peter II Volckamer and his wife Apollonia Mendel were commemorated by an
altar in the church of the Katharinenkloster endowed in 1493 by their son Nikolaus V, whose wife was
Barbara Melber (d. 1521). The altar depicts the Mass of Saint Gregory, the *Vierzehn Heiligen* and the
mystic marriage (*Kataloge des Germanischen Nationalmuseums, Textband*, pp. 130–1; vol. 2, *Bildband*,
plates 80 and 81).

25   Earlier Peter I Volckamer had acted as one of Nuremberg's representatives at the Council of
Constance in 1415 which had condemned Jan Hus to the stake. In 1485, when Friedrich had visited
Nuremberg, Paulus Volckamer had been amongst those chosen by the *Rat* (along with Ruprecht Haller,
Niclos Groß, Gabriel Nützel) to honour Friedrich by presenting to him 'nach der Statt Gewonheit ein
Clainot, achthundert Gulden werth' [according to the custom of the city a jewel worth 800 gulden]
(Müllner, *Annalen*, vol. 3, p. 71).

26   Müllner, *Annalen*, vol. 1, p. 58. The Lorenzkirche was not the only church with which the
family was involved: in 1444 Lienhard and Wilhelm Volckamer can be found amongst the brothers in
the Carthusian monastery, to which they donated more than 2,000 florins; Georg Volckamer became
its *Schaffer* in 1480; Paulus Volckamer was *Pfleger* of the monastery in 1475 (Müllner, *Annalen*, vol. 2
pp. 81–2). Paulus Volckamer was *Kirchenpfleger* of the Sebalduskirche in 1489 (Müllner, *Annalen*, vol.
1, p. 21) and Georg Volckamer in 1613 (Müllner, *Annalen*, vol. 1, p. 22). Kathrina Volckamerin had

Empire and by advertising their alliances with other Patrician families. At the bottom, supporting the sleeping Jesse, stand the name saints of the Volckamer family depicted in the window: Saints Nicholas, Sebaldus, Apollonia[27] and Barbara. On their left kneel, with the coat-of-arms, Peter II Volckamer, his son Nikolaus (died 1497) and grandson Sebald; on the right the donor's wife, Apollonia Mendel,[28] their daughter-in-law Barbara Melber with her coat-of-arms and her two daughters, Veronika (born 1472) and Apollonia (born 1474).[29] For the viewer standing beneath the window, then, the Volckamer both support and guide access to salvatory events.[30] Immediately above the donor figures are, on the left, Saint George and the dragon, on the right, Saint Sebastian; they flank Jesse, above whom one sees Joel, Habakuk, Aaron and various kings and prophets. On the fourth level the mystic marriage is framed by, on the left, Saints John the Evangelist[31] and Ursula;[32] on the right Saints Dorothy and Andrew, again with various kings and prophets, including another ancestor of Christ, King David, son of Jesse. On the sixth level Christ as *ecce homo* and the sorrowing Mary stand as sculptures in a framework of architectural tracery. At the top of the window God the Father raises His hand in blessing; the Holy Ghost, Old Testament symbol of peace and reconciliation, hovers immediately below Him, emitting rays of grace.[33]

been Abbess of the Klarissenkloster from 1420 to 1430 and Margretha Volckamerin from 1439 to 1441 (Müllner, *Annalen*, vol. 1, p. 76). Pauluß Volckamer was *Pfleger* of the Egidienkloster in 1477 (Müllner, *Annalen*, vol. 1, p. 116). Dr. Sebald Volckamer was buried in the Barfüsserkloster in 1468 (Müllner, *Annalen*, vol. 1, p. 196); whilst the Volckamer (and the Mendel) had their 'Jahrtäg und Begängnus' celebrated in the Predigerkloster (Müllner, *Annalen*, vol. 1, p. 201).

[27]   Saint Apollonia lived in Alexandria. She was taken prisoner in a mob-driven pogrom against Christians during the reign of Emperor Phillip Augustus (244–9). Her teeth were knocked out; eventually she was burnt. Apollonia was the patron saint of dentists and sufferers from toothache (Funk, *Glasfensterkunst*, p. 165).

[28]   A Katharina Mentlerin is listed as abbess/prioress of the Katharinenkloster in 1394 (Müllner, *Annalen*, vol. 1, p. 273). Peter Mendel was *Pfleger* of the convent in 1420. A Katharina Mentlerin is listed as abbess/prioress of the Katharinenkloster in 1394 (Müllner, *Annalen*, vol. 1, p. 273). Peter Mendel was *Pfleger* of the Egidienkloster in 1401 (Müllner, *Annalen*, p. 116); a Peter Mendel had his 'Jahrtäg' in the Egidienkloster (Müllner, *Annalen*, p. 117). A Marquard Mendel was *Pfleger* of the *Karthäuserkloster* in 1380 and a Peter Mendel in 1470 (Müllner, *Annalen*, vol. 2, p. 82).

[29]   Barbara Melber was the daughter of Veit Melber and Katharina Pfinzing (Biedermann, fol. Xxx3ʳ).

[30]   The bottom of the window is just above head height. The window is 7.40 metres high and 4.15 metres wide. Funk compares it in size and layout to late-Gothic carved altars (*Glasfensterkunst*, p. 163).

[31]   The feast day of Saint John the Evangelist is 27 December. Especially important is the consecration of the Communion wine on this day. See 'Johannes d. Evangelist', in *Handwörterbuch des deutschen Aberglaubens*, vol. 4, pp. 703ff.

[32]   Saint Ursula was massacred in Cologne along with 11,000 maidens on their return from a pilgrimage to Rome (*Hall's Dictionary*, pp. 317–18).

[33]   The dove also symbolized the Church, the Christian soul and the Seven Gifts of the Holy Spirit (*Sapientia, Intellectus, Consilium, Fortitudo, Scientia, Pietas, Timor*) or the Twelve Apostles (Murray and

Since Jesse's appearance resembles that of God the Father, the Tree leads Christ's human lineage and the viewer's gaze from the Volckamer at its roots upwards to His divine lineage in God the Father at the top of the window. Amongst other things, then, the window signals the primacy of paternal authority and the family network.

The viewer's gaze is further guided by the Tree itself to the Virgin, the Christ Child and Saint Katherine in the exact centre of the window.[34] The baldachins in gold glass above Saint George's slaying of the dragon and the martyrdom of Saint Sebastian serve to separate the "worldly" (as these events took place on earth) from the "divine" (the "already-saints" above the baldachin).[35] The branches of the Jesse Tree are the only route from the creation of saints and martyrs on earth to their calm exemplarity in Heaven. Moreover, the layout of the window, with its use of gold and silver architectural framework', locates Katherine, Mary and the Child in the centre of the Cross where the crucified Christ would have hung.[36] Blendinger makes the following comment: 'Die Einheit des Fensters wird durch die Schmuckzonen in Silber und Gold hergestellt. Der formalen Einheit entspricht die des theologischen Konzepts: Inkarnation als umfassende Verheißung und verändernde Wirklichkeit'.[37] Gold and silver are more than just visually unifying factors: as the colours of majesty and transfiguration they recall Matthew 17:1–2:

> And after six days Jesus taketh Peter, James, and John his brother, and bringeth them up into an high mountain apart,

> And was transfigured before them: and his face did shine as the sun, and his raiment was white as the light.[38]

Murray, *The Oxford Companion to Christian Art and Architecture*, p. 144).

[34]   The association of Mary with the Tree of Jesse is found as early as 1140 (*virga* = *Reis* (twig) // *virgo* = *Jungfrau* (virgin); see the *Lexikon für Theologie und Kirche*, ed. Walter Kaspar, vol. 10 (Freiburg, Basel and Vienna: Herder, 2006; rev. version of 3rd edn, 1993–2001), col. 1333–4).

[35]   Saints George and Sebastian are two of the *Vierzehn Heiligen*, the significance of whom will be discussed in conjunction with the Konhofer window.

[36]   The reading of Jesse as Adam confirms the echo of the Cross in the layout of the window, as Adam's skull is frequently depicted lying at the foot of the Cross, recalling the legend that the wood used in its construction grew out of a seed that came from the Tree of Knowledge in the Garden of Eden and was planted in the dead Adam's skull. The Jesse tree thus leads upwards from original Sin to redemption through God's sacrifice of His Son.

[37]   The unity of the window is created through the ornamental areas of silver and gold. Unity of form corresponds to that of the theological concept: the Incarnation as the promise that embraces and reality that changes the world' (Christian Blendinger, 'Der Lorenzer Hallenchor. Schatzkammer und Ort der Verkündung', in *500 Jahre Hallenchor St. Lorenz zu Nürnberg*, pp. 41–62 (p. 52)).

[38]   The passage continues: 'And, behold, there appeared unto them Moses and Elias talking with him. Then answered Peter, and said unto Jesus, Lord, it is good for us to be here: if thou wilt, let

As symbols of majesty and transfiguration, the gold and silver of the architectural tracery perform three further tasks: first, they frame and signal the transformation of Christ from infant, the Word made Flesh, to the humiliated, scourged flesh of God-become-man crucified on the Cross, to resurrected King of Heaven; second, they highlight the paradox between these two figures; third, they render visible the potentially transformative effect of Christ's incarnation and sacrifice on a pious believer's life. The colours also symbolize Christ as the sun, source of light and symbolic of royalty, divinity, resurrection and immortality.[39] This symbolism of colour and Cross are activated by the light of the actual sun rising in the East, so that the Volckamer window, as the transfigured Christ, conducts the salvatory radiance of the Resurrection, the sight of which will illuminate and transform the viewer's soul.[40] Since light was a manifestation of God, the window functions as His conduit into and signal of His presence within the Lorenzkirche. As Kurmann-Schwarz maintains:

> Dabei spielt eine besondere Rolle, daß die Scheiben [der Glasfenster] die Wand an der Stelle ihres Durchbruchs abschließen, ohne aber das Tageslicht daran zu hindern, ins Innere der Kirche einzudringen. Aufgrund dieser Eigenschaft werden die Glasmalereien mit dem Wort Gottes gleichgesetzt, das wie die Bilder auf ihrem gläsernen Träger die Gläubigen erleuchtet und sie vor dem Schlechten schützt.[41]

> [At the same time the fact that the panes of glass seal the wall at the point where they break through it but without preventing daylight from penetrating the

---

us make here three tabernacles; one for thee, and one for Moses, and one for Elias. While he yet spake, behold, a bright cloud overshadowed them: and behold a voice out of the cloud, which said, This is my beloved Son, in whom I am well pleased; hear ye him' (Matthew 17:3–5). The Transfiguration of Christ is celebrated on 6 August. God's words confirm the lineage depicted in the Tree of Jesse in the Volckamer window. Matthew 16 is about Christ's nature as Son of God and about preparation for His last days in Jerusalem. Here we see the essentialness and potency of vision: light is linked to, even a vehicle for, a vision (i.e. non-corporeal sight) of Moses and Elias, in other words provides access to a higher level of truth, here teleological. The passage also contains the different levels of speech (human and divine) typical of Katherine's legend and miracles: disciples to Christ; dead Moses and Elias to each other; God to disciples.

[39] The sun further symbolizes paternal authority, fame, victory, willpower and vitality; it was the particularly associated with Christ as Chronokrator (Hans Biedermann (ed.), *Knaurs Lexikon der Symbole* (Munich: Droemer Knaur, 1989, 1994), pp. 408–11).

[40] Especially the soul of a viewer standing beneath the window and bathed in the silver and gold transmitted light.

[41] Brigitte Kurmann-Schwarz, '"Fenestre vitree ... significant Sacram Scripturam". Zur Medialität mittelalterlicher Glasmalerei des 12. und 13. Jahrhunderts', in *Anzeiger des Germanischen Nationalmuseums*, Wissenschaftliche Beibände 25 (Nuremberg: Verlag des Germanischen Nationalmuseums, 2005), p. 63.

interior of the church plays a special role. Because of this quality the stained glass is equated with the Word of God, that, like the pictures on the glass that bears them, illuminates the believers and protects them from evil].

To return to the mystic marriage: Madelaine Caviness points out that, in stained-glass windows, the rising sun at Lauds would light up the blue glass, here the background to the mystic marriage,[42] since 'the low wave length of blue is compatible with low levels of light. With the dawn, following the first office, the darkness of the blue became light whilst the other colours (purple, yellow red, green) were still in shadow'.[43] These would glow around midday. In other

---

[42] Blue was 'used as a background colour to evoke the majesty of rulers and prelates; as a celestial colour signifying divine presence and intervention' (Michael Pastoureau, *Blue. The History of a Color*, trans. Markus I. Cruse (Princeton and Oxford: Princeton University Press, 2001), p. 41 (original French edition: *Bleu: Histoire d'une couleur* (Paris: Editions du Seuil, 2000)).

[43] This phenomenon is known as the Purkinje Shift (Caviness, 'Stained Glass Windows', pp. 140–1). According to Camille, glass was most often associated with the intense colour of gems, which Abbot Suger saw as possessing 'sacred virtues' (Camille, *Gothic Art*, pp. 44–6). Both glass and gems helped turn church space into an analogy for the celestial Jerusalem: 'In der Tat verbinden gemeinsame Eigenschaften Flachglas und Edelsteine, denn beide Materialien vermögen das Licht farbig zu brechen und werden zusammen mit den weißen Steinen als Baumaterialien des himmlischen Jerusalem erwähnt' [Indeed, shared characteristics connect sheet glass and precious stones for both materials are able to refract light into its different colours and, together with the white stones, are mentioned a building materials for the celestial city of Jerusalem] (Kurmann-Schwarz, '"Fenestre vitree"', p. 65). Thus the viewer standing in the transmitted light from the window could be symbolically transported to Heaven. Moreover, in a number of prayers, Saint Katherine is compared to a gemstone, for example: 'O du kospere gim du scheinende garit' [O you precious gem, you radiant garnet] (Stadtbibliothek Nürnberg, Cod. Cent. VII, 65, fol. 3ʳ⁻ᵛ); or 'Gegrüßt seistu edels gestein der klarheit · zu gleichen dem karfunkel' [Hail noble jewel of clarity, comparable to the carbuncle] (Stadtbibliothek Nürnberg, Cod. Cent. V, App. 81, fol. 103ᵛ). See also the *Gebetbuch* for Graf Ulrich VII (1515): 'GEgrüset sygest du katherina ain edel gestain der Clarheit ain glichnuß des karfunckels' [Hail Katherine, a precious jewel of clarity, like to the carbuncle] (Germanisches Nationalmuseum Hs. 1737, fol. 2ʳ⁻ᵛ). "Carbuncle" was originally used by Pliny to designate carbuncles, garnets and rubies. From the thirteenth century onwards they were distinguished from one another. All three were fiery, radiant red stones; the genuine carbuncle, however, was reputed to shine so brightly that it illuminated a completely dark room as if it were the sun. The carbuncle was also thought to possess in itself all the properties ascribed to all other precious stones ('Karfunkel', in *Handwörterbuch des deutschen Aberglaubens*, vol. 4, p. 1005). Radiance symbolizes virtue; carbuncles, garnets and rubies were symbols of ardent love. Directly in front of Katherine is a marguerite or daisy, to which she is often compared in prayers and which symbolizes tears, here possibly the tears shed at the Crucifixion, referred to in the Man of Sorrows at the top of the Volckamer window. To the bottom left of Katherine (from the viewer's perspective) is the

words, the mystic marriage would be one of the first objects in the church to be lit by the light from the East that betokens Christ's resurrection and immortality and symbolizes the resurrection of the soul in Christ. Since the mystic marriage symbolizes God's becoming one with the human soul,[44] the window illuminates the believer's spiritual union with the King of Heaven, highlighted by the fact that the ring held out by Christ to Saint Katherine occupies almost the exact centre of the window. Just as in the written life of Saint Katherine the ring remains on her finger when she awakes from her vision as tangible confirmation of its truth and link between the human and the divine, so the depiction of the ring in the glass of the Volckamer window renders it tangible to the viewer in the Lorenzkirche, its centrality confirming the real possibility of the worshipper's union with God.[45] Moreover, the light transmitted by the window is linked to the Virgin Mary on whose lap the Christ Child sits as he weds Saint Katherine: 'She [the Virgin] is the window through which Christ, the Light of the World, entered the terrestrial realm ... The purest form of light, that seen by mystics, was a manifestation of divine grace'.[46] Hence the window becomes the visualization for the viewer of a grace and perfect spiritual bliss, normally 'beyond their own powers of sight',[47] radiant with divine truth and God's sacrifice. Through their donation of the window and their support of the events depicted therein, the Volckamer act as a model of one path to this bliss and situate themselves at the locus of this grace. As its filter into the church, they, too, are transfigured by the light; acting as a conduit for transfiguration in their turn, since the coloured light that falls through them and the saints and onto the church floor and the viewer beneath the window bathes the latter in grace and virtue, aiding his transfiguration:

---

red rose, symbol of martyrdom; behind her the white lily symbolic of purity and commonly associated with the Virgin Mary. The symbolism of the flowers reinforces the message of the window, which in turn constitutes a visual (rather than textual/oral) prayer. Finally, in an eighth-century Irish pontifical the novice taking her vows is addressed as 'tu margaretas et gemmulas carbunculis' [you marguerite and carbuncle gem], further merging the Virgin, Saint Katherine and the consecrated nun (Gussone, 'Die Jungfrauenweihe', p. 36).

[44] Blendinger, 'Der Lorenzer Hallenchor', p. 53.

[45] The version of Saint Katherine's legend in *Der Heiligen Leben*, published only three to four years before the installation of the window, says: 'da erwachet sy vnd fand daz fingerlein an der hant vnd bekant / daz allesz das war waz daz sie in dem schlaff gesehen hett' [Then she awoke and found the ring on her hand and recognized that everything she had seen in her sleep was true] ([fol. cclij^v]).

[46] The light shining through the Volckamer window could here symbolize the actual conception of Christ, subsequently rendered visible by the child on the Virgin's knee.

[47] Camille, *Gothic Art*, p. 19. Vocabulary for light: *lux* = the souce of light such as that emitted by luminous bodies like the sun; *lumen* = light which was multiplied in space; *splendor* = light reflected off object. (Camille, *Gothic Art*, p. 42).

Within this system, images held a privileged place, since they were themselves appreciated as mediating *vincula* par excellence, that is, media that appealed equally to man's earthly and divine powers – his motive and perceptual faculties on the one hand (associated with the sensitive soul), his rational faculties on the other (associated with the intellective soul). Images in other words activated the full spectrum of operations by which the soul might be not only experienced, but also monitored, measured, and ultimately, manipulated.[48]

From the top of the window, the rays of grace emitted by the Holy Spirit are transmitted through the stone tracery of the window to the believer below. The cross of which the mystic marriage forms the centre – where the Crucified Christ would normally hang – is crowned by the image of the Man of Sorrows and the grieving Virgin;[49] God's blessing of the worshippers in the church is attainable only through the suffering of Christ and Mary. The mother of the dead Christ stands directly above the mother of the living Christ, a juxtaposition that links Mary's joy in her infant son to her sorrow over her sacrificed one but also recalls the prophecy from Isaiah and common belief that Mary became the receptacle for Christ knowing He was born to die. The white of the cloth across her lap, symbolic of the virginal purity of herself and her son, pre-empts the white of the mourning robes in the grieving Virgin frozen in sorrow.[50] In addition, the infant Christ who is God-made-flesh in the mystic marriage foreshadows the adult Christ whose self-same flesh is mortified as part of His sacrifice for mankind.[51] This row of the window leads upwards from the two name saints Nikolaus and Sebaldus, the latter the patron saint of Nuremberg, to the roots of the Tree growing out of Jesse's heart[52] to the prophets who foretold the coming of Christ and through their word

---

[48]   Walter S. Melion, 'Introduction: Meditative Images and the Psychology of Soul', in Reindert Falkenburg, Walter S. Melion and Todd M. Richardson (eds), *Image and Imagination of the Religious Self in Late Medieval and Early Modern Europe*, Proteus: Studies in Early Modern Identity Formation 1 (Turnhout: Brepols, 2007), pp. 1–36 (p. 2).

[49]   The replacement of the Crucifixion by the mystic marriage suggests the latter's importance for the spiritual and theological identity of Nuremberg, possibly because of the Katharinenkloster, possibly because of the hope encapsulated in the marriage as fruit of the Crucifixion and part of the spreading of Christianity throughout the Roman Empire, to which the Holy Roman Empire was heir.

[50]   So swathed is Mary in her mourning robes, in fact, that she is barely recognizable as a figure.

[51]   Christ as the Man of Sorrows holds, in a cross-shape, two of the instruments of His Passion, the bundle of twigs from the Flagellation and the spear with the sponge.

[52]   If Jesse symbolizes Adam, the Crucifixion present in the cross-shape at the centre of the window and in the *ecce homo* symbolizes the overcoming of the Old Adam (and Original Sin) by the New, Christ. In this, too, the Volckamer window signals and aids penance and redemption.

helped construct the faith for which Saint Katherine herself was martyred to the mystic marriage to the realization of prophecy in Christ as Man of Sorrows on the verge of Crucifixion to God and angels rejoicing in the salvation of mankind. Hence the viewer's eyes are led upwards from this world to the next one, devotion to and emulation of Saint Katherine representing one route for its attainment.

Caviness writes of stained-glass windows that they 'unlike the service books, or the Latin readings' were 'accessible to the laity' and could be prayed to 'at other times than the associated feast days'. Hence windows 'function to focus prayers in place of the liturgy, and as mnemonic devices to remind viewers of a life story that was rarely read during the office'.[53] The Volckamer window, as a possible site of prayer and focussed meditation, what Baxandall terms a 'visualizing meditation', may have prompted, first, an intensely imagined recreation of Saint Katherine's own vision of the mystic marriage and bliss of union with Christ; second, meditation on her life and miracles, possibly based on Sensenschmied's edition of *Der Heiligen Leben*; third, via the saints depicted with her – Sebastian, Ursula,[54] Dorothy, Andrew,[55] George and John the Evangelist[56] – martyrs in the early Church who gave their lives in the fight to establish Christianity, contemplation of the martyrdom that had helped convert the pagan Roman Empire into the Holy Roman Empire, of which Nuremberg was 'the imaginary capital'[57] and whose then ruler was represented in the *Kaiserfenster* (Imperial window) two windows to the left. Just as Saint Katherine is located at the heart of the family tree of Christ, so Nuremberg was situated at the spiritual heart of the Empire, housing the imperial coronation insignia and relics that included Longinus' spear and a splinter from the Cross, tangible links to the Crucifixion recalled by the colour-created cross in which the mystic marriage is located.[58] Through their endowment of the window

---

[53]   Caviness, 'Stained Glass Windows', p. 141.

[54]   Saint Ursula was massacred in Cologne along with 11,000 maidens on their return from a pilgrimage to Rome (*Hall's Dictionary*, pp. 317–18).

[55]   Saint Andrew is associated with marriage: 'Der Bursche, der am A.tage einem Mädchen zuerst begegnet, wird ihr Mann' [The first lad a girl meets on Saint Andrew's Day becomes her husband] ('Andreas', in *Handwörterbuch des deutschen Aberglaubens*, vol. 1, pp. 398–9).

[56]   Saint John the Evangelist is closely linked to the Crucifixion: not only did he and Mary stand at the foot of the Cross; his feast day, 27 December, is the day on which the Communion wine that commemorates the blood shed by Christ on the Cross is consecrated (*Handwörterbuch des deutschen Aberglaubens*, vol. 4, pp. 703ff.).

[57]   Stephen Brockmann, *Nuremberg: The Imaginary Capital*, Studies in German literature, linguistics, and culture (Rochester and Woodbridge: Camden House, 2006).

[58]   The Nuremberg Augustinerkloster also housed two splinters of the Cross, a piece of the rock on which it stood, some of the earth in which it was found, some of the earth from the hollow in which it stood and two thorns from Christ's crown, all donated (amongst many other relics) by Emperor Karl IV (Müllner, *Annalen*, vol. 1, p. 157).

and the Deocarus Altar, the Volckamer both facilitate and shape other worshippers' devotion and publicly anchor themselves at the heart of Nuremberg and hence of the Empire. More than that: in foregrounding the union of the believer's soul with the King of Heaven and Earth, the Volckamer window may symbolize that of Nuremberg with the Empire since Saint Katherine was so closely associated with the city. The window thus becomes an attempt to locate Nuremberg at the heart of the Kingdom of Heaven as well as a billboard for the importance of the Volckamer at the heart of Nuremberg.

Let us turn now to the other window to depict the mystic marriage, that endowed by the lawyer Konrad Konhofer (c. 1375–1452), Professor of Theology in Prague from 1398,[59] Doctor of Canon and Civil Law and Medicine and Master of the Liberal Arts.[60] Konhofer served the Bishops of Bamberg, Eichstätt and Passau and as canon in the cathedrals of Passau and Regensburg. In 1424 he travelled to Rome and obtained a letter of indulgence for seven years for pilgrims to the *Heiltumsweisung*.[61] On his return from Rome Konhofer was appointed legal advisor to Nuremberg, in which role he accompanied Peter I Volckamer to the Bishop's court in Bamberg in 1431 to intercede for the citizens of Nuremberg.[62] Consecrated priest (*Pfarrer*) of the Lorenzkirche on 1 June 1438, Konhofer was responsible for overseeing the building of the new choir, which he initiated in 1439 and which almost doubled the space available in the church. While representing Nuremberg at the Council of Basel in 1440, he there obtained permission for the entire revenue of the Lorenzkirche to be used for the building project for 10 years; he also contributed financially.[63] Every week for a year he gave 10 pounds Haller towards its construction and renounced his revenue as chaplain of the Kunigundenkapelle (next to the Lorenzkirche; now

---

[59]   Konhofer was consecrated priest in Prague in the same year.

[60]   Funk, *Glasfensterkunst*, p. 33 and p. 142.

[61]   Funk, *Glasfensterkunst*, p. 142.

[62]   Possibly to request permission to establish a parish in Wöhrd as a daughter parish of the Sebalduskirche and to consecrate a cemetery there (Gerhard Gruner, *Nürnberg in Jahreszahlen* (Nuremberg: Korn & Berg, 1999), p. 66.

[63]   Konhofer remained living in Regensburg, where he was a member of the cathedral chapter. For his efforts on behalf of the Lorenzkirche see Herbert Bauer, 'Zwischen Andrang und Entfremdung. Der Lorenzer Hallenchor und die Erfahrung der Gemeinde', in *500 Jahre Hallenchor St.*, pp. 22–4 (p. 22); and Corine Schleif, *Donatio et Memoria. Stifter, Stiftungen und Motivationen an Beispielen aus der Lorenzkirche in Nürnberg*, Kunstwissenschaftliche Studien 58 (Munich: Deutscher Kunstverlag, 1990), p. 159). A Herdegen, Jacob and Heinrich Kunhofer are mentioned by Müllner as living in Nuremberg in 1387, though he is not sure whether they were burghers; a Cunrad Kunhofer, possibly the donor's father, became a burgher of the city in 1389 (Müllner, *Annalen*, vol. 2, p. 162).

destroyed) in favour of the building project.[64] In addition, Konhofer collected money for a new organ, for the repair of the small organ, for the bells and for two Psalters. He endowed various liturgical objects and two altars: one dedicated to Saint Konrad and the *Vierzehn Heiligen*; the other to the Four Church Fathers (the *Vier-Lehrer-Altar*), also known as Saint Jerome's altar.[65]

The Konhofer window was installed posthumously in 1478/9 as the new choir had not yet been roofed at the time of his death in 1452; Konhofer, who died in Regensburg, was buried in the choir near the *Vier-Lehrer-Altar*. The inscription on his window reads: 'Nach cristi gepurt M°CCCC°LII°. an sant Wilbaltstag verschid der erwirdig vnd hochgelert Herr Conrat Kunhofer Doctor all*er* faculte*ten*, thumprobst zu rege*n*spurg vn*d* pfar*rer* hije zu sa*n*t lore*n*tzen, de*m* got gnädig seij' [On Saint Willibald's Day in the year MCCCCLII after the birth of Christ died the honourable and learned Herr Konrad Konhofer, Doctor of all Faculties, Cathedral Prebend in Regensburg and Parish Priest here at Saint Laurence's. May God have mercy on his soul].[66] The window occupies the most prestigious place in the church after the East window.[67] On the bottom row Konhofer[68] kneels at a prayer stool, dressed in a white pluvial and praying to the three saints in front of him: Bishop Konrad of Konstanz (his name saint);[69] Deocarus; and Saint Laurence, to whom the church is dedicated. Behind Konhofer stand Nuremberg's patron saint, Sebaldus, whose official canonization by Pope Martin V he had been charged to obtain and which had taken place on 26 March 1425,[70] and Saint Stephen, the first Christian martyr.[71] In Deocarus, Sebaldus and Laurence, then, Konhofer is

---

[64]   Stolz, 'Die zwei Schwestern', pp. 9–11.

[65]   Schleif, *Donatio et Memoria*, pp. 11–12. Konhofer also had his 'Jahrtäg' (*todestag mit kirchlicher feier*) in the Egidienkloster (Müllner, *Annalen*, vol. 1, p. 117).

[66]   Johann Wolfgang Hilpert, *Nürnbergs Merkwürdigkeiten*, Heft 2, *Die Kirche des heiligen Laurentius* (Nuremberg: Friedrich Campe, 1831), p. 28.

[67]   Both the *Konhoferfenster* and the neighbouring *Kaiserfenster* are the products of Michael Wolgemut's workshop, taken over from Hans Pleydenwurff in 1473 (Funk, *Glasfensterkunst*, p. 162; Scholz, 'Aktuelle Forschung', p. 59). Pleydenwurff and Wolgemut were also responsible for the woodcuts in Stephan Fridolin's *Der Schatzbehalter* (Nuremberg: Anton Koberger, 1491) and Hartmann Schedel's *Weltchronik* (Nuremberg: Anton Koberger, 1493).

[68]   The white pluvial was worn only at solemn vespers (*der feierlichen Vesper*) and processions of the sacraments.

[69]   Saint Konrad (d. 975) was Bishop of Konstanz. According to his legend he swallowed a poisonous spider when taking the wine during communion but remained unharmed, hence his attributes of chalice and spider (Funk, *Glasfensterkunst*, p. 143).

[70]   Funk, *Glasfensterkunst*, p. 35.

[71]   According to Funk, since their joint burial in San Lorenzo fuori le Mura in Rome c. 330 Saints Laurence and Stephen were usually honoured together (Funk, *Glasfensterkunst*, p. 35). Furthermore, all three are connected to the Holy Roman Empire and the spread of Christianity

aligning himself with three locally important saints whose cults he had helped to promote to the financial and political benefit of Nuremberg. In so doing he uses the window to remind the city of his service in increasing and consolidating its spiritual importance within the Empire, so like the Volckamer anchors himself at the centre of the city and the Holy Roman Empire. Furthermore, the depiction of Charlemagne's confessor in the window echoes the Deocarus Altar donated by Andreas Volckamer and hence serves to raise the profile within both church and city of a saint responsible for the spiritual welfare of the very founder of this Empire. Saints Stephen and Laurence strengthen the imperial connexion since the church in which they lie buried in Rome, San Lorenzo fuori le Mura, was built at the behest of Constantine the Great, the emperor who signed an edict of tolerance for Christians in 311 and whose conversion to Christianity on his deathbed sealed Christianity as the official religion of the Empire. Hence the entire bottom row of the window refers to the foundation and consolidation of the Roman Empire as a Christian political entity with Konhofer and Nuremberg as its central pillar.

Above Konhofer sit the four Church Fathers Augustine, Gregory, Jerome and Ambrose. As Schleif points out, the choice of saints in the window echoes that for the two altars endowed by Konhofer: one was dedicated to Saint Konrad and the *Vierzehn Heiligen*; the other to the four Church Fathers.[72] His choice of the Church Fathers, whose writings clarified and established fundamental Christian doctrine, continues the theme of Christianizing the Empire and reflects the learned Konhofer's own interest in education: in 1443 he had donated his personal library to the city council[73] and in 1445 endowed stipends of 50 florins a year each for three young men from Nuremberg to study Theology, Law or

---

within it: Laurence as martyr in the early Church; Deocarus as confessor to the first Holy Roman Emperor; and Sebaldus as a missionary in the Reichswald surrounding Nuremberg.

[72]   See also Müllner, *Annalen*, p. 52. Konhofer also endowed a living for the *Vier-Lehrer-Altar*, another of the 12 main altars of the Lorenzkirche.

[73]   Konhofer's library formed the basis of the *Ratsbibliothek* (City Council Library), which, although first mentioned in 1370, was considerably extended and improved by the donation. The *Ratsbibliothek* was the largest and most comprehensive in Germany, as well as one of the oldest. More than just a specialist library (i.e. legal/historical) for the support of Council business, it was housed in the specially enlarged *Losungsstube* (Sheriffs' Chamber) in the town hall. The Council commissioned and bought books for it; Nuremberg printers and booksellers deposited copies of their works; further donations were made. By 1500 the holdings amounted to 371 volumes on 33 desks and included works on law, theology, medicine; Classical and Humanist literature; a globe and a *mappa mundi* (Bernd Moeller, 'Die Anfänge kommunaler Bibliotheken in Deutschland', in Bernd Moeller, Hans Patze and Karl Stackmann (eds), *Studien zum städtischen Bildungswesen des späten Mittelalters und der frühen Neuzeit*, Abhandlungen der Akademie der Wissenschaften in Göttingen Philologisch-historische Klasse Dritte Folge 137 (Göttingen: Vandenhoeck & Ruprecht, 1983), pp. 136–72 (p. 143)).

Medicine for up to three years.[74] However, the Church Fathers also indicate that through learning the believer is led to God. Indeed, Konhofer himself models this devout learning as he kneels below Saint Jerome, reading from a volume that may be the Bible translated by the former into Latin. Moreover, Saint Katherine, who kneels above Saint Jerome, is linked by her own erudition and patronage of scholars, universities and libraries to the four Church Fathers.[75] The window, therefore, highlights (and hence reinforces the importance of) education as a means of access to knowledge of God.[76]

As in the Volckamer window, the architectural tracery depicted in the stained glass separates the lower and upper levels of the window and supports the events above it, though it does not form an explicit cross shape around the mystic marriage,

---

[74] Schleif, *Donatio et Memoria*, pp. 163–4; *Stadtlexikon*, p. 559. Müllner records the stipends as lasting five years (Müllner, *Annalen*, p. 54). There was a strong tradition of education in Nuremberg: the fourteenth century had seen the founding of Latin schools connected to the Lorenzkirche (mentioned 1325), the Sebalduskirche (mentioned 1337), the Heilig-Geist-Spital (mentioned 1339) and the Egidienkloster (mentioned 1396).

[75] About Saint Katherine's education the *Heiligen Leben* says the following: 'Vnd da sie bey sechs iaren waz da ließ man sie zu schul gen / da lernet sie gar wol / vnd da sie klug ward yn der kunst des ward sy gar volkummen darin daz man iren gleychen niedert fand / vnnd man hieß sie ein bewerte Meisterinn in den siben hochsten kunsten' [And when she was six years old she was allowed to attend school, where she learnt easily and well and when she became clever and knowledgeable in the Arts she developed such a degree of perfection that nowhere was her equal to be found and she was called a proven Master of the Seven Liberal Arts] (fol. cclij^r). Similarly, a Katharinenkloster prayer addresses her as follows: 'In der himelischen ewigen wunsamigkeit frew dich vnd frolock du heillige vnd weise katerina auß kuncklichen stam wolgeporn in freyen kunsten mit wolsprechenden wortten was du wol gelert in gramaticam loica · retorica vnd philosovia von gottes gnad dem kristenlichen glauben zu hilf' [Delight and rejoice in the eternal bliss of Heaven, you holy and wise Katherine, high-born from a royal line, you were most learned in the Liberal Arts with well-polished speech, in Grammar, Logic, Rhetoric and Philosophy by the grace of God and for the aid of the Christian Faith] (Stadtbibliothek Nürnberg, Cod. Cent. VII, 65, fol. 18^r-v). Another prayer addresses her as 'du heillige und weise katerina' and continues: 'in freyen kunsten mit wolsprechenden wortten was du wol gelert in gramaticam loica · retorica vnd philosovia von gottes gnad dem kristenlichen glauben zu hilf ... O katerina wie gar weislich argument furestu wider die heidenischen meister vor dem keißer mit eingebung des heilligen geistes' [You holy and wise Katherine ... you were most learned in Liberal Arts and well-polished speech, in Grammar, Logic, Rhetoric and Philosophy by the grace of God and for the aid of the Christian faith ... O, Katherine, what wise arguments you advanced against the heathen philosophers in the presence of the Emperor with inspiration from the Holy Spirit] (Stadtbibliothek Cod. Cent. VII, 65, fol. 18^r-v). Hence education and wisdom are explicitly validated when employed in the service of the Christian God and Katherine's inspiration by the Holy Ghost is a direct allusion to its descent over Mary and the Apostles at Whitsun (Acts of the Apostles 2:1–4).

[76] My thanks to Dr Nicola McLelland, University of Nottingham, for this insight.

which once again occupies the centre of the window. The portrayal of the union differs from that in the Volckamer window since from the viewer's perspective Saint Katherine kneels on the right rather than left; she rather than the infant Christ holds the ring; and the instrument of her martyrdom, the sword, is held in front of her, more immediately visible to the viewer.[77] However, the grapes in the ornamental Gothic tracery above the heads of Mary and Katherine symbolize the Blood of Christ and the sacrament of the mass, as may the red of the vaulting, so the Crucifixion is referred to symbolically. The Konhofer window was installed seven to eight years before the Volckamer so may have served as inspiration for the latter, which could thus represent a deliberate strengthening of, first, the presence of Saint Katherine in the church and, second, her link to the Holy Roman Empire in the form of the immediately adjacent East window donated by Friedrich III.

In the Konhofer window, however, Saint Katherine is embedded in a different, more local context. Although the architectural tracery above them distinguishes her and the Virgin from the other saints in the top half of the window, Katherine is still more integrated into the group of saints known as the *Vierzehn Heiligen*:[78] Katherine, Barbara, Margaret, George, Leonard, Nicholas, Sebastian, Egidius, Vitus, Christopher, Achatius, Blasius, Cyriacus of Rome, Erasmus, Eustachius, Dionysius, Anthony, Dorothy, Fridolin, Heinrich II, Laurence, Leodegar, Magnus, Rochus, Stephan, Theodul, Verenc, Wendelin, Wolfgang and Pantaleon (the group could vary from region to region).[79] They had been revered since the ninth century and were popular in Southern Germany, where their cult can first

---

[77]   In the Volckamer window Katherine kneels on the sword, barely visible under her robes. Its position symbolizes her overcoming of her martyrdom and triumphant status as Christ's eternal bride.

[78]   They are known in English as the Fourteen Holy Helpers. Their name derives from the legend that shortly before their martyrdom these saints are reputed to have asked God to grant aid to anyone asking for it in their name (Funk, *Glasfensterkunst*, p. 39; Schauber and Schindler, *Bildlexikon der Heiligen*, p. 416). Fries postulates a *Nothelferaltar* (altar dedicated to the *Vierzehn Heiligen*) in the Katharinenkirche as well (Fries, 'Kirche und Kloster', p. 109).

[79]   Luc Campana, *Die 14 Heiligen Nothelfer* (Lauerz: Theresia, 2008), p. 52; Funk, *Glasfensterkunst*, pp. 39–40. Barbara was called on for help in death, storms and fire; Katherine in diseases of the tongue, difficulty in speaking, headaches, difficulty in lactating; George in war and for the plague, fever, bewitchment, temptation; Sebastian for protection from the plague; Leonard by prisoners and for the protection of animals; Dionysius for syphilis, headaches, rabies, dog bites; Egidius (Giles) for help with infertility, mental illness, leprosy, plague; Nicholas for help with marriage prospects; Pantaleon for headaches, infections, physical decay and spiritual conflict; Vitus for protection from epilepsy and rabies, mental illness, lethargy and bed-wetting; Christopher for protection against sudden death, epidemics, eye problems and so forth (Funk, *Glasfensterkunst*, pp. 39–41; Campana, *Nothelfer*, pp. 86–7).

be identified in Regensburg, Bamberg, Würzburg and Nuremberg.[80] The date of their feast day was established as 1 November by Pope Gregory IV.[81] Three visions of the *Vierzehn Heiligen* had taken place between 24 September 1445 and 29 June 1446 (during Konhofer's lifetime) in Langheim in Frankenthal, north-east of Bamberg: a young shepherd, Hermann Leicht, son of the shepherd of the Cistercian abbey of Langheim near Staffelstein (which had been laid waste by Hussites in 1429),[82] twice saw a radiant child who disappeared when he approached him. The third time the child was surrounded by 14 other children, all bathed in light. Asked who he was and what he wanted, the child identified the group as the *Vierzehn Heiligen* and requested a chapel be built on that spot. The place became the famous pilgrimage destination Vierzehnheiligen, a Baroque basilica near Bad Staffelstein in Upper Franconia designed by Balthasar Neumann and completed in 1772. Pilgrimage to Vierzehnheiligen (as the place was known from 1446 onwards) from Nuremberg started in 1475; Emperor Friedrich III visited it in 1471 and 1475.[83] Leicht's visions are depicted in the second row from the top, above the mystic marriage. In the top row is Christ as ruler and judge of the world, flanked by the Virgin, John the Baptist and the Last Judgement. Schleif maintains that Konhofer's choice of the *Vierzehn Heiligen* expresses his 'enge Verbindung mit der Stadt Nürnberg und dem Stadtregiment'.[84] It may also be an attempt to link Nuremberg, where he spent considerable time, effort and personal money on the rebuilding of the choir of the Lorenzkirche, to Regensburg, where he continued to live and which was the centre of the cult, and to Bamberg, since Nuremberg belonged to that diocese. Due to her civic popularity, then, Saint Katherine functions as the bridge between Christ, Mary and the regionally significant saints anchored into the heart of Empire by Friedrich III's visit.[85]

---

[80] The earliest testimony to the cult of the *Vierzehn Heiligen* is a fresco (c. 1330) depicting them in the Dominikanerkirche Regensburg; a Regensburg Dominican may have been responsible for grouping the saints together. Katherine may have been included in the group as she had long been revered in Bamberg, to which diocese Nuremberg belonged. The cult spread to Landshut, Augsburg, Munich and Passau (Assion, *Mirakel*, p. 100; also citing Joself Dünninger, 'Die Wallfahrtslegende von Vierzehnheiligen', in *Festschrift für Wolfgang Stammler*, pp. 192–205).

[81] Campana, *Nothelfer*, p. 33.

[82] Schleif, *Donatio et memoria*, p. 163.

[83] *Basilika Vierzehnheiligen. Symphonie in Licht und* Farbe, Text P. Dominik Lutz, Bild A. Bornschlegel (Staffelstein: Obermain Buch- + Bildverlag Bornschlegel, 1986), pp. 13–14.

[84] 'close connection to the city of Nuremberg and the city government' (Schleif, *Donatio et memoria*, p. 163).

[85] Funk, *Glasfensterkunst*, p. 145.

In addition, Funk suggests that the window was an expression of the intensified cult of the Virgin and saints prompted by fear of the Hussites, who rejected the cult of Mary and the saints as unbiblical:[86] the four Church Fathers depicted in it could represent all the saints whilst Mary is the Queen of Heaven and of all saints. Nuremberg and Franconia had been severely affected by the Hussite Wars and the city was involved in efforts to quell the Hussites, despite having provided a stage for Hus himself.[87] The Hussite Wars raged from 1419 to 1433, causing unrest and destruction throughout Bohemia, Germany and Poland; damaging Nuremberg's trade;[88] and in 1430 coming within three miles of the city itself.[89] In May 1431, at the request of King Sigismund and Nuremberg, Konrad Konhofer and Peter Volckamer travelled to Eger to meet leading Hussites. The opposing sides achieved no reconciliation as the Roman curia and the princes demanded the Hussites submit themselves to the ruling of the Council of Constance.[90] Nuremberg sent 300 men for another military campaign against the Hussites, which ended in the German troops fleeing at

---

[86]   Funk, *Glasfensterkunst*, pp. 142–3.

[87]   On 20 October 1414 Johannes Hus had arrived in Nuremberg from Prague: 'Hat mit den zweien Pfarrern S. Sebalds und S. Lorenczen Pfarr disputirt, und weil sie nichts an ihme gewunnen, hat sich ein Cartheußer Münch, so ein Doctor gewest, an ihne gerichtet. Des Hußen Lehr hat vielen ansehenlichen Leuten zu Nürnberg, die der Disputation beigewohnet, wohlgefallen, dessen die Pfarrer sambt dem Münch übel zufrieden gewest. Er hat zu Nürnberg durch ein offentlich Programma, so er angeschlagen, jedermann wissend gemacht, daß er auf das Concilium reisete und daselbs seiner Lehr halben Rechenschaft geben wollte' [He conducted a disputation with the priests of Saint Sebaldus's and Saint Laurence's and because they did not win any arguments against him a Carthusian monk who was a doctor tried disputing with him. Hus's teaching appealed to many respectable people in Nuremberg who had been present at the disputation, something which greatly displeased the priests and the monk. By means of a public programme which he nailed up Hus let everyone know that he was travelling to the Council [of Constance] and would give an account of his doctrine there] (Müllner, *Annalen*, vol. 2, p. 218). In 1415 the *Rat* sent Peter Volckamer, Johann von Holfeld (the *Pfarrer* at the Lorenzkirche) and his *Schaffer und Meister* to the Council of Constance, which condemned Hus to death at the stake in 1415 (Müllner, *Annalen*, vol. 2, p. 219).

[88]   'Es ist dies Jahr [1428] abermals große Plackerei getrieben worden, ohne Zweifel aus Verursachung der hußitischen Kriegsläuft. Im Schwabenland und umb Sünßheimb sein den nürnbergischen Kaufleuten Güter aufgehalten und von den vereinten Ständen deswegen ein Tag gen Würzburg gelegt worden' [This year again saw much trouble and disturbance, doubtless caused by the Hussite campaigns. In Swabia and round Sinsheim [in Swabia] Nuremberg merchants had their goods trains held up and for that reason the combined Estates called a diet at Würzburg] (Müllner, *Annalen*, vol. 2, p. 269).

[89]   Müllner, *Annalen*, vol. 2, p. 275.

[90]   Funk, *Glasfensterkunst*, pp. 142–3.

Taus without having seen the enemy.[91] However, the more extreme Hussites, the Taborites, were eventually defeated in battle on 30 May 1434 and the Ultraquists agreed to the *Compactata* of Basel in 1436. Trouble did not really break out again until 1462, so after Konhofer's death and the probable determination of the iconic programme of the window. However, Konhofer's own experience of the Hussite Wars in his home region may have prompted this visual reassertion of, first, the centrality to Catholicism of the saints and their worship; second, the "real" presence of saints in and their protection of an area that had resisted heresy at no small cost.

However, none of this explains why Konhofer chose the mystic marriage as the subject of the window rather than having Saint Katherine depicted like the other Holy Helpers – static and with her attributes, the sword and the wheel. One reason may be that the sequence of Hermann Leicht's visions echoes that of Katherine herself, who also experienced two visions in which she was denied sight of Christ's face (her second vision was of the Virgin Mary alone) before her third, that of the mystic marriage. Katherine models exemplary service leading to privileged sight which is replicated almost a thousand years later in the diocese of Bamberg that Nuremberg had helped to protect during the Hussite Wars. Second, if the mystic marriage represents the union of the soul with God, the window may represent its donor's own wish to be unified with Him, not least since Saint Katherine kneels above Konhofer, functioning as a conduit to the Christ Child. Her location may also indicate that Konhofer is contemplating, even experiencing his own vision of, the mystic marriage, just as the viewer should engage in a visualizing meditation. Further, the window reassures the worshipper of Katherine's active concern for church, city and region by linking her to Saints Sebaldus and Laurence and depicting her recent presence in the area. Singled out by means of the mystic marriage as a particularly important representative of a locally significant cult, she is thus presented as the main source of aid in times of need. Saint Katherine functions, then, as a conduit to Christ not just for Konhofer but for the city as a whole.

How does all this relate Saint Katherine to the Holy Roman Empire? First, Saint Katherine belongs to a group of early martyrs whose dedication to God helped spread the Christian Empire of which the Holy Roman Empire is the continuation and at the heart of which Nuremberg stands. Second, the Konhofer and Volckamer windows show her united with the King of Heaven next to the window donated in 1477 by his chosen representative on earth, the Holy Roman Emperor Friedrich III.[92] The main themes of the window are

---

[91]   Müllner, *Annalen*, vol. 2, pp. 286–7.

[92]   Born 21 September 1415 in Innsbruck; died 19 August 1493 in Linz; ruled 1452–93. Friedrich was crowned German King in Aachen in 1442; he held his first

the establishment of Christianity in the Empire through Constantine's victory over his rival Maxentius in Rome in 312, his conversion and baptism and the subsequent discovery of the True Cross by Constantine's mother, Empress Helena (c. 255–330).[93] The third row depicts the theft of the Cross by the Persian king Chosrau (590–628) in 614[94] and its recovery by the Byzantine emperor Heraklius (610–41), who returned it to Jerusalem in 629.[95] Finally, Charlemagne's victorious military campaign against the Huns near Regensburg in 796 is shown.[96] Friedrich himself and his wife Eleonora of Portugal, whom he married in 1452, are depicted in a throne room beneath an elaborate Gothic tracery bearing the symbols of this Empire: the sceptre, orb, crown, all of which were kept in Nuremberg. A page holding the *Reichsschwert* (imperial sword) stands behind Friedrich.[97] The *Kaiserfenster*, then, narrates the incorporation of the mythology of the Cross into the mythology of the Christianized Empire, the Holy Roman Emperor himself being defined and legitimized by his defence and worship of the Cross.[98] Christ's Cross stands at the heart of the Empire; crucially, it stands at the heart of Nuremberg, literally in the relics and symbolically in both this window, illuminated every morning by the rising sun symbolic of Christ's Resurrection, and in the Cross that hangs behind the high altar, similarly illuminated by the light of Resurrection. That the light shines through the scenes

---

Reichstag in Nuremberg in 1444 and was crowned Emperor by Pope Nicholas V in Rome in 1452. Friedrich visited Nuremberg in 1444, 1456, 1471, 1481, 1485 and 1487 (Funk, *Glasfensterkunst*, p. 136). Image of *Kaiserfenster* at http://www.lorenzkirche.citykirche-magazin.de/index.php?option=com_content&task=view&id=23&Itemid=147.

[93]   The liturgical year celebrates two feasts for the Cross: the Discovery on 3 May and the Elevation on 14 September. An antependium (c. 1430–40) formerly on the Kreuzaltar (Altar of the Cross) in the Lorenzkirche also depicts the finding and testing of the Cross. It was probably donated by the Rummel and Haller families, whose coats-of-arms it boasts. It is now in the Germanisches Nationalmuseum (Gew 3715).

[94]   Possibly an allusion to the fear of the loss of the *Reichsreliquien* (including a fragment of the True Cross) to the advancing Hussites that led to their relocation to Nuremberg.

[95]   Funk, *Glasfensterkunst*, p. 21. According to Funk, the *Legenda aurea* is the source of the legends of the Cross; *Religion in Geschichte und Gegenwart* states Ambrosius (d. 397) was the first to record it (vol. 4, 'Kreuzesfest', p. 52). The repatriation of the True Cross by Heraclius gave considerable impetus to its veneration.

[96]   Funk, *Glasfensterkunst*, p. 23. Funk maintains that the imperial legends refer to the contemporary threat to Christendom from the Ottoman Turks, who had conquered Constantinople in 1453 and were advancing through the Balkans and Austria (Funk, *Glasfensterkunst*, p. 24).

[97]   Saint Christopher, one of the *Vierzehn Heiligen* and along with Andrew patron saint of the House of Hapsburg, is portrayed on the lowest row.

[98]   Angels appeared to both Constantine and Charlemagne announcing future victory if they fought under the sign of the Cross. For the former see *Der Heiligen Leben*, fol. xxiiij[r].

from the legend of the Cross symbolizes Christ's own transcendence of death and the role of His death in enabling man to overcome the everlasting death of the soul. Hence every morning God, present in the light that filters through the *Kaiserfenster* and fills the East choir with radiance and colour, renews the Empire and His bond to it, as well as to the viewer bathed in that light.

In foregrounding the indissoluble fusion between the Cross, the Holy Roman Empire and the Holy Roman Emperors, the *Kaiserfenster* acts as an advertisement for the relics of the Crucifixion held in the Frauenkirche,[99] in the church of the Heilig-Geist-Spital (a piece of the True Cross, Longinus's Lance and a nail from the Cross)[100] and in the Krell Altar immediately below it.[101] Endowed by the

---

[99]   Müllner lists the relics, including Crucifixion relics, given to the Frauenkirche by Emperor Karl IV: 'zwen Spän des heiligen Kreuzes, ein Stück des Steins, darinnen das Kreuz gestanden, etwas von dem Erdreich, da das Kreuz gefunden worden, ein Stück von der Krippen, ein Stück von der Säuln Christi, von dem Grab zwei Stück, ein Stück von dem Stein, so ob dem Grab gelegen, ein Stück von dem Stein, darauf Christus am Ölberg gekniet, etwas von dem Kleid Christi, zween Dorn von der Kron Christi, etwas vom Schwammen, damit man ihme am Kreuz getränket, etwas von Unser Frauen Haar, drei Stück von ihrem Schleier, etwas von Unser Frauen Milch, etwas von ihrem Gespinst, ein ganze Gürtel Unser Frauen, Unser Frauen Hembd, ein Börtlein, so sie selbs gewirkt, etwas von Unser Frauen Grab im Tal Josaphat, ein Stück von dem Stein, darauf Unser Frau gestorben, etliche Gebein von den Evangelisten, zwölf Boten und andern Heiligen, insonderheit etliche Stück von den Gebeinen der Altväter Abraham, Isaac und Jacob, und was des Lappenwerks mehr ist' [two splinters from the Holy Cross; a piece of the rock in which the Cross stood; some of the soil in which the Cross was found; a piece of the manger; a piece of the column [to which Christ was tied for His Flagellation]; two pieces of the Tomb; a piece of the rock that lay on top of the Tomb; a piece of the rock on which Christ kneeled on the Mount of Olives; a fragment of Christ's robe; two thorns from Christ's Crown of Thorns; some of the sponge with which he was given to drink when on the Cross; some of Our Lady's hair; three pieces of her veil; some of Our Lady's milk; some of her weaving; an entire girdle belonging to Our Lady; Our Lady's shift; a belt she embroidered herself; some of Our Lady's tomb in the Valley of Jehoshaphat; a piece of the rock on which Our Lady died; various bones belonging to the Four Evangelists, the Twelve Apostles and other saints, in particular various bits of bone from the Patriarchs Abraham and Isaac; and other bits of roguish nonsense] (Müllner, *Annalen*, vol. 2, pp. 10–13).

[100]   A relic of the Lance was also present in the Katharinenkirche, where it was associated with a miraculous image of the Virgin Mary that became a pilgrimage shrine in the fourteenth century (Fries, 'Kloster und Kirche', p. 16). In an altar (now missing) dedicated to Saint Katherine in the sacristy was a fragment of the pillar to which Christ was tied during His flagellation (Fries, 'Kloster und Kirche', p. 117).

[101]   The altar was known also known as the *Bartholomäusaltar*, as Saints Bartholomew and Barbara are shown on either side of the Virgin Mary. According to Hilpert on either side of the altar stood two panels with scenes from the legends of Saints Barbara and Bartholomew that Krell had endowed in memory of his parents. On a pillar next to this altar had also hung Jodokus Krell's epitaph with the Virgin Mary and Saints Helena, Barbara, James the Greater

Lorenzkirche priest Jodokus Krell before 1480, the altar depicts, and contains relics of, Saint Helena, as well as a splinter from the Cross and pieces of Mount Calvary, Christ's tomb and sites of His Passion.[102] In late-fifteenth-century sources the altar is overwhelmingly referred to by the name of its secondary patron (*Nebenpatronin*) Helena.[103] In 1484–5 Saint Helena's feast was incorporated into the liturgy at the Lorenzkirche. Emperor Friedrich III himself was particularly devoted to the worship of the Cross and to Saint Helena,[104] whose name Pope Nicholas V reputedly allowed Eleonora to adopt.[105] Dormeier speculates that Nuremberg was trying to win support from the imperial couple for the rebuilding of the choir and the exploitation of the Deocarus relics by upgrading the cult of Saint Helena.[106] However, enhancing her cult may have had four further purposes:

(Jodokus) and Bartholomew. This disappeared from the church in 1812 (Hilpert, *Die Kirche des heiligen Laurentius*, pp. 15–16). It is now in the Germanisches Nationalmuseum, Nuremberg, Inv. Gm 141 and is attributed to the workshop of Michael Wolgemut. Krell came from an honourable ("ehrbar") Nuremberg merchant family, which meant that, although non-Patrician, they were permitted to attend dances at the *Rathaus* and could sit on the *Großer Rat*, the larger of Nuremberg's two governing bodies. Families known as *Ehrbare* were members of the professional classes such as lawyers, apothecaries, doctors and so forth (Franz Machilek, 'Magister Jobst Krell, Vikar bei St. Lorenz in Nürnberg († 1483)', *Mitteilungen des Vereins für Geschichte der Stadt Nürnberg*, 59 (1972): 85–104 (p. 92)). The *Rat* approved Krell's taking the post of vicar at the *Lorenzkirche* on 20 September 1446. He was confirmed in it by the Bishop of Bamberg, Anton von Rotenhan, on 6 May 1447 (Machilek, 'Jobst Krell', p. 92). Dormeier mentions that a Franz Krell was *Kirchenmeister* of the Lorenzkirche in 1484 so there was a family connexion (Heinrich Dormeier, 'Kirchenjahr, Heiligenverehrung und große Politik im Almosengefällbuch der Nürnberger Lorenzpfarrei (1454–1516)', *Mitteilungen des Vereins für Geschichte der Stadt Nürnberg*, 84 (1997): 1–60 (pp. 3–4)). The Germanisches Nationalmuseum also houses the epitaph for Ursula Haller (c. 1482) Inv. Gm 152, which used to hang in the choir of the Lorenzkirche as the pendant to the Krell epitaph. It depicts Ursula Haller, Lorenz Haller (the donor) and another small female figure kneeling in front of Saints Helena, Bartholomew, Laurence and Barbara who flank Christ as Man of Sorrows. Fragments of the Cross were also housed in the Johannes Altar (endowed by the Imhoff family c. 1412 and again 1521). Image of Krell Altar at http://www.lorenzkirche.citykirche-magazin.de/index. php?option=com_content&task=view&id=23&Itemid=147.

[102]   Dormeier, 'Kirchenjahr', 37. On the door of the *mensa* (*Reliquientürchen*) are the heads of Jesus, Mary, the Twelve Apostles, Sebastian, Levinus, Nicholas, Laurence, Agnes, Dorothy, Katherine and Lucy (Hilpert, *Die Kirche des heiligen Laurentius*, p. 16).

[103]   Dormeier, 'Kirchenjahr', p. 35.

[104]   On 3 May 1442 (Feast of the Discovery of the True Cross) Friedrich III requested a private viewing of the *Reichskleinodien* in the Heilig-Geist-Kirche; he also had the feast of Saint Helena included in one of his private prayer books (Dormeier, 'Kirchenjahr', p. 38).

[105]   Dormeier, 'Kirchenjahr', p. 37.

[106]   Dormeier, 'Kirchenjahr', p. 37. On 26 August 1471 Emperor Friedrich III had attended a mass in the Lorenzkirche and given two gulden for the cult of Deocarus (Dormeier,

first, to promote the Crucifixion relics by foregrounding their civic presence in the Lorenzkirche and the church of the Heilig-Geist-Spital; second, thereby to highlight Nuremberg's privileged status within and fundamental importance to the Holy Roman Empire as chosen guardian of the relics and the coronation insignia; third, to tie Nuremberg, its governing families and the Empire more closely together through mutually reinforcing patterns of endowment and representation; fourth, to improve Nuremberg's relationship with Friedrich, which was slightly troubled: he did not support the city in its battle again the expansionist policies of Margrave Albrecht Achilles of Kulmbach and Ansbach, from 1470 Electoral Prince of Brandenburg.[107] Furthermore, he granted Nuremberg no new privileges and even demanded the return of the imperial insignia and relics.[108]

Saint Katherine is woven into this pattern in two ways. First, her depiction on the Krell Altar *predella* echoes the Konhofer and Volckamer windows, forging a link between them, the altar and the East window and thereby tying saint and Empire closer together and anchoring Katherine into the history of salvation, of which the Holy Roman Empire forms the final stage.[109] Signalling Nuremberg's centrality in this history – the Krell Altar shows Mary, the Christ Child and Saints

---

'Kirchenjahr', p. 17). The Lorenzkirche also possessed a tapestry (c. 1430–40), used as an antependium, which depicts the discovery of the True Cross by Saint Helena and the proving of its authenticity. The tapestry displays the coats-of-arms of the Rummel and Haller. Probably in the nineteenth century the tapestry was moved to the Sebalduskirche; it is now in the Germanisches Nationalmuseum (Gew 3715) (*Nürnberg 1350–1550. Kunst der Gothik und Renaissance* (Munich: Prestel, 1986), p. 198).

[107]   *Stadtlexikon*, p. 310.

[108]   See Müllner, *Annalen*, vol. 2, p. 362. Berthold Volckamer and Carl Holzschuher were sent by the *Rat* to King Friedrich in Vienna in 1443 to obtain, amongst other things, confirmation of the 'Brief über das Heilthumb' [document about the relics]. King Friedrich refused and requested that the 'Heilthumb' be sent to him in Regensburg, 'dann es ihme als einem Römischen König zustünde' [because they were his by right as King of the Germans]. The dispute rolled on into the following year, when eventually Nuremberg appealed to the Seven Electoral Princes for support. They told Friedrich to leave the relics and insignia in Nuremberg. In 1486, year of the endowment of the Volckamer window, Charlemagne's crown, sword, sceptre, robes etc. were in Frankfurt for the coronation of Maximilian as *Deutscher König*, a ceremony at which Nuremberg was represented by its donor, Peter II Volckamer (Müllner, *Annalen*, vol. 3, pp. 74–5). In 1485, when Friedrich had visited Nuremberg, Paulus Volckamer had been amongst those chosen by the *Rat* to honour Friedrich by presenting him with an expensive gemstone (Müllner, *Annalen*, vol. 3, p. 71). The Volckamer family were thus an essential part of Nuremberg's attempt to maintain its spiritual (and hence political) importance to the Empire, a role that may have influenced their choice of Saint Katherine at the heart of Christ's lineage.

[109]   A further – albeit it tenuous – link between Saint Katherine and the Empire is that 'Charlemagne allegedly brought back a phial of oil from Katherine's tomb after his legendary

Barbara and Bartholomew against the backdrop of Nuremberg – might constitute an attempt to persuade Friedrich to renew its right to guard the relics, a major source of pilgrimage income. On this oldest known depiction of Nuremberg the Lorenzkirche can clearly be seen just to the left of Saint Barbara's halo and almost above the chalice and wafer she holds, reminders of the relics in the *predella* as they commemorate Christ's death on the Cross.[110] Hence, this location further associates the church with the Crucifixion, here as commemorated in the mass, a link strengthened by the gestures of the Christ Child: with His right hand He points to the future site of the wound in His side caused by Longinus' spear; with the middle finger of His left He indicates where the nail will pierce His hand. Thus the viewer can see the church in which he himself is standing looking at the Krell Altar with its holy relics on an altar depicting this very church and his home city as the site of salvation. Much like Saint Katherine in the Konhofer window, the Krell Altar functions as a conduit to redemption.

Second, worshippers in the church would already have seen Saints Helena and Katherine explicitly linked on the altar dedicated to Saint Katherine on the south side of the threshold to the choir. Its wings, endowed by Nuremberg judge Levinus Memminger around 1485/90,[111] show, on the inside right, the discovery of the

---

pilgrimage to the Holy Land' (Lewis, 'Pilgrimage and the Cult of Saint Katherine in Late Medieval England', p. 44).

[110]   The church is also prominent on the woodcut of Nuremberg in the *Weltchronik* published by Hartmann Schedel in Nuremberg in 1493. Furthermore, the Nuremberg woodcut is the only one to occupy an entire double-page spread (fol. LXXXXIXᵛ–Cʳ).

[111]   Levinus Memminger, who died in 1493, was the son of Lorenz Memminger, who had come to Nuremberg from Graz and rapidly established himself in the city (Peter Strieder, *Tafelmalerei in Nürnberg 1350–1550* (Königstein im Taunus: Karl Robert Langewiesche Nachfolger & Hans Köster Verlagsbuchhandlung, 1993), p. 76). Levinus was a bishop martyr whose feast was celebrated on 12 November. He is thought to have been Irish; was consecrated priest by Augustine of Canterbury in 600; went to Flanders and was for decades a successful missionary. He was martyred on 12 November 659, when, amongst other things, his tongue was ripped out of his mouth. Usually represented with pliers and his torn-out tongue, he is the patron saint of Ghent (*Bildlexikon der Heiligen*, p. 416). The wings were the work of Michael Wolgemut and his workshop (Günther P. Fehring and Anton Ress, *Die Stadt Nürnberg*, 2, p. 88). Hilpert, however, identifies the male saint as Saint Conrad, since Conrad Tracht's widow Kunigunde had donated the carved shrine and a benefice in 1392 (Hilpert, *Die Kirche des heiligen Laurentius*, p. 18); Müllner refers to the altar as 'S. Katharinen Altar, zu welchem Kungundt Conradt Trächtin Anno 1392 eine Pfründ gestiftet' [Saint Katherine's altar for which Kunigunde, wife of Konrad Tracht, endowed a living in 1392] (Müllner, *Annalen*, vol. 2, p. 51) and identifies it as one of the 12 main altars in the Lorenzkirche. Murr, on the other hand, identifies the male saint as Saint Nicholas and fails to identify Saint Helena at all (Murr, *Beschreibung der vornehmsten Merkwürdigkeiten*, p. 111). Image at http://www.lorenzkirche. citykirche-magazin.de/index.php?option=com_content&task=view&id=23&Itemid=147.

True Cross by Saint Helena and its return to Jerusalem by Emperor Heraklius; on the left, the mystic marriage, with Katherine, the Virgin and the Christ Child surrounded by the *Vierzehn Heiligen*.[112] On the left outside wing are seen the shattering of the wheel and the beheading of Saint Katherine; on the right the beheading of Saint Levinus. According to Strieder, the iconography of the wings is determined by the family's patron saints: Levinus Memminger was married to Katharina Armauer; their daughters were Helena and Anna.[113] The carved altar shrine presents Saint Katherine with her traditional attributes as the central figure; Helena and Levinus stand on either side of her. Through the proximity to Saint Helena she is linked to the relics of the Cross and of Saint Helena housed in the Krell Altar and beyond them to the *Kaiserfenster*. In other words, she is tied into the Empire itself through a web of association that stretches throughout the Lorenzkirche, a connexion further strengthened by the altar wings: the finding of the True Cross and the mystic marriage foreground two high-status women crucial in the establishment of the early Church. Further, since the colour and pattern of Helen's robe, cloak and crown are virtually identical to Mary's,[114] the Christian Empress of earth is merged with the Christian Queen of Heaven. Both are mothers, one of the secular ruler, Constantine the Great, who made Christianity the religion of the Roman Empire; the other of the King of Heaven, whom Constantine served. The gold of Mary's robe is echoed in that of Katherine's; in fact, the gold, red and blue robes connect the three women to one another visually, creating a trinity of ideal Christian womanhood for the viewer and linking Saint Katherine in his mind with the very coming-into-being of the Christian empire.

However, the web is spun further than this: a further link to the *Kaiserfenster* and the relics of the Cross is provided by the same two key scenes from the story of Heraklius, which on the Memminger Altar play out as the background to the Discovery of the True Cross: the barring of Heraklius's triumphal entrance into Jerusalem by an angel when he returns, on horseback and richly dressed, with

---

[112]   Gümbel describes the celebratory ritual at the altar on Saint Katherine's feast day and also the altar furnishings belonging to it, which included an altar hanging depicting the Virgin, Katherine and Saint Ursula and one depicting the Virgin, Katherine, Saint Laurence and 'ein parmherzikait' (pietà). The altar was also decorated on Saint Kunigunde's feast day (Albert Gümbel, *Das Mesnerpflichtbuch von St Lorenz in Nürnberg*, Einzelarbeiten aus der Kirchengeschichte Bayerns 8 (Munich: Chr. Kaiser, 1928), p. 17 and p. 44).

[113]   Memminger's daughter Helena married Peter Imhoff in 1506; Anna married Bartholmess Haller in 1507. Strieder postulates that Memminger commissioned the altar from Wolgemut around 1485/6 as Helena cannot have been much older than 20 at the time of the wedding (although he offers no evidence) and Anna is not included in its iconography (Strieder, *Tafelmalerei*, p. 76).

[114]   Both wear dresses of red and gold brocade and a blue cloak round their shoulders.

the Cross; and his subsequent entry into the city on foot and in a white shift.[115] The colours and fabric of Heraklius's discarded robe match those of Saints Mary and Helena exactly, a small detail that further fuses the three female saints with the legend of the Cross. That Christ promises life after death is literally realized in the revival of the dead man through the laying on of the Cross.[116] Through their presence at the mystic marriage on the left-hand wing, the *Vierzehn Heiligen* also become more closely associated with the Cross and Empire. On this panel Wolgemut fuses, possibly at the behest of donor Levinus Memminger, two visions – Saint Katherine's of the mystic marriage and Hermann Leicht's of the *Vierzehn Heiligen* – not normally associated with each other except on the Konhofer window. Within the *hortus conclusus*, symbol of Mary's virginity, the heads and haloes of the helper saints surround the Christ Child and to some extent Saint Katherine, the circle they form both symbolizing eternity and echoing the shape of the wedding ring, itself a symbol of eternity. The circle also makes the mystic marriage – and hence Saint Katherine's status as the bride of Christ – more prominent. The wedding ring forms the centre of the panel and of a cross formed by the central vertical and horizontal lines,[117] so is highlighted by its position, just as it is in the Konhofer and Volckamer windows, the themes and composition of which it echoes. Through their presence within the *hortus conclusus* the *Vierzehn Heiligen* – and with them Nuremberg and Franconia, the region with which they are most closely associated – are locked into the history of salvation and the history of salvation is locked into the region.[118] At the centre of the circle of *Vierzehn Heiligen* Katherine, as in the Konhofer window, acts as the main bridge between the regional and the divine. One of the Helpers, Saint Vitus, is a portrait of Levinus Memminger, who, part of a vision (Hermann

---

[115]   Panels 4e and 4f on the *Kaiserfenster*.

[116]   On the opposite pillar at the threshold to the choir hangs the Keyper Epitaph, the Lamentation, also by Wolgemut (c. 1485). The obvious similarities in style and colouring link Christ's death on the Cross to the revivification of the corpse on which the True Cross is laid to test its authenticity. As in the Volckamer window, Mary as young mother in the mystic marriage is paralleled to Mary mourning the death of her son.

[117]   The central vertical line goes down through the tower and Saint Barbara's head to the head of Saint Egidius. The central horizontal line goes from the book on Saint Margaret's lap (the book symbolizing Christ as the Word made flesh) to the head of Saint Christopher carrying the infant Christ.

[118]   In the background of both panels, Discovery of the True Cross and mystic marriage, stands a fortress, especially prominent in the depiction of Jerusalem behind Saint Helena. As the fortress would inevitably remind the viewer of the *Kaiserburg* (imperial fortress) in Nuremberg, the city is, as in the Krell Altar, identified as the locus of divine events.

Leicht's), thus becomes an eyewitness to an earlier vision (Saint Katherine's).[119] Thus the "real" person that is Memminger confirms the reality of the mystic marriage whilst himself being assimilated into a divine reality normally beyond his and the viewer's "own powers of sight" yet presented here to the latter's physical eye.[120] Memminger's presence serves as testimony to his personal piety, a characteristic to which the whole city can bear witness as it is showcased in this painting; the cock in his hands symbolizes his spiritual watchfulness. However, the significance of Memminger's attendance at the mystic marriage goes further: as city judge he can be read as a representative of Nuremberg itself, so the entire city is rendered holier by its presence at the mystic marriage. Like Saint Katherine's ring, Memminger remains behind as tangible evidence of a truth beyond the vision of the ordinary worshipper. Since the Middle Ages placed considerable value on 'images as ... the basis of cognition and even epistemology', since they make their way to the human soul, the ultimate agent of perception and knowledge,[121] the Memminger Altar stamps on the viewer's psyche images which literally mould his thought, behaviour and soul. As the altar draws together the Cross, the imperial relics, Saint Helena, the establishment of Christianity in the Empire and the regional cult of the *Vierzehn Heiligen* with Saint Katherine at its heart, a worshipper who has seen it approaches the choir windows with this fusion imprinted on his physical and spiritual eye, shaping his reception of these windows and reinforcing his devotion to the saint and the Empire.

 Why did Saint Katherine and the mystic marriage occupy such an important place at the heart of the Lorenzkirche? In *Der Heiligen Leben* the mystic marriage enjoys no greater prominence in her legend than any other aspect of her life.[122] In fact, more space is devoted to her martyrdom and that of the 50

---

[119]   Might the fact that the Helpers surround Katherine, Mary and the Christ Child yet are not looking at them but in various directions suggest that they themselves are having a vision of the mystic marriage, so the viewer of the altarpiece sees the subjects of a vision themselves having a vision? In other words, three layers of sight are in operation – the Chinese boxes effect again.

[120]   Camille, *Gothic Art*, p. 19.

[121]   Camille, 'Before the Gaze', p. 216.

[122]   However, at the end of the account of Katherine's miracles the 'zwelff grosse mynnezeyche*n* vn*d* edler mynnreicher gabe*n*' [the twelve great signs of love and noble gifts of His love] accorded Katherine by Christ are recorded, the twelfth being His giving her communion in both kinds with His own hands when He visits her in jail. The text continues: 'Dye genad hett sye vo*n* de*r* haffnu*n*g dye sy zu got het / Da tet ir vnser her noch eyn grosser vberflussiges liebe zeiche*n* vn*d* ein lieblich gab da er sy gemahelt vn*d* er ir eyn klar guldin vingerlin an iren gold vinger stiß mit seyner gotlichen hand vn*d* sprach zu ir O Katherina mein ausserwelte gemahel mytt dem vingerlin vermahel ich dich mir in eynem rechten cristenliche*n* gelaube*n* das sal ein rechtes wares zeichen sein eyner steten gancze*n*

heathen philosophers, Maxentius's Empress and his captain of the guard, all of whom Katherine converts. In the Lorenzkirche, by contrast, the Memminger Altar constitutes the only representation of Katherine's beheading.[123] However, three possible reasons present themselves. First, Nuremberg was a centre of the spice trade. Veneration of Saint Katherine may have been intended to gain her favour as a representative of the city in Alexandria, a sort of divine insurance policy for a business that was highly lucrative but equally hazardous, as Nuremberg merchants in Alexandria were at the mercy of the sultan and the Mameluke authorities.[124] Both the Volckamer and Mendel dealt in spices; indeed, the

---

lieb zwischen mir vnd dir hye vnd dort ewiglichen / *daz* solt du behalten bis an deinen tod / die gnad lyst man von keinem heyligen mer / aber darumb das sie der almechtig got sunderlich lieb het fur alheyligen / so hatt er sy vermahelt im selbs mit einnem fruntlichen mahelsthacz [*sic*] vnd erczeyget ir dye grossen lyeb dar an die er czu ir hett da von mocht sye furbaß weder lieb noch leyd noch der tod vo*n* got gescheyden' [She enjoyed this grace on account of the hope she placed in God. Then Our Lord showed her yet another great sign of His overflowing love and a loving gift when He married her and placed a slender, radiant gold ring on her ring finger with His own divine hand and said to her, 'O, Katherine, my chosen spouse, with this ring I thee wed in the one true Christian faith. This shall be a true token of a constant, flawless love between me and you here and in the eternal hereafter. You should keep it until the hour of your death'. You cannot read about an act of such grace towards any other saint; but because God Almighty loved her especially above all other saints He took her unto Himself as His bride with a wedding gift that demonstrates His affection and showed her the great love He felt for her. Thenceforth neither love nor pain nor death itself could separate her from God] (*Der Heiligen Leben*, fol. cclxj^r).

123   The beheading of Saint Katherine is depicted in the foreground; Maxentius and a courtier look on. In the background is the miracle of the shattering of the wheel.

124   Tucher records the taxes and duties merchants had to pay; an attack on himself and Otto Spiegel in Alexandria which led to their being thrown into prison; his being stabbed in the neck; the fixing of prices for pepper and the outrageous means by which payment was extracted (Tucher, *'Reise'*, pp. 576–99). The need to establish favourable relations with the sultan found its way into literature as well: 'Vnd Fortunatus begert daß man mann jm für den Künig hülff / er brecht jm ein schanckung / Dann jeder kauffmann pflag dem Soldan ein schanckung zuthůn / wann er erst ghen Alexandria kam / Dazů / weil er bracht / waren des Soldans diener / wie noch an vil Fürsten *höffen* / gar geflissen' [Fortunatus wanted them to help him to obtain an audience with the King and he would bring him [the King] a gift for it is customary for every merchant to present the sultan with a gift when he first arrives in Alexandria. Because he had brought a present the sultan's servants were most assiduous in helping him achieve his goal, as they are today at many princes' courts] (*Fortunatus* (Augsburg: Heinrich Steiner, 1548), fol. L^{r,v}; first published Augsburg 1509). In return the sultan gives Fortunatus 'c. Crag pfeffer / die waren so vil werdt / als die kleinot die er jm gesche*n*ckt hett' [one hundred measures of pepper, which were worth as much as the jewels he had given him [namely, 5,000 ducats]] (*Fortunatus*, fol. L^v). The text also mentions 'der Venediger / Florentzer / Genueser / vnd Cathelonier leger

Mendel owed a large proportion of their considerable wealth to this trade.[125] Second, Nuremberg cultivated learning: in its early Humanist circles, the city schools and Saint Katherine's convent, which after the reform of 1428 became widely known for the erudition of its nuns and the size of its library. These nuns, themselves brides of Christ, were members of the immensely powerful Patrician elite, interrelated through ties of blood and marriage. Hence the mystic marriage, also depicted on two convent church altars, may have symbolized a) a model marriage in a Patrician community fused by marriage alliances; b) the cohesion of the governing class so crucial to the city's political and economic success; c) the integration into civic life of an influential convent community which enhanced Nuremberg's intellectual and spiritual capital further afield. Third, the key theme of Isaiah 11 is the righteousness of the new king's rule, so the Volckamer window especially may constitute a hint to Friedrich III and to Maximilian to treat the "imaginary capital" – represented by Saint Katherine – more graciously.[126] This possibility is supported by the fact that in 1486, year of the endowment of the Volckamer window, its donor Peter II Volckamer represented Nuremberg at the coronation of Maximilian as *Deutscher König* in Frankfurt.[127] The mystic marriage thus symbolizes the ideal union between the city and the Empire, which it supported loyally and in which, until the Reformation, it played a central financial, political and spiritual role. In Katherine, therefore, we have a showcased saint who became a civic logo.

Herrn' [the Venetians, Florentines, Genoese and Catalonians] who were in Alexandria (fol. L'), the competition for Nuremberg merchants.

[125]   Fleischmann, *Rat und Patriziat*, 31/2, p. 397.

[126]   In April 1442 Berthold Volckamer had been one of the three representatives (with Paulus Vo[r]chtel and Sebald Pömer) sent by the *Rat* to greet King Friedrich outside Nuremberg on his first visit to the city after his election as *Deutscher König* (Müllner, *Annalen*, vol. 2, p. 354). In 1444 he performed this office again when the King entered Nuremberg on 1 August for a major *Reichstag* (Müllner, *Annalen*, vol. 2, p. 371). Paulus Volckamer represented Nuremberg at the *Reichstag* in Speyer and Frankfurt called by Friedrich and Maximilian in January 1489. Maximilian first visited Nuremberg on 15 August 1489.

[127]   Müllner, *Annalen*, vol. 3, pp. 74–5.

Chapter 5

Spinning the Web: The Katharinenkloster and the City

The body-ego-space is territorialised, deterritorialised and reterritorialised – by modalities of identification, by psychic defence mechanisms, by internalised authorities, by intense feelings, by flows of power and meaning. Bodies are made within particular constellations of object relations – the family, the army, the state, the movies, the nation, and so on. These are not, however, passive bodies which simply have a space and are a space: they also make space. They draw their maps of desire, disgust, pleasure, pain, loathing, love. They negotiate their feelings, their place in the world. In their body-ego-spaces, people speak their internal-external border dialogues. Finally, bodies occupy, produce themselves in, make and reproduce themselves in multiple real, imaginary and symbolic spaces, which are never innocent of power and resistance.[1]

Thus does Steve Pile characterize the contemporary body in its relationship to the contemporary city, a place that is 'attractive, vibrant and cultured'; which offers 'multiple opportunities for business and pleasure, [its] multiple social worlds perpetually throwing up new ideas, food, music and fashion'; a place that is 'the seat of culture, learning, government and civil order', an 'icon of progress, enlightenment and opportunity'.[2] Medieval cities, on the other hand, are perceived as somehow "less": less diverse; less redolent of possibilities; one-sided in their self-presentation; symbolic rather than lived spaces:

Complex techniques for elaborating an image of the city had already existed in the Middle Ages, but for the most part they had enhanced the celebration of political or religious power or the progressiveness, wealth, or military strength of the city, as expressed in imposing architecture. These techniques were striking for their decisively symbolic, ideological, even metaphysical character.[3]

---

[1] Pile, *The Body and the City*, p. 209.

[2] Phil Hubbard, *city*, Key Ideas in Geography (London and New York: Routledge, 2006), pp. 64–5.

[3] Chiara Frugoni, *A Distant City: Images of Urban Experience in the Medieval World*, trans. William McCuaig (Princeton: Princeton University Press, 1991), p. 49. No evidence, examples or explanations of the "complex techniques" are offered by Frugoni.

Such reductiveness, however, completely ignores the lived reality of a city like Nuremberg: one of the largest in the German territories;[4] an organism grown on manufacturing, trade and political savvy; thanks to its visiting and resident merchants, pilgrims, rulers, diplomats, scholars and craftsmen ethnically and culturally diverse; through its Patricians, *Ehrbare*, scholars, clergy, artisans, beggars, soldiers, prostitutes and market traders socially diverse; seat of imperial diets as instruments of law and governance; home to the Meistersinger, *Fastnachtspiele* and some of the most celebrated, internationally active artists and Humanist scholars of the fifteenth and sixteenth centuries[5] – Nuremberg was, for all its symbolic status as guardian of the *Reichskleinodien*, a city as 'vibrant' and full of 'opportunity' as any twenty-first century counterpart. Hence, the 'body-ego-space' that is Saint Katherine stands at the centre of the web of stone, wood, water, earth, metal, flesh, psyche, intellect, family, business, trade, piety, civic rule and the spaces between them that constituted late-medieval Nuremberg, what Adrian Meyer describes as a 'dauerhaften Stoff aus Formen, Räumen, Geschichte und Erinnerungen', a 'komplexe[s] Beziehungssystem[s], eine[r] Vermengung von Dinglichem der Architektur und Dingen des Lebens'.[6] Katherine's body-driven ego, 'territorialised' 'by internalised authorities, by intense feelings, by flows of power and meaning', 'drew her map of desire' in another city, late-Antique/early medieval Alexandria, as a bridegroom commensurate with her beauty and status. Her desire, mapped onto the political and spiritual realities of her civic space, led to an abnegation of her ego-driven body that claimed territory beyond the corporeal: namely, visions of the transcendent and the bridal *unio mystica* with Christ. Her mystic marriage (with an infant, that is, de-sexualized, physically reduced male) occupies the 'symbolic space' at the centre of the symbolic space that is Saint Katherine, leaving her body unterritorialized physically, because virginal, but her ego 'occupied' by Christ and reproducing itself in the "mirror" Katherines woven into her legend.

---

[4]   In the early-sixteenth century Cologne is thought to have been the largest city in Germany with 30,000 inhabitants; Ulm, Strasbourg, Hamburg, Lübeck and Nuremberg are thought to have had approximately 20,000 to 25,000; Augsburg around 18,000 and Frankfurt am Main around 10,000. However, by another reckoning Nuremberg grew from between 20,000 and 25,000 in 1431 to between 40,000 and 50,000 in 1560.

[5]   Willibald Pirckheimer (1470–1530); Konrad Celtis (1459–1508); Michael Wolgemut (1434–1519); Albrecht Dürer (1471–1528); Veit Stoss (c. 1450–1533); Adam Kraft (1460?–1509); Peter Vischer (c. 1455–1529); Caritas Pirckheimer (1467–1532).

[6]   'lasting fabric fashioned out of forms, spaces, history and memories'; 'a complex system of relationships, a mixing of the material substance of architecture with objects from everyday life' (Adrian Meyer, *Stadt und Architektur. Ein Geflecht aus Geschichte, Erinnerung, Theorie und Praxis* (Baden: Lars Müller, 2003), p. 7).

Saint Katherine's dismembered and re-assembled body – 'deterritorialised' by Maxentius and 'reterritorialised' by God – 'occupies' and 'reproduces itself' in the 'multiple real, imaginary and symbolic spaces ... never innocent of power and resistance' that constitute her miracle stories and beyond them medieval Europe. Body, legend and miracle stories are 'made within', and according to the needs of, 'particular constellations of object relations' – the 'body-ego-spaces' of individual women or men; wealthy Patrician and *ehrbaren* families; the community of the Katharinenkloster, for whom the convent *was* their city, negotiable in the same way as the civic space beyond its walls; the wider urban community of Nuremberg; the material out of which the physical city is constructed. With all these, separately or mutually permeable, the miracle stories 'speak their internal-external border dialogues' and create 'modalities of identification' that bind animate bodies and inanimate stone, wood, canvas and so forth into the web 'of desire, disgust, pleasure, pain, loathing, love' that fused late-medieval Nuremberg into a single, multi-strand organism within its defensive walls. Chapter 1 claims that such was the presence of Saint Katherine within Nuremberg that 'the entire city could be read as a map of devotion to her'. This chapter will attempt to read this map by exploring further ways in which her body and legend spin out from the text into the convent into the physical space of the surrounding city, for 'the body is traced with the values of culture: the contours of the body are the contours of society: each reproduces the "nature" of both the powers and dangers credited to social structure'.[7]

At the centre of the map lies the textual Saint Katherine, whose legend as related in *Der Heiligen Leben* already prepares the reader to spin the core out into a broader urban context: after the concluding miracle story the narrative comes full circle by returning to the beginning of Saint Katherine's legend and to her lived secular life. Like the walls of Nuremberg the text encircles and contains her primary identity (bride of Christ), which is located, first, in her earthly, physical body; second, in that body's lived experience of transcendent joy (the mystic marriage may be a vision, but it is one experienced by Katherine-as-living-corporeal-being in the human state of sleep) and flesh-bound pain (her martyrdom); and, third, the post-mortem division (relics) and self-reproduction (oil) of that body. Katherine's body in its various locations – physical (Cyprus, Alexandria, Sinai); metaphysical (devotees' visions; invisible interventions; inhabitation of a devotee's body; loan of a body part); and adopted (home of relics and cult) – forms the centre of the complex of representations and responses spread across Germany and Europe in which Nuremberg embodies

---

[7] Pile, *The Body and the City*, p. 186.

the exemplary interaction of all aspects of devotion to the saint, the city as an extension of her body. As Pile observes:

> the body is an appropriate place to begin a 'psychoanalysis of space', partly because it is one site for the intensifying articulation of power, desire and disgust, of the individual, the social and the spatial. Moreover, the body is never merely a passive surface, a leaky container of visceral fluids, a collection of orifices, limbs, feelings, organs, and so on.[8]

However, textually and symbolically Katherine's body is precisely that: 'a leaky container of visceral fluids' that spill over into her tomb, permeating the monastic community on Sinai; the lives and spiritual experience of pilgrims; the devotion, dependence and identification of worshippers; the construction of her incorporation into narrative; her "embodiment" in image, civic space, economy, corporate/individual self-representation and academic scholarship. Hence her legend in *Der Heiligen Leben* concludes on a condensed recapitulation of her life that highlights her key attributes, namely her royal birth, status as bride of Christ, education and martyrdom:

> Sant Katherin was eines edlen geschlechtes vnd eynes edlen kuniges tocher / vnd was eyn eyniger erb des kunigkreychs vnd ist eyn gemahelte brutt vnsers herren Jhesu Cristi / vnd ist eyn bewerte Meisterin in den Syben hochsten kunsten / vnd ist eyn grosse mertrerin die groß peyn vnd marter gelytten hatt mit rechter gedult vnd in rechter gotlicher lyeb / vnd dar czu den bittern tod mit dem schwert. (fol. cclx^r)

> [Saint Katherine came of a noble lineage and was the daughter of a noble king and was the sole heir to the kingdom and is a wedded spouse of Our Lord Jesus Christ and is a proven mistress in the Seven Liberal Arts and is a great martyr who suffered great pain and martyrdom with true patience and out of true love for God and over and above that suffered bitter death by the sword].

The salient brevity of this passage renders it a spiritual "take-away", an *aide-mémoire* for the believer (or young child receiving religious instruction) of the sort found in an *Ars memorativa*.[9] Moreover, the possibility of its use as a devotional *aide-mémoire* is reinforced by prayers from Katharinenkloster

---

[8]   Pile, *The Body and the City*, p. 184.
[9]   See Chapter 1 for examples of the genre.

manuscripts which recapitulate the *vita* in much the same way as does *Der Heiligen Leben*:

> Gegrusset seistu sancta katerina du edele kungin du praut *christi* des kungs aller kung Gegrusset seistu wore nachfolgerin *christi* du lawtre ros vnd lilg du seist gegrust du starcke streitterin mit dem tracken das ist mit dem teufel vnd mit dem keiser maxentio Gegrusset seistu die funftzig meister prochtest zu dem himel das sÿ vber wunden wurden mit deinen worten vnd inder prunst der greülichen flamen Gegrust seistu die die kunigin mit den rittern host angeweist mit himelischer lere Gegrußet seistu die geslagen ist worden mit slegen vnd besloßen in den vinstern kerker do du geprauchest das liecht des himels Gegrusset seistu du heillige katerina wann du vber winden host das rad das all zu mal ver̈kert ward zu verderben die heiden ... Gegrusset seistu die nach deinem tod rast auf dem perg sinaÿ ... Gegrusset seistu von der grab ol fleusset das da heillet die seuchen aller der die do siech sein.[10]

> [Hail, Saint Katherine, you noble queen, you bride of Christ, King of Kings. Hail, true follower of Christ, you pure rose and lily. Hail, you doughty warrior against the dragon, that is, the Devil, and against Emperor Maxentius. Hail, you who caused the Fifty Masters to go to Heaven because they were overcome by your words and by the fierce heat of the cruel flames. Hail, you who instructed the Queen and the knights with divine teaching. Hail, you who were beaten with blows and shut into the dark dungeon and where you saw by the light of Heaven. Hail, Saint Katherine, for you overcame the wheel that was then turned against the heathens to destroy them ... Hail, you who after your death rested on Mount Sinai ... Hail, you from whose grave flows oil that cures the sickness of all those who are sick].

Again, key events in the saint's life are singled out for memorization: the mystic marriage; her defiance of Maxentius (here aligned with the Devil); her conversion of the philosophers, Faustina and the imperial knights; her martyrdom and final resting place on Sinai, goal of contemporary Patrician pilgrimage, subject of the cloister frescoes and hence available for the imaginative pilgrimage practised by those unable to travel in person.[11] The phrase "Gegrusset seistu" echoes the

---

[10]   Stadtbibliothek Nürnberg, Cod. Cent. VII, 65, fol. 11ʳ–13ʳ.

[11]   The Béguinage in Bruges, although a different type of institution, provides an instructive example: above each cell door is painted the name of a pilgrimage shrine in the Holy Land. Pia F. Cuneo describes a cycle of six panel paintings in the chapter house of Saint Katherine's convent in Augsburg: 'The painting depict the seven basilicas of Rome and were used by the convent's members as goals of a spiritual pilgrimage for which they obtained

"Ave Maria" of Gabriel's salutation to Mary in the Annunciation; combined with the exhortation of Saint Katherine as "du lawtre ros vnd lilg",[12] a metaphor commonly used for Mary, it binds Saint Katherine to the Virgin, with whom she is depicted in the Mystic Marriage (the Volckamer window depicts Saint Katherine and the Virgin with a lily and a rose), and underscores her exemplary status still further. Katherine's privileged position in the sacred hierarchy, one that mirrors her royal birth in the secular, renders her a powerful and hence attractive object of devotion. Constant repetition of the prayer would have left a double imprint on a nun's mind: the exemplary *vita* for emulation; and exemplary language for the personal formulation of spiritual aspiration or even for daily interaction. However, repetition may have had a further effect: in yet another Katharinenkloster prayer Saint Katherine is referred to as 'Du schone ros des himelischen paradis';[13] in a third as 'du lawtre ros vnd lilg'.[14] The repetition (even with variations) of key phrases, as well as stressing Katherine's purity and martyrdom, sparks a visual and verbal intertextuality (since words conjure images) with Mary, further prayers, the *vita*, sermons and images in the convent and city, magnifying and enriching the devotional experience in a three-dimensional intellectual, spiritual, emotional and even sensory collage effect. Returning the narrative to the saint's lived virtue at the end of the *Wunderanhang* imprints on the reader the facets of Katherine's life which flowed into the miracles translated for his benefit from Sinai to Europe; it does so in two forms: first, physically through the various relics (and the endlessly reproductive possibility of contact relics); second, verbally – in oral accounts, in written and printed text and – again physically – through the book in front of him in his own home.

Thus the reader, whether lay or cloistered, could use this memorized extract from Katherine's *vita* as a trigger for recalling either further textual details of the saint's legend or visual depictions of the same;[15] or for devotion and meditation.

---

papal indulgences' (Pia F. Cuneo, 'The Basilica Cycle of Saint Katherine's Convent. Art and Female Community in Early-Renaissance Augsburg', *Women's Art Journal*, 19 (1998): 21–5).

[12]   'you pure rose and lily'.

[13]   'you beautiful rose of the heavenly paradise'.

[14]   Stadtbibliothek Nürnberg Cod. Cent VII, 65, fol. 3ᵛ (and fol. 11ʳ⁻ᵛ). There are other examples.

[15]   Basing his analysis on the Princeton Index of Christian Art, Beattie identifies 32 distinct scenes from Katherine's life, of which 11 are particularly frequent: the mystic marriage; her refusal to worship an idol; the dispute with the philosophers; the martyrdom of the philosophers; the flagellation of Katherine; Faustina's visit to Katherine in prison; the torture of Katherine on the wheel; the breaking of the wheel by angels; Katherine facing beheading; Katherine post-beheading; her entombment by angels on Sinai (Beatie, 'Medieval German Illustrative Cycles', p. 144).

For a Nuremberg reader, lay or cloistered, the retrieved images might include any number or combination of the representations of Katherine throughout the city or the Katharinenkloster. In the convent church a stained-glass window portrayed the Virgin with Saint Katherine on the right and Barbara on the left;[16] the frescoes inside the convent church and the cloisters (c. 1380/90) depicted episodes from Katherine's life and passion: those in the east and south cloisters included her youth; her dispute with the heathen philosophers; their burning; her flagellation; the destruction of the wheel; the conversion and martyrdom of Faustina and Porphyrius; the beheading of Katherine; her burial on Sinai; the Last Judgement, the Annunciation and the Nativity;[17] whilst those inside the church depicted her defence of Christianity to Maxentius, her speech to Faustina and Porphyrius (both c. 1420) and the mystic marriage (circle of Hans Pleydenwurff, c. 1460–70).[18] Murals in the nuns' choir at the west end of church showed the Resurrection, the Crucifixion with Mary Magdalene on the left and Saint Dominic on the right, a Man of Sorrows and Katherine of Alexandria.[19] Thus Katherine's *vita*, woven into key stages in the history of salvation, formed part of the material physicality of the convent; it was the protective support structure on which the community's life and worship were based.[20] The

---

[16]   'Im Chore sind sehr schöne gemalte Fenster. Hinter dem Altare ist in der Mitte die allerseligste Jungfrau, zu ihrer rechten Katharina, zur linken Barbara. Im Fenster zur rechten sind 15 Heilige gemalet, unten ist Christus am Kreuze' [In the choir there are very lovely stained-glass windows. Behind the altar the Blessed Virgin is in the middle; Katherine on her right; Barbara on her left. In the window to the right 15 saints are represented; beneath them is Christ on the Cross] (Murr, *Merkwürdigkeiten*, p. 290). See Chapter 4, this volume, for the function of windows and their impact on the worshipper.

[17]   Fries, 'Kirche und Kloster', pp. 87–8; Hamburger, *The Visual and the Visionary*, p. 454. Hamburger dates the frescoes in the cloisters to c. 1400; those in the church to c. 1320–30 and c. 1350–70.

[18]   Fries, 'Kirche und Kloster', p. 90; Murr, *Merkwürdigkeiten*, p. 286. Cloisters, church and frescoes were destroyed in the Second World War.

[19]   Hamburger, *The Visual and the Visionary*, p. 454.

[20]   See Olaf Siart for a discussion of the various functions of cloisters, including as a site for private meditation; for teaching; for ritual processions, especially during Lent; and as a burial place for the sisters and for lay benefactors and members of the nobility (Olaf Siart, *Kreuzgänge mittelalterlicher Frauenklöster. Bildprogramme und Funktionen* (Petersberg: Michael Imhof, 2008), p. 16). Thus the cloisters and the images adorning them formed an integral element of the community's daily devotion, as unshakable as the convent walls themselves. Indeed, Siart continues: 'Er war Abbild des Paradieses und Reminiszenz an den Tempelvorhof von Jerusalem ... Er bot den Konventualinnen, die in apostolischer Eintracht und Demut dem Herrn nachfolgen wollten, einen für die Anforderungen ihres Lebens geeigneten Raum und die dafür angemessenen Bilder' [They [the cloisters] were a replica of Paradise and echo of the Temple forecourt in Jerusalem ... They offered the conventuals

Annunciation illustrated the potency of the Word that was made Flesh in the infant Christ, whom Katherine married and who formed the foundation of the nuns' daily existence and liturgical practice. Christ as Word, as *language*, generates a narrative that culminates in the Crucifixion, Resurrection and Last Judgement but which also flows through the texts produced and read by the nuns, thereby formulating convent life.

This structure was reinforced by the convent altars, which strengthened the saint's presence in the foundation but also situated her within the whole community of saints, whose histories and patronages in turn privileged different aspects of Katherine's own. An altar painted by a follower of Hans Pleydenwurff and endowed between 1468 and 1475 by Marx Landauer and his daughter Elisabeth, a nun in the convent (or by Elisabeth in her father's memory),[21] has a carved middle shrine of Christ on the Cross flanked by the Virgin, John the Baptist and Katherine on His right; John the Evangelist, Dominic and Thomas Aquinas on His left. The extant wings depict the Nativity, the mystic marriage, the Crucifixion and the Resurrection on the inside; the original wings (now disappeared) showed the Annunciation and Whitsun miracle on the inside, the Crucifixion and the beheading of Katherine on the outside. Birth, death, eternal life and the spread of Christianity embed Katherine as Christ's bride into the history of salvation, her martyrdom visually on a par with Christ's sacrifice of Himself to redeem mankind. Not just the nuns' patron saint but their order as a whole is privileged, since Dominic and Thomas Aquinas also act as witnesses to Christianity's defining event and, like John the Baptist preaching the advent of Christ or the Apostles dispersing to preach the Word after the descent of the Holy Spirit at Whitsun, participated in spreading the faith. Each holds a book, vessel for the Word and sign of the Dominicans' dedication to learning, one cultivated in the Katharinenkloster itself. Whenever mass was celebrated at

---

who wanted to follow the Lord in apostolic harmony and humility a suitable space for the demands of their life as well as the images appropriate to it] (p. 295). The cloisters of the Dominican monastery also constituted a didactic space: 'In dem Kreuzgang dies Klosters [Dominican] haben die Münch an den Wänden ein ganzes Chronicon von Anfang der Welt her teils gemalet, teils geschrieben, also daß man im Kreuzgang spazieren gehen und zugleich studieren können. Ist, wie zu vermuten, aus Hartmann Schedels Chronico genummen gewest' [In the cloisters of this [the Dominican] monastery the monks have a whole history of the world from Creation onwards in both text and image on the walls, so that one can walk in the cloisters and study it at the same time. It is probably taken from Hartmann Schedel's *Chronicle*] (Müllner, *Annalen*, vol. 1, p. 201).

[21]   Strieder, *Tafelmalerei*, p. 198. Marx Landauer was named a *Genannter* in 1454, married on 27 August 1438, was widowed in 1457 and died in 1468. His daughter Elisabeth died in 1475 (Lutze and Weigand, *Kataloge des Germanischen Nationalmuseums*, vol. 1, *Textband*, pp. 151–2).

this altar, the nuns, brides of Christ on taking the veil, could see themselves in Katherine as witnesses to the Crucifixion, itself commemorated in the Eucharist for which, as we saw in Chapter 2, they had prepared through reading and prayer. Moreover, since Mary and Katherine stand on the hierarchically more prestigious right hand of Christ, women are, within this female space, accorded greater honour than men in the flow of grace from Christ's wounds.

Similarly, Katherine is bound to other exemplars of the virginal Christian life who have rejected marriage in order to dedicate themselves to Christ: 'Zur rechten Hand des großen Altars ist an der Wand ein kleines Altärchen, in dessen Mitte die heil. Katharina in Holz geschnitzt ist. Auf dem rechten Flügel ist St. Barbara, auf dem linken Margareta gemalet, aussen aber der h. Johannes und Sebald'.[22] Katherine is frequently depicted with Saints Barbara and Margaret, both *Vierzehn Heiligen*, so their association reminds the worshipper of her – and their – care for Franconia as a whole. The saint's "local patriotism" is further signalled though the presence on the altar of Sebaldus, Nuremberg's patron saint and a male exemplar of virginity in the service of Christ, having abandoned his bride on their wedding night to go into the imperial forest surrounding Nuremberg and become a hermit. Like the Konhofer window and Memminger Altar, this altar, 'traced with the values of [civic] culture', negotiates the 'internal-external border' of nuns' bodies, convent walls, city walls and regional topography to fuse these spaces together under the protection of high-status civic and regional saints. The altar reminds the nuns of their location within the guardianship of civic and regional power structures, but also of their duty to protect these structures by directing their prayer outwards to cover Nuremberg and Franconia in a web of worship and intercessory devotion.

Just as the mystic marriage occupies the core of Katherine's 'body-ego-space', laying the foundation stone of her identity, representations of it structured convent space in altars as well as frescoes:

> Neben diesem [the altar discussed above] ist auf einer großen Tafel St. Anna und Maria gemalet, vor welchen die heil. Katharina kniet, und sich mit dem Jesuskinde vermählet.

---

[22] 'To the right of the main altar there is a small altar against the wall in the middle of which is a carving of Saint Katherine. Saint Barbara is depicted on the right wing; Saint Margaret on the left. On the outer wings are Saint John and Saint Sebaldus' (Murr, *Merkwürdigkeiten*, pp. 286–7). 'Vor dem Altare lieget Friedrich Behaim begraben' [Friedrich Behaim lies buried in front of the altar] (p. 287).

Zur rechten Hand des großen Altars ist oben an der Mauer die Jungfrau Maria mit dem Jesuskinde gemalet, vor welcher St. Katharina kniet.[23]

[Next to this altar is a large picture that showing Saint Anne and Saint Mary with Saint Katherine kneeling in front of them, marrying the Christ Child.

A picture on the wall to the right of the great altar shows Mary and the Christ Child with Saint Katherine kneeling in front of them].

From there the worshipper might proceed to the Behaim Altar:

Wenn man vom Chore in die Kirche kommt, so ist zur rechten Hand ein Behaimischer Altar, in dessen Mitte die Jungfrau Maria von Holz ist, vor welcher die heil. Katharina kniet. Auf dem rechten und linken Altarflügel ist eben diese Heilige gemalet. Aussen sind rechts zwo heilige Frauen, links St. Katharina und Barbara stehend. Das Reliquienschränkchen hat zween Deckel. Auf dem zur rechten ist inwendig die heil. Katharina als Braut, St. Katharina von Siena, und St. Barbara; auf dem zur linken Hand aber St. Johannes der Täufer, St. Dominicus, und St. Hieronymus gemalet. Außern sieht man zur rechten sechs Felder mit Martern der heiligen Märyrer.[24]

[When one enters the church from the choir the Behaim Altar is on the right. In its centre is a Virgin Mary carved out of wood in front of whom Saint Katherine kneels. On the right and left altar wings this same saint is painted. On the right outer wing are two holy women; on the left stand Saints Katherine and Barbara. The *mensa* has two doors. On the inside of the right-hand one are Saint Katherine as the Bride of Christ, Saint Katherine of Sienna and Saint Barbara; on the left-hand one are depicted Saint John the Baptist, Saint Dominic and Saint Jerome. On the outside six panels with martyrdom scenes can be seen on the right].

Church space was, then, defined by worshippers' 'body-ego-space[s]', was a chart of innumerable intersecting trajectories between doors, windows, murals, altars and sculptures that were overlain by the differing moods and memories carried with them by worshippers on single or repeated visits and merged into a 'komplexe[s] Beziehungssystem[s], eine[r] Vermengung von Dinglichem der

---

[23]   Murr, *Merkwürdigkeiten*, p. 287.

[24]   Murr, *Merkwürdigkeiten*, p. 290. He also mentions an image of Katherine and other figures from 1518 (p. 291).

Architektur und Dingen des Lebens'.[25] Furthermore, a nun's steps might also take her to the following:

> Zur linken Seite in der Mitte dieses Nonnenchores ist ein anderes Behälterlein. In der Mitte kniet die heil. Katharina vor Marien, in Holz von Bildhauerarbeit, rechts steht ein Heiliger, links Katharina von Senis. Gegen über ist ein gar kleines Altärchen, mit einem hölzernen Crucifixe. Am rechten Thürlein ist oben Christus am Oelberge, unten wie ihn Judas verräth; am linken oben das Handwaschen Pilatus, unten St. Veronica zu sehen. Aussen sind acht Heilige gemalet.[26]

> [On the left-hand side in the middle of the nuns' choir is another small container. In the middle a carved wooden Saint Katherine kneels in front of Mary. On the right stands a saint; on the left Katherine of Siena. Opposite stands a very small altar with a wooden crucifix. On the right-hand door can be seen Christ on the Mount of Olives in the top half; beneath Him the scene of Judas's betrayal. On the top half of the left-hand door can be seen Pilate washing his hands; underneath him Saint Veronica. On the outside eight saints are depicted].

Every time the nuns entered the church or walked through the cloisters Katherine's status as bride of Christ reminded them of their own such status and of the daily duty of dedicated, self-abnegating virtue it entailed, so that to negotiate convent space was to negotiate a space of memory, commemoration, contemplation, exhortation and promised reward. Thus the cloistered nuns conducted their daily lives and spiritual routines within a virtual reconstruction,[27] a three-dimensional staging of the saint's life and miracles that resonated with the textual versions of her legend (read to them at meals; poured over by them in private meditation; spoken by them in prayer; memorized by them in condensed form; recited by them like the beads of prayer on the rosary when moving through the convent) and spun the text into the web of a convent community

---

[25] 'a complex systems of relationships, a mixing of the material substance of architecture with objects from everyday life' (Meyer, *Stadt und Architektur*, p. 7).

[26] Murr, *Merkwürdigkeiten*, pp. 294–5.

[27] 'Living the Dream' discusses the episodes from Katherine's life highlighted on the Fütterer Altar: her vision of the Virgin and Christ Child; the debate with the 50 heathen philosophers; Faustina and Porphyrius visiting her in jail; the burning of the philosophers; the shattering of the wheel; the execution; and the entombment. Judging by the visual evidence, for the Katharinenkloster, at least, the key elements of the saint's legend were the mystic marriage; Katherine's education (expressed in the debate with the philosophers); and her martyrdom. The beauty mentioned in her condensed *vita* would have been illustrated in depictions of her.

founded on dedication to Saint Katherine.[28] To walk through the convent was to walk through the saint's life, proselytizing and martyrdom; combined with the recitation of extracts from her legend or the personal dialogue represented by prayer, movement through this particular map of spirituality could become an act of conscious meditation on the saint in the all-encompassing presence of the saint. Any communal absorption of text may have affected individual visualization of events from the narrative and served to bond the convent community by training nuns in shared devotional-contemplative practices. As Carola Jäggi puts it:

> Wann, wo, in welcher Art und zu welchem Zweck, bzw. mit welchem Ziel traten die Nonnen mit den jeweiligen Kunstwerken in Kontakt? Gab es bestimmte Zeiten innerhalb des Klosteralltags (Messe, Chorgebet, 'Meditation' bzw. Privatgebet), in denen solche 'Kontaktnahmen' besonders häufig waren? Hatten Bildwerke einen festen Platz in kollektiven Betrachtungsübungen oder spielten sie lediglich in der privaten Frömmigkeit der einzelnen Schwestern eine Rolle?[29]

> [When, where, how and to what purpose or to what end did the nuns come into contact with the respective works of art? Were there set times during the daily routine of the convent (mass; prayer in the choir; 'meditation' or private prayer) at which such contact was particularly frequent? Did works of art occupy a fixed place in collective contemplational exercises or did they merely play a part in the private piety of individual sisters?]

Communally practised modes of visualization and devotion based on images physically present in the daily routine of convent life, cross-linked and combined

---

[28]   The "staging" echoes the performativity of many of the miracle stories and, of course, the plays performed about saints' lives such as the Thuringian *Katharinenspiel*.

[29]   Carola Jäggi, "'Sy bettet och gewonlich vor únser frowen bild ...'": Überlegungen zur Funktion von Kunstwerken in spätmittelalterlichen Frauenklöstern', in Jean-Claude Schmitt (ed.), *Femmes, art et religion au Moyen Âge* (Strasbourg: Presses Universitaires de Strasbourg, 2004), pp. 62–86 (p. 64). She further argues that the Schwesternbücher from Dominican convents: 'lassen ... den Schluss zu, dass Bildwerke in den betreffenden Konventen keineswegs ausschliesslich dazu dienten, einen Heilsinhalt darzustellen und die Betrachterin zu dessen Nachvollzug anzuregen, sondern oft genau jene Rolle spielten, die der Kirche stets suspekt war: die Rolle als Stellvertreter, als Repräsentanten ("imagines") der dargestellten *persona*' [allow the conclusion that works of art in the respective convents were by no means exclusively intended to present a salvational content and encourage the observer to emulate it. On the contrary, they often performed the role which the Church had always viewed with suspicion: namely, the role of substitutes, of representatives ("imagines") of the *persona* depicted] (p. 64).

in multiple and varying ways, shaped nuns' private prayer and meditation in their own cells,[30] where they may have focussed on an image in front of them or imagined themselves, either alone or as part of the community, praying at a given altar and, if suitably prepared and penitent, granted a vision of Christ.[31] Discussing the function of images in the religious practice of late-medieval nuns, Elisabeth Vavra remarks:

> Bilder können ähnlich wie Texte zur Meditation eingesetzt werden. Allgemein wird anerkannt, dass für die Laienunterweisung, für die Unterweisung der Nonnen und Konversen das Heranziehen bildlicher Darstellungen notwendig ist … Bilder in jeglicher Form erleichtern das verlangte Miterleben und Miterleiden, das schliesslich bis zur Imitatio der heiligen Person führen kann, einer Imitatio, die so weit gehen kann, dass Schwestern Anzeichen der Schwangerschaft an sich fühlen oder in Visionen das ihnen erscheinende Christuskind säugen.[32]

---

[30]   The Germanisches Nationalmuseum houses a picture of a seated Franciscan nun, chin in one hand, lost in contemplation of a book she has just been reading. It is one of a series of four depicting everyday convent life (the other three show nuns weaving, reading and sleeping). Hanging on the wall behind the nun is a piece of paper with the word "Betrachterin" (contemplator) written on it. This confirms that private meditation, based on reading, formed an integral part of a nun's daily routine (*Spiegel der Seligkeit*, pp. 167–9).

[31]   Writing about the use of woodcuts as instruments of private devotion in convents, Peter Schmidt observes: 'Doch war die Eindämmung der *vita privata*, zu der offiziell auch der Besitz von Bildern gehörte, Bestandteil aller monastischen Reformprogramme, auch der dominikanischen des 14. und 15. Jahrhunderts. Private Bilderverehrung abseits der Kontrolle der Klostergemeinschaft wurde von Johannes Meyer, dem Reformchronisten des Domminkanerordens, kritisch gesehen. Doch der grundlegenden Reserviertheit der reformorientierten Ordensführungen steht häufig eine bilderfreundliche Praxis gegenüber – vor allem in den Frauenklöstern und im Zusammenhang mit der *cura monialium*' [yet the restriction of one's *vita privata*, which included the ownership of pictures, was a component of all monastic reform programmes, including that of the Dominicans in the fourteenth and fifteenth centuries. Johannes Meyer, the chronicler of reform in the Dominican Order, took a very critical view of the private worship of pictures uncontrolled by the convent community. Yet the fundamental reservations on the part of the reform-orientated leadership often goes hand in hand with an actual devotional practice that viewed images benevolently – above all in women's foundations and in connexion with the *cura monialium*] (Schmidt, 'Die Rolle der Bilder in der Kommunikation', p. 50.

[32]   Vavra, 'Bildmotiv', p. 221. Hamburger confirms the primacy of sight as a trigger for the participation in devotion of the entire body: 'Mittelalterliche Andacht ergriff den ganzen Menschen, nicht nur Geist, Emotionen oder Phantasie, sondern auch den Körper. Der Vorgang der Andacht wandte sich an alle Sinne, körperliche und geistige, durch Sprache, Sicht und Gestus. Andachtsbilder wurden oft als der Anfangspunkt für eine imaginäre Flucht aus dem Körper interpretiert. Mehr und mehr führte dieser Vorgang zu einem Eintauchen in die Sinne' [Medieval devotion seized hold of the whole person, not just the spirit, emotions

[Pictures could be used for meditation in much the same way as texts. It is generally recognized that the employment of visual representations was necessary in the instruction of lay people as well as of nuns and lay sisters ... Pictures of all kinds facilitate the required imaginative experiencing and empathy that can ultimately lead to the *imitatio* of the holy person, an *imitatio* that can be taken to such lengths that sisters experienced symptoms of pregnancy in their own bodies or give suck to the Christ Child who appears to them in visions].

Meditation, fused with collective devotion and private prayer, may have moulded the psyche of individual nuns by infusing them routinely with an exemplary sanctity contained and focussed inwards by the convent walls[33] and imbued with a sense of that particular sacred and, indeed, civic space as the convent was, in turn, encircled and contained by the city fortifications, singled out in Hartmann Schedel's *Weltchronik* (1493) as a key marker of Nuremberg's identity:[34]

Sunder sie [the city] ist zu de*n* zeitte*n* Karls des vierden *römischen keysers vnd konigs zu Beheym mit weiterm vmbkrais eingefangen vn*d* mit newen zinne*n* vn*d* mit eim weytte*n* vn*d* tieffe*n* geri*n*gs vmb die stat gefürte*n* grabe*n*. vn*d* mit. iij^c.lxv.

---

or imagination but also the body. The process of devotion addressed all the senses, physical and mental, through language, sight and gesture. Devotional images were often interpreted as the starting point for the worshipper, in his imagination, to take flight out of his body. This process increasingly led to an immersion in the senses] (Hamburger, 'Am Anfang war das Bild', pp. 21–2).

[33]   As Seegets remarks in relation to the Katharinenkloster and Klarissenkloster in Nuremberg: 'Auch wenn die zum Buchbestand der Gemeinschaften gehörende Literatur größtenteils nicht durch die Nonnen selbst verfaßt, sondern lediglich durch sie kopiert wurde, so daß wir sie nicht als zu Papier gebrachte Gedanken und Überzeugungen einzelner Schwestern, nicht als vox ipsissima der Klosterfrauen werten können, ist ihre Prägekraft nicht zu unterschätzen: Da Auswahl und Zusammenstellung der Texte in der Regel zielgerichtet erfolgte und viele Bände in der privaten oder gemeinschaftlichen Lektüre Verwendung fanden, sind sie als Ankerpunkte der klösterlich-theologischen Tradition der einzelnen Konvente zu betrachten' [Even if the majority of the literature that formed part of the book holdings of convent communities had not been composed by the nuns themselves but merely copied by them, so cannot be evaluated as the recorded thoughts and convictions of individual sisters, not as the *vox ipsissima* of the nuns, nevertheless, their power to shape should not be underestimated. Because the choice and compilation of texts was as a rule undertaken with a particular purpose in mind and because many volumes were used either for private or communal reading, they must be regarded as the anchor for the monastic-theological tradition of individual convents] (Seegets, 'Leben und Streben', p. 29). In 1458 the Katharinenkloster nuns were allowed to raise the height of their garden wall, *Nürnberger Ratsverlässe*, vol. 2, p. 21.

[34]   The convent was enclosed within the extended city walls in 1379.

thürne*n*. ergkern*n* vn*d* vorwern and de*n* zwaye*n* innern mawrn gemeret vn*d* mit
fast weite*n* vn*d* feste*n* inwonu*n*ge*n* gezieret.[35]

[However, it was encircled by extensive fortifications during the reign of the
Holy Roman Emperor and King of Bohemia Karl IV; new battlements were
erected; a broad, deep moat was dug right round the city; and the fortifications
were strengthened by 365 towers, protruding spy windows, bulwarks and the two
inner ring walls that contain spacious, secure living quarters].

In a further step, a nun could have relocated herself to an earlier stage in the
history of salvation, inserted herself into Saint Katherine's 'body-ego space' and
re-lived the saint's life as if she were the saint, becoming a miniature version
or mirror image of Katherine similar to those encountered in the miracle
stories. Through intense meditation and spiritual re-enactment, text, image
and individual may have fused into a new entity as close to a "reincarnation"
of the saint as was possible within the urban web of Nuremberg. As we have
seen, after the reform of 1428 nuns from the Katharinenkloster were dispatched
to reform Dominican convents in other towns, so like the divine light encountered
so frequently in the miracle stories or illuminating the Lorenzkirche through the
Volckamer window, the learned piety of the Katharinenkloster radiated outwards,
transforming communities further afield.

The narrative then constructs the second stage in the spinning of the saint's
web beyond the convent by cementing her exemplarity through further iteration
of her attributes: her chastity; beauty; charity; wisdom; eloquence; successful
proselytizing; and a God-given faith so profound that she freely and willingly
embraces martyrdom for His sake.[36] Thus her divinely acknowledged virtue
constructs the edifice that generates its own reproduction: namely, her cult and
its manifestations. Whilst the reader in already-Christian Nuremberg – heart
of the Holy Roman Empire and home to the imperial relics that testify to the
truth of Christ's sacrifice[37] – might have been denied the opportunity to emulate
Katherine in every respect, he might still emulate the saint's chastity, charity,
learning and faith, benefitting both himself and his community in the same way
as the oil flowing from the saint's bones benefitted her followers through her
grace. We return to the 'body … traced with the values of culture: the contours of

[35]   Hartmann Schedel, *Weltchronik*, fol. CIʳ. For a lengthy description of the
fortifications see also Conrad Celtis, *Norimberga*, trans. and ed. Gerhard Fink (Nuremberg:
Nürnberger Presse, 2000), pp. 32–4.
[36]   *Der Heiligen Leben*, fol. cclxʳ.
[37]   The relics also testify to the success of early martyrs like Katherine in spreading
Christianity, without which they would not have been preserved.

the body' as 'the contours of society': Saint Katherine's body – as physical entity and as text – traces the values of Christianity but is also inscribed with those of the city viewed by contemporaries as the political and economic centre of the Christian Empire; a city which deposits in her its piety, its zeal for learning, its political ambition, its pursuit of wealth and its striving for prestige in expectation of economic and spiritual return.

In a third narrative stage, Katherine is located within the wider community of saints, a holy body mirrored by Nuremberg Patricians, who named their children after saints, celebrated their feast days and were welded through intermarriage and shared mercantile interests into a privileged, pious elite. The situating of Katherine onto the cosmic stage takes the form of a reward: 'het ir vnser lieber herr Jhesus Christus zwelff grosse mynnezeychen vnd edler mynnreicher gaben erzeyget da mit er ander heyligen zwelf begabet hat'.[38] Her exemplarity, then, is further showcased by her sole reception of all 12 signs of love bestowed singly by Christ on other saints, a gift, reminiscent of a wedding present, that renders Katherine more potent an intercessor than other members of the divine assembly.[39] Katherine's tangible physical body becomes, in her legend, the locus of intangible divine grace. Twelve is, of course, symbolic as the number of Christ's Disciples (three of whom Katherine out-trumps in the favoured-martyr stakes); but also suggests that the follower of Saint Katherine receives more for his money in a divine dozen-for-the-price-of-one devotional deal. In profit-orientated Nuremberg, reliant on the spice trade with Alexandria for a large part of its wealth, privileging the cult of Saint Katherine was prudent in the secular as well as the salvatory economy, since she "represented" the city in Egypt, protecting its business interests in a hostile, precarious religious and commercial environment.[40] Thus enumerating the signs

---

[38]   'Our dear Lord Jesus Christ bestowed on her all twelve great signs of His love and noble, loving gifts that He bestowed individually on twelve other saints' (fol. cclx[r]).

[39]   Eis comments: 'Sie [the gifts] haben nur insofern eine Bedeutung für den Wunderanhang als sie zeigen, daß man sich dies Vorkommen gleicher Motive in verschiedenen Legenden durchaus bewußt war und darin keineswegs einen Mangel (etwa Phantasiearmut), sondern eher einen Vorzug (nämlich den der wechselseitigen Beglaubigung) erblickte' [They [the gifts] are significant for the appendix containing the miracle stories only in as much as they demonstrate a clear awareness of the repetition of the same motifs in different legends, a practice which was seen not as a failing (such as lack of imagination) but rather as an advantage (namely, mutual confirmation)] (Eis, 'Lupold von Wiltingen', p. 79).

[40]   Tucher describes being stabbed in the neck with a bread knife and imprisoned; also how European merchants were thrown into jail by Mameluke authories and released only if they purchased pepper from the sultan at vastly inflated prices (Tucher, 'Reise', pp. 579–82 and 596–8). Family connexions and the forging of advantageous business partnerships through marriage alliances was also important, so for shrewd, status-conscious Patricians Saint Katherine's lineage and family ties, as clearly displayed in the Volckamer window, may have been a factor in her

of Christ's love serves three purposes. First, it places Katherine at the top of the spiritual hierarchy, favoured by her bridegroom and hence firmly enmeshed in the heavenly family – as, indeed, she is showcased in the Volckamer window.[41] Second, it locates her in spiritual geography, namely, at the centre of a net of sanctity that originated in Cyprus, transferred to Alexandria, spread across Heaven and thence stretches out to encompass earth. On earth iconographic links to other saints with whom she is portrayed anchor her in this net devotionally and physically, since the association with Saint Katherine may reverberate, say, in prayers to other recipients of God's special favour such as Saints Peter, Stephen and Margaret; prayers said in the convent, the home, or in front of an altar such as Saint Peter's Altar in the Sebalduskirche or Saint Veit's Altar in the Augustinerkirche, which depicts Katherine with Saints Margaret and George, both recipients of a 'mynnezeychen' from Christ.[42] Third, it recalls the saying of the rosary, a cult promoted by the Dominicans and introduced into Nuremberg by the Katharinenkloster nuns in 1490.[43] Hence this enumeration may serve as another mnemonic device and meditational focus for subsequent readers, anchoring the rosary itself into a landscape of familiar devotional practice. The device of weaving shadow-Katherines into the text is here reversed, as the narrative culminates in Saint Katherine as the potentized version of some of the most powerful saints in the Christian pantheon. However, since Christ's gifts are explicitly linked to the progression of Katherine's *passio*, they subliminally reinforce her status as a shadow-Christ by staging a

---

popularity: as Christ's bride she was, in secular terms, the daughter-in-law of the Virgin and of God Himself.

[41]   She is firmly enmeshed in secular families, too, as the name "Katharina" (in various spellings) was very popular amongst the Patricians, especially the Löffelholz, the Volckamer, the Tucher and the Imhoff.

[42]   The altar (1487), also depicts other *Vierzehn Heiligen*, namely Saint Vitus (or Veit) himself, Saint Christopher and Saint Sebastian. Attributed to the workshop of Hans Traut, it is now in the Germanisches Nationalmuseum. See also Strieder, *Tafelmalerei*, pp. 87–90 and pp. 221–7.

[43]   *Hall's Dictionary*, pp. 333–4; Grote, *Die Tucher*, p. 70; and Ochsenbein, 'Handschrift und Druck'. An altar dedicated to the rosary (*Rosenkranzaltar*) (c. 1490–5) by Michael Wolgemut stood in the Dominikanerkirche until well into the eighteenth century. Two side panels are now in the Lorenzkirche; the *Maria im Rosenkranz* from the central panel is now in the Germanisches Nationalmuseum (*Nürnberg 1350–1550*, pp. 166–7). The Hayd-Paumgartner Epitaph (1502) in the Lorenzkirche depicts Patriarchs, prophets, martyrs and other saints surrounded by a rosary, amongst them Saint Helena and some of the *Vierzehn Heiligen* (George, Sebastian, Nicholas, Christopher, Barbara and Katherine) (Gerhardt Weilandt, *Die Sebalduskirche in Nürnberg. Bild und Gesellschaft im Zeitalter der Gotik und Renaissance* (Petersberg: Michael Imhof, 2007), p. 138).

narrative mirroring of the Stations of the Cross.[44] Imaginatively or physically – by designating as the sites of Saint Katherine's martyrdom objects within the convent or home or buildings within Nuremberg – the reader could progress from one Station to the next, pausing at and meditating on each one, mapping Katherine's desires onto his/her own body by empathetically imagining him/herself as the saint and living her suffering on him/herself. In this way the reader, whether a travelled merchant or a cloistered nun, could become both a location of Saint Katherine's martyrdom and a secondary recipient of Christ's gifts.

The first of Christ's "mynnezeychen" aligns Katherine with Saint John the Evangelist:

> Des ersten list man von sant Johans dem zwelffboten / das vnser her czu im kam ee er starb mit seynen Jungern vnd sucht yn heim / also kam er auch zu sant Katherinen in den kerker mit eyner grossen schar der Engel / vnd der iunckfrawen vnd sprach Tochter erkenn deynen schopfer durch des willen du die marter leydest / vnnd byst vastmuttig wann ich wil mit dir sein die gnad geschach ir von der grossen sunderlichen lieb die sy czu gott hett / da vonn sucht er sye heym von sundern genaden wegen. (fol. cclxʳ⁻ᵛ)

> [The first [sign] one reads about is that shown to Saint John the Apostle. Our Lord came to him with His Apostles before he died and visited him. In the same way He visited Saint Katherine in jail with a great host of angels and virgins and said, 'Daughter, know your Creator on whose account you suffered martyrdom and be steadfast for I shall be with you'. This grace was bestowed on her because of the great and special love she had for God. For this reason He visited her and bestowed singular grace upon her].

As John was the most beloved of Christ's disciples, so Katherine is the most beloved of His saints, vehicle for God's grace and transmitter of His Word in the post-Crucifixion world. This gift replays in condensed form two scenes from Katherine's *vita*: the angels' visiting her in jail and Christ's ministering of the sacrament to her during her incarceration, itself a reminder of His own imprisonment prior to His martyrdom on the Cross. Thus this first sign fuses Christ, John and Katherine into an alternative Trinity who comfort those unjustly imprisoned and functions as a spiritual incentive by demonstrating God's reward of unswerving commitment. The next sign of love is His sending of a white dove to feed Katherine for 12 days and nights during her imprisonment,

---

44   Initially there were seven Stations of the Cross; the number later rose to and remained at 14. Although there are only 12 stages to Katherine's martyrdom, the analogy is valid.

just as He had fed Mary Magdalene for more than 30 years in a cave.[45] The comparison to Mary Magdalene does not mark Saint Katherine as a prostitute; rather, it highlights both her rejection of worldly love for the love of Christ and the denial of her body, and sexuality, through fasting. The white dove embodies His grace and reminds the reader of potential redemption through the sustenance of the mass. Saint Katherine is next compared to Saint Blasius and other saints to whom God promised the granting of any request made to them in His name:

> Daz gelobt er auch Sant Katherin an yrem end / wer si anruffet vnd eret / in welchen notten der mensch wer / so wolt er yn erhoren vnnd sprach czu yr Kum her meyn ausserwelte waz du gebeten hast das solt du gewerrt seyn Dye genad het sy von ir grossen heilikeit / wan erhorung des gebetes ist eyn czeichen eynes heyligen lebens. (fol. cclx^v)

> [He also promised to Saint Katherine at her death that whoever calls upon her and honours her, in whatever dire distress that person finds himself, He would heed their call. He said to Saint Katherine, 'Come here, my chosen one. What you have prayed for will be granted you'. This grace was a result of her great sanctity, for the heeding of prayer is a sign of a holy life].

As Saint Blasius was one of the *Vierzehn Heiligen*, reference to him again foregrounds the regional cult, like the Konhofer window and the Memminger Altar anchoring Katherine and the other saints in Franconia and explicitly stressing the ready availability of their help to a worshipper in Nuremberg and the surrounding region. The Katharinenkirche may have contained a *Nothelferaltar* (dedicated to the *Vierzehn Heiligen*), so the cult was represented at the heart of the convent as well as the civic community.[46] Moreover, the same worshipper is encouraged by the highlighted efficacy of prayer to lead a model prayerful life himself. Saint Katherine as exemplary martyr is the message of the fourth sign of love, as Saint Stephen, to whom she is now compared, was the first Christian martyr.[47] Just before his death by stoning Christ granted him a vision of Heaven standing open; in the same way Katherine, immediately prior to her

---

[45]   According to Provençal legend Mary Magdalene lived in a cave near Sainte-Baume for 30 years, fasting and doing penance; seven times a day she was lifted to Heaven by angels and allowed a glimpse of the bliss that awaited her (*Hall's Dictionary*, p. 203).

[46]   Fries mentions the Königschlager Epitaph from c. 1505 that depicts Saints Katherine and Blasius with Maria, Barbara and a pilgrim, possibly Saint Sebaldus (Fries, 'Kloster und Kirche', 112).

[47]   Saint Stephen is also allied with Katherine in the Konhofer window.

execution, hears a voice saying, 'Kum her du ausserwelter gemahel des hymels tur ist dyr offen' (fol. cclx[v]).[48] However, Katherine exceeds Stephen in that a soundtrack accompanies her vision, aligning her by implication with Saint Paul, who was blinded by light from Heaven and heard Christ's voice.[49] Auditory as well as visual signals of divine grace within the text model and legitimize such phenomena outside the text, providing readers/listeners with a safe narrative structure for their own potential visionary aspirations or experience. Katherine's transcendence of Saint Margaret, another of the *Vierzehn Heiligen*, is the next sign of Christ's love: during the latter's martyrdom God sent a host of angels; similarly, He sends the Archangel Michael to Saint Katherine to comfort her in jail. In fact, Katherine enjoys three angelic visitations: to foretell the conversion of philosophers; to salve her wounds; and to break the wheel. Angels are virgins by nature, hence as the outward manifestation of her intactness their visit foregrounds the saint's own 'edle reinikeit';[50] their role as messengers suggests her communication with God in the cause of those for whom she intercedes. Christ's sixth sign of His love for Katherine are the milk and blood that flow from her neck on her martyrdom since they further align her with Saints Paul and Peter, the latter the founder of the Christian Church and another saint who was scourged, imprisoned and eventually beheaded (Acts 16:25–34). Furthermore, Paul is sometimes depicted with three jets of blood (symbolic of Faith, Hope and Charity) spurting from his severed head.[51] In both Paul and Katherine the literal – and miraculous – flow of milk and blood is transformed, like Christ's body and blood during the mass, into the flow of their exemplarity from the site of their martyrdom through text (Paul's *Epistles*, oral transmission and later *Der Heiligen Leben*) into the world around them, where this textual witness to God's power and mercy exercises a similarly transformative effect by baptizing converts to Christianity. In addition, as seen in Chapter 2, the nun's taking of vows on entering the convent was regarded as a second baptism that placed her into a sin-free state.[52] The flow of Saint Katherine's blood draws a symbolic parallel between the cleansing of the nun's sins through the profession that allows her access to the convent community and the cleansing of Katherine's sins through the bloody baptism that allows her access to the community of saints. As in

---

48   'Come here, you chosen bride, the door of Heaven stands open to you'.

49   'And as he journeyed, he came near Damascus : and suddenly there shined round about him a light from heaven : And he fell to the earth, and heard a voice saying unto him, Saul, Saul, why persecutest thou me?' (Acts 9:4–5). Paul enjoyed a second, ecstatic, vision reminiscent of Saint John's (II Corinthians 12:1–3).

50   'noble purity' (*Der Heiligen Leben*, fol. cclx[v])

51   *Hall's Dictionary*, p. 237.

52   Steinke, *Paradisgarten*, pp. 129–32.

Katherine's actual *passio*, blood and milk become metaphors for the function of *Der Heiligen Leben*; and her status is validated through association with a key foundation stone of the early Church. Moreover, she is thus singled out because of the 'lauterkeyt irß herczen / wann sye het sich gebaschenn in dem blutt vnsers herrenn Jesu Cristi myt rechtter andacht' (fol. cclx[v]).[53] Katherine models the exemplary 'visualizing meditation' as her own devotion has resulted in her being cleansed by Christ's blood in a metaphorical baptism through His martyrdom.[54]

In an analogy to the other cornerstone of early Christianity, Peter, who on his death was granted a vision of light[55] and the ascension in that light of his soul to eternal bliss, Katherine, when in jail, is surrounded by great radiance, reward for the strength of her faith and the seventh sign of Christ's love. Sight of this radiance converts Faustina and Porphyrius, enabling their martyrdom and eternal bliss, so Katherine's sanctity literally and metaphorically illuminates others, leading them from the darkness of pagan sin to the light of eternal life. Eighth, God compares her to Saint George, another of the *Vierzehn Heiligen*, whose martyr's wheel was also broken in answer to his prayers. Saint George symbolizes 'the victory of the Christian faith',[56] a victory lived out by Katherine in her vanquishing of the wheel and the miracles following her martyrdom.[57] She receives this grace thanks to her great patience throughout her martyrdom. The stages of Katherine's *passio* are thus explicitly linked to exemplary Christian virtues, as she owes the ninth sign of Christ's love, the similarity to Saint Clement in the angelic burial, to her humility. Clement, an early pope (end of the first century AD), was banished to work in marble quarries in the Crimea as punishment for refusing to give up his faith, then martyred by having an anchor

---

[53]   'purity of her heart for she had bathed herself in the blood of Our Lord Jesus Christ with true devotion'.

[54]   It may also be a literal baptism as it recalls the scene from Katherine's *passio* in which she is bound to a pillar and so severely whipped that her blood flows, a obvious allusion to the Flagellation of Christ: 'Da ward der keiser zornig vnd sye ab czehen vnd ward ann ein sewl gebunden vnd schlug si ser mit gerten vnd mit geyseln das das blut von ir floß' [Then the Emperor became angry and ordered her to be taken away and she was bound to a pillar and whipped so hard with rods and with whips that her blood flowed] (*Der Heiligen Leben*, fol. ccliij[r]).

[55]   On his way from Rome Peter also experienced a vision of Christ that prompted him to return to Rome to experience martyrdom (*Hall's Dictionary*, p. 243). Peter 'led the apostles in the teaching of the gospel' so his function as teacher and converter matches Katherine's (*Hall's Dictionary*, p. 239).

[56]   *Hall's Dictionary*, p. 137.

[57]   The wheel is a symbol of infinity, so the monstrous, knife-edged wheel of Katherine's legend may symbolize the eternal cycle of evil and persecution over which she triumphs through her eternal life as bride of Christ and object of devotion.

(symbol of steadfastness and hope) tied round his neck and being thrown into the sea.[58] Love, denial of the flesh, prayer, exemplary conduct, chastity, purity of heart, faith, patience, humility, steadfastness are subsequently joined by charity, since Katherine's sale of her paternal heritage and donation of alms to the poor earn her, as they did Saint Nicholas, the healing oil that flows from her grave, the tenth sign of Christ's love. The oil, then, symbolizes the effects of a charity that flows from its giver to aid those in need, itself a model for charitable provision in a city like Nuremberg, where the care of the poor, sick and elderly depended on the churches, monastic foundations and endowment by wealthy Patricians of alms-houses such as the Heilig-Geist-Spital (in whose church the imperial insignia and relics were kept from 1424 to 1796)[59] and the Zwölfbrüderhausstiftungen.[60]

The eleventh act of grace, contempt for worldly goods and honour, is illustrated by the comparison between Saint Katherine and another of the *Vierzehn Heiligen*, Saint Margaret, in which the legend of each is summarized:[61]

> Die eilfft gnad tet vnser her Sant Margreten daz sy schon vnd edel was / da von gewann der Richter groß lieb zu ir vnd gelobt ir vil eren vnd gutz / da tet ir gott dye genad das sy in ver schmacht vn*d* alles zeitlichs gut vnd ere durch die lyeben cristi Die gnad tet auch cristus seiner gemaheln sa*n*t Katherin / dye w*a*z noch vyl edler wann sye was eines edlen kunges tochter vnd was zu mal scho*n* vnd von der vberflussigen schon vnnd edle sye an ir was het der keiser grosse lieb czu ir vnd sprach czu ir Du solt dye aller nechst nach mir seyn / vn*d* gelobt ir vil gucz vnd eren / vn*d* wolt eyn bild nach ir machen lassen vnnd wer fur gieng der mußt im neigen vn*d* must es anbeten / Da tet ir vnser her die genad daz sy in verschmacht vnd alle die ere vnd gut die er ir gelobt het durch die lieb gottes / Die gnad het sy vo*n* ire*m* rechten leben. (fol. cclxj*ʳ*)

---

[58]   *Hall's Dictionary*, pp. 70–1.

[59]   Founded by Konrad Groß in 1339.

[60]   For elderly handworkers. Konrad Mendel founded one in 1388; Matthäus Landauer in 1510 (*Stadtlexikon*, p. 688 and p. 607).

[61]   Saint Margaret of Antioch was a very popular saint. According to her legend the Prefect of Antioch wanted to marry her. When she refused him on the grounds that she was a Christian virgin she was tortured and cast into prison, where Satan visited her in the form of a dragon and consumed her. The cross Margaret was holding made the dragon burst asunder and the saint emerged unharmed, eventually to be beheaded. She is the patron saint of women in childbirth and is frequently represented with the Virgin and Saint Katherine (*Hall's Dictionary*, p. 198).

[The eleventh sign of grace was bestowed by Our Lord on Saint Margaret, that she was beautiful and noble. For this reason the judge was seized by great love for her and promised her great worldly honour and wealth. Then God showed her His grace in causing her to despise the judge and all worldly possessions for love of Christ. Christ bestowed this grace on his spouse Saint Katherine, who was even nobler as she was a king's daughter and in addition was beautiful. Thanks to her extraordinary beauty and nobility the Emperor was seized by great love for her and said to her, 'You shall be second only to me in status'. He promised her great wealth and honour and wanted to have an image created in her likeness that anyone passing would have to bow to and worship. Then Our Lord showed her His grace by causing her to despise the Emperor and all the honour and wealth he had promised her for the love of God. She was given this grace because of her righteous life].

As throughout this section, mention of another saint serves only for a lengthier, consolidative exposition of Saint Katherine's own virtues, each extract from her legend serving as a self-contained *aide-mémoire* within a given context. Frequent repetition may in itself have constituted a form of meditation, here on the transitory nature of earthly goods symbolized by Maxentius' proposed image of Katherine and the promise of worldly wealth and honour. To worship Katherine as a beautiful king's daughter would have been to worship a false, because non-Christian, idol[62] and to render Katherine a parody of a saint, one elevated not by God but by His opposite. The proposed statue also acts as a metaphor for the choice between the right life and the wrong one, since Katherine's refusal to be deflected from the worship of Christ, or to deflect others by being cast as idol, results in her commemoration in the text of *Der Heiligen Leben* and images worshipped "legitimately" in Christian spaces. Finally, the twelfth sign of Christ's love for his bride transcends all others:

> Zu dem czwelfften mal tet vnser her Sant dyonisio dye genad da er in dem kerker lag vnnd meß dar in sprach vnd die oblat gesegnet het / da kam vnser her zu im vnd gab ym selber seinen fronleychnam vn*d* sprach bis fro wan dein lon ist gros bey myr / dye genad tet ir vnser her auch da er zu ir kam in den kerker an dem zwelfften tag Da gab er ir selber seinen zarten fronleichnam mit seinen gotlichen henden vnd seyn rosenfarbes blut das was eyn edle gab vnd eyn zeiche*n* der vberflussigen lieb dye er zu ir hat Dye genad hett sye vo*n* *der* haffnu*n*g dye sy zu got het. (fol. cclxj^r)

---

[62]   Much as the Israelites worshipped the golden calf (Exodus 32:4–5).

[The twelfth time Our Lord bestowed a sign of grace was on Saint Dionysius when he was imprisoned in jail and celebrating mass there. When he had blessed the host Our Lord came to him and gave him His body with His own hands and said, 'Rejoice, for you have great merit with me'. Our Lord showed the same grace to her [Katherine] when He also came to her in jail on the twelfth day and gave her His own tender body and His rose-red blood with His own hands. That was a noble gift and a sign of the abundant love He feels for her. She received this grace because of the hope she placed in God].

Here Saint Katherine is compared to the third-century patron saint of France, Saint Dionysius or Denis, another of the *Vierzehn Heiligen*.[63] Saint Dionysius, like Katherine, witnesses a host miracle, with the difference that he, as a male cleric, may, in an echo of the Mass of Saint Gregory, bless the host and quasi-initiate the miracle, whereas Katherine, as a woman, is its passive recipient. Notably, however, Katherine's experience is "talked up" by being described in greater detail, the colouring of Christ's blood forging an explicit link to her legend and reminder of the martyrdom theme running through both legend and miracle stories: 'vnd gab ir da seinen heyligen leichnam vnd sein roßenfarbeß blut mit seinen gotlichen henden / das was eyn edle gab / vnd was eyn czeychen der grossen lieb dy er zu yr hett' (fol. ccliijᵛ).[64] The mass as ritual remembrance of God's love for all mankind in the sacrifice of His only son is here transformed into an explicit sign of His love for this particular representative of it, Katherine's reward for her faith in Him. Trust in God and hope for mankind's redemption as promised by Christ's sacrifice are the final message from this section of the *Lobrede*.

In a fourth stage, the narrative circles back once more to the mystic marriage as the ultimate sign of God's love and grace and, together with the wheel, primary marker of Katherine's identity, advertised as such in the Volckamer window, Konhofer window and Katharinenkloster images. In a further echo of her legend, Christ's words to Katherine are recorded in direct speech, the dialogue

---

[63]   Saint Dionysius was sent with other bishops to convert Gaul in roughly 250 AD and was probably martyred in Paris by order of the Roman prefect (in another version by one of the local pagan chieftains). His body then rose and carried its severed head (his attribute) to his grave on Montmartre. His remains were later transferred to the site of the Abbey of Saint-Denis (*Hall's Dictionary*, p. 98; Edward and Lorna Mornin, *Saints. A Visual Guide* (Toronto: Novalis, 2006), p. 82). Dionysius is represented on the Memminger Altar in the Lorenzkirche.

[64]   'And gave her His holy body and His rose-red blood with His divine hands. That was a noble gift and was a sign of the great love He feels for her'. This extract describes Christ's ministering of the sacraments to Saint Katherine while she is in jail.

incorporating Christ into the narrative as a real, living, interactive presence rather than one accessible only through secondary signs such as the host:

> Da tet ir vnser her noch eyn grosser vberflussiges liebe zeichen vnd ein lieblich gab
> da er sy gemahelt vnd er ir eyn klar guldin vingerlin an iren gold vinger stiß mit
> seyner gotlichen hand vnd sprach zu ir O Katherina mein ausserwelte gemahel
> mytt dem vingerlin vermahel ich dich mir in eynem rechten cristenlichen
> gelauben das sal ein rechtes wares zeichen sein eyner steten ganczen lieb zwischen
> mir vnd dir hye vnd dort ewigklichen / daz solt du behalten bis an deinen tod /
> die gnad lyst man von keinem heyligen mer / aber darumb das sie der almechtig
> got sunderlichen lieb het fur alheyligen / so hatt er sy vermahelt im selbs mit
> einnem fruntlichen mahelsthacz [*sic*] / vnd erczeyget ir dye grossen lyeb dar an
> die er czu ir hett da von mocht sye furbaß weder lieb noch leyd noch der tod von
> got gescheyden. (fol. cclxj^r)

[Then Our Lord bestowed on her another great and abundant sign of His love and a loving gift when He took her as His bride and placed a radiant gold ring on her ring finger with His divine hand and said to her, 'O Katherine, my chosen spouse, with the ring I wed myself to you in the true Christian faith. This shall be a proper and true sign of a constant, perfect love between me and you in this life and the next for ever after. You should keep this until your death'. This grace is not to be found in the legend of any other saint, but because Almighty God loved her above all other saints He took her as His own bride with a loving dowry and thereby demonstrated the great love He felt for her. For this reason neither joy nor sorrow nor death can separate her from God].

Christ's speech to Katherine is recorded in much fuller detail than in the legend, which thus becomes the precursor of His commitment to her in the same way Old Testament prophets are the types of their New Testament realization.[65] The formulation of the marriage vow, core of Katherine's legend, may echo the vow

---

65   The legend runs: 'da erschein yr vnser Frau mit irem Sun in kunigklicher gezird vnd klarheyt / da sach sie ein antluczt gar klarlichen vnd recht minneklichen vnd redt mit yr von der gemahelschaft vnd gemahelt sich ir / vnd styeß ir ein kleines guldeins fingerlein ann vnd sprach / O mein liebe Katherina Ich wil mich dir in dem gelauben gemaheln da erwachet sy vnd fand daz fingerlein an der hand vnd bekant / daz alleß das war waz daz sie in dem schlaff gesehen hett' [Then Our Lady and her Son appeared to her dressed royally and radiant. Then she saw a radiant, truly lovely face and He spoke to her of marriage and took her as His bride and placed a small gold ring on her finger and said, 'O my dear Katherine, I wish to take you as my bride in the faith'. Then she awoke and found the ring on her finger and realized that everything she had seen in her sleep was true] (*Der Heiligen Leben*, fol. cclij^v).

made by nuns on taking the veil. Whether religious or lay, a reader could, in his mind's eye, 'occupy' the 'body-ego space' of Saint Katherine and enter into spiritual wedlock with God, becoming a shadow-Katherine, even a Katherine "relic", the thing-left-over in late-fifteenth-century Nuremberg by the impact of her legend and its textual embodiment. The circling of the narrative back to the mystic marriage echoes the ring placed on her finger by Christ, the circle of gold a symbol for their mutual loyalty and the eternity of their union.[66] It is the most prominent sign of their "special relationship", being associated with no other saint: Agnes also claimed to be a bride of Christ but normally a ring is neither mentioned nor associated with her; she is usually shown with her attribute the lamb.[67] Text, then, itself becomes 'eyn klar guldin vingerlin';[68] and by memorizing it the reader/listener can wear the ring imaginatively and spiritually as a sign of his/her inseparability from God.[69] In this way the cult of Saint Katherine lasts for the whole of human history, to be subsumed into the a-temporal truth of eschatological fulfilment after Judgement Day.

The account of Saint Katherine's life and miracles concludes with the emphasis on her primacy as recipient of God's grace and as intercessor with Him: 'so tut er [God] ir dort noch tausent stund mer genaden in den ewigen freuden ymmer ewiklichen an end Darumb sullen wir keinen zweyfel habenn sy vermag nach vnser frawenn mer bey got dan kein heilig / wann sy hat mer dyner vnd dynerin wan kein heilig' (fol. cclxjʳ).[70] This rallying call to the troops reassures the reader by binding him into an immeasurable community of devotees on earth, strengthening both his faith and his readiness to support the saint's cult through

---

[66]   Gussone describes the role of the ring in the consecration of a nun, one that aligns her with Saint Katherine: 'Als erstes wird ein Ring übergeben mit der Formel: "Empfange den Ring der Treue, das Zeichen des Heiligen Geistes, damit Du Braut Gottes genannt wirst, wenn du ihm treu dienst"' [First she is handed a ring with the ritual formula, 'Receive this ring of fidelity, the sign of the Holy Ghost, so that you may be called a bride of Christ if you serve Him faithfully'] (Gussone, 'Die Jungfrauenweihe', p. 34).

[67]   However, the Germanisches Nationalmuseum does contain a Mystic Marriage of Saint Agnes (Gm 1634) by the Master of the Bartholomew Altarpiece, who was active in Utrecht and Cologne between 1475 and 1510. It closely resembles depictions of the Mystic Marriage of Saint Katherine, only the saint is here identified as Agnes by her lamb.

[68]   'a radiant gold ring'.

[69]   In a further closing of the circle the texts harks back to the qualities endowed on Katherine by God, 'daz ir geleich in der welt an schone / an adel / an richtumb nie ward' [that the world had never seen her like for beauty, nobility and wealth], qualities which she in turn looks for in a bridegroom.

[70]   'Thus He bestows on her there a thousand times more grace in eternal bliss, ever eternal without end. For that reason we should not doubt that after Our Lady she is able to petition God more successfully than any other saint for she has more servants than any other saint'.

financial or artistic endowment within Nuremberg. Then the text reminds him once more of Katherine's loyalty to her followers as one of the *Vierzehn Heiligen*: 'Sie ist wol lieb zu habe*n* vn*d* yr ist gut zy dynen / wan an zweyfel sie gibt wyder gelt vnd let keynen dienst verloren er sey gros od*er* klein ... vnd ist ein genedige fursprecheri*n* vor got allen den menschen die sy anruffen vn*d* eren' (fol. cclxj^r).[71] Through devotion to Saint Katherine the reader is bound into and protected by the larger heavenly community of God and all His saints.

Finally, this section of *Der Heiligen Leben* ends on a prayer which fuses Saint Katherine with the Trinity:

> Nun helff vns dye heylig iunckfraw Sant Katherin vmb got vnsern herren Jhesum Christu*m* iren lyeben gemaheln erwerben durch all ir wirdikeyt dye sye ewiglich mit ym hat / d*az* wir hye menschen werden nach gottes lob / vnnd vnsers lebens eyn gucz end vnd dar nach das ewig lebe*n* / das helf vns got der vater vnd gott der sun vn*d* got der heylig geyst Amen. (fol. cclxj^r)

> [Now, for the sake of God, Our Lord Jesus Christ, her dear spouse, may the holy virgin Saint Katherine help us, through all the worthiness she eternally enjoys in His eyes, to become people worthy of God's praise in this world and to die a good death and enjoy eternal life thereafter. May God the Father and God the Son and God the Holy Ghost aid us in this. Amen].

The prayer reads like a summarizing guide through the physical-devotional web of Katharinenkloster life. Easily memorized, it could also be transported by the lay reader when he moved into the wider civic community, mapping Saint Katherine onto the physical city and informing his interaction with fellow citizens. Thus the imaginative reconstruction of Saint Katherine's life and miracles that took place within the enclosed community of the convent and within the walled community of Nuremberg turned convent and city into a Petri dish for the breeding of appropriately contained and pious women (and appropriately pious and loyal citizens). Whilst these women were to a certain extent removed from the mercantile and marital economy of the city,[72] they

---

[71] 'She deserves to be loved and it is good to serve her for without a doubt she rewards service and lets no act of service be in vain, whether it be great or small ... And she intercedes graciously with God on behalf of all the people who call on her and honour her'. We have discussed these factors in Chapter 4 in connexion with the Volckamer and Konhofer windows and Memminger Altar. The explicit favouring of Saint Katherine would, of course, appeal particularly to a Dominican readership such as the convent.

[72] The convent received income from Patrician families for the celebration of commemorative masses and livings for priests; it also owned mills and land and enjoyed

participated actively in its spiritual economy in a number of ways: first, the enclosed and enclosing meditation on Saint Katherine focussed rays of devotion in the convent like a lens focusses rays of light onto tinder which then bursts into flame. Second, the light and fire generated by the convent's piety radiated out from the convent, flowing through prayer, letters, manuscripts copied for individuals and monastic foundations, as well as through *Der Heiligen Leben* itself, to illuminate and ignite the entire city and its extra-mural territories with love for Saint Katherine. This channelled illumination brought the convent into the external space that was the city but also the city into the convent in the form of *Totenschilder*, epitaphs, endowments (altars, windows, masses, land) and the Patricians buried in its church.[73] The interaction between convent

---

income from tithes (Müllner, *Annalen*, vol. 1, pp. 270–3). Moreover, as letters written by the Birgittine nun Katerina Lemmel show, Patrician nuns still controlled considerable sums of money invested outside their convents, so were actively present in the financial economy of Nuremberg (see Schleif and Schier, *Katerina's Windows*).

[73]   Those recorded by Biedermann include, for example, many members of the Behaim family: Albrecht (d. 1207), buried in the Lorenzkirche; *Totenschild* [death shield] in the Katharinenkirche; Friederich Behaim, d. 1295, buried in the Katharinenkirche, 'allwo er sein Totenschild, wie auch das Gedächtniß in einem Fenster zu St. Sebald hat' [although he has his death shield and an epitaph in a window in the Sebalduskirche]; Albrecht V Behaim, d. 1342, buried in the Katharinenkirche; Albrecht VI Behaim, d. 1359, buried in the Katharinenkirche and *Totenschild* there; Agnes Behaim, d. 1344, wife of Michael Pfintzing, buried in the choir of the Katharinenkirche; Berthold Behaim, 'Pfleger zu St. Catharinen' [*custos* at Saint Katherine's], d. 7.4.1405, 'liegt bey St. Catharinen' [lies in Saint Katherine's] and has his *Totenschild* there; Albrecht VIII Behaim, buried in the Katharinenkirche; Friederich II Behaim, d. 1365, buried in the choir of the Katharinenkirche; Crafft Behaim, b. 1326, d. 1406, buried in Katharinenkirche and has *Totenschild* there; Michael I Behaim, b. 1315, d. 1389, buried in the Katharinenkirche and has *Totenschild* there; his three wives (Cunegunde Stromerin; Margaretha Kumptin; Margaretha Wagnerin) are buried there too; Peter I Behaim, b. 1356, d. 1414, 'liegt bey St. Catharinen' and has *Totenschild* there; Michael II Behaim, b. 1373, d. 1446, buried in the Katharinenkirche and has *Totenschild* and other monuments there; his four wives (Dorothea Vetterin; Barbara Stromerin; Elisabetha Rieterin; Christina Ortliebin) are buried there too; Martin II Behaim has his *Totenschild* in the Katharinenkirche (erected by his son Martin III in 1519); Stephan Behaim d. 1511, buried in Katharinenkirche; Michael V Behaim has his *Totenschild* in the Katharinenkirche (and the Sebalduskirche); Michael VI Behaim, b. 1536, d. 1597, has his *Totenschild* in the Katharinenkirche (and Sebalduskirche); Leonhard Behaim b. 1433 (on St. Katherine's Day), d. 1486, buried in the Sebalduskirche, *Totenschild* in the Katharinenkirche (and Sebalduskirche); Margaretha Volckamerin, d. 1393, wife of Craft Behaim, lies next to him in the Katharinenkirche; Anna Schürstabin von Oberndorf, 1440; second wife of Conrad Imhoff; lies buried in the Katharinenkirche, where both their memorials are; he died in Venice in 1396 and lies in the Chapel of Saints John and Paul there; Raphael Behaim (21.7.1542–14.1.1592) has *Totenschilde* in the Sebalduskirche and Katharinenkirche.

and civic space, intensified by Patrician family ties (and the use by printers of convent manuscripts), rendered the walls between them permeable and merged the two spaces into a larger whole.[74] Indeed, the Katharinenkloster could be viewed as an extension of Patrician domestic space, territorialized by *memoria* as commemoration in the stone, painted, wooden and glass monuments that, ultimately, represented financial clout as much as spiritual aspiration; and by the members of leading Patrician families routinely assigned by the Council to the convent to keep an eye on its affairs.[75] Thus Patrician identity helped direct the 'flows of power and meaning' even within the cloistered community.

Hence this version of Saint Katherine's legend, found in Katharinenkloster manuscripts, reinforced in the Katharinenkloster prayers and transported into

---

Schlotheuber underlines the importance to lay people of burial in convents: 'Für die Familien waren die Grabstätten in den Frauenklöstern attraktiv, da das Gebet der unberührten Jungfrauen als besonders wirkmächtig galt. Die weiblichen Familienmitglieder beteten hier für das Seelenheil der Verstorbenen und der Lebenden und hielten damit die memoria der Familie wach. Damit übernahmen sie wichtige identitätsstiftende Aufgaben, die freilich bedingten, dass möglichst immer ein Mitglied dem Konvent angehörte' [For the families, tombs in the convents were attractive, as the prayers of the untouched virgins were reputed to be particularly efficacious. Here the female members of the family prayed for the salvation of the departed and the living and by so doing kept memory of the family alive. In this way they assumed important tasks of constructing and perpetuating their family identity; these naturally meant, that if at all possible at least one member of the family should always be a member of the convent community] (Eva Schlotheuber, 'Die Bedeutung der Jungfräulichkeit für das Selbstverständnis der Nonnen der alten Orden', in Jeffrey F. Hamburger, Carola Jäggi, Susan Marti and Hedwig Röckelein (eds), *Frauen – Kloster – Kunst. Neue Forschungen zur Kulturgeschichte des Mittelalters* (Brepols, 2007), pp. 43–55 (p. 47)).

74   This is further confirmed by the findings of Werner Williams-Krapp: 'Es bestanden nur selten inhaltliche oder terminologische Barrieren, daß solche ursprünglich für eine geistliche Leserschaft bestimmte Werke auch von Laien rezipiert werden konnten. Und in der Tat ist die große Masse der geistlichen Literatur, offensichtlich ohne daß größere textliche Eingriffe nötig gewesen wären, auch in Laienbibliotheken nachweisbar, und zwar abgeschrieben von Vorlagen, die sich in den örtlichen Klöstern befanden. Auch die Drucker bezogen ihre Vorlagen in der Regel aus monastischen Sammlungen' [Rarely did there exist barriers of content or terminology that prevented works originally conceived for an ecclesiastic readership from being read by lay readers. Indeed, the vast majority of devotional literature can be traced in lay libraries as well, apparently without the need for major textual alterations. Moreover, this literature had been copied from source texts found in local monastic foundations. Printers, too, as a rule obtained their source copies from monastic collections] (Williams-Krapp, 'Ordensreform und Literatur', p. 42).

75   For example, Cunradt Groß (1329), Jobst Tetzel der Ältere (1394), Peter Mendel (1420), Berthold Behaim (d. 1405), Sigmundt Stromer (1430) (Müllner, *Annalen*, vol. 1, p. 275). However, the convent is rarely mentioned in the *Ratsverlässe* (the minutes of Council meetings).

Der Heiligen Leben sits, Arachne-like,[76] amidst a complex web of associations that both alter the mental, spiritual, emotional and economic geography of Nuremberg and reach beyond the city into other local and regional foundations (with their libraries, altars, sculpture, tapestries and stained glass) as far as Alexandria. For example, the church of the Pilgrimspital zum Heiligen Kreuz, founded by Bertold Haller (c. 1310–79) in 1352/3 outside the city walls as a hospice for non-local pilgrims, poor priests, students and scholars, housed a *Nothelferaltar* (c. 1430).[77] The central panel shows the mystic marriage with Saints Barbara and Margaret on Katherine's right and Saints Sixtus, Nikolaus and Egidius on the Virgin's left; the wings depict Eustachius, Pantaleon, Sebastian and George on the left, Leonhard, Erasmus and Blasius on the right. The backs of the wing panels depict Saint Helena's discovery of the True Cross on the left and the worship of the True Cross by Emperor Heraklius on the right. Saint Katherine, then, is found amidst the same nexus of regionally important saints, devotion to the True Cross and through it incorporation into the Holy Roman Empire that characterizes her presence in the Lorenzkirche. Furthermore, depiction of the Cross prepares travellers for its presence amongst the Crucifixion relics in Nuremberg churches and, of course, for the *Reichskleinodien*. The pilgrims and scholars who stayed at the Pilgrimspital zum Heiligen Kreuz travelled along trade routes; and trade may have helped spin the web of Saint Katherine's cult if she functioned as Nuremberg's representative not just in Alexandria but in other cities that conducted significant business with the Franconian metropolis.

---

[76]   The myth of Arachne can be found in Ovid, *Metamorphoses*, 6:129–45. Rather unfortunately for this argument, Arachne is turned into a spider because she enrages Minerva; and in Christian mythology the spider represents the 'tempting devil, who weaves his web to capture the souls of men' (Impelluso, *Nature and Its Symbols*, p. 281).

[77]   No extant evidence exists as to who donated the altar and when (Strieder, *Tafelmalerei*, pp. 33–4 and pp. 176–7; *Stadtlexikon*, pp. 431–2; Helmut Freiherr von Hallerstein and Ernst Eichhorn, *Das Pilgrimspital zum Heiligen Kreuz vor Nürnberg. Geschichte und Kunstdenkmäler*, Nürnberger Forschungen 12 (Nuremberg: Verein für Geschichte der Stadt Nürnberg, 1969), pp. 116–32). Von Hallerstein and Eichhorn mention further *Nothelfer* altars around the Nuremberg region, namely in Heilsbronn, Osternohe, Reutles, Kalchreuth, Wolframseschenbach, Ottensoos (the *predella* of the Katherine altar) and Kornburg (pp. 124–5). They link the spread of their cult to the Black Death; and the popularity of Saint Katherine in Franconia as a whole to the fact that she was the patron saint of lepers (p. 127). An altar dedicated to Saint Katherine is documented in the town church in Windsheim in 1317 (p. 129); other evidence of her cult could be found in Rezelsdorf and Schwabach (p. 128). The Allerheiligenkapelle near Kleinschwarzenlohe by Kornburg contained a votive picture (now in the Germanisches Nationalmuseum) of a cleric kneeling in front of the mystic marriage with Saints Egidius and Bartholomew on either side (*Kataloge des Germanischen Nationalmuseums zu Nürnberg. Die Gemälde des 13. bis 16. Jahrhunderts*, vol. 1, *Textband*, p. 152).

One such is Cracow, where the Marienkirche housed not just Saint Mary's Altar (1477–89) by Nuremberg sculptor Veit Stoß but an altar dedicated to Saint Katherine (1514/15) by Hans Süß von Kulmbach, pupil of Albrecht Dürer and responsible for the *Tucher-Gedächtnisbild* (1513) in the Lorenzkirche, which also depicts Katherine.[78] The Cracow altar displays Katherine's conversion by the picture of the Virgin and Christ; the disputation with the heathen philosophers; the burning of the philosophers; the shattering of the wheel; Faustina and Porphyrius visiting Saint Katherine in jail; the execution of Faustina; the execution of Saint Katherine; the transport of Katherine's body to Mount Sinai and its burial there, topics familiar from the Fütterer Altar and designed to present the whole narrative of sanctity to a worshipping public. The coat-of-arms on the altar identifies the donor as the prominent merchant and financial advisor to King Sigismund I of Poland, the German-born Jan Boner (before 1463–1523), who commissioned it for his family chapel in the Marienkirche.[79] One of the wealthiest men of the age, Boner dealt in cloth, metal, spices, glass and cattle. Hence the choice of Katherine as subject of the altar may have been influenced by close trade links to the city in which she was particularly revered or by a similar desire for a divine insurance policy to protect business dealings with Alexandria.

To return to Nuremberg itself: Phil Hubbard claims of our perception of modern urban space that there is a:

> cognitive or mental picture of a city which we carry in our heads and refer to when we make decisions about how we get from one area of the city to another, for example, or decide where we want to rent a house. Far from being an accurate and scale map of the city, this is a map full of contradictions and inconsistencies, in which 'real' distances are distorted and routes misplaced.[80]

---

[78] Cracow and Nuremberg have officially been twin cities since 1979; the Krakauer Haus in Nuremberg acts as a venue for intercultural contact.

[79] Strieder, *Tafelmalerei*, p. 135 and pp. 260–1. The panels of the jail visit and Katherine's beheading disappeared after the Second World War. Jan Boner was born in Landau (Palatinate) of an old Patrician family and was a merchant in Nuremberg before moving to Poland. In 1483 he became a citizen of Cracow and, together with his father-in-law Severin Betmann, founded the firm Boner und Genossen. He was the most important supplier to and creditor of the Polish court and aristocracy. He acquired huge tracts of land, numerous town houses, salt and metal ore mines. Responsible for rebuilding the royal castle in Cracow, he commissioned artists from Germany to do work for it. In 1520 he was raised to the Polish nobility (*Neue Deutsche Biographie*, ed. die Historische Kommission bei der Bayerischen Akademie der Wissenschaften, vol. 2 (Berlin: Duncker & Humblot, 1955), pp. 442–3).

[80] Hubbard, *city*, p. 31.

Centralizing the cult of Saint Katherine in the believer's spiritual landscape results in an altered topography of Nuremberg and an altered negotiation of the physical city by the believing body. First, the location of the Katharinenkloster at the heart of the web renders what was marginal (the convent stood outside city walls until 1379, on the edge of the city's daily working geography) central, thereby changing the spatial relationships within the city. For example, its economic hub, the Hauptmarkt (main market square), enlarged in 1349 in a strategic bid to boost Nuremberg's trade, moves from being at the heart of the city to a marginal space, linked to the Katharinenkloster by sculptures of the saint on the portal of the Frauenkirche (1352), which dominates the square.[81] Similarly, the two main parish churches, the Sebalduskirche (just off the Hauptmarkt and opposite the town hall) and the Lorenzkirche (on the main thoroughfare from the Königstor to the Hauptmarkt) become, in a worshipper's mental geography, satellites of the Katharinenkloster, as does the Egidienkirche to its north with its altar of the mystic marriage. The Egidienkirche probably dates back to 1120/30 and was built on the second, northern *Königshof* (royal farm), itself founded in 1040.[82] Due to its location on royal ground, the original chapel enjoyed the status of a royal church.[83] A large Romanesque church was constructed in Nuremberg

---

[81]   The Frauenkirche stands on the site of the old Jewish synagogue. Since the Hauptmarkt stands on what was undesirably swampy ground, it was settled by the Jewish population, who were evicted and slain by permission of Emperor Karl IV when the *Rat* wished to create a more central, attractive, and hence more profitable, venue for trade.

[82]   The first, southerly, *Königshof* (c. 1040/50) stood on what became the *Deutschordensgelände* (commandery of the Teutonic Order), where the Jakobskirche now stands (Kurt Pilz, *Die St. Egidienkirche in Nürnberg. Ihre Geschichte und ihre Kunstwerke*, Einzelarbeiten aus der Kirchengeschichte Bayerns 4 (Nuremberg: Selbstverlag des Vereins für bayerische Kirchengeschichte, 1972), p. 1. The *Königshöfe* were administrative centres for the royal lands and forests scattered across the region.

[83]   Little is known about the origins of Saint Egidius (or Giles), although he was the abbot of the Benedictine monastery Saint-Gilles near Arles (the centre of his cult) in the late-seventh or early eighth century and popular in the Late Middle Ages (*Hall's Dictionary*, p. 138). His attribute is an arrow or a stag, since according to his legend he saved a stag shot at by the king whilst out hunting by protecting it in his arms; the arrow pierced his own body. (For the symbolism of the stag as the soul yearning for God (derived from Psalm 42) see Impelluso, *Nature and Its Symbols*, pp. 244–5). Egidius is the patron saint of beggars and cripples and one of the *Vierzehn Heiligen*. Wigbodo, a canon of Bamberg Cathedral, went on a pilgrimage to Saint-Gilles in 1120 and reportedly returned with a relic of the saint, so the building of the Egidienkirche in Nuremberg c. 1120/30 may be linked to the foundation on the Michaelsberg in Bamberg by Bishop Otto I (1102–39) of a hospice and chapel dedicated to Saint Egidius. In 1140 the first Staufer Emperor Konrad III (r. 1138–52) and his wife Gertrud (d. 1146) transferred supervision of the Nuremberg church to the abbot of the Schottenkloster in Regensburg and raised the former to the status of an abbey

1150 that incorporated the original Egidienkapelle, now the Euchariuskapelle. The whole complex lies beneath the Kaiserburg to the south-east, outside the city walls until they were extended in 1350–1452. As the church was destroyed by fire in 1696 and again by Allied bombs on 2 January 1945, few of the original medieval endowments remain. However, the Euchariuskapelle survived and with it an altar dedicated to Saint Katherine endowed in 1498 by Jörg Beck (d. 1498) and his wife Dorothea (d. 1503). The carved central shrine shows the mystic marriage in front of a cloth of honour held by three angels;[84] the painted wings depict on the inside the burning of the philosophers, the shattering of the wheel, the execution and Katherine's entombment by angels; on the outside Katherine with sword and wheel and Barbara with chalice and host. In addition, the wings represent Saint Wolfgang, Bishop of Regensburg (972–94), and Saint Leonhard, patron saint of prisoners and cattle and another of the *Vierzehn Heiligen*. This altar is integrated into the associations with Saint Katherine that structure the spiritual landscape of Nuremberg in a number of ways.[85] First, the typical focus in the Egidienkirche altar on key episodes from Katherine's life resonates with the Löffelholz Altar in the Sebalduskirche (its carved central shrine depicts the miracle of the wheel and the execution; the wings the disputation with and burning of the philosophers). Second, the carved mystic marriage at its centre bears a stylistic resemblance to the carved altar shrine (c. 1480) of the same subject in the Katharinenkirche, including the three angels at the back holding the cloth of honour, so sanctity resonates visually across civic space. Moreover,

---

subject to the Emperor alone. Its first monks came from the Schottenkloster Sankt Jakob in Regensburg and from Würzburg when the monastery was established in Nuremberg in 1146. ("Schottenkloster" is the name given in Germany to monasteries founded by Irish monks.) In 1418 the monastery was reformed by Benedictine monks from Reichenbach in the Upper Palatinate; it was dissolved in 1525. Information on the Egidienkirche is taken from Pilz, *Die St. Egidienkirche in Nürnberg*.

[84]   The shrine is attributed to the 'Meister der hl. Katharina', also responsible for the carved shrine on the Fütterer Altar and stylistically influenced by Veit Stoß; the wings to a pupil of the Meister des Augustineraltars (Pilz, *Egidienkirche*, p. 170 and plate 20). Murr mentions the altar and donors but fails to identify the mystic marriage: 'Zur rechten Hand am Schwibbogen, der in die dritte Kapelle hinaus weiset, ist ein kleiner Altar mit dem Marienbilde, welches das Jesuskind auf dem Schoose hält. Auf den Altardeckeln ist die heil. Dorothea' [On the right by the flying buttress, which juts out into the third chapel, stands a small altar with an image of Mary holding the Christ Child on her lap. Saint Dorothy is on the altar wings] (Murr, *Merkwürdigkeiten*, p. 146).

[85]   By 1498 the royal associations of the Egidienkirche may have faded somewhat, but they do serve to bind Katherine into the Holy Roman Empire, as we have seen in the Lorenzkirche.

the subject matter alone calls to mind the Volckamer and Konhofer windows.[86] Third, its painted wings and shrine show more episodes from the saint's life than any extant altar apart from the Fütterer Altar, which it echoes in the depiction of Katherine's entombment and similarities in the execution scene (Katherine's hairstyle; dress; the executioner's hand on her shoulder). Fourth, through Saints Egidius, Leonhard and Barbara the altar blends with other depictions of the *Vierzehn Heiligen* in Nuremberg, particularly with the Memminger Altar in the Lorenzkirche, in the foreground of which sits Egidius with his attribute, a stag. Fifth, the Egidienkirche contained two paintings of the Mass of Saint Gregory: one at which an indulgence of 20,024 years and 24 days could be obtained in return for five Our Father and five Hail Marys; the other an epitaph for the Zingel family (1447–1531).[87] Thus, as in Saint Katherine's legend, Katherine and Gregory, Katharinenkirche and Egidienkirche, are spatially and thematically connected through the Eucharist. A further connexion is established through the Ketzel window (1510/15), endowed by Wolf Ketzel, merchant and in 1493 Jerusalem pilgrim,[88] and designed by Hans Süß von Kulmbach, who was also responsible for the frescoes of Empress Faustina commissioned by Anton II Tucher around 1511 for the Haus zur Krone, the *Stammhaus* of the senior Tucher line.[89] The window shows the Four Church Fathers or *Vier Lehrer*, subject also of the altar commissioned for the Lorenzkirche by Konrad Konhofer. Hence a devotee of Saint Katherine could plot a spiritual pilgrimage through Nuremberg that took him from the Lorenzkirche to the Katharinenkloster to the Egidienkirche to the Sebalduskirche, stopping at each altar, tapestry, sculpture or window to reinforce the saint's impress on his/her soul through prayer, to recall passages from her legend and imaginatively to relive on his/her body key episodes from her life, like the conversion of the philosophers, the martyrdom or the mystic marriage.

If mental or physical movement through the city takes the Katharinenkloster as its orientation point, the convent, identified by the statue of Saint Katherine on its gateway, becomes the hub of contours of devotion on the urban map – as does the worshipper's body, since it forms the axis from which lines of association flow. As the body negotiates Nuremberg, so the cognitive map of the city and the mental/emotional/devotional pathways linking texts about and images of Katherine shift, since this axis occupies a constantly changing location

---

86   The Volckamer and Mendel enjoyed a long association with the Egidienkirche as well: in 1401 and 1420 a Peter Mendel was *Pfleger* of the Egidienkloster (Müllner, *Annalen*, vol. 1, p. 116); Paulus Volckamer in 1477 (Müllner, vol. 1, p. 116); a Peter Mendel had his 'Jahrtäg' celebrated in the Egidienkloster (Müllner, *Annalen*, vol. 1, p. 117).

87   Pilz, *Egidienkirche*, p. 98 and pp. 164–5.

88   He lived from 1472 to 1544 and married Barbara Tetzel in 1504.

89   Grote, *Die Tucher*, p. 22; plate 50.

in relation to them. Noise, smells, weather, light conditions, mood, health, individual finances, personal encounters, family ties – elements that modern scholarship can no longer reconstruct – all overlay the city and the moving axis with mutable cognitive 'maps of desire, disgust, pleasure, pain, loathing, love'.[90] For example, a member of the Löffelholz family may, literally, spiritually and emotionally, have been more "invested" in the Sebalduskirche Löffelholz Altar than a member of, for example, the Imhoff family; and Löffelholz worship of Saint Katherine been overlaid with personal memories, shared family history and shared family piety.

Second, her legend as recorded in the manuscript basis for *Der Heiligen Leben* leaves its impact upon the cognitive map of the city by stretching from the Katharinenkloster to copies of this work in Nuremberg households and beyond,[91] thereby constructing virtual intellectual and spiritual links between the convent and those families as well as between the families themselves.[92] Individual or shared readings of *Der Heiligen Leben* may have been shaped by individual or shared memories of Saint Katherine throughout the city. Thus the same member of the Löffelholz family may have read the legend in the mental shadow of the altar and endowed the textual saint with the carved or painted features of the altar saint. If that person were a Löffelholz woman named after the saint,[93] textual, visual, family and personal identification may have led her to read the legend with herself as the saint in the body of Katherine as depicted on the Löffelholz Altar.

Third, similar lines might be drawn between other families and other representations of the saint across Nuremberg, including those in the Katharinenkirche itself. For example, the Behaim Altar in the Katharinenkirche was probably donated by Martin II Behaim (1373–1446), a merchant who traded in various wares, mainly with Lübeck and Venice.[94] Only elected onto

---

[90]   Pile, *The Body and the City*, p. 209.

[91]   Other versions of the Katherine legend reflecting a different tradition are recorded in the convent manuscripts. One is Germanisches Nationalmuseum Sammelhandschrift 15131, which includes Katherine's conception and birth. These are possible only after her father and his subjects have sacrificed to a miraculous crucifix (fol. 2^r–7^r). This version is, as far as could be ascertained, less widespread and less reflected in iconographic tradition.

[92]   Moreover, the legend's inclusion in *Der Heiligen Leben* enmeshes other saints' lives into the web woven by Saint Katherine, forming implicit links between them as well.

[93]   For example, Katharina Löffelholz neé Dintner, wife of Dr Johann Löffelholz; or Katharina Löffelholz, daughter of Wilhelm Rumel and wife of Thomas Löffelholz (1503).

[94]   The Behaim are first mentioned in Nuremberg in 1285 and 1288; the focus of their trade was with Venice and Italy, also Salzburg, Styria and Corinthia. From at least 1318/23 (the oldest extant Council lists) they served on the *Rat*. In 1379 they donated to the Sebalduskirche a stained-glass window depicting the life of Mary in the south end of the East choir; and around the same time a *Schmerzensmann* (Man of Sorrows) in the

the *Kleiner Rat* as *Jüngerer Bürgermeister* (Junior Mayor) in 1416, he held that office for 16 years. In 1435, after a break of four years, he served again on the Council, this time as *Älterer Bürgermeister* (Senior Mayor) for 12 years. Martin II was married four times: in 1392 to Dorothea Vetter from Rothenburg ob der Tauber (d. 1409); in 1409 to Barbara Stromer (d. 1421); in 1423 to Elisabeth Rieter (d. 1425); and in 1426 to Christina Ortlieb (d. 1441). Twenty-nine children resulted from these unions, of whom 25 died before him. He, his wives and children are buried in the Katharinenkirche, as are many other family members, so the altar stood as an abiding emblem of their commitment to Saint Katherine and the convent community. Similarly, in 1493 Nikolaus V Volckamer endowed an altar for his parents, Peter (1431–93) and Apollonia neé Mendel, donor of and commemorated by the Volckamer window in the Lorenzkirche. Commemorated on the same altar are two Dominican nuns, identified by their coat-of-arms as belonging to the same family, possibly Gertrud V and Clara V (d. 1525). The central panel depicts the Mass of Saint Gregory, beneath which the nuns occupy the centre foreground, through their position signalling both their family's dedication to the crucified Christ and the significance of the Eucharist in convent devotion. Furthermore, they kneel beneath the Virgin and John the Evangelist (who support Christ displaying His wounds) and on either side of the line running down from the Cross (with the instruments of the Passion) through Christ's crucified body and the chalice on Gregory's altar to their coats-of-arms. More than passively devoted, the family actively witness and are integrated into Gregory's miraculous vision. The altar's inner wings portray the *Vierzehn Heiligen*, amongst whom Katherine is twice represented through the mystic marriage: once in the top left panel of the left inner wing, where the Virgin, flanked by Saint Margaret on her left and Saints Barbara and Katherine on her right, stands holding the Christ Child, who puts the ring onto Katherine's finger in front of the chalice and wafer held by Barbara; and once on an outside wing, where the mystic marriage occupies two full panels.[95] Under the second mystic marriage kneel the donor, his two sons, his wife Barbara Melber and their daughter-in-law; beneath them the Volckamer and Melber coats-of-

---

South choir. The family had a long association with the Katharinenkirche, which also boasts a Behaimfenster and where many members lie buried, such as Albrecht Behaim (d. 1342); and Berthold Behaim (d. 1405), one of the leading members of the *Kleiner Rat* from 1374 until his death. Friedrich III Behaim (d. 1379) endowed a prebend to the Katharinenkirche. The Behaim and Stromer had also intermarried before Martin: Michael I (d. 1389) married Kunigunde Stromer (d. 1360) (Fleischmann, *Rat und Patriziat*, 31/2, pp. 317–40).

[95]   Lutze and Weigand, *Kataloge des Germanischen Nationalmuseums*, vol. 1, *Textband*, p. 130; vol. 2, *Bildband*, plates 80 and 81. The other wing depicts Saint Anthony of Padua and an unidentified bishop.

arms. The melding of Saint Katherine with family identity, Patrician alliance and civic space could not be more clearly advertised, since the family "marry" themselves to the saint by supporting and worshipping the mystic marriage and to the Patrician community by echoing the Konhofer window, the Memminger Altar and their own window in the Lorenzkirche.

Even if a donation to the Katharinenkirche did not portray the saint herself, it served to associate the donors with her and her community. For example, Ortloph III Stromer (d. 1498) and his wife Katharina Harsdörfer (d. 1522) endowed the main altar for the church in 1490, the *Angstaltar* (Fear Altar), which depicts the Flagellation, Christ's Coronation with the Crown of Thorns, His praying in the Garden of Gethsemane and the Resurrection. It bore the Stromer-Harsdörfer coat-of-arms,[96] which in turn forged a link to the Behaim Altar, as the Stromer and Behaim were related by marriage. Similarly, Stephan and Lukas Paumgartner endowed an altar by Dürer in 1502/3 in memory of their father Martin I, who lies buried in the church.[97] The central panel shows the Nativity; Saint George (a portrait of Stephan Paumgartner (1462–1525))[98] is on the left panel and Saint Eustachius (a portrait of Lukas Paumgartner (d. 1518)) on the right. In the foreground on either side of the Nativity kneel other family members, including Barbara Paumgartner née Volckamer (d. 1494), the wife of Martin I Paumgartner (1436–78; m. 22 August 1458), and the widowed Barbara's second husband Hans Schönbach (m. 1480).[99] Through their portrayal as saints, Barbara and Martin's sons Stephan and Lukas (as Veit Memminger before them) clearly situate themselves in the spiritual life of the Katharinenkloster; whilst through their mother they are linked to the Volckamer family and its endowments throughout the city, including the Volckamer window in the Lorenzkirche. Since the Paumgartner were also related by marriage to the Löffelholz, their coat-of-arms on the Nativity Altar also creates a bridge to the

---

[96]   Strieder, *Tafelmalerei*, p. 238.

[97]   A Konrad Paumgartner (d. c. 1350) and his son of the same name (d. 1367) are first mentioned in 1338 as *Bürgen* [guarantors] at the oath-taking of new citizens. A member of the family, Konrad III, was first elected to the *Großer Rat* in 1367 but the Paumgartner only married into the leading families in the early fifteenth century, when they had amassed a considerable fortune through trade in cloth, pelts, cotton and spices with Venice, Flanders, Poland, Hungary and the Orient. Konrad VI (c. 1380–1464) Paumgartner acted as banker for Burgrave Friedrich I of Nuremberg, Emperor Sigismund, Duke Ludwig der Jüngere von Bayern-Ingolstadt and even the Roman curia. His daughters married members of the Tucher, Graser, Tetzel and Löffelholz families.

[98]   Stephan Paumgartner is known for his pilgrimage to the Holy Land in 1498.

[99]   Strieder, *Tafelmalerei*, p. 114 and pp. 242–3; Biedermann, *Geschlechtsregister*, Tabula DXXXII; Fleischmann, *Rat und Patriziat*, 31/2 *Anlagen*.

Sebalduskirche and Patrician alliances advertised on the Löffelholz Altar there.[100] However, the choice of saints signals that Paumgartner Altar fulfilled a purpose other than the advertisement of impressive connexions: George was called on for help in withstanding temptation, whilst Eustachius was turned to in times of adversity, grief in the family and loss of faith. Their patronage expresses the shame recently suffered by the Paumgartner and the family's response to it: after the scandalous bankruptcy, flight from Nuremberg and lawsuit against the city of Martin's elder brother Anton I in 1465, the family's upward trajectory was halted for four decades.[101] Commissioning an altar by an artist as prestigious as Dürer publicly announces both their remorse and, more forcefully, their return as major players on the civic stage, a return "sanctioned" by Saint Katherine as the altar stands in the space dedicated to her.[102]

Centralizing the cult of Saint Katherine in the believer's spiritual landscape alters the topography of Nuremberg in a fourth way. As discussed in Chapter 1, her followers may have traversed the streets of Nuremberg, actively using its physical structure to commemorate her and constructing a "new" city in the process: the overlaying of doors, windows and buildings with episodes from her legend peopled by images of her from the Sebalduskirche,[103] Lorenzkirche, Katharinenkirche and Frauenkirche, say, could have formed a web of interlocking mental and spiritual pathways through Nuremberg that altered its topography. The city thus becomes more than a map of devotion to the saint in which certain places of emotional, spiritual, family or economic importance to the walking body emerge in high profile and function as key orientation markers whilst others fade into its perceptual background: it becomes a three-dimensional reconstruction of Katherine's life and martyrdom which encompasses the walker and is activated differently either by different walkers at different times or by the same walker at different times and in different moods. In other words, the city morphs into 'a map full of contradictions and inconsistencies,

---

[100]   It was in memory of Konrad VI Paumgartner's daughter Kunigunde (d. 1462), Wilhelm Löffelholz's wife, that the Löffelholz Altar was commissioned.

[101]   See Müllner, *Annalen*, vol. 2, pp. 559–60.

[102]   Stephan was named *Genannter des Großen Rats* and *Jüngerer Bürgermeister* on the *Kleiner Rat* in 1507, so was the first member of his family to be *ratsfähig* (eligible to serve on the Council) for 40 years (Fleischmann, *Rat und Patriziat*, 31/2, pp. 757–79). George and Eustachius are, of course, two of the *Vierzehn Heiligen*. That Eustachius's faith was tested by suffering may be an allusion to the family's recent trials.

[103]   For example, in addition to the windows and altars, the Sebalduskirche displayed a number of tapestries with scenes from her life (for details see Friedrich Wilhelm Hoffmann, *Die Sebalduskirche in Nürnberg. Ihre Baugeschichte und ihre Kunstdenkmale*, rev. Th. Hampe, E. Mummenhoff and Jos. Schmitz (Vienna: Gerlach & Wiedling, 1912), p. 202 and p. 204).

in which "real" distances are distorted and routes misplaced',[104] becoming physically, topographically and spiritually unstable (and always open to further reconstruction by new texts or works of art).

Fifth, the web of memories and associations is not just internal to the city but stretches, as discussed above, beyond its walls to churches like the Katharinenkirche in Altenfurt on the outskirts of modern Nuremberg as well as to regional and foreign foundations.[105] This web would have been spun by, amongst others, artists and craftsmen, who, given their highly trained visual memories, would effortlessly have slotted the altars, windows, tapestries, frescoes and statues of the saint into their mental library of images and retrieved them to compare to images of her outside the city or when commissioned to represent her themselves. Non-residents, once returned home, may mentally have merged her legend and stored images of Katherine from Nuremberg with those of her in and around their own city. For example, devotion to Katherine flourished in Augsburg, a major Southern German merchant city which enjoyed close business and family ties to Nuremberg and had seen the building of a Dominican convent dedicated to the saint between 1251 and 1259.[106] Its nuns came, like those in the Nuremberg convent, from local Patrician families. Augsburg merchants visiting Nuremberg on business could compare images of Katherine in public and private spaces with those in their own city and, indeed, their own homes. Casting the net still further, pilgrims and merchants who visited Alexandria could have included in their mental baggage Katherine's textual[107] and visual presence in Nuremberg and, by imagining the saint active in these places in her "Nuremberg identity", have mapped it onto the site of her tomb at Sinai or martyrdom in Alexandria,[108] thereby transposing Nuremberg into Egypt. Pilgrims' experience was coloured by multiple 'modalities of identification', 'psychic defence mechanisms', 'internalised authorities', layers of 'intense feelings' and 'flows of power and meaning': identified and self-identifying as Christians, they were removed from their accustomed status

---

[104]   Hubbard, *city*, p. 31.

[105]   The first documented reference to a round church in Altenfurt dates from 2 July 1225, when King Heinrich VII awarded a privilege to the Nuremberg *Schottenkloster* Sankt Egidien, to which Altenfurt belonged; next to the round church were a hermit's cell, a farm and a forester's house. For a history and description of the church see *Stadtlexikon*, p. 63; and Fritz Traugott Schulz, *Die Rundkapelle zu Altenfurt bei Nürnberg*, Studien zur deutschen Kunstgeschichte 94 (Strassburg: Heitz (Heitz & Mündel), 1908).

[106]   See Cuneo, 'The Basilica Cycle of Saint Katherine's Convent'.

[107]   In the form of a prayer or memorized extract from her legend such as those discussed at the beginning of this chapter.

[108]   Namely, her prison; the red marble pillars onto which the wheel was tied; two red marble pillars marking the site of execution outside the city gates (Tucher, '*Reise*', pp. 589–91).

in the fixed hierarchy of their city or state; ethnically foreign yet claiming their "legitimate" religious homeland in the sites of Christ's ministry and His followers' martyrdom; spiritually unsettled because travelling through territory onto which Islam had inscribed its dominance;[109] vulnerable because linguistically inept and both physically and psychologically unaccustomed to the heat, dirt, thirst, food, insects, discomfort and strain of travel through the vast and empty desert; on the defensive because in fear of attack from local populations;[110] wrestling with the conflict between the 'internalised authority' of their superiority as Christians and the external authority of Muslim political, cultural and financial control. Their bodies, 'made within [the] particular constellations of object relations' that was medieval Nuremberg, would have been forced to negotiate a new, less stable and less dominant, 'place in the world', 'territorialised' by an awareness of conflicting power structures and new 'maps of desire, disgust, pleasure, pain, loathing, love'. On their return to Nuremberg, these same pilgrims and merchants may have fused this experience of the saint in Egypt with their experience of her in the city by merging three layers of time – Katherine's life, their visit to her shrines, their present – with three layers of place – Alexandria, Sinai, Nuremberg – and multiple layers of recalled and present emotion. Memory embedded Alexandria and Sinai into their own home space, but in a more fragmented, possibly more resistant way. We saw in Chapter 1 that Hans Tucher compares Saint Katherine's monastery at Sinai to the Heilsbronner Hof,[111] but a different traveller – a Hans Rieter (1384), a Bernhard Kress (1433), a Heinrich Ketzel (1438) – may have compared it to a different Nuremberg location, one with more personal associations, an act binding the saint even more closely into that traveller's daily life and environment.[112]

---

[109]   The Mamelukes controlled the Holy Land until 1517, when it fell to the Ottoman Turks.

[110]   Fabri mentions, for example, threatening behaviour from the Saracens at the caves in Jaffa where pilgrims had to spend three days after disembarkation: 'lo! Of a sudden they fell into a fury about I know not what, and drove us back again into our cave, threatening us with sticks, and spurned us from them into the cave as though we had been beasts' (Fabri, *Wanderings*, vol. 1, 1, p. 234). Pilgrims were also maltreated by those who profited from them: 'for pilgrims often suffer great annoyance from the ass-drivers, in being struck by them and thrown from their asses and having their property stolen' (Fabri, *Wanderings*, vol. 1, 1, p. 242). Bedouins were always feared: 'We were much alarmed at meeting any people soever, because it had been foretold to us that we should suffer much evil at the hands of the Arabs in the wilderness' (Fabri, *Wanderings*, vol. 2, 2, p. 499).

[111]   Tucher, '*Reise*', p. 524.

[112]   That pilgrims prolonged their spiritual journey by altering the urban landscape is illustrated by, for example, Jörg Ketzel, who undertook a pilgrimage to the Holy Land with Kurfürst Friedrich II von Brandenburg in 1453 and in 1459 endowed, in the courtyard of the Heilig-Geist-Spital, a Heilig-Geist-Kapelle that closely resembled the Jerusalem original. His

Sixth, the associative web spun out through patronage of art and architecture wove Patricians, *Ehrbare* and clergy within the city into a corporate whole, publicized the ties of blood and marriage that bound them and rendered permeable their individual and collective body-ego boundaries. As we have seen, coats-of-arms on endowments in public spaces advertised family marital allegiance across the city. Just how extensive and complex were the strands connecting families and spaces will be demonstrated by two final examples, one of which is the Volckamer window in the Sebalduskirche,[113] donated in 1488 by the brothers Peter III and Paulus I Volckamer to replace the original window endowed c. 1379 by their forbears Hartwig II and Heinrich II Volckamer (d. 1379 and 1389 respectively).[114] The latter and their wives, Anna Nützel and Elisabeth Rasp,[115] are shown kneeling in prayer in the bottom row of the window, supporting and worshipping the scenes from the life of Mary and Christ (Annunciation; Adoration of the Magi; Presentation of Christ in the Temple) that play out above them. Hartwig I Volckamer (d. 1375) was the first of the family to come to Nuremberg (1337) and a member of the *Kleiner Rat* from 1362,[116] so through the window Peter and Paulus Volckamer document and publicly commemorate their family's long association with Nuremberg and central role in its governance.[117] In the second row we see the donors themselves and their wives Apollonia and Magdalena Mendel. Peter Volckamer was, of course, responsible for endowing the Volckamer window in the Lorenzkirche in

relocation of the holiest site in Christendom to the home of the *Reichskleinodien* (kept in the Heilig-Geist-Spital) altered the latter's spiritual topography. Steffan Paumgartner remarks on the similarity between the chapel and Christ's tomb in the Church of the Holy Sepulchre in Jerusalem (*Stadtlexikon*, p. 431). The Ketzel, who had arrived in Nuremberg from Augsburg in 1422/35, were *ehrbar* and not entitled to serve on the *Kleiner Rat*. Heinrich Ketzel der Ältere had undertaken a pilgrimage to the Holy Land in 1389. In 1438 Heinrich der Jüngere was made *Genannter des Großen Rats*. The Ketzel were merchants, trading in saffron, metal and textiles (*Stadtlexikon*, p. 532). Endowments such as the Heilig-Geist-Kapelle also served to establish a family in the city and to raise their public profile.

[113]   Attributed to the workshop of Veit Hirsvogel der Ältere.

[114]   Scholz, 'Aktuelle Forschung', p. 61. According to Fleischmann, Heinrich II Volckamer died in 1389 (*Rat und Patriziat*, 31/2 *Anlagen*). The Volckamer and the Behaim erected their Begräbnisstätte underneath the windows they endowed, which are adjacent to one another (Weilandt, *Sebalduskirche*, p. 318).

[115]   Heinrich II Volckamer was married twice: first to Anna Schürstab, daughter of Ratsherr Leopold IV; then to Elisabeth Rasp, a *Bürgerin* (Müllner, *Annalen*, vol. 1, p. 50; Fleischmann, *Rat und Patriziat*, 31/2, p. 1044 and *Anlagen*).

[116]   His daughter Kungundt was a nun in the Katharinenkloster in 1359.

[117]   The Volckamer belonged to the prestigious inner circle of 20 *alte Geschlechter*, the families with the longest record of service on the powerful *Kleiner Rat*. The Nützel and Schürstab were also *alte Geschlechter* (Fleischmann, *Rat und Patriziat*, 31/2, pp. 223–4).

memory of his wife Apollonia and, whilst the Sebalduskirche window may not depict Saint Katherine, it does include the family coat-of-arms, which features half a Katherine wheel and figures prominently in the Lorenzkirche window as well. Volckamer and Mendel are further linked in the Sebalduskirche since its Volckamer window also displays the coat-of-arms of Margarethe Mendel (d. 1492),[118] the first wife of Paulus Volckamer (1448–1505);[119] whilst more or less opposite the Volckamer window in the north aisle of the church is the Mendel window, endowed in 1385 by the three brothers Marquard I (d. 1385), Konrad I (d. 1414) and Peter I (d. 1423) Mendel and depicting scenes from the lives of Saint Anne and the Virgin.[120] As the daughter of Peter III Mendel and Apollonia Waldstromer, Apollonia Mendel was the great-granddaughter of Peter I, so three windows in two churches unite families across generations.

To document all traces of Saint Katherine in Nuremberg, to analyse their interaction and their fusion of different realms of civic, cloistered and domestic space would exceed the limits of any academic study so one final example must suffice, the Löffelholz window in the Lorenzkirche, which takes us back full textual circle to the first chapter of this monograph. Endowed by Johann Löffelholz (1448–1509) and his wife Katharina Tintner (1472–1511),[121] and executed by Hans Baldung Grien in 1505/6,[122] it illustrates the life of Mary as

---

[118]   Fleischmann has date of death for Margarethe Mendel as 1495 (Fleischmann, *Rat und Patriziat*, 31/2, pp. 1049–50), whilst Weilandt has 1492 (*Sebalduskirche*, p. 598).

[119]   Weilandt, *Sebalduskirche*, p. 598. Weilandt also unfolds the interaction of the works of art endowed in the rivalry between the Volckamer and the Behaim (*Sebalduskirche*, pp. 318–40).

[120]   The two windows are on either side of the shrine containing the relics of Saint Sebaldus, Nuremberg's patron saint. Marquard I married Kunigunde Schürstab in 1370; Konrad I married Elisabeth Stromer (no date given in Fleischmann); Peter I married Anna Stromer (Fleischmann, *Rat und Patriziat*, 31/2 *Anlagen*).

[121]   Johann Löffelholz studied Law in Erfurt and Padua, then entered the service of the Bishop of Bamberg and the Archbishop of Mainz. In 1475 he became councillor to Duke Ludwig of Bavaria-Landshut; in 1474 *Rechtskonsulent* of Nuremberg; from 1503 onwards he was Assessor to the *Reichskammergericht*. He was a bibliophile, a Humanist and enjoyed a reputation for considerable learning. In 1488 he married Katharina Tintner (1472–1511), the only daughter of wealthy merchant Friedrich Tintner (d. 1503). To commemorate the death of their son Wilhelm, Johann and Katharina Löffelholz also endowed an altar in the Georgskapelle in the Augustinerkloster in 1501 (Fleischmann, *Rat und Patriziat*, vol. 31/2, p. 674 and *Anlagen*). Funk dates the marriage to 1484 (*Glasfensterkunst*, p 187). Strieder mentions an epitaph for their son Johannes (1492–1504) by Hans Traut der Jüngere; it depicts the *Heilige Sippe* [holy clan] and hangs in the Lorenzkirche (Strieder, *Tafelmalerei*, p. 233). Spellings of Katharina's surname vary: Tintner, Dintner, Dietner.

[122]   At this time Hans Baldung Grien was a pupil in Albrecht Dürer's workshop; he took over the commission for the window as Dürer had left Nuremberg in 1505 for his second trip

encapsulated in the Annunciation, the Nativity and the Adoration of the Magi. Beneath these scenes are showcased the family coats-of-arms, publicly joining the Löffelholz and Tintner within ecclesiastic and urban space; and the donors' name saints, John the Baptist and Saint Katherine. According to Funk:

> So stehen die beiden Heiligen zueinander in ikonographischer Beziehung. Sie weisen auf den Anfang des Heiles und auf dessen Vollendung hin. Beide stellen aber auch eine Verbindung zur Ikonologie der darüberliegenden Fensterzeile her mit der Verkündigung an Maria, Jesu Geburt und der Anbetung Christi. Johannes weist auf seine Ankunft und Menschwerdung hin, Katharina auf seine Anbetung und damit auf seine göttliche Verehrung.[123]

[Thus the two saints stand in an iconographic relationship to each other. They point to the beginning of salvation and to its accomplishment. However, both also establish a connexion to the iconography of the row above them in the window, with the Annunciation, the Birth and Adoration of Christ. John points to His advent and becoming Man; Katherine to adoration of Him and thus to His adoration as God].

Within the window Katherine serves a fourfold purpose: as a symbol for Katharina Tintner's piety; as a signpost to her location on the map of Patrician marital alliances; as a reminder of a model Christian marriage (that of Saint Katherine to Christ, emulated by Katherine Tintner and Johann Löffelholz); and as a model for the worship of Christ (as the lamb in the Löffelholz coat-of-arms He is literally integrated into the family identity), above whom Saint Katherine holds the symbol of her martyrdom, her wheel.[124] Like the Volckamer, the Tintner and Löffelholz model exemplary piety in their literal support of the Virgin's life. Their coats-of-arms unite families across generations, too, since, in addition to the donors themselves, they represent Johann Löffelholz's great-grandparents Friedrich Löffelholz (d. 1439) and Agnes Haßfurter (d. 1432); his grandparents Hans Löffelholz (d. 1455) and Barbara Haller (d. 1467); and his parents, Wilhelm Löffelholz (d. 1474) and Kunigunde Paumgartner.[125] Chapter 1 discusses Wilhelm Löffelholz's endowment of the Löffelholz Altar (1462/4) in the West choir of the Sebalduskirche in memory of his wife Kunigunde,

---

to Venice (Funk, *Glasfensterkunst*, p. 187; Fleischmann, *Rat und Patriziat*, 31/2, p. 674).

[123]   Funk, *Glasfensterkunst*, pp. 189–90.

[124]   As Funk points out, the inclusion of the Löffelholz coat-of-arms at the feet of both John the Baptist and Katherine integrate the saints into the family tradition (Funk, *Glasfensterkunst*, p. 190).

[125]   Funk, *Glasfensterkunst*, p. 189.

who had died in 1462. Thus parents and children are trans-spatially and trans-temporally bound by endowments which link both churches and are publicized through their coats-of-arms. Moreover, the coats-of-arms on both the window in the Lorenzkirche and the altar in the Sebalduskirche include those of Löffelholz spouses (the Tintner, Paumgartner, Löffelholz, Löffelholz-Tintner, Löffelholz-Stromer-Sachs, Löffelholz-Züngel, Löffelholz-Kreß and Löffelholz-Stromer),[126] so the wider web of family ties connecting the Patricians is also privileged in and blessed by its sacred location in the two main parish churches.[127] Saint Katherine is thus fused into a system of visual markers that both align families within distinct, civically significant spaces and span the distance between those spaces, merging them into one extensive map of Patrician dominance over the city and its economic, political and religious policies.

Should the worshipper take a few more steps in the Lorenzkirche, he would see a sandstone sculpture (c. 1410) carved into a pillar in the north aisle and depicting three virgin saints: Katherine holding her wheel and a sword; Agnes the Lamb of God; and Barbara (probably – the stone is damaged) a chalice and wafer in commemoration of her request that those who honoured her martyrdom should receive the sacrament.[128] Barbara's other attribute, a tower, symbolizes chastity; she is frequently portrayed with Saint Katherine and, like the latter, was one of the *Vierzehn Heiligen*; while Saint Agnes (d. 304) was one of the earliest

---

[126]   Wilhelm Löffelholz's second wife was Barbara Hirschvogelin, daughter of Wilhelm Hirschvogel and Christina Haller and widow of Sebald Tucher. She, too, is included on the Löffelholz Altar. The Hirschvogel window in the Lorenzkirche depicts the *Heilige Sippe* and would thus have been visually linked to the Volckamer window, even if it does not depict Saint Katherine. However, these panes were not acquired by the parish of the Lorenzkirche until 1836 so obviously do not form part of the medieval context.

[127]   Implicitly the trading alliances between them as well, as Patrician fathers tended to marry off their daughters to families whose trade interests matched theirs or who owned resources (such as tin or copper mines) that they needed for trade or manufacture (Fleischmann, *Rat und Patriziat*, 31/1, p. 231).

[128]   The third-century martyr Saint Barbara was locked away in a tower by her possessive father, the pagan Dioscurus, to hide her beauty from potential suitors. Her conversion to Christianity in his absence was revealed to her father through her request that a third window be knocked into the tower in witness to the Holy Trinity. Escaping death at her father's hands, Barbara was tortured at the behest of the Roman authorities and eventually, in some versions of the legend, beheaded on a mountain top by her father, who was himself struck by lightning and consumed by fire. She became the patron saint of milliners, knights, soldiers, gunsmiths, armourers, architects, builders, miners, firemen and all those in danger of sudden, unexpected death (Apostolos-Cappadona, *Women in Religious Art*, pp. 35–6; *Hall's Dictionary*, pp. 40–1). In the edition of *Der Heiligen Leben* published in Nuremberg by Anton Koberger in 1488, Saint Barbara is described as "vnmeßlichen schön" [immeasurably beautiful] (fol. CCLXIIIʳ).

virgin martyrs to be venerated.[129] All three saints are young girls who resisted marriage to dedicate themselves to Christ; two (Katherine and Agnes) are explicitly brides of Christ, who Himself is present in the lamb held by Agnes.[130] The lamb's mirroring by the coats-of-arms in the nearby Löffelholz window sets up another ripple of resonances throughout the church and beyond. The striking similarity of three virgins[131] suggests they represent an ideal of female chastity that is further reinforced by their constituting a shadow Trinity. The Trinity, in turn, is doubly present in the six spokes of Saint Katherine's wheel, unusually shown complete. Barbara and Agnes point to their attributes: the former's chalice and host symbolize the commemoration of Christ's death in the Eucharist; the latter's lamb and pennant the victory of the Lamb of God over death. However, they also point past these attributes to Saint Katherine herself, whose importance is signalled by her central position. Since for the Middle Ages the wheel frequently symbolized Fortune and denoted inconstancy, its intactness in the carving may be intended to recall the opposite, namely the infinity (perfect circle) of God and His constant love for mankind. Since the three saints are carved into the very stone of the pillar, the Lorenzkirche may be said to rest on them, just as the Church itself rested on the sacrifices brought by the early martyrs in their spreading of Christianity throughout the (Holy) Roman Empire. The "territory" of the Lorenzkirche, like the entire city of Nuremberg, maps the centrality of Saint Katherine to the Christian endeavour and her status in Patrician eyes as a pillar of Empire. Katherine's imperial eminence is exemplified by the personal piety of Emperor Karl IV, whose favourite saint she was since he ascribed his victory over the Milan League at San Felice near Modena on Saint Katherine's Day 1332 to her protection. She was the patron saint of knights and on that same day Karl and 200 of his companions were knighted. The Emperor attributed a second victory to

---

[129]   Saint Agnes lived in Rome during the persecution of Christians under Diocletian. Courted by the son of the Prefect of Rome, she declined his hand in marriage, claiming she was already wed to her heavenly bridegroom. The Prefect demanded Agnes perform sacrifice to the Roman gods or be thrown into a brothel. She chose the latter, so was led naked through the streets of Rome, covered by hair that had conveniently grown to her feet and so concealed her body. In the brothel an angel hid her body from the sight of others by means of a bright light that surrounded it. On his attempt to ravish her, Agnes's suitor was killed by a demon, only to be restored to life through her prayers. Agnes herself was meant to be burnt as a witch but the flames burnt her executioners, leaving her unscathed; eventually she was beheaded. She is the patron saint of young maidens, engaged couples, rape victims, gardeners and chastity (*Hall's Dictionary*, pp. 10–11; Apostolos-Cappadona, *Women in Religious Art*, p. 6).

[130]   Depictions of Agnes in a mystic marriage are rare. The Germanisches Nationalmuseum houses one by the Master of the Saint Bartholomew Altar) (c. 1495/1500).

[131]   They exhibit same faces, same long flowing hair, same crowns, same drapery, same cloaks, same chaste dress.

her, that over Milanese troops at Castle Penede on Lake Garda on her feast day in 1340. His second daughter (b. 1342) from his first marriage was named after Saint Katherine. Karl had a fresco of the saint painted on the side of the altar table in his private oratory in Saint Mary's Tower on Burg Karlstein; she was also portrayed in the castle Chapel of the Holy Cross.[132] Nuremberg was indebted to Karl IV for permitting, in 1349, the expulsion of the Jews that allowed the expansion of the Hauptmarkt at the heart of the city as a key part of Nuremberg's drive for greater economic prosperity. As in Karl IV, represented on the Frauenkirche on the Hauptmarkt (as is Katherine herself on the portal),[133] Empire, trade, individual devotion and artistic patronage merge in the Patricians who governed Nuremberg to create an intensely experienced personal relationship between saint and city that guaranteed her protection in return for their fidelity.[134] Depicted on an altar in the Walpurgiskapelle on the Kaiserburg,[135] Katherine looked down on her city from above, making it her enduring 'body-ego-space', the disparate locations of her worship joined – like her body by the angels – into a single map of desire.

---

[132]   Franz Machilek, 'Privatfrömmigkeit und Staatsfrömmigkeit', in *Kaiser Karl IV. Staatsmann und Mäzen*, ed. Ferdinand Seibt (Munich: Prestel, 1978), pp. 87–101 (p. 88). Initially the oratory was dedicated to Mary; later it was rededicated to Katherine.

[133]   A mechanical clock on the church façade shows the "Männleinlaufen" every day at 12 o'clock: the Seven Electoral Princes circle three times, performing obeisance to Karl IV. The clock was built by the locksmith Georg Heuß and the coppersmith Sebastian Lindenast and installed in 1509. Publicly, then, the city expresses its gratitude to one of its principal guardians.

[134]   Goodich notes a 'religious cult and its trappings had become one of the major expressions of social and political unity in the later middle ages' (Goodich, *Violence and Miracle*, p. 14).

[135]   Murr, *Merkwürdigkeiten*, p. 28.

Bibliography

Manuscripts

Germanisches Nationalmuseum Hs. 877.
Germanisches Nationalmuseum Hs 1733.
Germanisches Nationalmuseum Hs. 1737.
Germanisches Nationalmuseum Hs. 1738.
Germanisches Nationalmuseum Hs 7054.
Germanisches Nationalmuseum Hs. 15131.
Germanisches Nationalmuseum Hs. 117 254
Germanisches Nationalmuseum Sammelhandschrift 86 409.
Stadtbibliothek Nürnberg, Cod. Cent. V, App. 81.
Stadtbibliothek Cod. Cent. VII, 65.

Primary Sources

Ars memorativa (Augsburg: Johann Bämler, 1480).
Außlegung der heÿligen messe (Augsburg [Johannes Bämler], 1484).
Bernhard von Breidenbach, *Die heyligen reyssen gen Jherusalem* (Mainz: Erhard Reuwich, 1486).
Das Reisebuch der Familie Rieter, ed. Reinhold Röhricht and Heinrich Meisner (Tübingen: Bibliothek des litterarischen Vereins in Stuttgart, 1884).
Der Heiligen Leben (Nuremberg: Hans Sensenschmid, 28 July 1474).
Der Heiligen Leben (Nuremberg: Anton Koberger, 1488).
Eusebius, *The History of the Church*, trans. G.A. Williamson (London: Penguin, 1965; rev. reprint 1989).
Fabri, Felix, *The Wanderings of Felix Fabri*, trans. Aubrey Stewart, 2 vols, The Library of the Palestine Pilgrims' Text Society 7–10 (London: Committee of the Palestine Exploration Fund, 1897).
Fortunatus (Augsburg: Johann Otmar, 1509).
Fortunatus. Studienausgabe nach der editio princeps von 1509, ed. Hans-Gert Roloff, Universal-Bibliothek 7721 (Stuttgart: Reclam, 1981).
Fridolin, Stephan, *Schatzbehalter* (Nuremberg: Anton Koberger, 1491).

Gebetbüchlein (Augsburg: Günter Zainer, 1471).

Geoffroy de la Tour Landry, *The Book of the Knight of the Tower. Translated by William Caxton*, ed. M.Y. Offord, Early English Text Society, Supplementary Series 2 (London, New York and Toronto: Oxford University Press, 1971).

Gottfried von Strassburg, *Tristan*, ed. Karl Marold (Berlin: de Gruyter, 1969).

Gottfried von Strassburg, *Tristan*, trans. and intro. Arthur Hatto (Harmondsworth: Penguin, 1960).

Hartmann von Aue, *Erec*, ed. Christoph Cormeau and Kurt Gärtner, Altdeutsche Textbibliothek 39 (Tübingen: Niemeyer, 1985).

Hartmann von Aue, *Iwein*, ed. G.F. Benecke and K. Lachmann, rev. Ludwig Wolff (7th edn Berlin: de Gruyter, 1968).

Herbort von Fritslâr, *Liet von Troye*, ed. Ge. Karl Frommann (Quedlingburg and Leipzig: Basse, 1837; reprint Amsterdam: Rodopi, 1966).

Jacobus de Voragine, *The Golden Legend. Readings on the Saints*, trans. William Granger Ryan, vol. 2 (Princeton: Princeton University Press, 1993), pp. 334–41.

Katharinen Martyr, ed. Johann Lambel, *Germania*, 8 (1863): 129–86.

Konrad von Megenberg, *Buch der Natur* (Augsburg: Johannes Bämler, 1475).

Ludolf von Sudheim, *Ludolph von Suchem's Description of the Holy Land and of the Way Thither. Written in the Year 1350*, trans. Aubrey Stewart, Palestine Pilgrims' Text Society 27 (London: Palestine Pilgrims' Text Society, 1895).

Marquard vom Stein, *Marquard vom Stein. Der Ritter vom Turn*, ed. Ruth Harvey, Texte des späten Mittelalters und der frühen Neuzeit 32 (Berlin: Erich Schmidt, 1988).

Mirabilia Romae (Nuremberg: [Peter Wagner], 1491).

Paumgartner, Steffan, 'Die Jerusalemfahrt des Herzogs Heinrich des Frommen von Sachsen (1498)', ed. Reinhold Röhricht, *Zeitschrift des deutschen Palästina-Vereins*, 24 (1901): 1–25.

Schedel, Hartmann, *Weltchronik* (Nuremberg: Anton Koberger, 23 December 1493).

Seuse, Heinrich, *Stundenbuch der Weisheit*, trans. Sandra Fenten (Würzburg: Königshausen & Neumann, 2007).

Tucher, Hans, *Reise zum Heiligen Grab* (Augsburg: Johann Schönsperger, 1482).

Tucher, Hans, *Die 'Reise ins Gelobte Land' Hans Tuchers des Älteren (1479–1480)*, ed. Randall Herz, Wissensliteratur im Mittelalter 38 (Wiesbaden: Reichert, 2002).

Wolfram von Eschenbach, *Parzival*, ed. Karl Lachmann (6th edn Berlin and Leipzig: de Gruyter, 1926; reprint 1965).

Wolfram von Eschenbach, *Parzival*, trans. A.T. Hatto (Harmondsworth: Penguin, 1980).

Secondary Sources

Allgemeine Deutsche Biographie, ed. die historische Commission bei der königl. Akademie der Wissenschaften (Leipzig: Duncker & Humblot, 1884).

Angenendt, Arnold and Kren Meiners, 'Erscheinungsformen spätmittelalterlicher Religiosität', in *Divina Officia. Liturgie und Frömmigkeit im Mittelalter*, Ausstellungskataloge der Herzog August Bibliothek 83 (Wolfenbüttel: Herzog August Bibliothek, 2000), pp. 25–35.

Apostolos-Cappadona, Diane, *Dictionary of Women in Religious Art* (1st edn New York: Continnuum, 1996; reprint New York and Oxford: Oxford University Press, 1998).

Arnold, Klaus, 'Wallfahrten als Nürnberger Familientradition um 1500', in Klaus Arnold (ed.), *Wallfahrten in Nürnberg um 1500. Akten des interdisziplinären Symposions vom 29. und 30. September 2000 im Caritas Pirckheimer-Haus in Nürnberg, Pirckheimer Jahrbuch*, 17 (2002): 133–41.

Assion, Peter, *Die Mirakel der Hl. Katharina von Alexandrien. Untersuchungen und Texte zur Entstehung und Nachwirkung mittelalterlicher Wunderliteratur* (Diss. Phil. Heidelberg 1969).

Assion, Peter, 'Katharina von Alexandrien', in *Die deutsche Literatur des Mittelalters. Verfasserlexikon*, vol. 4 (Berlin and New York: de Gruyter, 1983), col. 1055–73.

d'Avray, D.L., 'Katharine of Alexandria and Mass Communication in Germany: Woman as Intellectual', in Nicole Bériou and David L. d'Avray (eds), *Modern Questions about Medieval Sermons. Essays on Marriage, Death, History and Sanctity*, Biblioteca di Medioevo Latino 11 (Spoleto: Centro Italiano di Studi sull'Alto Medioevo, 1994), pp. 401–8.

Baker, Sharon J., *Sachs and the City: Staged Avarice as a Barometer for Civic Confusion* (MA Diss. Bristol 2009).

Barth, Susanne, *Jungfrauenzucht: Literaturwissenschaftliche und pädagogische Studien zur Mädchenerziehungsliteratur zwischen 1200 und 1600* (Diss. Phil. Cologne 1993) (Stuttgart: M&P, 1994).

Basilika Vierzehnheiligen. Symphonie in Licht und Farbe, Text P. Dominik Lutz, Bild A. Bornschlegel (Staffelstein: Obermain Buch- + Bildverlag Bornschlegel, 1986).

Bauer, Herbert, 'Zwischen Andrang und Entfremdung. Der Lorenzer Hallenchor und die Erfahrung der Gemeinde', in Herbert Bauer, Gerhard Hirschmann and Georg Stolz (eds), *500 Jahre Hallenchor St. Lorenz zu Nürnberg 1477–1977*, Nürnberger Forschungen 20 (Nuremberg: Selbstverlag des Vereins für Geschichte der Stadt Nürnberg, 1977), pp. 22–40.

Baxandall, Michael, *Painting & Experience in Fifteenth-Century Italy* (Oxford and New York: Oxford University Press, 1972).

Beatie, Bruce A., 'Saint Katharine of Alexandria: Traditional Themes and the Development of a Medieval German Narrative', *Speculum*, 52 (1977): 785–800.

Beatie, Bruce A., 'St. Katharine of Alexandria in Medieval German Illustrative Cycles: A Problem beyond Genre', in Hubert Heinen and Ingeborg Henderson (eds), *Genres in Medieval German Literature*, GAG 439 (Göppingen: Kümmerle, 1986), pp. 140–56.

Becksmann, Rüdiger (ed.), *Glasmalerei im Kontext. Bildprogramme und Raumfunktionen. Akten des XXII. Internationalen Colloquiums des Corpus Vitrearum Nürnberg, 29. August – 1. September 2004*, Wissenschaftliche Beibände zum Anzeiger des Germanischen Nationalmuseums 25 (Nuremberg: Germanisches Nationalmuseum, 2005).

Belzyt, Leszek, 'Nürnberger Kaufleute, Handwerker und Künstler in Krakau', in Helmut Neuhaus (ed.), *Nürnberg – Europäische Stadt in Mittelalter und Neuzeit*, Nürnberger Forschungen 29 (Nuremberg: Selbstverlag des Vereins für Geschichte der Stadt Nürnberg, 2000), pp. 249–61.

Benecke, Georg Friedrich, *Mittelhochdeutsches Wörterbuch*, 4 vols (Leipzig: Hirzel, 1854-66).

Biedermann, Johann Gottfried, *Geschlechtsregister des Hochadelichen Patriciats zu Nürnberg* (Bayreuth: Friederich Elias Dietzel, 1748; reprint Neustadt an der Aisch: Christoph Schmidt, 1982).

Binski, Paul, *Medieval Death. Ritual and Representation* (London: British Museum Press, 1996).

Blendinger, Christian, 'Der Lorenzer Hallenchor. Schatzkammer und Ort der Verkündung', in Herbert Bauer, Gerhard Hirschmann and Georg Stolz (eds), *500 Jahre Hallenchor St. Lorenz zu Nürnberg 1477–1977*, Nürnberger Forschungen 20 (Nuremberg: Selbstverlag des Vereins für Geschichte der Stadt Nürnberg, 1977), pp. 41–62.

Bock, Franz, *Die Werke des Matthias Grünewald*, Studien zur deutschen Kunstgeschichte 54 (Strasbourg: J.H. Ed. Heitz, 1904).

Bornstein, Diane, *The Lady in the Tower: Medieval Courtesy Literature for Women* (Hamden: Archon, for Shoe String Press, 1983).

Bowie, Fiona and Oliver Davies (ed. and intro.), *Hildegard of Bingen. An Anthology* (London: SPCK, 1990).

Brandl, Rainer, 'Der Katharinenaltar des Georg Fütterer. Anmerkungen zu seinem wiederentdeckten Stifterbild', *Anzeiger des Germanischen Nationalmuseums* (1988): 95–115.

Bray, Jennifer Relvyn, *The Legend of St Katherine in Later Middle English Literature* (PhD Diss. London 1984).

Brockmann, Stephen, *Nuremberg: The Imaginary Capital*, Studies in German literature, linguistics, and culture (Rochester and Woodbridge: Camden House, 2006).

Brüggemann, Theodor, in conjunction with Otto Brunken. *Handbuch zur Kinder- und Jugendliteratur: Vom Beginn des Buchdrucks bis 1570* (Stuttgart, 1987).

Bull, Marcus (intro. and trans.), *The Miracles of Our Lady of Rocamadour* (Woodbridge: Boydell, 1999).

Burghartz, Susanna, 'Ehebruch und eheherrliche Gewalt. Literarische und außerliterarische Bezüge im "Ritter vom Turn"', in Hans-Jürgen Bachorski (ed.), *Ordnung und Lust. Bilder von Liebe, Ehe und Sexualität in Spätmittelalter und Früher Neuzeit*, Literatur – Imagination – Realität 1 (Trier: Wissenschaftlicher Verlag, 1991), pp. 123–40.

Camille, Michael, *Gothic Art: Visions and Revelations of the Medieval World*, Everyman Art Library (London: Weidenfeld & Nicolson, 1996).

Camille, Michael, *The Medieval Art of Love* (London: Laurence King, 1998).

Camille, Michael, 'Before the Gaze. The Internal Senses and Late Medieval Practices of Seeing', in Robert S. Nelson (ed.), *Visuality before and beyond the Renaissance. Seeing as Others Saw* (Cambridge: Cambridge University Press, 2000), pp. 197–223.

Campana, Luc, *Die 14 Heiligen Nothelfer* (Lauerz: Theresia, 2008).

Campbell, Joseph, *The Hero with a Thousand Faces* (Princeton: Princeton University Press: 1949; reprint London: Fontana, 1993).

Carbach, Johann Jacob, *Nürnbergisches Zion / Das ist: Wahrhaffte Beschreibung Aller Kirchen und Schulen in= und ausserhalb Der Reichs=Stadt Nürnberg [..]*. (s.l., 1733).

Carroll, Jane L., 'Woven Devotions. Reform and Piety in Tapestries by Dominican Nuns', in Jane L. Carroll and Alison G. Stewart (eds), *Saints, Sinners and Sisters. Gender and Northern Art in Medieval and Early Modern Europe* (Aldershot: Ashgate, 2003), pp. 182–201.

Carruthers, Mary, *The Book of Memory. A Study of Memory in Medieval Culture* (Cambridge: Cambridge University Press, 1990).

Caviness, Madeline H., 'Stained Glass Windows in Gothic Chapels, and the Feasts of the Saints', in *Kunst und Liturgie im Mittelalter. Akten des internationalen Kongresses der Bibliotheca Hertziana und des Nederlands Instituut te Rome. Rom, 28.–30. September 1997, Römisches Jahrbuch der Bibliotheca Hertziana*, Beiheft zu Band 33 (1999/2000) (Munich: Hirmer, 2000), pp. 135–48.

Celtis, Conrad, *Norimberga*, trans. and ed. Gerhard Fink (Nuremberg: Nürnberger Presse, 2000).

Conklin Akbari, Suzanne, *Seeing through the Veil* (Toronto, Buffalo and London: University of Toronto Press, 2004).

Cuneo, Pia F., 'The Basilica Cycle of Saint Katherine's Convent. Art and Female Community in Early-Renaissance Augsburg', *Women's Art Journal*, 19 (1998): 21–5.

Curtius, Andreas, 'Die Hauskapelle als architektonischer Rahmen der privaten Andacht', in *Spiegel der Seligkeit. Privates Bild und Frömmigkeit im Spätmittelalter*, Ausstellungskatalog Germanisches Nationalmuseum, Nürnberg (Nuremberg: Verlag des Germanischen Nationalmuseums, 2000), pp. 34–48.

Die deutsche Literatur des Mittelalters. Verfasserlexikon, 13 vols (Berlin and New York: de Gruyter, 1978–2007).

Die Religion in Geschichte und Gegenwart, Handwörterbuch für Theologie und Religionswissenschaft, ed. Friedrich Michael Schiele and Leopold Zscharnack (Tübingen: J.C.B. Mohr, 1909–1913; 3rd edn ed. Kurt Galling et al. (Tübingen: Mohr Siebeck, 1957–65).

Deutsche Pilgerreisen nach dem Heiligen Lande, ed. Reinhold Röhricht (Innsbruck: Wagner'schen Universitätsbuchhandlung, 1900).

Dinzelbacher, Peter, 'Die Visionen des Mittelalters. Ein geschichtlicher Umriß', *Zeitschrift für Religions- und Geistesgeschichte*, 30 (1978): 116–28.

Dinzelbacher, Peter, 'Katharina von Alexandrien', in *Die deutsche Literatur des Mittelalters. Verfasserlexikon*, vol. 4 (Berlin and New York: de Gruyter, 1983), col. 1055–75.

Dormeier, Heinrich, 'Kirchenjahr, Heiligenverehrung und große Politik im Almosengefällbuch der Nürnberger Lorenzpfarrei (1454–1516)', *Mitteilungen des Vereins für Geschichte der Stadt Nürnberg*, 84 (1997): 1–60.

The Dramas of Hrotsvit of Gandersheim, trans. and intro. Katharina M. Wilson, Matrologia Latina (Saskatoon: Peregrina, 1985).

Drewer, Lois, 'Jephthah and His Daughter in Medieval Art: Ambiguities of Heroism and Sacrifice', in Colum Hourihane (ed.), *Insights and Interpretations*, Index of Christian Art Occasional Papers 5 (Princeton: Department of Art and Archaeology, Princeton University, in association with Princeton University Press, 2002), pp. 35–59.

Dubbini, Renzo, *Geography of the Gaze. Urban and Rural Vision in Early Modern Europe*, trans. Lydia G. Cochrane (Chicago and London: University of Chicago Press, 2002) (First published as *Geografie dello sguardo: Visione e paesaggio in età moderna* (Turin: Giulio Einaudi editore, 1994)).

Dünninger, Joself, 'Die Wallfahrtslegende von Vierzehnheiligen', in *Festschrift für Wolfgang Stammler zu seinem 65. Geburtstag*, ed. Wolfgang Stammler, Gerhard Eis, Johannes Hansel and Richard Kienast (Berlin: Erich Schmidt, 1953), pp. 192–205.

Ehrenschwendtner, Marie-Luise, 'A Library Collected by and for the Use of Nuns: St Catherine's Convent, Nuremberg', in Jane H.M. Taylor and Lesley Smith (eds), *Women and the Book. Assessing the Visual Evidence* (London and Toronto: British Library and University of Toronto Press, 1996), pp. 123–32.

Eichhorn, Ernst, 'Der Sebalder Engelschor. Ein Beitrag zur mittelalterlichen Sakralarchitektur Nürnbergs', in Helmut Baier im Auftrag des Evang.-Luth. Pfarramts St. Sebald (ed.), *600 Jahre Ostchor St. Sebald – 1379–1979* (Neustadt a. d. Aisch: Ph. C. W. Schmidt, 1979), pp. 94–116.

Eis, Gerhard, 'Lupold von Wiltingen. Eine Studie zum Wunderanhang der Katharinenlegende', in *Festschrift für Wolfgang Stammler zu seinem 65. Geburtstag*, ed. Wolfgang Stammler, Gerhard Eis, Johannes Hansel and Richard Kienast (Berlin: Erich Schmidt, 1953), pp. 78–91.

Eisermann, Falk, review of Antje Willing, *Literatur und Ordensreform im 15. Jahrhundert. Deutsche Abendmahlsschriften im Nürnberger Katharinenkloster*, Studien und Texte zum Mittelalter und zur frühen Neuzeit 4 (Münster: Waxmann, 2004), in *IASL Online* at http://iasl.uni-muenchen.de/rezensio/liste/Eisermann3830913311-1032.html.

Elsevier's Dictionary of Symbols and Imagery. Second, Enlarged Edition by Ad de Vries. Revised and Updated by Arthur de Vries (Amsterdam: Elsevier, 2004).

Endres, Rudolf, 'Das Schulwesen in Franken im ausgehenden Mittelalter', in Bernd Moeller, Hans Patze and Karl Stackmann (eds), *Studien zum städtischen Bildungswesen des späten Mittelalters und der frühen Neuzeit*, Abhandlungen der Akademie der Wissenschaften in Göttingen Philologisch-historische Klasse Dritte Folge 137 (Göttingen: Vandenhoeck & Ruprecht, 1983), pp. 173–214.

Falkenburg, Reindert, Walter S. Melion and Todd M. Richardson (eds), *Image and Imagination of the Religious Self in Late Medieval and Early Modern Europe*, Proteus: Studies in Early Modern Identity Formation 1 (Turnhout: Brepols, 2007).

Fehring, P. and Anton Ress, *Die Stadt Nürnberg*, 2nd edition revised by Wilhelm Schwemmer, Bayerische Kunstdenkmale 10 (1st edn 1961; Munich: Deutscher Kunstverlag, 1977).

Fisher, Sally, *The Square Halo & Other Mysteries of Western Art Images and the Stories that Inspired Them* (New York: Harry N. Abrams, 1995).

Fleischmann, Peter, *Nürnberg mit Fürth und Erlangen. Von der Reichsstadt zur fränkischen Metropole*, Dumont Kunstreiseführer (Cologne: Dumont, 2003).

Fleischmann, Peter, *Rat und Patriziat in Nürnberg. Die Herrschaft der Ratsgeschlechter vom 13. bis zum 18. Jahrhundert*, 3. vols, Nürnberger Forschungen 31 (Neustadt an der Aisch: Schmidt, 2008).

Fries, Walter, 'Kirche und Kloster zu St. Katharina in Nürnberg', *Mitteilungen des Vereins für Geschichte der Stadt Nürnberg*, 25 (1924): 1–143 and illustrations.

Frugoni, Chiara, *A Distant City: Images of Urban Experience in the Medieval World*, trans. William McCuaig (Princeton: Princeton University Press, 1991).

Funk, Veit, *Glasfensterkunst in St. Lorenz. Michael Wolgemut, Peter Hemmel von Andlau, Hans Baldung Grien, Albrecht Dürer* (Nuremberg: A. Hofmann, 1995).

Gilchrist, Roberta, 'Medieval Bodies in the Material World: Gender, Stigma and the Body', in Sarah Kay and Miri Rubin (eds), *Framing Medieval Bodies* (Manchester: Manchester University Press, 1994), pp. 43–61.

Goodich, Michael E., *Violence and Miracle in the Fourteenth Century. Private Grief and Public Salvation* (Chicago and London: University of Chicago Press, 1995).

Gormans, Andreas and Thomas Lentes (eds), *Das Bild der Erscheinung. Die Gregorsmesse im Mittelalter*, KultBild. Religion und Visualität in der Vormoderne 3 (Berlin: Reimer, 2007).

Grigsby, J.L., 'Miroir des bonnes femmes', *Romania*, 82 (1961): 458–81 and *Romania*, 83 (1962): 30–51.

Grigsby, J.L., 'A New Source of the *Livre du Chevalier de la Tour Landry*', *Romania*, 84 (1963): 171–208.

Grote, Ludwig, *Die Tucher. Bildnis einer Patrizierfamilie*, Bibliothek des Germanischen Nationalmuseums Nürnberg zur deutschen Kunst- und Kulturgeschichte 15/16 (Munich: Prestel, 1961).

Gruner, Gerhard, *Nürnberg in Jahreszahlen* (Nuremberg: Korn & Berg, 1999).

Gümbel, Albert, *Das Mesnerpflichtbuch von St Lorenz in Nürnberg*, Einzelarbeiten aus der Kirchengeschichte Bayerns 8 (Munich: Chr. Kaiser, 1928).

Gussone, Nikolaus, 'Die Jungfrauenweihe in ottonischer Zeit nach dem Ritus im *Pontificale Romano-Germanicum*', in Jeffrey F. Hamburger, Carola Jäggi, Susan Marti and Hedwig Röckelein (eds), *Frauen – Kloster – Kunst. Neue Forschungen zur Kulturgeschichte des Mittelalters* (Turnhout: Brepols, 2007), pp. 25–41.

Hall, James, *Hall's Dictionary of Subjects & Symbols in Art*, intro. Kenneth Clark (1st edn 1974; London: John Murray, 2000).

Hallerstein, Helmut Freiherr von and Ernst Eichhorn, *Das Pilgrimspital zum Heiligen Kreuz vor Nürnberg. Geschichte und Kunstdenkmäler*, Nürnberger Forschungen 12 (Nuremberg: Verein für Geschichte der Stadt Nürnberg, 1969).

Hamburger, Jeffrey F., *Nuns as Artists. The Visual Culture of a Medieval Convent* (Berkeley, Los Angeles and London: University of California Press, 1997).

Hamburger, Jeffrey F., *The Visual and the Visionary. Art and Female Spirituality in Late Medieval Germany* (New York: Zone, 1998).

Hamburger, Jeffrey F., 'Am Anfang war das Bild: Kunst und Frauenspiritualität im Spätmittelalter', in Falk Eisermann, Eva Schlotheuber and Volker Honemann (eds), *Studien und Texte zur literarischen und materiellen Kultur der Frauenklöster im späten Mittelalter*, Studies in Medieval and Reformation Thought 99 (Leiden and Boston: Brill, 2004), pp. 1–43.

Handwörterbuch des deutschen Aberglaubens, ed. Hanns Bächtold-Stäubli, 10 vols (Berlin: de Gruyter, 1927–42).

Harper's Bible Dictionary, ed. Paul J. Achtemeier et al. (New York: HarperCollins, 1985).

Harvey, Ruth, 'Prolegomena to an edition of "Der Ritter vom Turn"', in Peter F. Ganz and Werner Schröder (eds), *Probleme mittelalterlicher Überlieferung und Textkritik. Oxforder Colloquium 1966* (Berlin: Erich Schmidt, 1968), pp. 162–82.

Heinrichs-Schreiber, Ulrike, 'Sehen als Anwendung von Wissen. Aussage und Wirkung der Bilder in Stephan Fridolins *Schatzbehalter* und bei Albrecht Dürer', in Gerd Dicke and Klaus Grübmüller (eds), *Die Gleichzeitigkeit von Handschrift und Buchdruck* (Wiesbaden: Harrassowitz, 2003), pp. 49–104.

Herz, Randall, 'Hans Tuchers des Ä. "Reise ins Gelobte Land"', in Klaus Arnold (ed.), *Wallfahrten in Nürnberg um 1500. Akten des interdisziplinären Symposions vom 29. und 30. September 2000 im Caritas Pirckheimer-Haus in Nürnberg*, *Pirckheimer Jahrbuch*, 17 (2002): 79–104.

Hilpert, Johann Wolfgang, *Nürnbergs Merkwürdigkeiten und Kunstschätze*, Heft 2, *Die Kirche des heiligen Laurentius* (Nuremberg: Friedrich Campe, 1831).

Hoffmann, Friedrich Wilhelm, *Die Sebalduskirche in Nürnberg. Ihre Baugeschichte und ihre Kunstdenkmale*, rev. Th. Hampe, E. Mummenhoff and Jos. Schmitz (Vienna: Gerlach & Wiedling, 1912).

Hubbard, Phil, *city*, Key Ideas in Geography (London and New York: Routledge, 2006).

Humphreys, Colin J., *The Miracles of Exodus. A Scientist's Discovery of the Extraordinary Natural Causes of the Biblical Stories* (London: Continuum, 2003).

Hurukawa, N., N. Seto, H. Inoue, K. Nishigami, I. Marzouk, A. Megahed, E.M. Ibrahim, H. Murakami, M. Nakamura, T. Haneda, S. Sugiyama, T. Ohkura, Y. Fujii, H.M. Hussein, A.S. Megahed, H.F. Mohammed, R. Abdel-Fattah, M. Mizoue, S. Hashimoto, M. Kobayasi and D. Suetsugu, 'Seismological Observations in and around the Southern Part of the Gulf of Suez, Egypt', *Bulletin of the Seismological Society of America*, 91 (2001), 4: 708–17.

Impelluso, Lucia, *Nature and Its Symbols*, trans. Stephen Sartarelli, A Guide to Imagery (Los Angeles: The J. Paul Getty Museum, 2004).

Jäggi, Carola, '"Sy bettet och gewonlich vor únser frowen bild ...": Überlegungen zur Funktion von Kunstwerken in spätmittelalterlichen Frauenklöstern', in Jean-Claude Schmitt (ed.), *Femmes, art et religion au Moyen Âge* (Strasbourg: Presses Universitaires de Strasbourg, 2004), pp. 62–86.

Jäggi, Carola, *Frauenklöster im Spätmittelalter. Die Kirchen der Klarissen und Dominikanerinnen im 13. und 14. Jahrhundert*, Studien zur internationalen Architektur- und Kunstgeschichte 34 (Petersberg: Michael Imhof, 2006).

Jenkins, Jacqueline and Katherine J. Lewis, 'Introduction', in Jacqueline Jenkins and Katherine J. Lewis (eds), *St Katherine of Alexandria. Texts and Contexts in Western Medieval Europe*, Medieval Women: Texts and Contexts 8 (Turnhout: Brepols, 2003).

Jolles, André, *Einfache Formen. Legende · Sage · Mythe · Rätsel · Memorabile · Märchen · Witz*, Studienausgabe der 5., unveränderten Auflage (Tübingen: Niemeyer, 1974).

Kaiser, Otto, *Isaiah 1–12. A Commentary*, trans. John Bowden, Old Testament Library (1st edn London: SMC, 1972; new edn 1983) (German: Otto Kaiser, *Das Buch des Propheten Jesaja*, Das alte Testament Deutsch 17 (Göttingen: Vandenhoeck & Ruprecht, 1981)).

Kamann, J., 'Die Pilgerfahrten Nürnberger Bürger nach Jerusalem im 15. Jahrhundert, namentlich die Reisebereichte des Dr. med. Hans Lochner und des Jörg Pfinzing', *Mitteilungen des Vereins für Geschichte der Stadt Nürnberg*, 2 (1880): 78–163.

Käppeli, Thomas, *Dominikanerinnenkloster St. Katharina. Ein Abriß seiner Geschichte* (Wil: St. Katharina, 1957).

Kataloge des Germanischen Nationalmuseums zu Nürnberg. Die Werke plastischer Kunst, ed. Walter Josephi (Nuremberg: Verlag des Germanischen Nationalmuseums, 1910).

Kataloge des Germanischen Nationalmuseums zu Nürnberg. Die Gemälde des 13. bis 16. Jahrhunderts, ed. Eberhard Lutze and Eberhard Weigand, 2 vols (Leipzig: Koehler, 1937).

'Das Katharinenspiel', ed. Otto Beckers, *Germanistische Abhandlungen*, 24 (1905): 125–57.

Kautzsch, Rudolf, *Die Holzschnitte zum Ritter vom Turn (Basel 1493). Mit einer Einleitung*, Studien zur deutschen Kunstgeschichte 44 (Strasbourg: J.H. Ed. Heitz, 1903).

Kelberg, Karsten, *Die Darstellung der Gregorsmesse in Deutschland* (Diss. Phil. Münster 1983).

Kern, Theodor von, 'Die Reformation des Katharinenklosters zu Nürnberg', *Jahresbericht des Historischen Vereins in Mittelfranken*, 31 (1863): 1–20.

Klarer, Mario, 'Die mentale imago im Mittelalter: Geoffrey Chaucers Ekphrasen', in Christine Ratkowitsch (ed.), *Die poetische Ekphrasis*, Österreichische Akademie der Wissenschaften Sitzungsberichte der phil.-hist. Klasse 735 (Vienna: Österreichische Akademie der Wissenschaften, 2006), pp. 77–96.

Knaurs Lexikon der Symbole, ed. Hans Biedermann (Munich: Droemer Knaur, 1989, 1994).

Koegler, Hans, 'Die Basler Gebetholzschnitte vom Illustrator des Narrenschiffs und Ritters vom Turn', *Gutenberg-Jahrbuch* (1926): 117–31.

Kreutzer, Hans Joachim, 'Marquart von Stein', in *Die deutsche Literatur des Mittelalters. Verfasserlexikon*, 2nd edition, vol. 6 (Berlin and New York: Walter de Gruyter, 1987), col. 129–35.

Kunze, Konrad, 'Der Heiligen Leben', *Verfasserlexikon*, vol. 3 (Berlin and New York: de Gruyter, 1981), col. 617–25.

Kunze, Konrad, 'Jacobus de Voragine', *Verfasserlexikon*, vol. 4 (Berlin and New York: de Gruyter, 1983), col. 448–66.

Kurmann-Schwarz, Brigitte, '"Fenestre vitree ... significant Sacram Scripturam". Zur Medialität mittelalterlicher Glasmalerei des 12. und 13. Jahrhunderts', in *Anzeiger des Germanischen Nationalmuseums*, Wissenschaftliche Beibände 25 (Nuremberg: Verlag des Germanischen Nationalmuseums, 2005), pp. 61–73.

Lentes, Thomas, 'Inneres Auge, äußerer Blick und heilige Schau. Ein Diskussionsbeitrag zur visuellen Praxis in Frömmigkeit und Moraldidaxe des späten Mittelalters', in Klaus Schreiner (ed.), *Frömmigkeit im Mittelalter: Politisch-soziale Kontexte, visuelle Praxis, körperliche Ausdrucksformen* (Munich: Fink, 2002), pp. 179–220.

Lewis, Katherine J., 'Pilgrimage and the Cult of Saint Katherine in Late Medieval England', in Jacqueline Jenkins and Katherine J. Lewis (eds), *St Katherine of Alexandria. Texts and Contexts in Western Medieval Europe* (Turnhout: Brepols, 2003), pp. 37–52.

Lexikon des Mittelalters, 9 vols (1st edn Lachen: Coron Verlag Monika Schoeller, 1999; reprint Frankfurt am Main: dtv, 2002).

Lexikon für Theologie und Kirche, ed. Walter Kaspar (Freiburg, Basel and Vienna: Herder, 2006; rev. version of 3rd edition, 1993–2001).

Lilley, Keith D., *City and Cosmos. The Medieval World in Urban Form* (London: Reaktion, 2009).

Lindberg, David C., *Theories of Vision from Al-Kindi to Kepler*, University of Chicago History of Science and Medicine (Chicago and London: University of Chicago Press, 1976).

Lindberg, David C., 'The Science of Optics', in David C. Lindberg (ed.), *Science in the Middle Ages*, The Chicago History of Science and Medicine (Chicago and London: University of Chicago Press, 1978).

Lusiardi, Ralf, *Stiftung und städtische Gemeinschaft. Religiöse und soziale Aspekte des Stiftungsverhaltens im spätmittelalterlichen Stralsund*, Stiftungsgeschichten 2 (Berlin: Akademie Verlag, 2000).

Macardle, Peter, 'Die Gesänge des "St. Galler Mittelrheinischen Passionsspiels". Ein Beitrag zur Rekonstruktion und Lokalisierung', in Timothy Jackson, Nigel F. Palmer and Almut Suerbaum (eds), *Die Vermittlung geistlicher Inhalte im deutschen Mittelalter. Internationales Symposium Roscrea 1994* (Tübingen: Niemeyer, 1996), pp. 255–70.

Machilek, Franz, 'Magister Jobst Krell, Vikar bei St. Lorenz in Nürnberg († 1483)', *Mitteilungen des Vereins für Geschichte der Stadt Nürnberg*, 59 (1972): 85–104.

Machilek, Franz, 'Klosterhumanismus in Nürnberg um 1500', *Mitteilungen des Vereins für Geschichte der Stadt Nürnberg*, 64 (1977): 10–45.

Machilek, Franz, 'Privatfrömmigkeit und Staatsfrömmigkeit', in Ferdinand Seibt (ed.), *Kaiser Karl IV. Staatsmann und Mäzen* (Munich: Prestel, 1978), pp. 87–101.

Machilek, Franz, 'Dedicationes Ecclesiae Sancti Sebaldi. Die mittelalterlichen Kirch- und Altarweihen bei St. Sebald in Nürnberg', in Helmut Baier im Auftrag des Evang. –Luth. Pfarramtes St. Sebald (ed.), *600 Jahre Ostchor St. Sebald – 1379–1979* (Neustadt a. d. Aisch: Ph. C. W. Schmidt, 1979), pp. 143–59.

Maijer, Moritz Maximilian, *Denkwürdigkeiten und Kunstschätze*, 1. Heft, *Die Kirche des heiligen Sebaldus* (Nuremberg: Friedrich Campe, 1831).

Marquard vom Stein: Der Ritter vom Turn. Kommentar, posthumously ed. Peter Ganz, Nigel Palmer, Lothar Schmitt and Christopher Wells, Texte des späten Mittelalters und der frühen Neuzeit 37 (Berlin: Erich Schmidt, 1996).

Meier, Esther, *Die Gregorsmesse. Funktionen eines spätmittelalterlichen Bildtypus* (Cologne, Weimar and Vienna: Böhlau, 2006).

Meiss, Millard and Elizabeth H. Beatson (eds), *Les Belles Heures de Jean Duc de Berry. The Cloisters. The Metropolitan Museum of Art* (London: Thames and Hudson, 1974).

Meyer, Adrian, *Stadt und Architektur. Ein Geflecht aus Geschichte, Erinnerung, Theorie und Praxis* (Baden: Lars Müller, 2003).

Meyer, Heinz and Rudolf Suntrup, *Lexikon der mittelalterlichen Zahlenbedeutungen*, Münstersche Mittelalter-Schriften 56 (Munich: Fink, 1987).

Mills, Bob, *Suspended Animation. Pain, Pleasure & Punishment in Medieval Culture* (London: Reaktion, 2005).

Moeller, Bernd, 'Die Anfänge kommunaler Bibliotheken in Deutschland', in Bernd Moeller, Hans Patze and Karl Stackmann (eds), *Studien zum städtischen Bildungswesen des späten Mittelalters und der frühen Neuzeit*, Abhandlungen der Akademie der Wissenschaften in Göttingen Philologisch-historische Klasse Dritte Folge 137 (Göttingen: Vandenhoeck & Ruprecht, 1983), pp. 136–72.

Mornin, Edward and Lorna Mornin, *Saints. A Visual Guide* (Toronto: Novalis, 2006).

Müllner, Johannes, *Die Annalen der Reichsstadt Nürnberg von 1623*, vol. 1 *Von den Anfängen bis 1350*, ed. and intro. Gerhard Hirschmann, Quellen zur Geschichte und Kultur der Stadt Nürnberg 8 (Nuremberg: im Selbstverlag des Stadtrats zu Nürnberg, 1972); vol. 2 *Von 1351–1469*, ed. Gerhard Hirschmann, Quellen zur Geschichte und Kultur der Stadt Nürnberg 11 (Nuremberg: im Selbstverlag des Stadtrats zu Nürnberg, 1984); vol. 3 *1470–1544*, ed. Michael Diefenbacher in collaboration with Walter Gebhardt, Quellen zur Geschichte und Kultur der Stadt Nürnberg 32 (Nuremberg: im Selbstverlag des Stadtarchivs Nürnberg, 2003).

Murr, Christoph Gottlieb von, *Beschreibung der vornehmsten Merkwürdigkeiten in des H. R. Reichs freyen Stadt Nürnberg und auf der hohen Schule zu Altdorf* (Nuremberg: Johann Eberhard Zeh, 1778).

Murray, Peter and Linda Murray, *The Oxford Companion to Christian Art & Architecture* (Oxford and New York: Oxford University Press, 1996).

Neue Deutsche Biographie, ed. die Historische Kommission bei der Bayerischen Akademie der Wissenschaften, vol. 2 (Berlin: Duncker & Humblot, 1955).

Nicholls, Theodor Jonathan, *The Matter of Courtesy. Medieval Courtesy Books and the Gawain-Poet* (Cambridge: Brewer, 1985).

Northemann, Yvonne, *Zwischen Vergessen und Erinnern. Die Nürnberger Klöster im medialen Geflecht* (Petersberg: Michael Imhof, 2011).

Nürnberg 1350–1550. Kunst der Gothik und Renaissance (Munich: Prestel, 1986).

Die Nürnberger Ratsverlässe, Schriften des Zentralinstituts für fränkische Landeskunde und allgemeine Regionalforschung an der Universität Erlangen–Nürnberg 23, vol. 1 *1449–1450*, ed. Irene Stahl (Neustadt an der

Aisch: Degener, 1983); vol. 2 *1452–1471*, ed. Martin Schieber (Neustadt an der Aisch: Degener, 1995).

Ochsenbein, Peter, 'Latein und Deutsch im Alltag oberrheinischer Dominikanerinnenklöster des Spätmittelalters', in Nikolaus Henkel and Nigel F. Palmer (eds), *Latein und Volkssprache im deutschen Mittelalter. Regensburger Colloquium 1988* (Tübingen: Niemeyer, 1992), pp. 42–51.

Ochsenbein, Peter, 'Handschrift und Druck in der Gebetbuchliteratur zwischen 1470 und 1520', in Gerd Dicke and Klaus Grubmüller (eds), *Die Gleichzeitigkeit von Handschrift und Buchdruck*, Wolfenbütteler Mittelalter-Studien 16 (Wiesbaden: Harrassowitz, 2003), pp. 113–27.

Os, Henk van, with Hans Nieuwdorp, Bernhard Ridderbos and Eugène Honée, *The Art of Devotion in the Late Middle Ages in Europe 1300–1500*, trans. Michael Hoyle (Princeton: Princeton University Press, 1994).

Panofsky, Erwin, *The Life and Art of Albrecht Dürer* (Princeton: Princeton University Press, 1943).

Pastoureau, Michael, *Blue. The History of a Color*, trans. Markus I. Cruse (Princeton and Oxford: Princeton University Press, 2001) (original French: *Bleu: Histoire d'une couleur* (Paris: Editions du Seuil, 2000)).

Pechloff, Ursula, *Nürnberg. St. Egidien* (Nuremberg: ev.-luth. Pfarramt St. Egidien, 1996).

Pfeiffer, Gerhard (ed.), *Nürnberg. Geschichte einer europäischen Stadt* (Munich: Beck, 1982).

Pile, Steve, *The Body and the City: Psychoanalysis, Space and Subjectivity* (London and New York: Routledge, 1996).

Pilz, Kurt, *Die Egidienkirche in Nürnberg. Ihre Geschichte und ihre Kunstwerke*, Einzelarbeiten aus der Kirchengeschichte Bayerns 4 (Nuremberg: Selbstverlag des Vereins für bayerische Kirchengeschichte, 1972).

Poulain, Louis, *Der Ritter vom Turn von Marquart von Stein* (Diss. Phil. Basel 1906).

Reske, Christoph, *Die Produktion der Schedelschen Weltchronik in Nürnberg*, Mainzer Studien zur Buchwissenschaft 10 (Wiesbaden: Harrassowitz, 2000).

Röttinger, Heinrich, 'Die Holzschnitte der Druckerei des Jacob Cammerlander in Straßburg', *Gutenberg-Jahrbuch* (1936).

Schauber, Vera and Hanns Michael Schindler, *Bildlexikon der Heiligen* (Munich, 1999).

Schieber, Martin, *Nürnberg. Eine illustrierte Geschichte der Stadt* (Munich: Beck, 2000).

Schiewer, Hans-Jochen, 'Auditionen und Visionen einer Begine. Die "Selige Schererin", Johannes Mulberg und der Basler Beginenstreit. Mit einem Textabdruck', in Timothy Jackson, Nigel F. Palmer and Almut Suerbaum (eds), *Die Vermittlung geistlicher Inhalte im deutschen Mittelalter. Internationales Symposium Roscrea 1994* (Tübingen: Niemeyer, 1996), pp. 289–317.

Schleif, Corine, *Donatio et Memoria. Stifter, Stiftungen und Motivationen an Beispielen aus der Lorenzkirche in Nürnberg*, Kunstwissenschaftliche Studien 58 (Munich: Deutscher Kunstverlag, 1990).

Schleif, Corine, 'Forgotten Roles of Women as Donors: Sister Katerina Lemmel's Negotiated Exchanges in the Care for the Here and the Hereafter', in Truus van Bueren in collaboration with Andrea van Leerdam (eds), *Care for the Here and the Hereafter:* Memoria, *Art and Ritual in the Middle Ages* (Turnhout: Brepols, 2005), pp. 137–54.

Schleif, Corine and Volker Schier, *Katerina's Windows* (Philadelphia: Pennsylvania State University Press, 2009).

Schlie, Heike, 'Die Autoritätsmuster der "Gregorsmesse" – Umdeutungen und Auflösungen eines Zeichensystems', in Frank Büttner and Gabriele Wimböck (eds), *Das Bild als Autorität. Die normierende Kraft des Bildes* (Münster: LIT, 2004), pp. 73–101.

Schlotheuber, Eva, 'Die Bedeutung der Jungfräulichkeit für das Selbstverständnis der Nonnen der alten Orden', in Jeffrey F. Hamburger, Carola Jäggi, Susan Marti and Hedwig Röckelein (eds), *Frauen – Kloster – Kunst. Neue Forschungen zur Kulturgeschichte des Mittelalters* (Brepols, 2007), pp. 43–55.

Schmid, Josef J., 'Die Reichskleinodien. Objekte zwischen Liturgie, Kult und Mythos', in Bernd Heidenreich and Frank-Lothar Kroll (eds), *Wahl und Krönung* (Frankfurt: Societätsverlag, 2006), pp. 123–49.

Schmidt, Peter, 'Die Rolle der Bilder in der Kommunikation zwischen Frauen und Männern, Kloster und Welt: Schenken und Tauschen bei den Nürnberger Dominikanerinnen', in Jean-Claude Schmitt (ed.), *Femmes, art et religion au Moyen Âge* (Strasbourg: Presses Universitaires de Strasbourg, 2004), pp. 34–61.

Schneider, Karin, 'Die Bibliothek des Katharinenklosters in Nürnberg und die städtische Gesellschaft', in Bernd Moeller, Hans Patze and Karl Stackmann (eds), *Studien zum städtischen Bildungswesen des späten Mittelalters und der frühen Neuzeit*, Abhandlungen der Akademie der Wissenschaften in Göttingen Philologisch-historische Klasse Dritte Folge 137 (Göttingen: Vandenhoeck & Ruprecht, 1983), pp. 70–82.

Schnitzler, Norbert, 'Illusion, Täuschung und schöner Schein. Probleme der Bildverehrung im späten Mittelalter. Schaufrömmigkeit – ein Mißverständnis', in Klaus Schreiner (ed.), *Frömmigkeit im Mittelalter: Politisch-soziale Kontexte, visuelle Praxis, körperliche Ausdrucksformen* (Munich: Fink, 2002), pp. 221–39.

Scholz, Hartmut, *Entwurf und Ausführung. Werkstattpraxis in der Nürnberger Glasmalerei der Dürerzeit*, Corpus vitrearum medii aevi Deutschland, Studien 1 (Berlin: Deutscher Verlag für Kunstwissenschaft, 1991) (Diss. Phil. Stuttgart 1988).

Scholz, Hartmut, 'Aktuelle Forschung zur Glasmalerei in St. Lorenz', in Christian Schmidt and Georg Stolz (eds), *Hundert Jahre Verein zur Erhaltung 1903–2003*, Schriftenreihe des Vereins zur Erhaltung der St. Lorenzkirche in Nürnberg 2 (Nuremberg, 2004), pp. 52–9.

Scholz, Hartmut, *St. Sebald in Nürnberg*, Meisterwerke der Glasmalerei 3 (Regensburg: Schnell + Steiner, 2007).

Schraut, Elizabeth, *Stifterinnen und Künstlerinnen im mittelalterlichen Nürnberg*, Ausstellungskataloge des Stadtarchivs Nürnberg 1 (Nuremberg: Selbstverlag der Stadt Nürnberg, 1987).

Schreiner, Klaus (ed.), *Frömmigkeit im Mittelalter. Politisch-soziale Kontexte, visuelle Praxis, körperliche Ausdrucksformen* (Munich: Fink, 2002).

Schriften aus der Gottesfreund-Literatur, 1. Heft, *Sieben bisher unveröffentlichte Traktate und Lektionen*, ed. Philipp Strauch, Altdeutsche Textbibliothek 22 (Halle: Niemeyer, 1927), pp. x–xii and pp. 1–21.

Schulz, Fritz Traugott, *Die Rundkapelle zu Altenfurt bei Nürnberg*, Studien zur deutschen Kunstgeschichte 94 (Strassburg: Heitz (Heitz & Mündel), 1908).

Seegets, Petra, 'Leben und Streben in spätmittelalterlichen Frauenklöstern', in Berndt Hamm and Thomas Lentes (eds), *Spätmittelalterliche Frömmigkeit zwischen Ideal und Praxis*, Spätmittelalter und Reformation. Neue Reihe 15 (Tübingen: Mohr Siebeck, 2001), pp. 24–44.

Sennett, Richard, *Flesh and Stone. The Body and the City in Western Civilization* (New York and London: Norton, 1994).

Siart, Olaf, *Kreuzgänge mittelalterlicher Frauenklöster. Bildprogramme und Funktionen* (Petersberg: Michael Imhof, 2008).

Smith, Susan L., 'The Gothic Mirror and the Female Gaze', in Jane L. Carroll and Alison G. Stewart (eds), *Saints, Sinners and Sisters. Gender and Northern Art in Medieval and Early Modern Europe* (Aldershot: Ashgate, 2003), pp. 73–92.

Spiegel der Seligkeit. Privates Bild und Frömmigkeit im Spätmittelalter, ed. G. Ulrich Großmann, Ausstellungskatalog des Germanischen Nationalmuseums (Nuremberg: Verlag des Germanischen Nationalmuseums, 2000).

Spilling, Harald, *Die Visio Tnugdali. Eigenart und Stellung in der mittelalterlichen Visionsliteratur bis zum Ende des 12. Jahrhunderts*, Münchener Beiträge zur Mediävistik und Renaissance-Forschung, 21 (Munich: Bei der Arbeo-Gesellschaft, 1975).

Stadtlexikon Nürnberg, ed. Michael Diefenbacher and Rudolf Endres (Nuremberg: Tümmels, 1999; 2nd edn 2000).

Steer, Georg, 'Geistliche Prosa', in *Geschichte der deutschen Literatur von den Anfängen bis zur Gegenwart*, vol. 3, *Die deutsche Literatur im Spätmittelalter 1250–1370*, Teil 2, *Reimpaargedichte, Drama, Prosa*, ed. Ingeborg Glier (Munich: Beck, 1987), Chapter 6, pp. 306–70.

Steinke, Barbara, *Paradisgarten oder Gefängnis? Das Nürnberger Katharinenkloster zwischen Klosterreform und Reformation*, Spätmittelaltar und Reformation. Neue Reihe 30 (Tübingen: Mohr Siebeck, 2006).

Stolz, Georg, 'Die zwei Schwestern. Gedanken zum Bau des Lorenzer Hallenchors 1439–77', in Herbert Bauer, Gerhard Hirschmann and Georg Stolz (eds), *500 Jahre Hallenchor St. Lorenz zu Nürnberg 1477–1977*, Nürnberger Forschungen 20 (Nuremberg: Selbstverlag des Vereins für Geschichte der Stadt Nürnberg, 1977), pp. 1–21.

Strieder, Peter, *Tafelmalerei in Nürnberg 1350–1550* (Königstein im Taunus: Karl Robert Langewiesche Nachfolger & Hans Köster Verlagsbuchhandlung, 1993).

Theologisches Begriffslexikon zum Neuen Testament, ed. Lothar Coenen, Erich Bayreuther and Hans Bietenhard, 3 vols (Wuppertal: Brockhaus, 1969–71).

Tobin, Rosemary Barton, *Vincent of Beauvais' 'De Eruditione Filiorum Nobilium'. The Education of Women*, American University Studies, Series XIV Education, 5 (New York, Berne and Frankfurt am Main: Lang, 1984).

Vavra, Elisabeth, 'Bildmotiv und Frauenmystik – Funktion und Rezeption', in Peter Dinzelbacher and Dieter R. Bauer (eds), *Frauenmystik im Mittelalter* (Ostfildern: Schwabenverlag, 1985), pp. 201–30.

Veit, Ludwig, *Handel und Wandel mit aller Welt*, Bibliothek des Germanischen National-Museums Nürnberg zur deutschen Kunst- und Kulturgeschichte 14 (Munich: Sporer, 1960).

Walker Bynum, Caroline, 'Seeing and Seeing Beyond: The Mass of St. Gregory in the Fifteenth Century', in Jeffrey F. Hamburger and Anne-Marie Bouché (eds), *The Mind's Eye: Art and Theological Argument in the Middle Ages* (Princeton: Department of Art and Archaeology Princeton University in association with Princeton University Press, 2006), pp. 208–40.

Walker Bynum, Caroline, *Wonderful Blood. Theology and Practice in Late Medieval Northern Germany and Beyond* (Philadelphia: University of Pennsylvania Press, 2007).

Walsh, Christine, *The Cult of St Katherine of Alexandria in Early Medieval Europe*, Church, Faith and Culture in the Medieval West (Aldershot and Burlington, VT: Ashgate, 2007).

Weilandt, Gerhardt, 'Heiligen-Konjunktur. Reliquienpräsentation, Reliquienverehrung und wirtschaftliche Situation an der Nürnberger Lorenzkirche im Spätmittelalter', in Markus Mayr (ed.), *Von Goldenen Gebeinen. Wirtschaft und Reliquie im Mittelalter*, Geschichte und Ökonomie 9 (Innsbruck, Vienna and Munich: Studien-Verlag, 2001), pp. 186–220.

Weilandt, Gerhardt, 'Pilgrimage in the Medieval City. The Example of Nuremberg in the 15th Century', *Peregrinationes*, 1, 4, 20 at http://peregrinations.kenyon.edu/vol1-4/articles/weilandt.pdf.

Weilandt, Gerhardt, *Die Sebalduskirche in Nürnberg. Bild und Gesellschaft im Zeitalter der Gotik und Renaissance* (Petersberg: Michael Imhof, 2007).

Weisbach, Werner, *Der Meister der Bergmannschen Offizin und Albrecht Dürers Beziehungen zur Basler Buchillustration. Ein Beitrag zur Geschichte des deutschen Holzschnittes*, Studien zur deutschen Kunstgeschichte 6 (Strasbourg: J.H. Ed. Heitz, 1896).

Weisbach, Werner, *Die Baseler Buchillustration des XV. Jahrhunderts*, Studien zur deutschen Kunstgeschichte 8 (Strasbourg: J.H. Ed. Heitz, 1896).

White, Stephen D., 'The Politics of Anger', in Barbara H. Rosenwein (ed.), *Anger's Past. The Social Uses of Emotion in the Middle Ages* (Ithaca and London: Cornell University Press, 1998), pp. 127–52.

Wilckens, Leonie von, 'Die Teppiche der Sebalduskirche', in Helmut Baier im Auftrag des Evang.-Luth. Pfarramts St. Sebald (ed.), *600 Jahre Ostchor St. Sebald – 1379–1979* (Neustadt a. d. Aisch: Ph. C. W. Schmidt, 1979), pp. 133–42.

Wilhelm, Friedrich, *Die Sebalduskirche in Nürnberg. Ihre Baugeschichte und ihre Kunstdenkmale*, rev. Th. Hampe, E. Mummenhof and Jos. Schmitz (Vienna: Gerlach & Wiedling, 1912).

Williams-Krapp, Werner, 'Ordensreform und Literatur im 15. Jahrhundert', *Jahrbuch der Oswald von Wolkenstein Gesellschaft*, 4 (1986/7): 41–51.

Williams-Krapp, Werner, 'Die Bedeutung der reformierten Klöster des Predigerordens für das literarische Leben in Nürnberg im 15. Jahrhundert', in Falk Eisermann, Eva Schlotheuber and Volker Honemann (eds), *Studien und Texte zur literarischen und materiellen Kultur der Frauenklöster im späten Mittelalter*, Studies in Medieval and Reformation Thought 99 (Leiden and Boston: Brill, 2004), pp. 311–29.

Willing, Antje, *Literatur und Ordensreform im 15. Jahrhundert. Deutsche Abendmahlsschriften im Nürnberger Katharinenkloster*, Studien und Texte zum Mittelalter und zur frühen Neuzeit 4 (Münster: Waxmann, 2004).

Winkler, Friedrich, *Dürer und die Illustrationen zum Narrenschiff* (Berlin: Deutscher Verein für Kunstwissenschaft, 1951).

Wogan-Browne, Jocelyn, *Saints' Lives and Women's Literary Culture c. 1150–1300* (Oxford and New York: Oxford University Press, 2001).

Wolf, Gerhard, 'Zur Hölle mit dem Teufel! Die Höllenfahrt Christi in den Passions- und Osterspielen des Mittelalters', in Timothy Jackson, Nigel F. Palmer and Almut Suerbaum (eds), *Die Vermittlung geistlicher Inhalte im deutschen Mittelalter. Internationales Symposium Roscrea 1994* (Tübingen: Niemeyer, 1996), pp. 271–88.

Woodford, Charlotte, *Nuns as Historians in Early Modern Germany* (Oxford: Clarendon, 2002).

Worringer, Wilhelm, *Die altdeutsche Buchillustration* (Munich and Leipzig: R. Piper, 1912).

Online Resources

Primary Sources

Ars memorativa: digitized Latin version (Ingolstadt 1499): http://dfg-viewer.de/show/?set%5Bmets%5D=http%3A%2F%2Fdaten.digitale-sammlungen.de%2F%7Edb%2Fmets%2Fbsb00025100_mets.xml.

Bayerische Staatsbibliothek München Digital Collections: www.digitale-sammlungen.de/index.html?c=digitale_sammlungen&l=de.

Bayerische Staatsbibliothek München Incunabula: http://inkunabeln.digitale-sammlungen.de/start.html.

Bernhard von Breidenbach, *Die heyligen reyssen gen Jherusalem*: digitized version (Speyer 1505): http://dfg-viewer.de/show/?set%5Bmets%5D=http%3A%2F%2Fdaten.digitale-sammlungen.de%2F%7Edb%2Fmets%2Fbsb00002034_mets.xml.

Fortunatus: English translation with illustrations: www.michaelhaldane.com/FortunatusIllustrated.htm.

Fridolin, Stephan, *Schatzbehalter*: digitized extracts: http://daten.digitale-sammlungen.de/~db/0003/bsb00034562/images/; and http://daten.digitale-sammlungen.de/~db/0003/bsb00034574/images/.

Der Heiligen Leben: digitized version (Nuremberg 1488): http://dfg-viewer.de/show/?set%5Bimage%5D=1&set%5Bzoom%5D=default&set%5Bdebug%5D=0&set%5Bdouble%5D=0&set%5Bmets%5D=http%3A%2F%2Fdaten.digitale-sammlungen.de%2F~db%2Fmets%2Fbsb00027260_mets.xml.

Die Hausbücher der Nürnberger Zwölfbrüderstiftungen: www.nuernberger-hausbuecher.de/.

Konrad von Megenberg, *Buch der Natur*: digitized manuscript (from workshop of Diebold Lauber): http://digi.ub.uni-heidelberg.de/diglit/cpg300; and (Regensburg, third quarter of the ninth century): http://daten.digitale-sammlungen.de/~db/0004/bsb00043227/images/.

Manuscripta Mediaevalia: www.manuscripta-mediaevalia.de/#|4.

Mirabilia Romae urbis: digitized English translation: www.archive.org/stream/marvelsromeorap00nichgoog#page/n10/mode/2up.

Schedel, Hartmann, *Weltchronik*: digitized Latin edition: http://dfg-viewer.de/show/?set%5Bmets%5D=http%3A%2F%2Fdaten.digitale-sammlungen.de%2F%7Edb%2Fmets%2Fbsb00034024_mets.xml; digitized German edition: http://inkunabeln.digitale-sammlungen.de/Seite_S-199,1,a1a.html.

Secondary Sources

Germanisches Nationalmuseum: www.gnm.de.

Handschriftencensus: www.handschriftencensus.de.

Mitteilungen des Vereins für Geschichte der Stadt Nürnberg: www.bayerische-landesbibliothek-online.de/mvgn.

Stadtbibliothek Nürnberg: www.nuernberg.de/internet/stadtbibliothek/altbestaende.html.

Stadtlexikon Nürnberg: www.stadtarchiv.nuernberg.de/stadtlexikon/.

Das Verzeichnis der im deutschen Sprachbereich erschienenen Drucke des 16. Jahrhunderts (VD 16): www.bsb-muenchen.de/1681.0.html.

Das Verzeichnis der im deutschen Sprachraum erschienenen Drucke des 17. Jahrhunderts (VD 17): http://gso.gbv.de/DB=1.28/.

Index

For Product Safety Concerns and Information please contact our EU
representative GPSR@taylorandfrancis.com
Taylor & Francis Verlag GmbH, Kaufingerstraße 24, 80331 München, Germany